GENDERING THE
MASTER NARRATIVE

GENDERING THE MASTER NARRATIVE

Women and Power
in the Middle Ages

Edited by

MARY C. ERLER

AND

MARYANNE KOWALESKI

CORNELL UNIVERSITY PRESS

ITHACA AND LONDON

First published 2003 by Cornell University Press
First printing, Cornell Paperbacks, 2003

Printed in the United States of America

Library of Congress Cataloging-in-Publication Data

Gendering the master narrative : women and power in the Middle Ages / edited by Mary C. Erler and Maryanne Kowaleski.
    p. cm.
Includes bibliographical references and index.
  ISBN 0-8014-4112-9 (alk. paper) — ISBN 0-8014-8830-3 (pbk. : alk. paper)
  1. Women—History—Middle Ages, 500-1500. 2. Literature, Medieval—Women authors—History and criticism. 3. Women and literature—History—To 1500. 4. Social history—Medieval, 500–1500. 5. Power (Social sciences) 6. Narration (Rhetoric) 7. Women in literature. 8. Rhetoric, Medieval. I. Erler, Mary Carpenter. II. Kowaleski, Maryanne. III. Title.
  HQ1143.G46 2003
  305.4'09'02—dc21
                                               2002151956

1 3 5 7 9 Cloth printing   10 8 6 4 2

1 3 5 7 9 Paperback printing   10 8 6 4 2

The editors dedicate this volume to Jo Ann McNamara, whose pioneering work over the last three decades has done so much to stimulate investigations into the issues of women and power. An energetic and devoted teacher of undergraduates at Hunter College, City University of New York, Jo Ann has also served as friend, adviser, and informal mentor to a crucial generation of feminist medievalists, many of whose work is included in this volume.

CONTENTS

ABBREVIATIONS

AA SS	*Acta Sanctorum*
ANTS	Anglo-Norman Text Society
Archiv	*Archiv für das Studium der neueren Sprachen und Literaturen*
ASV	Archivio di Stato di Venezia
BL	British Library, London
BN	Bibliothèque Nationale, Paris
CWA	Churchwardens' Accounts
EETS	Early English Text Society
HBS	Henry Bradshaw Society
MGH SS	*Monumenta Germania Historica, Scriptores*
MLR	*Modern Language Review*
OP	Occasional Publication
o.s.	ordinary series
VC	Vicars Choral, York
VCH	*Victoria County History*
WCA	Westminster City Archives, London
YML	York Minster Library
ZRPh	*Zeitschrift für romanische Philologie*

Introduction

A New Economy of Power Relations: Female Agency in the Middle Ages

Mary C. Erler and Maryanne Kowaleski

> What we need is a new economy of power relations—the word
> "economy" being used in its theoretical and practical sense.
> MICHEL FOUCAULT, "The Subject and Power"

In 1988 we published an overview of research on medieval women's power that prefaced a collection of essays. The task of that book was to recover and make visible ways that women acted in history—specifically, around the issue of what we then called *power* and what is now often called *agency*.[1] In the 1970s and 1980s, groundbreaking work in anthropology and sociology that asked about women's relation to culture had prepared the

All but one of these chapters were first offered as papers at the annual conference of the Center for Medieval Studies held at Fordham University from March 31 to April 1, 2001. The conference, "Medieval Women and Power Revisited: Challenging the Master Narrative," proposed to reexamine the issues raised by Fordham's 1985 conference "Women and Power in the Middle Ages" and addressed in much subsequent work over the past decade and a half. Our aim was to assess the impact of recent scholarship—in part by confronting clashing interpretations and varying perspectives—to discover how far we had come in formulating new narratives of female empowerment in the middle ages. We were particularly interested in how research on female agency (power) had challenged the master narrative in various medieval disciplines.

For financial support of the conference, we are indebted to Professor Robert Himmelberg, former dean of the Graduate School of Arts and Sciences at Fordham, and to his successor, Professor Nancy Busch. We would also like to acknowledge the help of the staff and graduate assistants of the Center for Medieval Studies, particularly Janine Larmon Peterson, and the staff of the Graduate School, Maureen Hanratty and Megan Healy, for their invaluable logistical support of the conference.

[1] Mary C. Erler and Maryanne Kowaleski, eds., *Women and Power in the Middle Ages* (Athens, Ga., 1988). The contents are largely papers offered at a 1985 Fordham University conference. This introduction thus concentrates on research published after 1985.

way for our more specific interest in women's relation to power within a particular historical period, the middle ages.[2] We wanted to provide some fresh ways of analyzing women's agency (thus we attempted to complexify the use of the public/private dichotomy) and to suggest some fresh forms in which female influence could be seen (through social networks instead of patronage, for instance, or family membership as opposed to accounts of "great women"). By broadening the conventional understanding of power as public authority and by focusing on distinctively female forms of exerting influence and achieving goals, we aimed to provide a more nuanced and inclusive analysis that would demonstrate *how* female agency functioned and *when* conditions enabling the exercise of female power occurred.

The fifteen years that have intervened and the volume of work that they have produced have brought us to different perspectives. Two theorists in particular have affected not only the writing of feminist history but the foundation of most disciplines in the humanities. Foremost we think of Michel Foucault's writing on power: its widespread acceptance makes it a current running below much contemporary thought on this topic.[3] Foucault's awareness of the constructed nature of subjectivity goes hand in hand with Judith Butler's consciousness of the performative nature of gender.[4] One result of these philosophers' work has been to make it difficult to speak, on the one hand, of agency, and on the other, of "women." Foucault's demonstration of historic forces beyond individual control has made the task of posing models of resistance to hierarchical domination more complex, while Butler's work, together with the experience of women of color, has removed the concept of a unitary "women's experience."

Both these perspectives are poststructural, part of what scholars have learned to call "the linguistic turn"—a handy shorthand for the view, springing from literature and linguistics, that historical inquiry does not investigate social reality but rather a text. Feminism has also been at least partly responsible for this direction of inquiry because in its search for an

[2] For example, Sherry B. Ortner, "Is Female to Male as Nature Is to Culture?" in *Woman, Culture, and Society*, ed. Michelle Zimbalist Rosaldo and Louise Lamphere (Stanford, 1974), 67–87; M. Z. Rosaldo, "Women, Culture, and Society: A Theoretical Overview," ibid., 17–42; idem, "The Use and Abuse of Anthropology: Reflections on Feminist and Cross-Cultural Understanding," *Signs* 5 (1980): 389–427; Peggy Reeves Sanday, *Female Power and Male Dominance: On the Origins of Sexual Inequality* (Cambridge, 1981). See also the introduction to Sherry B. Ortner and Harriet Whitehead, *Sexual Meanings: The Cultural Construction of Gender and Sexuality* (Cambridge, 1981).

[3] Foucault's widely scattered writings and interviews on this topic have been collected in *Power*, ed. James D. Faubion, trans. Robert Hurley et al., vol. 3, *Essential Works of Foucault 1954–1984* (New York, 2000); see also Foucault, *Power/Knowledge: Selected Interviews and Other Writings 1972–1977*, ed. Colin Gordon, trans. Colin Gordon et al. (New York, 1980). Also relevant is Foucault, *The History of Sexuality*, vol. 1, *An Introduction*, trans. Robert Hurley (New York, 1978), esp. 41–49.

[4] Judith Butler, *Gender Trouble: Feminism and the Subversion of Identity* (New York, 1990).

explanation of the inequality between the sexes, feminism saw early on the power of discourse to construct social reality.[5] Nevertheless, the deconstruction of the notion of a historical subject or agent has been troubling for feminists who had previously defined their task as the recovery of that reality, now categorized as an illusion. Others have attempted to provide a less totalizing reading, and indeed Foucault's work can be seen as vital to feminist efforts, for instance, in his stress on the powerful shaping of the subject through practices of identity formation, particularly the way oppression is internalized. His emphasis on the forces that determine the possibility of agency is present in several of the contributions in this book.

Through our earlier volume, we hoped to illustrate how forms of experience classically defined as subordinate provided a broad and recognizable arena for activity. As a result, the explicit claims for female power made there were read by some as polemical. The chapters in this book instead often embody a push-pull movement that simultaneously notes women's opportunities and the ways in which these apparent advances were shadowed by real losses. As one writer says, "Feminist praxis is continually caught between appeals to a free subject and an awareness of victimization."[6] The old question of whether the glass is half full or half empty translates theory into domestic metaphor and expresses the somewhat baffled sense that some feminists share at this point.

As a result of such uncertainty, the chapters that follow use the term *"power"* infrequently. Although all are concerned with presenting versions of women's agency, often a sobering perspective insists on the necessarily limited nature of such claims. Dyan Elliott's history of women and confession (chapter 2), for example, shows how the sacrament empowered women as well as impaired them. With tongue slightly in cheek, Elliott suggests that as the Fourth Lateran Council created a class of professional confessors, so it demanded a class of professional penitents—a role filled by the Beguines' "confessional virtuosity." Elliott's analysis, like others in this book, examines both women and men in relationship. Consequently she points out that the benefits of confession were mutual: the male confessor and the female mystic legitimized each other in their respective roles. Confession could disempower women, however, since heretical revelations often came in confessional form. Further, the practice of regular confession was often a function of spiritual direction, and such relations between men

[5] See, e.g., Joan Scott, *Gender and the Politics of History* (New York, 1988); Chris Weedon, *Feminist Practice and Poststructuralist Theory* (Oxford, 1987); Mary Poovey, "Feminism and Deconstruction," *Feminist Studies* 14, no. 1 (1988): 52–65; Kathleen Canning, "Feminist History after the Linguistic Turn: Historicizing Discourse and Experience," *Signs* 19 (1994): 368–404.

[6] Jana Sawicki, "Foucault and Feminism: A Critical Reappraisal," in *Critique and Power: Recasting the Foucault/Habermas Debate*, ed. Michael Kelly (Cambridge, Mass., 1994), 347–64, at 355.

and women dedicated to holiness always carried some element of danger. In sum, the problems inherent to the sacrament—the development of female scrupulosity, for instance—together with its attraction for women tended slightly to discredit it. Elliott's analysis is explicitly Foucauldian; confession is a power mechanism, its effectiveness increased by antifeminism and concern for clerical purity. Her research on confession might be considered paradigmatic for other feminist inquiry because it invites us to understand empowerment/disempowerment as swings of the same pendulum, produced by the precarious balance of power inherent in every male-female relationship.

Like confession, the social organization of the medieval parish provided women with opportunities: a venue for collective action, the possibility of socially recognized work, an outlet for individual piety, female fellowship, and support. At the same time women's parish activities provoked reaffirmations of conventional gender roles. These took the form of clerical warnings, for instance, on female purchase of pews as an expression of status (women both purchased and changed their seats more often than men). Katherine French (chapter 8) points out how women's participation in parish guilds and in fund-raising gave them leadership experience but also reinforced their separate and secondary position. A survey of the services offered to the parish shows that women's contributions of laundry and cleaning, identical with the work they did elsewhere, were less valued than men's, who more often held the important administrative positions of churchwardens. So, although the limits of gender-related behavior were expanded in some directions by parish activity, at the same time other forces worked to strengthen conventional gender roles. This push/pull perspective also emerges in French's assessment of the Reformation's effect on the parish's female subculture. She suggests that the Reformation's abolition of traditional parish celebrations like Hocktide, its destruction of saint's images and of the guilds attached to such devotions, and its new seating arrangements by family rather than gender may have represented a diminution in the power of women in the parish. Thus French is asking us to gender the traditional understanding of "Reformation."

Similarly, Holly Hurlburt's study of public ritual (chapter 9) points to the tension between the real and the symbolic contained in the frequent, albeit silent, tableaus of women marching in the Venetian dogaresse's entrance procession. The ceremony constituted a visual reminder of the consort's physical proximity to the locus of political power and presented the rare public vision of a community of women. Because the doge was not present, and the dogaresse was seated in his chair surrounded by other women, it would seem that models of female power were here deployed for society's observation, particularly since Hurlburt suggests that the entrance ceremony constituted a symbolic marriage, like many other Venetian ceremonies. Yet no woman was unchaperoned and all were married—their

honor symbolically safeguarded by the Venetian social system of patriarchy and the honor of the state. The dogaresse thus represented the con-
stricted power of Venetian patrician women, whose responsibility was to
increase the political mobility of their natal family through marriage.
Hence the visual statement of this female ceremony was mixed and contained both encouraging and discouraging messages.

All three of these chapters focus on gender relations—the social organization of the relationship between men and women—to analyze when and
how medieval women were able to act.[7] The authors try to avoid simple binary oppositions of "male" versus "female" culture, or rigid distinctions
between public and domestic spheres, concentrating instead on showing
how female relations of power are best understood through women's connections with men. Felicity Riddy's meditative exploration of the idea of
"home" (chapter 11) is perhaps the most explicit of all the volume's chapters in discussing the interactions of men and women. She concludes that
in the home the realities of domesticity made it impossible to speak simply
of male power and female subordination and that the home was responsible for the development of an "egalitarian discourse of intimacy" perhaps
not possible elsewhere. Most unexpected is her contention that it was
women's provision of physical care (a position formally servile) that allowed such equality. By taking responsibility for the home, including the
messier functions of everyday life, women collapsed the dichotomy of
power and subordination because "bodily functions democratize hierarchies and are unimpressed by status." One sign of this domestic democra-
tization was the boldness with which many urban bourgeois women could
talk, and we might see the stereotype of the nagging wife as produced by
the home's relations of equality. In refusing the conventional oppositions of
male public/female private spheres and substituting a nexus of interaction, Riddy says what other contributors similarly insist on: that only fresh
structures of analysis will allow us to describe women's place in the world.

The starting point for the history of lay spirituality offered by Nicholas
Watson (chapter 3) is, like marriage, another traditional male-female pair-
ing: female anchorite and male spiritual director. Disagreeing with feminist readings that have emphasized the clerical misogyny of *Ancrene Wisse*,
Watson argues that the anonymous author's chiding was like a coach's
harshness to an athlete, meant to energize and inspire. The author offers
his readers a conception of the spiritual life at once heroic and accessible,
one that substitutes spiritual desire ("the heat of the hungry heart") for
physical asceticism. This shift was not only empowering for its original female audience but also for the increasingly male readership of the *Ancrene
Wisse* and its derivatives in the later middle ages, through which was

[7] Particularly important in the area of gender relations is Joan W. Scott, "Gender: A Useful Category of Historical Analysis," *American Historical Review* 91 (1986): 1053–75.

evolved a demanding spirituality lived in the world—one that might take St. Thomas More as its representative end point. Here the existence of an originally female audience created a space for a reinvented spiritual practice that through the centuries was repeatedly transformed, becoming an influential *via media*. This chapter (together with those by Elliott, Riddy, and Rees Jones) thus sees female power not as individual or group agency but as an effect produced by social forces acting on social conceptions of female nature—in this case the concept of interiority, a state conventionally associated with women.

Indeed, the consolations and the opportunities women found in religion have stimulated much research relevant to the subject of agency because spiritual experience was one way that assumptions about gender were challenged. When women had mystical visions, uttered prophecies, or represented their communities, they were wielding a universally recognized form of authority. Extreme ascetic practices could also empower mystics by allowing them to identify with the suffering and humanity of Christ and to exercise control over their lives and their families.[8] Grace Jantzen's recent redefinition of mysticism, in fact, sees it as inseparable from an agenda of power and intimately allied with gender. Since mysticism is "a way of defining power, whether institutional or individual, then the question of who counts as a mystic is of immediate importance."[9] And the relation of men and women in religion, the ways in which they conceded authority and claimed it, is not only Dyan Elliott's subject in this volume but has now produced a substantial body of work illustrating and analyzing this gendered relationship of power.[10] In addition the topic of women's public preaching or teaching occupied both holy women and men during the period and engaged the anxieties of important female mystics such as Julian of Norwich and Margery Kempe. It is difficult to say whether this form of public authority, based on private religious validation, was one that allowed women a degree of access or instead was more narrowly guarded than secular authority.[11] A related area, that of female spiritual authority in

[8] The classic work here is Caroline Walker Bynum, *Holy Feast and Holy Fast: The Religious Significance of Food to Medieval Women* (Berkeley, 1987).

[9] Grace Jantzen, *Power, Gender, and Christian Mysticism*, Cambridge Studies in Ideology and Religion 8 (Cambridge, 1995), 1–2.

[10] For instance the collection *Gendered Voices: Medieval Saints and Their Interpreters*, ed. Catherine M. Mooney (Philadelphia, 1999); Anne Clark Bartlett, "'A Reasonable Affection': Gender and Spiritual Friendship in Middle English Devotional Literature," in *Vox Mystica: Essays on Medieval Mysticism in Honor of Professor Valerie M. Lagorio*, ed. A. C. Bartlett et al. (Cambridge, 1995); John Coakley, "Friars as Confidants of Holy Women in Medieval Dominican Hagiography," in *Images of Sainthood in Medieval Europe*, ed. Renate Blumenfeld Kosinski and Timia Szell (Ithaca, 1991), 222–46.

[11] See Alcuin Blamires, "Women and Preaching in Medieval Orthodoxy, Heresy, and Saints' Lives," *Viator* 26 (1995): 135–52. Anneke B. Mulder-Bakker has suggested the importance of female age to public visibility in "The Prime of Their Lives: Women and Age, Wisdom and Religious Careers in Northern Europe," in *New Trends in Feminine Spirituality: The*

writing, rather than in public teaching, has received more attention from scholars. Female strategies of self-authorization in writing, according to Jane Chance, have been extensive enough to constitute a "tradition of dissonance" and, in authorizing the female writing subject, might be thought to constitute a political act.[12]

In deconstructing categories, searching for disruptive strategies, accommodating diversity, and reformulating paradigms, postmodernist critiques have also chipped away at the invidious domination of the historical and the literary-historical master narrative. As the chapters in this book attest, "master narrative" can have multiple meanings. To some it encompasses the standard unfolding of political events as related in history textbooks. Its literary corollary might be found in recent disputes about formation of the canon, its artistic parallel in the reverence for "old masters." To others it is the patriarchal narrative that privileges the actions, opinions, and texts of men. Such narratives can be written on a large scale—in the attention paid to church-state relations compared with changes in the institution of marriage—or on a smaller scale, in the discourse on a particular text or image. In revisiting the issue of medieval women and power, we asked contributors to address how their research might disturb the master narrative, how it might move toward the eventual formulation of a new synthesis.

Jo Ann McNamara (chapter 1) challenges the dominant historical narrative on its own terms by reassessing the claims she made in a classic essay written in 1973 (with Suzanne Wemple) on how aristocratic women could exert public power via their involvement in the family and kinship networks. She notes that two central tenets of the earlier article have withstood the test of time: (1) that elite women encountered fewer barriers to the acquisition of power in the early middle ages and (2) that as the power of aristocratic families waned, so too did that of aristocratic women. Although she continues to locate the decline in elite women's power around the year 1000, she now pushes back the first manifestations of this influence through the family to the days of the Roman Empire, thus rejecting traditional periodization, which locates a rupture between "ancient" and "medieval" centuries later. Her new formulation also more rigorously disputes the explanatory paradigms of the master narrative in arguing that

---

Holy Women of Liège and Their Impact, ed. Juliette Dor, Lesley Johnson, and Jocelyn Wogan-Browne, Medieval Women: Texts and Contexts 2 (Turnhout, Belgium, 1999), 215–36. For a recent approach that draws on art history, see Katherine Ludwig Jansen, *The Making of the Magdalene: Preaching and Popular Devotion in the Late Middle Ages* (Princeton, 2000).

[12] Jane Chance, "Speaking *in Propria Persona*: Authorizing the Subject as a Political Act in Late Medieval Feminine Spirituality," in *New Trends in Feminine Spirituality*, 269–94. Classic essays on the topic of women's literary authority are Sarah Beckwith, "Problems of Authority in Late Medieval English Mysticism: Language, Agency, and Authority in *The Book of Margery Kempe*," *Exemplaria* 4 (1992): 172–99, and Lynn Staley Johnson, "The Trope of the Scribe and the Question of Literary Authority in the Works of Julian of Norwich and Margery Kempe," *Speculum* 66 (1991): 820–38.

the fundamental change took the form of a "shift in the gender system" that affected both men and women and substituted class for gender as the basic organizing principle of society. In pointing to the influence of the Gregorian "reforms," particularly the emphasis on clerical celibacy, she also queries the value of "reform" movements that are conventionally cast in a positive light.[13] Although her investigation focuses on the ruling elite, her deliberate challenge to the prevailing account of medieval history, here and as far back as 1973, is all the more compelling for the rigorous scrutiny, mounted by herself and others, that her ideas have sustained over the past three decades.

McNamara's reevaluation of historical periods, her insistence that the master narrative consider shifts in how gender was constructed, and her efforts to highlight changes in women's power reflect current, lively debates on whether, when, and why women's status may have changed during the middle ages.[14] McNamara, along with Susan Stuard and others, argues for what can be termed "change for the worse." These historians point in particular to the eleventh and twelfth centuries when women's access to education and positions of power in monasteries and in ruling circles dwindled.[15] Other scholars have singled out such major processes as the Carolingian reforms, the Norman conquest of England, and the rise of humanism as responsible for declines in the status of women.[16] Those who advocate these positions tend to focus on women from the upper ranks of society and to consider power in terms of public authority, over long periods of several centuries. In contrast, historians who point to improvements in the status of women tend to focus on working women and economic fluctuations over the shorter term, such as occurred after the Black Death when wages rose and opportunities for work widened in response to labor shortages.[17] Judith Bennett rejects both of these positions, preferring to emphasize long-term continuities in the status of women. In criticizing the

[13] This theme comes out even more strongly in her book, *Sisters in Arms: Catholic Nuns through Two Millennia* (Cambridge, Mass., 1996).

[14] For a summary of this debate, on which the following account draws, see Judith M. Bennett, *Medieval Women in Modern Perspective* (Washington, D.C., 2000), 19–25. The characterization "change for the worse" is also hers.

[15] Susan Mosher Stuard, "The Dominion of Gender: Women's Fortunes in the High Middle Ages," in *Becoming Visible: Women in European History*, 2d ed. (Boston, 1987), 153–72; McNamara, *Sisters in Arms*; and idem, essay in this volume.

[16] Suzanne Fonay Wemple, *Women in Frankish Society: Marriage and the Cloister 500 to 900* (Philadelphia, 1981); Jane Tibbetts Schulenburg, *Forgetful of Their Sex: Female Sanctity and Society, ca. 500–1100* (Chicago, 1998); Pauline Stafford, "Women and the Norman Conquest," *Transactions of the Royal Historical Society*, 6th ser., 4 (1996): 221–50; Margaret L. King, "Book-Lined Cells: Women and Humanism in the Early Italian Renaissance," in *Beyond Their Sex: Learned Women of the European Past*, ed. Patricia H. Labalme (New York, 1984), 91–116.

[17] See, e.g., P. J. P. Goldberg, *Women, Work, and Life Cycle in a Medieval Economy: Women in York and Yorkshire, c. 1300–1520* (Oxford, 1992); Caroline Barron, "The 'Golden Age' of Women in Medieval London," *Reading Medieval Studies* 15 (1989): 35–58.

tendency of many feminist scholars to overemphasize transformations in women's history, she suggests an alternative model of "patriarchal equilibrium" to describe how women's experiences might vary (for example, they received slightly higher wages after the Black Death), yet their status remained essentially the same (they still worked largely in humble, poorly paid positions).[18]

Whatever stance scholars adopt in analyzing changes in women's power and influence, however, the current trend—itself an outgrowth of poststructural inquiry—is to criticize the prevailing master narrative for its excessive reliance on political and institutional themes, its adherence to periodization that privileges clearly demarcated transformations in public authority, and its inattention to gender as a category of analysis. In one way or another, all the chapters in this book question some aspect of this conventional understanding.

Still, a new understanding has yet to emerge. Indeed, it has been suggested that efforts to provide a new textbook account of women in history have so far mostly consisted of "adding women and stirring."[19] Works such as McNamara's, however, which refuses to accept the Gregorian "reforms" as necessarily representing a move forward, and Elliott's, which rejects the post-Lateran development of frequent confession as simply positive and instead insists on the inclusion of pathology and power, demonstrate the sort of larger rethinking that an eventual synthesis must include.

Equally firm in its rejection of conventional "grand narratives" in literary history is Jocelyn Wogan-Browne's chapter, which calls for a collectively arrived at chronology that registers women's "informal, quotidian, underrecognized, significant, and continuous presence." This vision of a different sort of female history, as original in its way as McNamara's in hers, springs from a base that at first appears narrowly codicological—examination of a manuscript collection of saints' lives read in the East Anglian nunnery of Campsey—but expands from this specialist base to urge a reconsideration of how traditional "placement" of literary texts, as well as the audience for them, is connected with older narratives of nationalism. The early English text of *Ancrene Wisse*, for instance, was subsumed into a discourse of "Englishness," while Anglo-Norman texts that reveal a different, often fuller, women's literary history were ignored. The Campsey manuscript also re-

---

[18] Judith M. Bennett, "Medieval Women, Modern Women: Across the Great Divide," in *Culture and History 1350–1600: Essays on English Communities, Identities and Writing*, ed. David Aers (London, 1992), 147–75. For her ideas on "patriarchal equilibrium," see "Confronting Continuity," *Journal of Women's History* 9 (1997): 73–94.

[19] The phrase is from Judith M. Bennett, "When the Master Takes a Mistress" (paper delivered at Fordham University's Medieval Studies conference March 31, 2001) in which she discussed her experience with the master narrative in revising C. Warren Hollister's *Medieval Europe: A Short History* (New York, 8th ed., 1998).

veals how power relations were exercised through production of texts that catered to the nuns' interests, including references to real places associated with the manuscript's patrons in East Anglia and to precedents for the exercise of female power, particularly in the foundation of female monastic communities.

The topic of women's alliances with one another, raised here in several chapters, has received surprisingly little attention, although as a recent collection of essays points out, given the scarcity of institutional structures for women beyond the family, study of women's connections could provide a perspective on agency that goes beyond the individual.[20] In suggesting that women's networks and women's lineages remain substantially underexplored, Wogan-Browne's chapter, as well as research by French on women's parish guilds in England and by Hurlburt on the rare vision of a community of women in Venice, demonstrate that the work of historical recovery can never be seen merely as part of feminism's initial goal for itself, but must continue as an ongoing initiative—ideally, linked (as here) with bold retheorizing. Alliances between women, however, did not always produce positive results for them. The tensions inherent in religious community life, for both men and women, are revealed in bishops' visitation accounts. And the power of female gossip to reveal men's secrets and subvert patriarchal authority raised considerable anxiety and could provoke harsh retaliation. Such gossip, moreover, was often more likely to be aimed at other women than at men.[21] Institutionalized alliances of women, such as women's craft guilds, were not only rare but also less autonomous than men's guilds.[22]

The interest shown by scholars in women's reading and women's reading communities in the chapters by Wogan-Browne and Watson also represents an attempt to assess women's place in intellectual history. Recent stress on the communal and oral nature of medieval reading has seemed particularly relevant to the culture of reading women. Riddy has taught us to see this culture as emphatically devotional in its reading choices, composed of both nuns and laywomen, and characterized by the exchange of both books and ideas between members of these two female states.[23] His-

---

[20] Susan Frye and Karen Robertson, eds., *Maids and Mistresses, Cousins and Queens: Women's Alliances in Early Modern England* (Oxford, 1999), introduction.

[21] See, e.g., Karma Lochrie, *Covert Operations: The Medieval Uses of Secrecy* (Philadelphia, 1999), 66–79; Karen Jones and Michael Zell, "Bad Conversation? Gender and Social Control in a Kentish Borough, c. 1450–c. 1570," *Continuity and Change* 13 (1998): 11–31; Steve Hindle, "The Shaming of Margaret Knowsley: Gossip, Gender, and the Experience of Authority in Early Modern England," *Continuity and Change* 9 (1994): 371–93; Laura Gowing, *Domestic Dangers: Women, Words, and Sex in Early Modern London* (Oxford, 1996).

[22] Maryanne Kowaleski and Judith M. Bennett, "Crafts, Guilds, and Women in the Middle Ages: Fifty Years after Marian K. Dale," in *Sisters and Other Workers in the Middle Ages*, ed. J. M. Bennett et al. (Chicago, 1989), 11–38.

[23] Joyce Coleman, *Public Reading and the Reading Public* (Cambridge, 1998); Felicity Riddy, "'Women Talking about the Things of God': A Late Medieval Subculture," in *Women and Lit-*

torical recovery continues to be important here, as more books belonging to women are identified and as these material objects allow us to speak with more certainly about women's reading choices.[24]

Such a gendering of material culture is one of the approaches used in Sarah Rees Jones's chapter, which draws both on York's "built environment" and its tenantry records. Like many contributors, she situates her analysis in the larger context of gender relations, noting, for instance, the "overlapping gender identities" evident in the layout of bourgeois homes, which contained shops or offices alongside domestic accommodation. But a variety of changes did occur in housing practice that together fostered among the urban elite an attachment to the individual house as home, where women were acknowledged to have particular rights and interests, and where family identity was reproduced. This increasingly autonomous household was seen as the responsibility of the "housewife," whose care produced the discourse of "homeliness" analyzed by Riddy. The situation differed for poorer women (many of them widows or newly arrived singlewomen), who accounted for a larger share of renters after the Black Death, but at the lower end of the market. By the mid- to late fifteenth century, the numbers of these female tenants fell even below those of the period before the plague, a development Rees Jones explains chiefly in terms of declining work opportunities for women in York.

This changing proportion of female tenants in medieval York can also be interpreted as the measured response of working women—many of them widows or recent immigrants from the countryside—to the widening opportunities for waged work in post-plague towns. We know little about these women other than their names and tenant histories, yet these faceless women, when they react similarly to specific economic conditions, together represent a potent example of women's collective power. Although scholars hotly debate the effects of the plague on women's work, they recognize that peasant and urban working women were economic actors whose decisions influenced the rate of rural-urban immigration and the urban property market, as Rees Jones shows.

Recent attempts by medieval demographers to explain long-term population swings also emphasize women's agency by singling out the crucial role of nuptiality (at what age and whether a woman married) and fertility (the rate at which women bore children).[25] Indeed, early modern de-

---

erature in Britain c. 1100–1500, ed. Carol M. Meale (Cambridge, 1993), 104–27; Jocelyn Wogan-Browne, "Analytical Survey 5: 'Reading Is Good Prayer': Recent Research on Female Reading Communities," *New Medieval Literatures* 5 (2002): 229–97.

[24] Mary C. Erler, *Women, Reading and Piety in Late Medieval England* (Cambridge, 2002).

[25] For an overview of the debates and implications for women's history of recent demographic findings, see Maryanne Kowaleski, "Singlewomen in Medieval and Early Modern Europe: The Demographic Perspective," in *Singlewomen in the European Past, 1250–1800*, ed. Judith M. Bennett and Amy M. Froide (Philadelphia, 1999), 38–81, 325–44. For medievalists who offer evidence for a fertility-driven model of population change, see Richard M. Smith,

mographers now argue that the proportion of lifelong singlewomen exercised more influence over variations in the total size of communities than any other single factor.[26] Historical demography, therefore, along with methods such as prosopography, offers feminist medievalists valuable tools to recover the history of larger groups of women, not just the well-documented and elite members of society.[27] These methods also provide us with avenues to explore different forms of female agency, ones that may not immediately empower—or disempower—individual women, but which over the long run alter the structures of medieval society because of their aggregate effect. Such demographic analysis, whose focus is women in groups, will certainly take a central place in changing the historical narrative.

This view of women's collective impact is echoed in Wendy Larson's account of how female attachment to St. Margaret as childbirth advocate persisted despite clerical disapproval (chapter 5). Larson quotes the warnings of various clerical authorities against an overly literal reading of the saint's iconography, as she bursts forth from a dragon's belly. In the substantial survival of material artifacts displaying this devotion, however, women's own interpretation of the image—a mother's hope for herself and her child during birth—triumphed. Conventionally such perseverance might have been theorized as an instance of women's sustained resistance. Larson refuses this analysis and instead offers a model of power through utility: "the version of St. Margaret's legend that served the needs of a larger and apparently more influential set of patrons prevailed." Here, as in Rees Jones's chapter, the force of a continuing female collective reality is visible. In addition, Larson's redefinition of patronage to include a full range of practices (not just financial or intellectual sponsorship) allows us to rethink this traditional area of female power, which has recently come to seem rather too familiar, in a fresh way. Her definition moves patronage from an elite, individual level to a broadly popular

---

"Hypothèses sur la nuptialité en Angleterre aux XIIIe-XIVe siècles," *Annales E. S. C.* 38 (1983): 120–24; L. R. Poos, *A Rural Society after the Black Death: Essex 1350–1525* (Cambridge, 1991); Goldberg, *Women, Work, and Life Cycle.*

[26] David R. Weir, "Rather Never Than Late: Celibacy and Age at Marriage in English Cohort Fertility, 1541–1871," *Journal of Family History* 9 (1994): 340–54; Roger Schofield, "English Marriage Patterns Revisited," ibid. 10 (1985): 2–20. The proportion of women who never marry affects nuptiality, which in turn affects fertility, which many early modern demographers see as exercising the most influence over changes in population size. Thus far the data to prove these theories for the middle ages are sparse, but they have been persuasively argued for the early modern period when data are more abundant.

[27] *Prosopography* is "collective biography," or the history of specific groups; for an explanation of the methodology and overview of recent developments, see K. S. B. Keats-Rohan, "Prosopography and Computing: A Marriage Made in Heaven?" *History and Computing* 12 (2000): 1–11. For the application of the method to the history of women (in this instance, English nuns), see Marilyn Oliva, *The Convent and the Community in Late Medieval England: Female Monasteries in the Diocese of Norwich, 1350–1540* (Woodbridge, U.K., 1998).

one, allowing the possibility of viewing devout women as a patronage-dispensing *class*. Larson's rethinking of patronage is similar to McNamara's reconception of historical periods and Wogan-Browne's rejection of nationalist literary paradigms. All three chapters say, "the categories are different than we've thought" and move toward conceptual changes that go beyond the mere addition of remarkable women to the familiar narrative.

Like Wendy Larson, Pamela Sheingorn (chapter 6) investigates the proliferation of a specific visual image—in this case, St. Anne teaching the Virgin Mary—despite the absence of a scriptural foundation for this mother-daughter exchange. Depictions of St. Anne teaching from a book promoted ideas of mothers as instructors, daughters as diligent pupils, and literacy as the norm among elite women—ideas that trickled down, as demonstrated by the appearance of the image even in the wall paintings and inexpensive alabaster figures of ordinary parish churches. Sheingorn attributes the absence of this image from art history's master narrative to its replacement by Victorian ideologies of femininity as submissiveness and the tendency to focus on the affective relation of mother and son, as opposed to the domestic, household relationship of mother and daughter.[28] She notes the image's emphasis not only on the crucial role of mothers in the dissemination of learning but also on the potentially subversive power that literacy offered in making possible criticism and commentary. Sheingorn asks whether this image was particularly frequent in manuscripts owned by women. If this were so, we might see in such a continuing devotional practice evidence, as in Larson's chapter, of women's collective preference as a cultural force.

Women's seeming preference for particular female images raises the question of the extent to which it is possible to describe specific female cultures—for instance, women participants in the parish, or women readers and book owners—not as reduced, parallel versions of more visible male analogues but as sounding characteristic female notes. Even more vexing is the question of whether such female subcultures empowered women. Did they encourage women to shape their own lives? Did they help them develop coping strategies (such as the power of resistance, or gossip)? Did their very exclusion of men nourish powers of the powerless? On the one hand, such female cultures could provide emotional and even financial

---

[28] Appearing in the same year as Sheingorn's article on reading and St. Anne was an essay by Wendy Scase, "St. Anne and the Education of the Virgin: Literary and Artistic Traditions and Their Implications," in *England in the Fourteenth Century*, ed. Nicholas Rogers, Harlaxton Medieval Studies 3 (Stamford, 1993), 81–96. For more recent work that further develops this topic, see Patricia Cullum and Jeremy Goldberg, "How Margaret Blackburn Taught Her Daughters: Reading Devotional Instruction in a Book of Hours," in *Medieval Women: Texts and Contexts in Late Medieval Britain, Essays for Felicity Riddy*, ed. Jocelyn Wogan-Browne et al. (Turnhout, Belgium, 2000), 217–26.

support, instill self-confidence, and foster leadership skills, especially when occurring within institutionally sanctioned female communities such as monasteries. On the other hand, they were often informal, marginalized, viewed with mistrust, and open to attack when they began to exercise power that threatened the patriarchal status quo, as gossips and Beguines sadly discovered. The difficulty of recovering genuine female voices from the male-authored texts that survive must also be considered.[29] And of course efforts to identify elements of a putative female culture can easily fall into essentialism, and perhaps can only be viable when they issue from accounts of specific situations, as, for instance, in Wogan-Browne's characterization of upper-class female interests based on the Campsey manuscript's contents. Analyses that attempt a description of historically specific women's cultures represent one of the continuing directions of feminist scholarship.

Barbara Newman's chapter asks a related question, about how medieval culture understood the concept of nature as it was historically shaped by literature. The questions about what is "natural" to women, which both *Roman de Silence* and Christine de Pizan ask, are ones that vex us still. Newman examines the *Romance of the Rose* (in which Nature represents heterosexual fulfillment), *Roman de Silence* (which searchingly explores the notion of gender), and Christine's work (where Nature encompasses a broadly defined productivity, both intellectual and physical). In Newman's chapter, more than any other in this book, a powerful woman stands at the center of activity, as Christine reconceives and rewrites her predecessors' definitions of Nature, evolving a figure of all-purpose female creativity expressed equally through motherhood, domestic labor, or intellectual work. All opposition between nature and culture ceases as Nature becomes a promoter of women's cultural achievements.

By developing such an androgynous conception of Nature (a philosophical/literary abstraction of great historical power), Christine makes it possible for those who came after her to think differently about intellectual and cultural archetypes. Newman's account of Christine's work proceeds in the way a recent overview of medieval literature has called for: refusing the *grand recit* in favor of observing literature's cultural specificity, even slipperiness, its historical reformulation in "new textual configurations, generative of meanings undreamed of at the moment of first conception."[30] If Watson's chapter shows the power of literary work in shaping culture and woman's role in that work, Newman's chapter, unusually, assigns that power to a single influential female thinker. What the two chapters share is

[29] On this point, see in particular the essays in Mooney, ed., *Gendered Voices*.
[30] David Wallace, "General Preface," to *The Cambridge History of Medieval English Literature*, ed. David Wallace (Cambridge, 1999), xvii.

their interest in the process of textual and ideological transmission and women's part in it.

The chapters in this book all work to create a "new economy of power relations"[31] not only by acknowledging how deeply embedded power relations are in the social nexus but also by deconstructing the fixed categories of "female" and "male." In locating power relations in discourses on women, they also deliberately gender the master narrative by querying its interpretive efficacy, historicizing specific texts and experiences of women, and offering new paradigms that insist on understanding female relations of power through women's connections with men. They also bring these power relations to light not by examining the political level of the state, but by focusing attention on discourses at the micro-level of society, whether an official religious discourse such as confession, the everyday discourse of the home, or the discourse surrounding a specific ceremony. They also explore the mechanisms of power, showing how, for example, power relations could be exercised through the production of texts or images that catered to women's interests, or through the reinterpretation of conventional texts and images by women to suit their ends.

In our earlier volume, we identified several aims. One was the production of "realistically complex analyses of the power relations between men and women." A second desire was to identify "chronologies . . . which chart the rise and fall of women's power and link it to particular historical situations."[32] The contributors to this volume continue to see these as areas for further work. The evolution of gender studies has produced a great deal of new research in which the complexity of the interrelationship between men and women is a central theme. The call for new historical chronologies, specifically for revisions of periodization that take gender into account, is likewise regularly heard. The multiplicity of such chronologies has been impressed on us more forcibly since we first wrote. It has recently been pointed out that historical trajectories that move through the same set of circumstances can often be imagined as proceeding in opposite directions.[33] So, for instance, the rise of universities reduced educational opportunities for women while expanding them for men. At present, investigation of women's agency must develop a sensitivity to such multiple narratives, often coexisting or even conflicting, and

[31] Foucault's 1982 phrase, used in our epigraph, and the essay from which it is taken are reprinted in Foucault, "The Subject and Power," in *Power*, ed. Faubion, 328, but Foucault did not apply the phrase in a feminist context.

[32] Erler and Kowaleski, eds., *Women and Power in the Middle Ages*, 11. A third concern, resisting the divorce of literature from history, hardly seems necessary now because the marriage is obvious in most of the chapters that follow.

[33] Wallace, "General Preface," xviii.

must recognize lines of inquiry that run parallel rather than converging in a satisfying manner.

These topics from our earlier book—attention to the relations between men and women and revision of chronologies—continue to provide directions for fruitful work. New approaches, some of them illustrated in these chapters, will also gradually unfold further in future research. Prosopography and demography, for example, offer students of female agency an opportunity to facilitate study of women in groups, a focus that deemphasizes the "great woman" model. By developing new geographical and linguistic categories for texts, literary history can be revised, away from its earlier nationalist focus. Scholars must also attend to familiar categories of activity such as patronage and domesticity, refining and rethinking the apparently well-known. And, for the present at least, we will necessarily work with narratives that are partial rather than comprehensive.

CHAPTER ONE

Women and Power through the Family Revisited

Jo Ann McNamara

Heraclitus tells us that you cannot step into the same river twice, and later philosophers have added that, indeed, you cannot really step into the same river once. We try to build bridges, embankments, and dams, devices that will put us in a position to chart the flow of time, to get the past organized, and to capture it once and for all. But even as we try to fit time into categories, labeling the minutes, years, decades, and centuries, we find that we have been caught ourselves in its relentless current. In this chapter, it is my interesting duty to play a double role, as observer and as swimmer in the river.

Thirty years ago, Suzanne Wemple and I presented a joint paper to the first Berkshire Conference on women's history entitled, "The Power of Women through the Family in Medieval Europe, 500–1100." That paper was subsequently published in *Feminist Studies*, reprinted in a collection called *Clio's Consciousness Raised*, and reprinted again with the collected papers from the first "Women and Power in the Middle Ages" conference at Fordham University.[1] I have been asked to revisit that scene to determine how my view of the river has changed since I first attempted to step into it. I must emphasize that this time I am acting solely on my own without the insights and the scholarship of Professor Wemple. As a result, this has become a highly self-referential paper, pointing to conclusions drawn not

---

[1] Jo Ann McNamara and Suzanne Wemple, "The Power of Women through the Family," *Feminist Studies* 1 (1973): 126–41; reprinted in *Clio's Consciousness Raised*, ed. Mary Hartman and Lois Banner (New York, 1974), 103–18; and in *Women and Power in the Middle Ages*, ed. Mary C. Erler and Maryanne Kowaleski (Athens, Ga., 1988), 83–101.

from an initial encounter with the sources but from the thinking and re-thinking I have done about many of those same sources over the decades since, in the light of my own continuing research and the ever-swelling flood of interesting work produced by my contemporaries.

As our title indicated, our paper represented a preliminary sweep through a current full of shoals and rapids barely charted by scholarly explorers. In those days, the master narrative concentrated on the development of governments and institutions, quite indifferent to the fact that nearly all the actors were male. The middle ages were neatly framed by the fall of the Roman Empire and the Renaissance, with a lesser chapter ushered in by the twelfth-century renaissance and with a condescending dismissal of the claim that people at the turn of the millennium trembled in fear before the opening of a new era in history. Peter Brown's *World of Late Antiquity* had just been published.[2] No one had yet labeled Georges Duby's initial work "the feudal transformation" and thus refocused our sense of transition on the year 1000.[3] Neither of these great authorities framed their chronologies in terms of women's experience, and David Herlihy had barely begun the creative analyses that would enable him and his students to penetrate the documentary evidence of charters and other quantitative sources for social history.[4] In brief, our work was slightly in advance of the quickening currents of modern scholarship. It suffered from lack of the evidentiary and theoretical support that has developed over the ensuing decades, but it profited in prestige from the lucky fact that it anticipated views that have subsequently come to dominate the field.

Our paper generally respected the chronological markers favored at the time, fitting an account of women into the narrative of Rome's fall in the fifth century, followed by a barbaric age with Europe's revival developing in the twelfth century. Briefly, we proposed a scheme for the history of European ruling-class women that began with recognition of their private access to wealth and its privileges despite their exclusion from the public life of the Roman Empire.[5]

We explained the competitive success of individual women who accu-

[2] Peter Brown, *The World of Late Antiquity, AD 150–750* (London, 1971).

[3] Georges Duby, *La société aux XIe et XIIe siècles dans la région mâconnaise* (Paris, 1953) acted as the springboard for Pierre Bonnassie, *From Slavery to Feudalism*, trans. Jean Birrell (Cambridge, 1991), which outlined a dramatic social revolution in the early eleventh century. The concept was expanded by Jean-Pierre Poly and Eric Bournazel, *The Feudal Transformation, 900–1200*, trans. Caroline Higgitt (New York, 1991).

[4] His study, "Land, Family and Women in Continental Europe, 701–1200," which we cited from its original venue, *Traditio* 18 (1962): 89–113, was subsequently reprinted in *Women in Medieval Society*, ed. Susan M. Stuard (Philadelphia, 1976), 13–46.

[5] At the same conference, Sarah Pomeroy presented some of the early research that would go into her pioneer study of women in antiquity, *Goddesses, Whores, Wives, and Slaves* (New York, 1975).

mulated wealth and power in the violent world of deteriorating legal and political structures. That disorder was followed by the fortunate evolution of a legal system that benefited women's overlapping membership in natal and conjugal families. We devoted the bulk of the paper to women's active role in the power conflicts of the early middle ages and the developing European polities of the ninth, tenth, and eleventh centuries.[6]

To the best of my knowledge, no one has ever seriously challenged our conclusion that in this period aristocratic women encountered few structural barriers to the acquisition of power in almost every capacity except the priesthood. If this has appeared to some scholars to suggest a "golden age," it is because we did not dwell on the carnage that surrounded such women and to which they contributed.

Further, it has been commonly accepted that class was the decisive factor. Women derived their power from families intent on deploying all their human resources on a broad horizontal plane for the immediate acquisition of wealth and status in an expanding world. They endowed daughters and widows with wealth in pursuit of strategies dependent on marriage alliances and military enterprise. Eleanor Searle would eventually characterize this system as "predatory kinship."[7] At the time, Claude Levi-Strauss's work was just becoming familiar.[8] Gayle Rubin's powerful essay on the exchange of women was still several years in the future.[9] Our work turned out to be compatible with the passion for applying structural anthropology to medieval situations that would develop in the decade that followed.

To understand the dramatic presence of powerful women in the invasion period, we relied heavily on the efficacy of law codes devised under Roman influence but incorporating barbarian customs like bride price. We felt that the power later granted to queens and, by extension, women of noble rank further down in the political hierarchy, was drawn from their membership in the great kindreds of the Carolingian and post-Carolingian

---

[6] We accepted without question the framework established by Marc Bloch in *Feudal Society*, trans. L. A. Manyon, 2 vols. (Chicago, 1970). Today, Bloch's distinction between two feudal ages has been abandoned. No one seems to believe any longer in "the first feudal age," and growing numbers of medievalists have come to reject the entire concept of feudalism, largely because he broadened the concept to encompass every aspect of society. Nevertheless, the sense of a shift around the millennium has received very strong support even from those who do not see it as an abrupt revolution. A selection of the most important arguments in this debate can be found in Barbara Rosenwein and Lester Little, *Debating the Middle Ages* (New York, 1998), 105–210.

[7] Eleanor B. Searle, *Predatory Kinship and the Creation of Norman Power, 840–1066* (Berkeley, 1988).

[8] Claude Levi-Strauss, *The Elementary Structures of Kinship* (Boston, 1969) had a massive impact on scholars of the 1970s seeking the aid of other disciplines to make sense of the activity of women in history and in society in general.

[9] Gayle Rubin, "The Traffic in Women: Notes on the 'Political Economy' of Sex," in *Toward an Anthropology of Women*, ed. Rayna R. Reiter (New York, 1975), 157–210.

age. Relying on legal texts ornamented with anecdotal evidence, we were able to demonstrate a convergence of marriage settlements, inheritances, and gifts that enabled some women to accumulate wealth from both natal and conjugal families and enjoy it without legal hindrance. We attributed the widely attested presence of women in positions of influence and even juridical power to the continuing absence of a public authority powerful enough to curb their private enterprise. We noted briefly that women sometimes used these advantages for their own ends without predictable deference to family interests, but emphasized that they drew their importance from their familial roles.

We saw an evolution in women's ability to inherit and control property and the powers of jurisdiction and patronage that went with it. Subsequently, we proposed, the restoration of public authority, which we dated roughly to the twelfth century, came at the expense of the great kindreds. Facing a decline in status due to the rising power of central states and restricted opportunities to enlarge wealth through loot and territorial expansion, aristocratic families adopted new strategies, restricting the proportion of property that daughters or even younger sons might inherit or receive as dowries and limiting the dower rights of widows to use of a portion of the husband's income without the unrestricted power of alienation. Soon after, our thoughts on the evolution of a dowry system were expanded and strengthened by an important essay by Diane Owen Hughes.[10] We were all launched upon a stream of social history in which women's history was an indispensable component—a stream that swelled the original river far beyond its original narrow banks.

Even when we wrote, Georges Duby had begun to elaborate his theories concerning a change in family structure in the late eleventh and twelfth centuries that had an obvious impact on the position of women, though he never saw them as active agents in his sources. He proposed that the great kindreds that had accumulated power by means of a broad horizontal deployment of their branches in the expansive early middle ages began systematically to prune their family trees, aiming for a tight system of primogeniture that would guarantee the consolidation of wealth and power in the patrilineage.[11] It seems to me now that our paper was in some way imperceptibly enlisted in what became the reigning theory of recent decades to fill the gap left by Duby's general inattention to women. I came myself to believe that we said considerably more on this subject than in fact we did say. Nevertheless, there can be no serious doubt that our thoughts ran on

[10] Diane Owen Hughes, "From Brideprice to Dowry in Mediterranean Europe," reprinted in *The Marriage Bargain: Women and Dowries in European History*, ed. Marion A. Kaplan (New York, 1985), 13–58.

[11] Georges Duby, *Medieval Marriage*, trans. Elborg Forester (Baltimore, 1978). These lectures were later expanded in the text of *The Knight, the Lady, and the Priest: The Making of Modern Marriage in Medieval France*, trans. Barbara Bray (New York, 1985).

the same lines, and I certainly based some of my own later work on Duby's proposition.

Duby's last work summarily relegated women of the twelfth century to silence and ineffectiveness, consigning them literally to an isolated domestic sphere.[12] These claims have not gained much credence. It is hard to imagine that anyone with the slightest knowledge of medieval history would seriously contend that individual women were not significant actors on its stage throughout the period. Duby himself eluded the problem by focusing on a peculiar body of texts that included women only as progenitors of noble families. His conclusions have elicited a powerful response in a collection of essays edited by Ted Evergates.[13] The authors focus on the broad variety of evidence for virtually every important province in France to assert that aristocratic women played active roles in public life. The data collected by the contributors are indisputable, and I would not be surprised to find that it could be extended to similar situations elsewhere in Europe. Evergates himself and Amy Livingstone in particular called into question at least one of the premises on which Wemple and I based our conclusions: the practice of primogeniture as the centerpiece of aristocratic family strategy and the shift from a horizontal to a vertical kinship structure. I would still contend, however, that those families that did not practice primogeniture, including the Counts of Champagne, eventually died out while those who did, like the French monarchs, absorbed their lands through their manipulation of the marriages of heiresses.[14] And no one, as far as I can tell, has challenged the limitations that developed on women's control of the dower: their inability to alienate the property they got from their husbands or to bring it away from his heirs into another marriage.

But I agree that we must free ourselves from the illusion of abrupt structural change in family development and factor in the vagaries of individual interests and affections and even miscalculations. A more realistic model is probably that developed by Martha Howell for the abundant evidence of bourgeois marriage and inheritance practices in late medieval Douai.[15] There, a shift from conjugal partnership to lineal inheritance becomes evident over several centuries as hundreds of individuals assessed their economic advantages. Nevertheless, I think our original conclusion still stands: the power of great families declined and that of aristocratic women declined with them. This might better be expressed, however, by use of a

---

[12] Georges Duby, *Women of the Twelfth Century*, trans. Jean Birrell, 3 vols. (Chicago, 1998).

[13] Theodore Evergates, ed., *Aristocratic Women in Medieval France* (Philadelphia, 1999).

[14] The same meticulous research without the concentration on women confirms these conclusions: Theodore Evergates, *Feudal Society in the Bailliage of Troyes under the Counts of Champagne, 1152–1284* (Baltimore, 1976).

[15] Martha C. Howell, *The Marriage Exchange: Property, Social Place, and Gender in Cities of the Low Countries, 1300–1550* (Chicago, 1998).

model advanced by Judith Bennett in her book on brewsters in England.[16] The aristocracy certainly continued to be powerful for many centuries, and women more or less held their position within the aristocracy. But other powers surpassed them in the high middle ages, and those powers did not incorporate women. Thus aristocratic women continued to derive power from their familial status, but that status was reduced as other roads to power, closed to women, were broadened.

These theories fit neatly into the larger debate over the ongoing rewrite of the master narrative focused on the reconstruction of the power structure around the year 1000, that ancient favorite among watersheds. Whether it should be characterized as a "feudal transformation" or formulated without the offensive construct altogether, I leave to others to contest. Whether we should imagine the turn as a gradual evolution or a violent revolution is also a matter of contention. But it seems clear to me that women were disadvantaged by the development of more centralized states, a more hierarchical church, and an urban society based on the money economy. Where women continued to inherit from fathers and husbands, their ability to enjoy their wealth was inhibited by lords able to control their marriages. The religious life continued to offer an alternative, but the opportunities for women within the church were severely limited by increasing concentration of spiritual power within the priesthood. Appointments to royal, comital, or ecclesiastical governments did not compensate women as they did their elder brothers. Their exclusion from universities guaranteed their ineligibility to enter the new bureaucracies and professions that absorbed their younger brothers. It is surprising that R. I. Moore, usually so sensitive to questions of exclusion, could have outlined the transfer of power from the aristocracy as a class to the *clerici* so cogently without noticing that this new ruling class deliberately excluded women. Instead, he mused that the proclamation of a gender revolution to complete the range of changes that constituted *The First European Revolution* could be far away.[17]

In fact, the publication of the papers presented in 1990 at the Fordham University conference on "Medieval Masculinities" constituted such a proclamation. It grew out of the recognition that a revision of the master narrative to include women must necessarily lead to the perception that men were gendered beings and that the tension between women and men and the roles they played against one another must be basic to our understanding of all history. My own address, along with a second paper written a year or so later, tied a shift in the gender system to the effects of the Gregorian revolution.[18] Today, I would go even further with that analysis and

---

[16] Judith Bennett, *Ale, Beer, and Brewsters: Women's Work in a Changing World, 1300–1600* (Oxford, 1996).

[17] R. I. Moore, *The First European Revolution, 900–1200* (Oxford, 1998), 4.

[18] "The Herrenfrage: The Restructuring of the Gender System, 1050–1150," in *Medieval Masculinities*, ed. Clare A. Lees (Minneapolis, 1994), 3–29; "Canossa: The Ungendered Man

claim that one of the most significant components in the millennial revolution was the substitution of gender for class as the basic organizing principle in the new society. In an ecclesiastical society where offspring did not officially exist, a certain egalitarianism could prevail among men whose talents brought them to the highest ranks. This is not to deny that those who sprang from wealthy and influential families had the best chance to develop their talents and win the positions they could be trained to fill. But it does mean that their sex alone endowed them with their initial eligibility.[19] The imposition of celibacy on the clergy created a womanless space within which men could discourse and organize. Men even came to define potency by the repudiation of women rather than by their domination.[20]

With a celibate clergy monopolizing the highest positions, determined by a combination of educational credentials and political skills, married men were reduced to second-class citizenship as were encratic (sexually abstinent) women.[21] But married men gained a privileged position once reserved for the celibate by virtue of a new gender theory emphasizing alterity or complementarity against the old Aristotelian continuum. Ironically, the theory was first delineated by Hildegard of Bingen, according to Prudence Allen, but it had a mighty future before it in the hands of men determined to consign women to the sphere of family life while they occupied the expanding public spaces of the second millennium.[22]

Throughout the early middle ages, a modified Aristotelian concept of gender prevailed, enabling some women to play masculine roles while maintaining their inherent inferiority. Indeed, it still survived in Thomas Aquinas's justification of women's subservience and, incidentally, their exclusion from the priesthood on the grounds that she was a misbegotten man. Our painful struggles with construction and deconstruction in the

---

and the Anthropomorphized Institution," in *Render Unto Caesar*, ed. Sabrina Petra Ramet and Donald Treadgold (Washington, D. C., 1995), 131–50. Institutional history has returned to the idea of the eleventh century as a turning point with renewed appreciation of the revolutionary character of the Gregorian movement, as in Harold J. Berman, *Law and Revolution: The Formation of the Western Legal Tradition* (Cambridge, Mass., 1983).

[19] I pushed this thesis further into the high middle ages and lower in the class structure with "City Air Makes Men Free and Women Bound," in *Text and Territory: Geography and Literature in the European Middle Ages*, ed. Sylvia Tomasch and Sealy Gilles (Philadelphia, 1998), 143–58.

[20] I have looked for the origins of this turn in the Cluniac movement in "Chastity as a Male Virtue in Odo of Cluny's Gerald of Aurillac," to be included in a Festschrift for James A. Brundage.

[21] *Encratic* is taken from early Christian usage, describing a heretical sect that preached that salvation could not be achieved without strict sexual abstention. It is a convenient term for anyone who wishes to retain *celibacy* to describe the unmarried clergy and acknowledges that *chastity* is often applied to the monogamous sexually active.

[22] Allen first advanced her theory in "Hildegard of Bingen's Philosophy of Sex Identity," *Thought* 64 (1989): 231–41, papers from an earlier Fordham conference. It then found its place in her larger work, *The Concept of Women: The Aristotelian Revolution, 750 BC–AD 1250* (Montreal, 1985).

last couple of decades have taken us a long way from the simple indignation we felt in 1970 at Aquinas's formulation.[23] As used by Aquinas, the proposition was subtly altered to fit a social system where gender took precedence over class. Subsequent studies of classical formulations have revealed a single-gender system, a continuum that allotted a greater or lesser degree of virility to every individual. Under this system, females as well as males were effectively masculine in gender, though the majority failed to achieve a high degree of potency. Now we can see that a theory that endows every individual with their own quotient of manliness introduced the probability that females of the right genetic mix would invariably be more manly than males from inferior races or classes. Thus aristocratic descent overcame deficiencies of gender in the early middle ages. In an issue of *Speculum* devoted to gender, Carol Clover illustrated this concept convincingly for Scandinavian women of the Viking age.[24] In general, early medievalists have been prone to accept the proposition that women could be drafted by their families to play the roles of men where a suitable male was lacking.[25]

When I started to write this chapter, I had no problem with that proposition and simply intended to draw on the more sophisticated theoretical principles of recent decades to support our original scheme. But looking back through the evidence we used, I was struck with the realization that few of the narrative sources chronicling female exercise of power (as opposed to legal sources) seem to bear out this quasi-anthropological scheme. We did find a handful of marriages being made for the sake of political alliances in the Carolingian period, and those, on the whole, ranged from unsatisfactory to disastrous. The marriages of Judith of Bavaria with Louis the Pious and of Teutberga with Lothar created far more political furor than any alliance could have been worth. Charlemagne himself was swift to repudiate his Lombard wife, and he decided against marrying off any of his daughters, presumably from fear of creating overpowerful sons-in-law. Similarly, Otto the Great preferred to endow his daughter with an ecclesiastical principality rather than risk a powerful son-in-law. Considering that he had become emperor in Italy as a result of his wife Adelheid's inheritance from her first husband, which she diverted from her children by that marriage, we can only admit that he was right to worry. Whatever the reason, it is actually extremely rare to find women deriving power from their

[23] When we wrote, collections of quotes from early and medieval Christian sources like those presented in Julia O'Faolain and Lauro Martinez's anthology *Not in God's Image* (New York, 1973) were the latest word in understanding gender relations.
[24] Carol J. Clover, "Regardless of Sex: Men, Women, and Power in Early Northern Europe," *Speculum* 68, no. 2 (1993): 364–88.
[25] An excellent example of integrating women into our view of the early medieval power structure is provided by Karl Leyser, *Rule and Conflict in an Early Medieval Society: Ottonian Saxony* (Bloomington, 1978).

positions in their natal families as daughters or sisters and rarer still to locate power in motherhood except at the child's expense.

The gender system that developed in the second millennium changed the nature of woman's position as part of a couple and advantaged the male, whether celibate or married, by divorcing men from the couple as a functioning social unit and barring women from the exercise of an inherent manliness that earlier theorists had recognized in them.[26] The homosocial bond facilitated male commensurability and relegated women to an ontological femininity that effectively barred them from potency.

Obviously, these changes did not fall like a thunderbolt on the stroke of midnight, 1000. But if the power of women through the family should actually be understood as the power of women as wives and, eventually, as widows, a shift in the nature of the couple would have a major impact on women's power. And this does seem to be the case. Even those women whose aristocratic connections were among their major qualifications to marry a highly placed man were significantly without family support in their public careers. This includes the German empresses, Adelheid and Theophano, and the Merovingian queens, Brunhild and Radegund.

On the other side, the Merovingian period produced some dramatic instances of queens who had made their way up from slavery through personal attraction alone. The Carolingian and post-Carolingian periods provide several dramatic examples of royal widows who appeared to carry a claim to their husband's crown with them into a new marriage.[27] If I were now to create an evolutionary scheme, I would say that women's importance as bearers of familial alliances had little significance until the end of the first millennium. Their importance as counters in aristocratic family strategies apparently emerged only when their personal autonomy was reduced by parental and public control of the passage of wealth and status, in effect, when their masculinity gave way to a heightened concept of femininity.

Now I would propose that manly women did indeed play powerful roles in the early middle ages, and no one was particularly surprised that they could do so successfully. They led armies and defended towns. They sat in judgment and made treaties. They controlled resources and deployed them to gain greater wealth and power. Their female sexuality provided an armory of seductive weapons whereby they attracted and held the most powerful men as their husbands. The virility that a single-gender

[26] I attempted some outline of these twists and turns in "An Unresolved Syllogism: The Search for a Christian Gender System," in *Conflicted Identities and Multiple Masculinities: Men in the Medieval West*, ed. Jacqueline Murray (New York, 1999), 1–24.

[27] The Empress Adelheid is an obvious example. This proposition appears to be the only explanation for the scandalous marriage of Charles the Bald's daughter Judith with her stepson, his father's heir to the English crown, and the marriage of Canute with his predecessor's widow, Emma of Normandy.

Aristotelian system conferred on them enabled them to use the position gained by marriage effectively.

As the church slowly imposed the principle of indissoluble monogamy, the corporate couple became ever stronger.[28] Joined as one flesh, their interests were also one. Once formed, the marriage alliance looks like the only one that a beleaguered potentate could trust, especially if his bride had no protector but himself. Clovis could kill all his relatives and then complain that he had no brothers at his side, but his wife was his true partner and confidante. Women like Brunhild and Fredegund, even the sainted Clothild, were ferocious to everyone but their husbands. Fierce Merovingian queens and saintly Ottonian empresses seemed immune from charges of sexual infidelity, perhaps because they acted as alter egos to their husbands.

During marriage, women acted as partners and surrogates for their husbands, and after marriage they often stepped into their roles. The most powerful women were those who took up the government of kingdoms and the leadership of armies after their husbands were dead. The evidence does not even bear out the proposition that widows acted for the sake of their children. Some had no children, and others seem to have had few scruples in dominating their children, shoving them aside for their political interests or even eliminating them from their public lives. Occasionally they went so far as murder. Thus it is the conjugal family that seems to harbor the key to women's power, and it is this thread that I mean to pursue backward in time.

In the partnerships of Germanic kings and queens, a gendered division of labor is often noticeable while the marriage lasts. The king plays the part of the violent warrior, stern judge, and mighty ruler. The queen develops the virtues of sanctity, healing and prayer, intercession for the guilty, and charity for the weak. This is what we might expect from the Ottonians, as shown by Patrick Corbet.[29] But in my own hagiographic studies, I came to realize that the same rule applied to the Merovingians whose kingdoms were not based on any notion of Christian polity.[30] Moreover, unless she elected to spend her widowhood in a convent, a Merovingian queen soon forsook her softer role when taking on the manly powers of her deceased husband.

Was this, as the Romans might have conjectured, a reflection of the bar-

[28] Jo Ann McNamara and Suzanne Wemple, "Marriage and Divorce in the Frankish Kingdom," in *Women in Medieval Society,* ed. Stuard, 95–124.

[29] Patrick Corbet, *Les saints ottoniens: Sainteté dynastique, sainteté royale et sainteté féminine autour de l'an Mil* (Sigmaringen, 1986).

[30] "The Need to Give: Suffering and Female Sanctity in the Middle Ages," in *Images of Sainthood in Medieval and Renaissance Europe,* ed. Renate Blumenfeld-Kosinski and Timea Szell (Ithaca, 1991), 199–221, and implicitly in the texts compiled in *Sainted Women of the Dark Ages* (with John E. Halborg and Gordon Whatley) (Durham, N.C., 1992).

barity of the northern European peoples, daughters of the Amazons, of Boudicca? Tacitus, more than any other author, created the barbarian woman and linked the partnership of women and men to the uncivilized and wild, to people with no proper sense of boundaries. Wemple and I began with the idea that despite their personal wealth, women were excluded from the public life of the Roman Empire and gained access to masculine roles only with the collapse of imperial power. But later research has shown that Theodosian empresses played the same game in the Christian Empire of the fourth and fifth centuries that the Ottonian empresses played in the tenth.[31] The sources themselves insist that the model of sainted queenship throughout that ever-lengthening period now known as "late antiquity" was Helena, the mother of Constantine, who played the role of his queen after the execution of his wife.[32]

Tracking the power of women through the conjugal family, therefore, has moved us back into the heyday of the Roman Empire and right through that wall that once divided the master narrative so unshakably into ancient and medieval history. Can we therefore look at Christianity as an instrument of power for women and insist on revising our chronological framework to incorporate the fourth and fifth centuries? To some extent, I think we can. The first ecclesiastical legislation aimed at imposing indissoluble monogamy appears in that period, and missionaries carried the principle with them into the northern forests. It was contested and partial throughout the settlement period until the ecclesiastical revolution of the eleventh century. Only then could we reasonably suggest that there was, at least theoretically, some sort of domestic sphere in Europe to which women could reasonably be assigned.

However, it now seems that Constantine and his immediate successors did little to interfere with the commitment to monogamous partnerships that characterized the pagan society of the empire.[33] Inspired by Stoic writers, Foucault and his followers have situated the Roman turn to couplehood in the early empire.[34] Plutarch and Paul alike preached mutual support and affection between husbands and wives.[35] In the first century, the outcry was very strong against the late Republican aristocratic habits of seeking family power through marriage alliances and frequent divorce. In

[31] Kenneth Holum, *Theodosian Empresses: Women and Imperial Dominion in Late Antiquity* (Berkeley, 1982).

[32] Jo Ann McNamara, "*Imitatio Helenae*: Sainthood as an Attribute of Queenship in the Early Middle Ages," in *Saints*, ed. Sandro Sticca (Binghamton, 1996), 51–80.

[33] Judith Evans Grubb, *Law and Family in Late Antiquity: The Emperor Constantine's Marriage Legislation* (Oxford, 1995).

[34] Michel Foucault, *The History of Sexuality*, vol. 3, *The Care of the Self*, trans. Robert Hurley (New York, 1988).

[35] Jo Ann McNamara, "Gendering Virtue," in Sarah B. Pomeroy, ed., *Plutarch's Advice to the Bride and Groom and a Consolation to His Wife: English Translations, Commentary, Interpretive Essays, and Bibliography* (Oxford, 1999), 151–61.

fact the family power and the activity of women as instruments of family power that I now see as characteristic of dynastic Europe after the turn of the millennium seems to belong also to the Roman Republican period. But the last great Roman who used his daughter in this way was Augustus. From the first century on, Roman sentiment was turned toward respecting the durability of marriage, the bond of the couple to one another, and the consent of the parties involved to seal the validity of the marriage. Christian law as it developed after Constantine put the seal on these sentiments and gave them legal force.

Moreover, if the fourth century seems to sanctify the role of the wife, the real power that empresses had over their husbands and, at least indirectly, their subjects extends much further back. Perhaps it is not entirely coincidental that Tacitus, the chronicler of the terrifying Boudicca, was no less the narrative creator of the frightful Livia. The partnership of husband and wife in wielding power and influence was inherent in the nature of the empire itself and if it is to be a marker in the history of the European gender system, its beginning must be placed in the Augustan age. Thus it would seem that we must look behind the fourth century for the roots of the power that aristocratic women carried into barbarian Europe.[36]

So the power of women as wives, sharers of a common destiny with their mates, did not arise out of the collapse of patriarchal institutions when Rome fell. It was the hallmark of the Roman Empire itself. Of course, the second great pillar of early western civilization developed in the same period. The Christian religion, from the beginning, privileged the couple over the natal family. Moreover, its female martyrs and ascetics, from at least the second century on, enjoyed the adjective "manly" outside the boundaries of the couple. Over the past three decades, this phenomenon has attracted a number of commentators.[37] In the monastic movement, women could be classed within a third gender in which males and females alike enjoyed the higher dominance of self-control envisioned by classical authors.[38] There, women could most effectively utilize the power and wealth of their natal families as abbesses and church administrators (*metropolitanae*), but the real enabling factor was their indissoluble marriage to Christ.

[36] This was the belief I pursued in two early articles on Christian women in the Roman family: "Cornelia's Daughters: Paula and Eustochium," *Women's Studies* 11 (1984): 9–27, and "Wives and Widows in Early Christian Thought," *International Journal of Women's Studies* 2, no. 6 (1979): 575–92.

[37] I first grappled with the question of the "manly woman" before there was a developed gender theory to enlighten my efforts, "Sexual Equality and the Cult of Virginity in Early Christian Thought," *Feminist Studies* 3, no. 3/4 (1976): 145–58. Newer thoughts on those lines have been offered by Gillian Cloke, *"This Female Man of God": Women and Spiritual Power in the Patristic Age (350–450)* (New York, 1995).

[38] I develop this idea at greater length in "Chastity as a Third Gender in the Work of Gregory of Tours," in Kathleen Mitchell and Ian Wood, eds., *The World of Gregory of Tours* (Leiden, 2002).

In the light of this new history of women, the family, and gender, I see the "middle ages" dissolving into nothing and the more recent "late antiquity" giving way to a simple division between the first and second millennia. Over the course of the first millennium, the European gender system underwent a series of shifts and changes. Still, there is a certain unity to be found in the dramatic presence of women in the master narrative. The first millennium began with the collapse of a gender system that excluded women firmly, even from the physical precincts of the Senate in Rome. The patriarchy of the Republic may be only a myth created by nostalgic imperial subjects. Its aristocracy was largely destroyed by the civil wars, but as late as the fourth and fifth centuries, we can still see a coterie of die-hard pagan senators clinging to those hoary traditions while their wives, their mothers, and their daughters were diverting their fortunes and obliterating their patrilines.

Thus I envisage European civilization emerging like the Nile out of a tangle of marsh and tributaries around the turn of the first century B.C.E. into the first century C.E. A new master narrative will, I hope, privilege the experiences of women and men over the destinies of institutions and polities. I believe that the relationships between the two sexes within the matrix of a single gender gives coherence to the entire first millennium. It also provides a metaphor for the ongoing development of western civilization. The imperial father and the ecclesiastical bride/mother were sometimes partners, sometimes rivals. The separation of church and state is a product of their dual beginning and like a first millennium marriage, it fluctuated erratically between rivalry and union. Sometimes they played out opposing roles as ruler and nurturer. Sometimes they competed for the same powers: acting out the tensions implicit in the dominant single-gender system. These institutional conflicts penetrated the real world of men and women as well; bishops competed with queens as imperial consorts, for example. This was a society in which women played vital roles in the ongoing history of dynasties. As a consort, the Roman Catholic church—not necessarily the religion that is shared by the Greek and Russian churches or converts spread as far away as China and India—shared and supported the imperial power. And with the death of her first partner, this same church became in some respects his heir, exercising his power by herself in Rome and, to strain my metaphor, carrying it to successive husbands among the Franks and Germans of the north.

Romanization and Christianization are grand terms. They give an intellectual framework to our study of those myriad peoples, slowly accumulating inherited or acquired skills, steadily clearing and populating the Latin West, hardly hampered at all by that event once known as the fall of the Roman Empire. It is a story centered on growth and the opportunities as well as the insecurities that went with it. Above all, it is a master narrative that proposes that in its origins, European civilization was based on the cooperation of men and women whether in the encratic union of a third gender or the intimacy of married consortium. I started once upon a time with a vision of women enjoying power in violent times and losing it to the oppressive security of a more ordered age. I now see that first age as a time of growth and creativity. It was not Arcadia nor even a golden age, but it was a time when the sexes collaborated for good or evil more closely than they did in the millennium that followed. I hope that the feminist movements of our own day may be pointing the way to a newer and better partnership.

CHAPTER TWO

Women and Confession:
From Empowerment to Pathology

Dyan Elliott

In the thirteenth century, western Europe (or, more precisely, Latin Christendom) witnessed a truly astonishing surge of popular piety. This wave of
religious fervor tended to foreground women, particularly laywomen, in
an unprecedented way. And, women, on the crest of this wave, would in
turn be conceived as confessing subjects.[1] There are some pragmatic reasons for this representation. First, we have to consider clerical bias. In the
life of any holy woman, the figure of the confessor usually hovers somewhere on the horizon. He could loom large or small, according to his discretion, since he was generally responsible for recording his penitent's life
and revelations.[2] Then there was the fact that confession was one of the
most basic ways of affirming a holy woman's orthodoxy, and a partisan
confessor would, of course, avail himself of this opportunity. But clerical
representations suggest that the association between women and confession extends far beyond pragmatism and that confession is positioned at
the very center of female spirituality. Women were not only regarded as especially prone to frequent confession, but their spiritual lives were seemingly organized around their confessional needs and desires. Yet assuming
that such a sacramental dependency did exist, I would argue that it was a
costly one. For if confession enriched the spiritual lives of some, it brought

---

[1] For a Foucauldian discussion of the construction of the "confessing subject" in the context of trials for heresy, see John Arnold's *Inquisition and Power: Catharism and the Confessing
Subject in Medieval Languedoc* (Philadelphia, 2001), esp. 98–110.

[2] See Dyan Elliott, "*Dominae* or *Dominatae*? Female Mystics and the Trauma of Textuality,"
in *Women, Marriage, and Family in Medieval Christendom: Essays in Memory of Michael M. Sheehan, C.S.B.*, ed. Constance Rousseau and Joel Rosenthal (Kalamazoo, 1998), 47–77.

infamy and danger to others. My purpose here is to assess the pendulum-like swing of the association between women and confession, with its many vacillations from empowerment to disempowerment, and the places in between.

Two roughly contemporaneous vignettes from northern Europe provide an interesting point of departure for an exploration of the vexed subject of women and confession. The first is from the life of Mary of Oignies, as rendered by her confessor Jacques de Vitry shortly before her death in 1213. The work constitutes one of the earliest notices of the Beguine movement. It is also considered to represent the ur-life of a female mystic.

> If sometimes it seemed to her that she had committed a little venial sin, she showed herself to the priest with such sorrow of heart, with such timidity and shame and with such contrition that she was often forced to shout like a woman giving birth from her intense anxiety of heart. Although she guarded herself against small and venial sins, she frequently could not discover for a fortnight even one disordered thought in her heart. Since it is a habit of good minds to recognize a sin where there is none, she frequently flew to the feet of priests and made her confession, all the while accusing herself and we could barely restrain [ourselves] from smiling when she remembered something she had idly said in her youth.[3]

The invocation of "the habit of good minds" is a direct, albeit silent, quotation from the letter to Augustine of Canterbury attributed to Gregory the Great.[4] Jacques then proceeds to describe how, every Vespers, Mary would carefully search her day's activities to ascertain that they had been properly regulated, and then proceed to make a fearful confession. The various clerics in the community could themselves discover no real faults in Mary's behavior: "in this alone we sometimes reprimanded her, seeking consolation for our own sloth, because she would confess these small sins we mentioned above more frequently than we would have wished."[5] Mary's exemplary confessional habits are framed by the lengthy prologue to her life in which Jacques reminds Bishop Fulk of Toulouse, to whom the life is dedicated, that when the latter was visiting Liège while on the run from Cathar heretics, he marveled over how many of the Beguines would weep more for a single venial sin than the men of his own country would have wept for a thousand mortal sins.[6]

[3] Jacques de Vitry, "Vita B. Mariae Oignacensis," in *Acta Sanctorum* (Paris and Rome: Victor Palmé, 1867)[hereafter *AA SS*], June, 5:551; *The Life of Marie d'Oignies*, trans. Margot King (Saskatoon, 1986), 20.

[4] Bede, *Ecclesiastical History of the English People* 1.27, ed. and trans. Bertram Colgrave and R. A. B. Mynors (Oxford, 1969), 92–93.

[5] *AA SS*, June, 5:551; *Life of Marie*, trans. King, 20–21; cf. *AA SS*, June, 5:567, *Life of Marie*, trans. King, 88.

[6] *AA SS*, June, 5:547; *Life of Marie*, trans. King, 3.

My second vignette, from the chronicle of the monk Richer of Sens, describes the nefarious activities of a certain Dominican, Robert of Paris—now identified as one of the earliest papal inquisitors, Robert le Bougre. Richer relates that one day a beautiful matron attended Robert's preaching. Sizing her up, Robert told her to wait for him after the sermon. When she obediently followed him to a private spot "where she expected to make her confession to him," he attempted to seduce her. Robert countered her resistance with the threat of having her burned for heresy. On the next day he made good his threat, interrogating her in public. Placing his hand (which contained a concealed piece of parchment inscribed with certain magical words) on her forehead, she was compelled to confess herself a heretic even though she was innocent of such an offense. The woman was saved by her son, who fortunately learned of the ruse from someone familiar with Robert's techniques. Thus appearing at the bishop's consistory where his mother was to be reexamined, the son wrested the parchment from Robert's hand, breaking the spell and permitting the woman to protest her innocence. Robert was perpetually enclosed in a stone prison.[7]

The two tales may, at first, seem to have little in common. In one, the confession is voluntary; in the other, magically constrained. One concerns an exemplary sacramental confession; the other, the devolution from sacramental confession into a bogus confession of heresy. Similarly, the clerics in question are at a variance: a sympathetic confessor versus a ruthless inquisitor.

But the stories are nevertheless united by deeper, more enduring structures. Confessor and inquisitor should in no way be construed as terms of opposition that cancel each other out. From its inception, the Dominican order was intended to help detect heresy and supplement the overtaxed parochial clergy in the hearing of confession. The Franciscans likewise assumed parallel pastoral and disciplinary functions. The potential conflation or perhaps even confusion in functions is suggested by the tale wherein the matron is drawn into a private interview with the confessor/inquisitor, anticipating the performance of one kind of confession, but enacting another. The respective roles are likewise fixed: the priestly interrogator is, by definition, male, even as the suppliant is female. And both tales suggest a pronouncedly female affinity for sacramental confession, intrinsic to which is—what most Christians would agree to be a virtue—a willingness to accuse oneself.

---

[7] *Richeri gesta Senoniensis ecclesiae* 4.18, ed. G. Waitz, *MGH SS* (Hanover, 1880), 25:307–308. On Robert's career, see Charles Homer Haskins, "Robert le Bougre and the Beginnings of the Inquisition in Northern France," in *Studies in Mediaeval Culture* (Oxford, 1929), 193–244, esp. 210 ff. The episode described here is translated on pp. 225–226. Cf. Robert's parallel persecution of the matron Petronilla of La Charité in 1236, whom Robert refused to acquit even after her canonical compurgation. She eventually appealed to the pope successfully (see Lucien Auvray, ed., *Registres de Grégoire IX* [Paris, 1896], vol. 2, no. 3106).

Auricular confession did not come easily to western Europe. When annual confession was first made mandatory at the Fourth Lateran Council of 1215 (Lateran IV), Christendom required considerable coaching—parish priests and the laity alike. The new mendicant orders were partially created and soon streamlined into teams of professional confessors, whose incursions into the parish structure were vigorously defended by mendicant spokespersons, such as Bonaventure.[8]

But the promotion of confession needed something more than just the right amount of clerical personnel. Professional confessors called out for professional penitents, and this personnel was very often female. Unlike the Franciscans, whose lay character was effaced within a couple of decades of the death of its founder, women, however pious, were frozen in an eternally lay condition that not only rendered them recipients, versus administrators, of the sacraments, but further cast the power of sacerdotal sacramentalism into sharp hierarchical relief. Thus Jacques de Vitry and Thomas of Cantimpré, early sponsors of the Beguine movement, were especially intent on modeling correct confessional habits by emphasizing the exemplarity of their holy charges. As is evident from the above description, Mary's confessional practices far outstripped the bare requirements of Lateran IV, anticipating the recommendation for daily confession that would later be advanced by authorities such as Raymond of Peñafort.[9] Moreover, this confessional avidity eddied outward. For example, Mary and the other Beguine mystics were miraculously sensitive to the unconfessed sins of others. Their supernatural radar was akin to the ability that this same group of women possessed to discern unconsecrated hosts, in keeping with female eucharistic piety described by Caroline Walker Bynum.[10] And indeed, the two types of sacramental devotion were closely connected insofar as confession was progressively understood as a precondition for communion.[11]

Moreover, Beguine spirituality, generally, did not only corroborate the newly emphasized importance of confession, but accommodated most as-

[8] Norman Tanner et al., ed. and trans., *Decrees of the Ecumenical Councils* (London, 1990), Lat. IV, c. 21, 1:245. Also Bonaventure, Opusc. XIV, "Quare fratres minores praedicent et confessiones audiant," in *S. Bonaventurae . . . Opera Omnia* (Florence, 1898), 8:375–385.

[9] See Raymond of Peñafort, *Summa de poenitentia et matrimonio* 3.34.6 (Rome, 1603; reprint Farnham, Hants., 1967), 442.

[10] Caroline Walker Bynum, *Holy Feast and Holy Fast: The Religious Significance of Food to Medieval Women* (Berkeley, 1987), 141, 228–29.

[11] As Louis Braeckmans demonstrates, this sequence was not mandatory until the Council of Trent. Even so, the association between confession and communion was already discernible in the mid-thirteenth century with the writings of Albert the Great, Thomas Aquinas, and Bonaventure (*Confession et communion au moyen age et au concile de Trente* [Gembloux, 1971], 14–15, 42–43, 46, 47). Note that many eminent confessors' manuals do not make this association (p. 72).

pects of the penitential system. Mary of Oignies can again be seen as representative here. Her vigorous acts of penance, both on behalf of herself and others, emphasized that certain works on earth could affect one's destiny in the afterlife. The visions and supplicatory interventions of Beguine mystics on behalf of individuals in purgatory not only secured the still nebulous existence of this supernatural zone of expiation but also helped to fill church coffers by reifying the need for indulgences and masses for the dead.[12] This kind of sponsorship, though perhaps beginning with the Beguine movement, did not stop there. Not surprisingly, it is a prominent part in the profile of sanctity for the few women who actually achieved formal canonization—mystics such as Bridget of Sweden and Frances of Rome.[13]

In fact, the institutional gains in the foregrounding of female confessional practice were so palpable that a skeptic might wonder whether the practice was invented to suit the exigencies of the church's sacramental program. But I doubt that clerical masterminds like Jacques de Vitry invented women's confessional virtuosity, nor do I think it originated with the Beguines. There is fragmentary but compelling evidence that this tendency was already present in female spirituality. For instance, when the penitential movement was beginning to make itself felt, one of the first life confessions on record was made by the German Empress Agnes to Peter Damian. (Many historians would argue that she had a lot to be sorry for in forwarding the goals of the papacy against the Empire.) Her care was such that she began to review her faults from the age of five—that is, two years before an individual is *capax doli* (capable of deceit) and considered truly culpable.[14] By the same token, the relations between Robert of Arbrissel

[12] On Beguine mysticism and its role in validating purgatory, see Jo Ann McNamara's important analysis arguing that certain economic shifts unfavorable to women between 1050 and 1150 transformed the role of the pious female from almsgiver and patron of the living to intercessor on behalf of the dead: "The Need to Give: Suffering and Female Sanctity in the Middle Ages," in *Images of Sainthood*, ed. Blumenfeld-Kosinski and Szell, 199–221, esp. 213ff. Cf. Barbara Newman's analysis of women's important intercessory role on behalf of souls in purgatory, *From Virile Woman to WomanChrist: Studies in Medieval Religion and Literature* (Philadelphia, 1995), 109–36.

[13] A number of Bridget's *Revelations* turned on this capacity. See particularly her vision of her deceased husband, Ulf, in *Revelaciones Extravagantes* 56, ed. Lennart Hollman, Samlingar utgivna av Svenska Fornskrifsällskapet, ser. 2, Latinska Skrifter, vol. 5 (Uppsala, 1956), 178–79. Cf. article 32 of Bridget's process, concerning her ability to see the destiny of souls (*Acta et processus canonizacionis Beate Birgitte*, ed. Isak Collijn, Samlingar utgivna av Svenska Fornskrifsällskapet, ser. 2, Latinska Skrifter, vol. 1 [Uppsala, 1924–1931]). Also see Barbara Obrist, "The Swedish Visionary: Saint Bridget of Sweden," in *Medieval Women Writers*, ed. Katharina Wilson (Athens, Ga., 1984), 234–35. Cf. Frances of Rome's visions of purgatory described in the life written by her confessor, John Matteotti in *AA SS*, March, 2:172, and her process of canonization in Placido Tommaso Lugano, ed., *I processi inediti per Francesca Bussa dei Ponziani (1440–1453)* (Vatican City, 1945), art. 40, 81–82; art. 43, 85.

[14] Henry Charles Lea, *A History of Auricular Confession and Indulgences in the Latin Church* (London, 1896), 1:196.

and the Countess Ermengard of Brittany in many ways anticipate the spiritual intimacy prevailing between later holy women and their confessors.[15] A socially constructed reading of this female drive is also close at hand. In the high middle ages, everything was expanding except women's social role, which was proportionately contracting. Men, socially enabled, could search the world. Women, socially hobbled, could search their souls. From the negative standpoint, women could be understood as victims who could not resist the pressures toward internalizing the rhetoric of blame that extended from Eden to medieval wives' manuals. From the positive standpoint, however, they could be seen as finally turning this disparaging rhetoric to their advantage.

Nor should these exemplary Beguine penitents be regarded as mere pawns in the church's larger sacramental agenda. Scholars such as John Coakley have made the mutual gains of confessor and female penitent sufficiently clear that my comments in this context will remain gestural.[16] The individual priest provided the mystic with an experience of the Godhead that was intrinsic to his office: paralleling the priest's Christological role in the course of the mass, the confessor, admitted to the secrets of the penitential forum, had the privilege of "knowing as God," and this authority was frequently played back to him by his penitents. The confessional relationship also provided the priest with the direct experience of divine alterity since the female penitent's mystical revelations were frequently revealed in the context of sacramental confession. Indeed, some clerical authorities, such as Jean Gerson, would assume confession to be the natural medium through which these revelations were disclosed.[17] But certain shared propensities make the confessional relationship potentially self-indulgent for both priest and penitent. From Gerson's perspective, clerics were often prone to the vice of curiosity, which he also characterizes as a quintessentially female character flaw. Women "itching with curiosity" are more inclined to turn away from the truth, both embracing and generating novel

[15] See René Nidurst, "Lettre inédite de Robert d'Arbrissel à la comtesse Ermengarde," *Bibliothèque de l'Ecole de Chartes* 3,5 (1854), esp. 232–35.

[16] See particularly John Coakley's "Gender and the Authority of the Friars: The Significance of Holy Women for Thirteenth-Century Franciscans and Dominicans," *Church History* 60 (1991): 445–60, and idem, "Friars as Confidants of Holy Women in Medieval Dominican Hagiography," in *Images of Sainthood*, ed. Blumenfeld-Kosinski and Szell, 222–46. Also see Elizabeth Petroff, *Body and Soul: Essays on Medieval Women and Mysticism* (New York, 1994), esp. pt. 3, 139–60; Elliott, "*Dominae* or *Dominatae*?" and the recent collection of articles assessing the relations between various holy women and their assisting clerics, *Gendered Voices: Medieval Saints and their Interpreters*, ed. Catherine Mooney (Philadelphia, 1999).

[17] See Jean Gerson, *De probatione spirituum*, in *Oeuvres complètes*, ed. Palémon Glorieux (Paris, 1960–1973), 9:184; trans. Paschal Boland, in *The Concept of "Discretio spirituum" in John Gerson's "De probatione spirituum" and "De distinctione verarum visionum a falsis"* (Washington, D.C., 1959), 39.

teachings.[18] Scholarly curiosity, a vice Gerson would frequently stigmatize in his writings, would render clerics especially susceptible to the novelty of female revelations.[19]

Female Hand Out of Patriarchal Glove

Thus far I have been examining ways in which women's confessional practice could be harnessed by the church in support of the penitential system to the advantage of both parties. But there are also ways in which women could make tactical use of confession to achieve certain personal goals that were frequently at odds with the interests of patriarchal authorities. Such an instance occurs in 1276 when Philip III sent two representatives on a delicate mission. He wanted to know if his beloved second wife, Mary of Brabant, had had a hand in poisoning his son by his first marriage, as his enemies claimed. At the time, there were three local "pseudo-prophets," two of whom were male. But the third and most efficacious of these soothsayers was a Beguine named Isabella, whom some scholars have since associated with the controversial stigmatic, Elisabeth of Spalbeek. The bishop of Laon, a relative to the chamberlain, Peter of Brocia, who was behind the campaign to malign the queen, got there earlier and had the advantage of questioning Isabella first. Indeed, by the time the other representative, the abbot of St. Denis, arrived, she refused to answer his questions altogether. Moreover, when the bishop returned to court, he likewise rebuffed questions, claiming that he had heard her testimony under the seal of sacramental confession. The exasperated king's retort was that he hadn't sent the bishop to hear her confession, but to learn the truth. A second application was made to the prescient Beguine, on which occasion she testified to the queen's innocence.[20]

[18] Gerson, *De probatione*, in *Oeuvres complètes*, 9:184; trans. Boland, in *Concept of 'Discretio spirituum'*, 37; cf. *De examinatione doctrinarum*, in *Oeuvres complètes*, 9:468, 473.

[19] See particularly his *Contra curiositatem studentium*, in *Oeuvres complètes*, 3:224–49. A section of this has been translated in Steven Ozment's, *Jean Gerson: Selections from A deo exivit, Contra curiositatem studentium and De mystica theologia speculativa*, Textus minores, 38 (Leiden, 1969), 26–45.

[20] William of Nangis, *Gesta Philippi tertii Francorum regis ann. 1276*, in *Recueil des historiens des Gaules et de la France*, ed. Danon and Naudet (Paris, 1840), 20:502. It is the French version that claims the Beguine was more renowned than the other two prophets. Also see Ch.-V. Langlois, *Histoire de France illustrée*, ed. E. Lavisse (Paris, 1901), 3, 2: 104–5; Ernest McDonnell, *Beguines and Beghards in Medieval Culture, with Special Emphasis on the Belgian Scene* (New Brunswick, N.J., 1954), 331–32. For an identification of the Beguine with Elisabeth of Spalbeek, see A. Mens, "L'Ombrie italienne et l'ombrie brabançonne: Deux courants religieux parallèles d'inspiration commune," *Etudes franciscaines* annual supplement 17 (1967), 27, n. 1. Elisabeth's life appears in the *Catalogus codicum hagiographicorum Bibliothecae regiae bruxellensis* (Brussels, 1886), pt. 1, 1:362–78. Also see W. Simons and J. E. Ziegler, "Pheonomenal Religion in the Thirteenth Century and Its Image: Elisabeth of Spalbeek and

Clearly the bishop cannily chose to avail himself of the seal of confession in order to frustrate the king's will. By agreeing to make her confession to the bishop, Isabella was either the unwitting dupe of his machinations or she was complicit with his aims. The fact that she initially refused to respond to the king's second messenger, the abbot of St. Denis, suggests the latter because the seal of confession only bound the priest—not the penitent. But temporary complicity with episcopal goals was, in itself, opportunistic. Since Isabella would eventually help to clear the queen's name, she may have fallen in with the bishop's plan momentarily in order to buy time. Presumably, prophecy has its own internal timing that may or may not be aloof from the exigencies of politics.

Isabella demonstrates a tactical use of sacramental confession that permitted her subtly to control and time her intervention in public affairs. A second instance, also from the thirteenth-century Beguine milieu, demonstrates ways in which the confessional relationship itself could be tactically deployed. The chronicler Richer balances his account of Robert le Bougre's deception by immediately following it up with a parallel example of female treachery. A certain woman of the city of Marsal in the archdiocese of Metz, appropriately named Sybil, was envious of the visibility achieved by the local Beguines, and self-consciously imitated their spiritual practices in order to con the entire diocese.[21] Her web of deception extended from the parish priest, to the bishop, to both mendicant orders—who were avidly preaching the virtues of Sybil. Some highlights of her fraudulent repertoire were her three-day raptures, during which she ostensibly refused food and drink, only to indulge herself late at night;[22] conversations with angels (after which she spread aromatic spices to simulate the angelic presence); struggles with demons (punctuated by the feathers of torn pillows); and conversations between demons and angels (with Sybil ventriloquizing each voice). For obvious reasons, most of Sybil's chicanery was perpetrated in privacy, with the admiring populace on the outside of a closed door, but

---

the Passion Cult," in *Women in the Church*, ed. W. J. Sheils and Diana Wood, *Studies in Church History*, vol. 27 (Oxford, 1990), 117–26.

[21] Richer, *Gesta* 4.9, *MGH SS*, 25:309–10.

[22] For another spectacular case of fraudulent raptures, see Dyan Elliott, "The Physiology of Rapture and Female Spirituality," in *Medieval Theology and the Natural Body*, ed. Peter Biller and Alastair Minnis (Woodbridge, 1997), 169–71. Note that fraudulent raptures were not invariably evil. See Caesarius of Heisterbach's account of how a cleric feigned raptures to win the trust of a heretical ring of theologians who were eventually burned at Paris (*Dialogus miraculorum* 5.22, ed. Joseph Strange [Cologne, 1851], 1:306; trans. H. Von E. Scott and C. C. Swinton Bland, *The Dialogue on Miracles* [London, 1929], 1:350). But generally, feigned miracles were associated with false prophets—biblical and those again anticipated in the period surrounding Antichrist. See especially Peter d'Ailly's discussion of feigned miracles in *De falsis prophetis*. Note, however, that he grants that sometimes false prophets can perform true miracles "for sometimes grace is infused in hypocrites by God not only for doing good works but also for performing miracles or predicting the future" (printed in L. E. du Pin's edition of Gerson's works, *Opera omnia* [Antwerp, 1706], vol. 1, col. 521).

there was one important exception. Sometimes in the evening she would sally forth dressed in a hairy demon-suit, which she fondly referred to as her *larva* (specter or hobgoblin), in order to terrify the populace with vociferous threats against that pious virgin Sybil. Thus disguised, she once railed against Sybil's intervention on behalf of a recently deceased individual, reputed to be wicked, whose soul she swept up in a three-day rapture. The "demon" complained that Sybil's tearful suffrages and prayers had managed to preserve the deceased from the flames that he had so richly deserved. And the demon had been so looking forward to leading his "friend" around his delightful field, "always scattered with the dew of sulfur and fire; there are my happy reptiles and viperous animals, and serpents, and snakes, and toads . . . [where] I live with my beloved friends and make jokes." Sybil's sartorial aspirations were not limited to representations of the demonic, but extended to material expressions of celestial glory. On the day after her successful demonic caper, the bishop entered her chamber to discover her rosy-faced, as if sleeping, beneath a subtle white material that did not seem to have been made by human hands. In answer to the bishop's questions, her host volunteered that Sybil was often discovered in this mode after her celestial raptures.[23] The angels themselves provided her with such otherworldly ornaments, in addition to making her bed. Clearly, Sybil's jaded imitation of Beguine spirituality would be immediately put to shame by the mere presence of a Christina Mirabilis,[24] but no such apologies are in order for her inventiveness, which is worthy of a Jean de Meun.

Sybil was eventually exposed while simulating a debate between angels and demons that ostensibly occurred while she was in rapture. Someone looked through a chink in the door to discover her holding this remarkable colloquy while making the bed herself. Sybil's short-lived success was entirely contingent on the assistance of her "familiar" priest—who secretly provided her with food and drink to sustain her during her raptures and acted as her intermediary with the world. It is not surprising that a vernacular source claimed that the whole ruse was initiated so the couple would have the opportunity for sexual dalliance.[25] But it is much more likely that

---

[23] Cf. an incident in Sulpicius Severus's life of St. Martin in which an individual, who claims communication with angels, promises to appear in angelic robe that will prove "the power of God." This beautiful robe of unidentifiable substance disappears when the attempt is made to lead him before Martin (*Vie de Saint Martin* c. 23, ed. Jacques Fontaine, *Sources Chrétiennes*, no. 133 [Paris, 1967], 1:304–7; trans. Alexander Roberts, *The Life of Saint Martin*, Select Library of Nicene and Post-Nicene Fathers of the Church, vol. 11 [Ann Arbor, 1964], 15).

[24] See Thomas of Cantimpré's *The Life of Christina of Saint-Trond*, trans. Margot King (Saskatoon, 1986). Also see Barbara Newman's discussion of Christina's career in "Possessed by the Spirit: Devout Women, Demoniacs, and the Apostolic Life in the Thirteenth Century," *Speculum* 73 (1998): 463–68.

[25] See *Gesta, MGH SS*, 25:308, n. 1.

theirs was not an affair of the heart, but the kind of relationship that would later be stigmatized by Gerson in his denunciations of "those who cherish the false miracles and revelations of these little women so that they will obtain profit or honor."[26] Thus, in addition to the exchange of sacramental power and supernatural services, we can see the deployment of the prophet for profit. Through her coalition with a small-scale patriarch, here signified by the "familiar" priest, Sybil took on and befuddled a large-scale patriarch, here represented by the bishop.

This point could have been made with practically any partnership between a mystic and her attendant priest. But I have chosen this rather provocative example because notable failures make visible the shared components that are seamlessly displayed, and hence, frequently concealed, in notable successes. Moreover, I want to draw attention to a fact that was never lost on the higher clergy: that the would-be mystic and attendant cleric legitimized one another in their respective roles—regardless of whether the mystical experiences at the center of their relationship were legitimate.

A Torn Glove, A Festering Hand (or Gloves Off?)

The very factors that render confession (or, in the largest sense, the penitential system) efficacious as a potential source of female empowerment contribute to its currency as a mechanism of disempowerment and containment. We need only remind ourselves of the conditions under which confession was introduced to ascertain why this should be so. When Lateran IV first made annual confession mandatory for Latin Christendom, this was part of its many-pronged initiative to counteract the threat of heresy. Even if confession was not precisely instituted with the detection of heresy in mind, a point that scholars such as Pierre-Marie Gy have vehemently urged, there is little doubt that within a couple of decades this understanding was annexed to confession.[27]

Moreover, women's prominent role as penitents would necessarily cast their less tractable sisters into unfavorable relief. Consider, for example, the well-known case of the Beguine mystic, Marguerite Porete. Her indiffer-

[26] Gerson, *Centilogium de impulsis*, no. 65, in *Oeuvres complètes*, 8:143. This invective is grounded in the comparison of these fraudulent contemporaries with the female prophet whom Paul condemned, despite her endorsement of his mission. He was thus persecuted by her followers in an effort to protect this valuable asset (Acts 16.16).

[27] See Pierre-Marie Gy's "Le Précepte de la confession annuelle (Latran IV, c. 21) et la détection des hérétiques: S. Bonaventure et S. Thomas contre S. Raymond de Peñafort," *Revue des sciences philosophiques et théologiques* 58 (1974): 444–50. Note, however, that in Bonaventure's later analysis of c. 21, one of his arguments is that regular confession helps priests to discern heretics (". . .ut discernantur obedientes ab inobedientibus vel hareticis per observantiam talis statuti," Bonaventure, Opusc. XIV, "Quare fratres minores praedicent et confessiones audiant," in *Opera*, 8:376).

ence to presenting herself in the context of some recognizable confessional relationship—whether from the perspective of a stable confessional practice or a confessor to vet and record her revelations—ultimately meant that she would end up at a different confessional tribunal altogether: an inquisitional tribunal for heresy. When the cleric, Guiard de Cressonessart, attempted to defend Marguerite before this dire forum, thus providing her with suitable clerical cover, she rebuffed his overtures.[28]

But compliance with Lateran IV could furnish as many difficulties for women as resistance to its strictures. From the beginning, there were problems with the observation of the celebrated seal of confession. An ominous exemplum by Jacques de Vitry, for example, relates some awkward confessional exchanges that occurred between the early Dominicans and various religious women in the Low Countries.

> Certain of the said women showed their infirmities and temptations and the failing of their fragile nature to those men just as they would to religious, so that they would be helped specially by their prayers. But those men not only suspected them with temerity to be otherwise but in different lay and clerical congregations . . . they preached that the renowned communities of holy virgins were really prostitutes rather than religious groups and thus the defects of the few were poured out to all . . . [and] they scandalized many.[29]

In the case of the Prussian mystic, Dorothea of Montau, a frank disclosure of her revelations to an unsympathetic priest in the course of confession led directly to an accusation of heresy, stimulating a handful of clerics to insist on her immolation.[30]

Furthermore, female volubility, however commendable, was almost immediately problematized, particularly among the mendicants. The Franciscan statutes of the general chapter at Narbonne in 1260 already determined that the frequency of women's confession should be limited. Noncompliant friars would be denounced to their superiors by well-wishing brethren.[31]

---

[28] The documents for the trial of Marguerite and Guiard have been edited by Paul Verdeyen as "Le Procès d'inquisition contre Marguerite Porete et Guiard de Cressonessart (1309–1310)," *Revue d'histoire ecclésiastique* 81 (1986): 47–94. Verdeyen also includes select chroniclers who discussed the trial.

[29] Jacques de Vitry, *The Exempla or Illustrative Stories from the Sermones Vulgares of Jacques de Vitry*, ed. Thomas Frederick Crane, Folklore Publications, no. 26 (London, 1890), no. 80, 36. The confessors in question are, in all likelihood, marked as mendicants—not only because they are designated preachers but also because their presence in the area was in order to preach and hear confession.

[30] I discuss this episode in "Authorizing a Life: The Collaboration of Dorothea of Montau and John Marienwerder" in *Gendered Voices*, ed. Mooney, 187–8.

[31] Michael Bihl, ed., "Statua generalia ordinis edita in capitulis generalibus celebratis Narbonae an. 1260, Assisii an. 1279 atque Parisiis an. 1292. Editio critica et synoptica," in *Archivum Franciscanum Historicum* 34 (1941): Narbonne, 1260, 6.5, 70. Also see Donato Soliman, *Il ministero della confessione nella legislazione dei frati minori,* Studi e testi Francescani, no.

Though these constraints were partially inspired by limited resources in personnel, fear of intimacy between the sexes was also undoubtedly an issue. St. Francis's reluctance to assume responsibilities for female orders is a case in point. A parallel caution is apparent on a more local level as well; the first rule of Francis already barred friars from receiving vows of obedience from women.[32] In a similar vein, Bonaventure would develop an elaborate twelve-point series of justifications for the Franciscan refusal to promote the Third Order, the sixth of which turns on the risk that pastoral responsibilities to women entail.[33]

But even those who worked hardest to foreground female virtuosity in the penitential system could rarely restrain their fears of the potential dangers that might arise from the privileged rapport between confessor and penitent. Despite his impeccable credentials as a promoter of the Beguine movement and his personal spiritual indebtedness to the influence of Lutgard of Aywières, Thomas of Cantimpré's anxieties are especially palpable.[34] In the course of his work *Concerning Bees*, in which he ostensibly sets out to write a history of the Dominican order but does so by meandering amid various contemporary scandals, a potentially staggering insight emerges: that many clerics are more tempted by women who appear to have embraced a religious way of life. Likewise women, who would automatically spurn the attractions of secular men—stimulated by the devil and spurred on by twisted minds—frequently cannot resist the allure of holy men, monks, or other ecclesiastics. Thomas associates the perverse logic informing such attractions with Pliny's ruminations on the nature of the pig which, when agitated by the furies of lust, will rush at any person dressed in white.[35]

---

28 (Rome, 1964), 145. Cf. fourteenth-century efforts to limit female frequency of confession (147).

[32] Caietanus Esser, *Opuscula sancti patris Francisci Assisiensis* (Rome, 1978), c. 12, 265. (This is what is, in fact, referred to as the first rule. The original rule, which Francis presented to Innocent III in 1209 or 1210, has not survived, however.) See Soliman, *Il ministero della confessione*, 145. Also see the general council of Narbonne in 1260, which forbids a friar to assume responsibility for a female house and repeats the first rule's prohibition against receiving a vow of obedience from a woman (ed. Bihl, "Statua generalia," 6.6, 70–71).

[33] See Bonaventure, Opusc. 17, pt. 2, q. 16, in *Opera*, 8:368–9.

[34] Thomas's *vita* of Lutgard has been translated by Margot King, *The Life of Lutgard of Aywières* (Saskatoon, 1987). See particularly 2.32, 59, where she is referred to explicitly as *mater spiritualis*. On Thomas and his instructions regarding confession in *De apibus*, see Alexander Murray, "Confession as a Historical Source in the Thirteenth Century," in *The Writing of History in the Middle Ages*, ed. R. H. C. Davies and J. M. Wallace-Hadrill (Oxford, 1981), 286–305.

[35] Thomas of Cantimpré, *Bonum universale de apibus* 2.30.44 (Douai, 1627), 348–49; cf. Pliny, *Hist. nat.* 10.63. Thomas also enlists a porcine analogy in the preceding warning to women to be resistant to masculine suasions even as the Virgin initially was to the angel Gabriel's words. Citing Aristotle, he invokes the behavior of the sow who, as long as she is holding her ears rigid, is resisting the male pig's sexual overtures. A relaxation in the ears corresponds to her sexual receptivity (2.30.42, 346–47). For more on the attraction between clerics and holy women, see 2.30.19, 329; 2.30.46, 351–53.

This not very edifying reflection is buttressed by an example concerning a friar named Dominic, who was a monk at the same monastery as the order's founder. The friar's reputation for sanctity had so impressed the king of Castile that when a certain prostitute claimed that she could seduce him, the outraged monarch threatened to execute her for slander—a charge that forced her to make good her boast. The prostitute accordingly attended Dominic's sermon, during which she feigned a tearful, credible conversion. The cleric felt exhilarated at such puissant proof of his impact as a preacher. He heard her confession and advised her to assume a more seemly manner of dress. For her part, the woman simulated the demeanor of a humble and obedient penitent to perfection. This performance was crowned with an exaggerated sorrow, punctuated by a becoming flood of tears, though the reason for her bitter compunction was veiled in mystery. Eventually, at the preacher's urging, she revealed the reason for her grief: that she needed to sleep with him once in order to be saved. Now fully alerted to her ruse, the preacher nevertheless promised to fulfill her desire at an appointed place and time. She accordingly summoned the king to witness the downfall of his saintly favorite. They arrived to find the holy man, in the spirit of the hagiographical ordeal, on a bed of live coals, from where he invited the woman to join him. The king's men rushed up to coax him out of the fire, while the prostitute took his place, being burned at the king's orders.[36] Thomas thus advises confessors to behave with circumspection, keeping their comments brief, harsh, and rigid.

> Nor should they be the less avoided if they seem to be of good character and honest life; because by how much more religious they are, by that much more do they entice; and under the guise of religion the vitals of lust [*viscus libidinis*] especially flourish. Believe me: I speak as a bishop [i.e., as bishop's penitentiary] and an expert.[37]

The capstone for such warnings recalls a recent and lamentable example from Cambrai, this time involving two individuals of good will. A cleric, chaste from youth, was a canon in a conventual church. Out of zeal for pastoral work, he relinquished his prebend for a parish, in which he piously toiled for seven years. But then on a fateful day, the sixty-year-old virgin who was accustomed to wash the priest's hair shirt entered his bedroom unattended: "Before the woman and the priest separated, they were both deprived of their long preserved lily of virginity and chastity." The woman

---

[36] Thomas of Cantimpré, *De apibus* 2.30.45, 349–51. For other instances in which saintly chastity is demonstrated through parallel ordeals involving fire, see Dyan Elliott, *Spiritual Marriage: Sexual Abstinence in Medieval Wedlock* (Princeton, 1993), 70, 77, 90, 129, 272.

[37] Thomas of Cantimpré, *De apibus* 2.30.46, 352. Note that when he claims to speak as a bishop he means as someone who hears confessions on behalf of the bishop.

soon died of sorrow; the man, reveling in his vice, went from bad to worse.[38]

Thomas's hortatory examples, though effective, lack the sophistication of some later treatments. The literature of spiritual discernment, which flourished in the later middle ages, would provide a slightly more dignified analysis on the transformation of spiritual into carnal love by interpreting it in terms of demonic occlusion. Hence Henry of Freimar censures the initially innocent, but all the more dangerous, impulse that will seek private and excessive conversations with a devout person.[39]

The manuals produced to assist the clergy in hearing confession would eventually become replete with detailed advice for deflecting the temptations afforded by female penitents. Raymond of Peñafort had instructed the priest to make a woman sit across from him and to avoid looking into her face. Gerson concurs, but adds that the confessor should assume a stance in which he is least likely to be aroused—even if this entails full prostration. By Antoninus of Florence's time, women were only to be confessed in public with witnesses. Nor should priests tarry, rather imposing a strict time limit on women "who wish to confess excessively frequently. . . . [The priest] should always use harsh and terse words with them rather than gentle."[40] Antoninus further condemns priests who hear daily confessions, thinking it a waste of time and source of scandal. Similar views would be expressed by John Nider.[41] Therefore, if we approach confession from the vantage point of social control or the kind of Foucauldian surveillance associated with power, the above discourse—grounded in a concern with clerical purity and peppered by antifeminism—would add an additional layer to these mechanisms of constraint. The net result would inevitably work to the diminution of female power.

Thus far, I have outlined some of the ways that women could be derailed from the careful observance of the sacrament through outer constraints. But there were also dangers that allegedly arose from within, whereby an exacting penitent might sink too deeply into the sacrament—inadvertently crossing a subtle barrier beyond which a virtue can be deformed into a vice. We can already see this transformation beginning in the thirteenth

[38] Ibid., 2.30.47, 353.

[39] See Henry of Freimar, *De quatuor instinctibus*, in *Insignis atque preclarus de singulari tractatu de quatuor instinctibus* (Venice, 1498), 4th sign, fol. 61r. Henry claims to be following the contours of Augustine's *De trinitate* and the Ps.- Augustinian treatise *De singularitate clericorum*.

[40] Raymond of Peñafort, *Summa de poenitentia* 3.34.30, 464–65; Gerson, *De cognitione castitatis*, in *Oeuvres complètes*, 9:63; Antoninus of Florence, *Confessionale Anthonini* (also known by its first word, *Defecerunt*) 3.11 (Paris: Jehan Petit, 1507?), fol. 28r.

[41] Antoninus of Florence, *Confessionale* 3.11, fol. 28v. Cf. John Nider's *Confessionale sue manuale confessorum fratris Johannis Nyder ad instructionem spiritualium pastorum valde necessarium* (Paris, n.d.), see 2.1, 6th rule. (This edition is unpaginated.)

century when theologians such as Thomas Aquinas went to work on Gregory's characterization of the "habit of good minds to recognize a sin where there is none" by asking if someone could go so far as to confess a sin that he or she had not really committed, concluding that this was impermissible.[42] This problematization of confessional practice continued apace among pastoral theologians, such as Jean Gerson, under the rubric of scrupulosity or pusillanimity.[43] Gerson's discussion is grounded in the premise that fear is a passion, and that someone predisposed to this passion is especially prone to suffer from scrupulosity of conscience.[44] Complexion might further be a contributing factor. If an individual had thin, cold blood, and their natural moisture was dominated by phlegmatic humors, he or she would be prone to fear and pusillanimity, which was frequently associated with a weakness of the heart.[45] Nor is Gerson oblivious to the potential good inherent in a fearful disposition. To this end, he foregrounds the statement in Proverbs "Blessed is the man that is always fearful" (Prov. 28:14) in his writings on spiritual discernment.[46] And yet, the devil, disguised as the angel of light, works on the passions in different ways. For instance, he is capable not merely of exciting lust but also repressing it, hence simulating spiritual tranquility and sweetness.[47] Similarly, pusillanimity can also masquerade as a virtue. The naturally timorous suffer from defects in their complexion that are open to demonic exploitation. The ensuing fear should thus be fled rather than embraced.[48]

From Gerson's perspective, a classic case of needless scrupulosity is an individual's concern about insufficient attention during prayers—something that, to Gerson's mind, is perfectly understandable, and hence excusable, considering human frailty. Even so, there are many who think themselves insufficiently contrite, wearing themselves and their confessors out over such light sins—hence putting their own deficiencies ahead of God's clemency. Such individuals who "from infirmity have accidentally excessively fluxible phantasies [*fluxibiles nimis habent phantasias*] and are dis-

[42] Thomas Aquinas, *Scriptum super sententiis,* bk. 4, dist. 21, q. 2, art. 3, resp. and resp. ad 4 (Paris, 1947), 4: 1066, 1067.

[43] On scrupulosity, see Thomas Tentler, *Sin and Confession on the Eve of the Reformation* (Princeton, 1977), 156ff.

[44] Gerson, *De remediis contra pusillanimitatem,* in *Oeuvres complètes,* 10:381. An alternative title to this work is *De scrupulis conscientiae.* Also see the French translation of this treatise in *Oeuvres complètes,* 8:386–398. Glorieux is unclear as to which version came first, but believes that the Latin was written before 30 July 1405 (see his introduction to the French, 8:386). Gerson returns to the problem of scrupulosity in many different contexts. See, e.g., his *Regulae mandatorum* no. 8, 9:97; *De signis bonis et malis,* 9:163; *De praeparatione ad missam* consideratio 3, 9:37–39; *De meditatione cordis* c. 17, 8:82, 83; *Traité des diverses tentations de l'ennemi,* 7:346, ff.

[45] Gerson, *De passionibus animae* c. 18, c. 20, in *Oeuvres complètes,* 9:17, 20.

[46] Gerson, *De distinctione revelationum,* in *Oeuvres complètes,* 3:49.

[47] Gerson, *De remediis contra pusillanimitatem,* in *Oeuvres complètes,* 10:378.

[48] Ibid., 10:379.

tracted willy nilly from their proposition by a light breeze of wind to other things" are not in any way culpable.[49]

But there were other dangers implicit in scrupulosity that were more costly than either the penitent's niggling self-torture or the confessor's exasperation. The impulse to confess every sinful or potentially blasphemous thought could have the effect of reinforcing the thought.[50] Even more alarming ramifications occur if an individual manages to convince him- or herself that a morally neutral act is sinful or that a venial sin is a mortal sin. Such convictions become self-fulfilling prophecies because the conscience constitutes a tribunal unto itself. To go against what conscience prompts is sinful, even if its dictates are wrong.[51] Moreover, while Gerson is constantly reproving the scrupulous that their fearfulness puts divine clemency and even divine grace in doubt, what is also at issue is the priest's power of absolution.[52]

In other words, the scrupulosity of the Beguine milieu had been an important prop in promoting the sacrament of confession, but by the time Gerson was writing, this same trait had come to undermine the sacrament. Mary of Oignies exhibited precisely the kind of sorrow over the commission of a venial sin that Gerson would target as suspect. The confessional profile of Mary's contemporary, Lutgard of Aywières, was even more vexed, at least when regarded through a late medieval lens. Not only was insufficient attention over the saying of her hours a constant concern for Lutgard, but this anxiety was not restricted to her own religious practice. She also (correctly) predicted a plague on the nuns who served in the infirmary of her community for similar inattention.[53] Moreover, Lutgard's fears for herself were eventually assuaged, not through confession, but through the mysterious arrival of a shepherd from afar who reassured her, in the presence of her entire community, that she was pleasing to God.[54]

Already in Gerson we find a predisposition to be especially concerned

[49] Gerson, *De remediis contra pusillanimitatem*, in *Oeuvres complètes*, 10:381. This exculpation does not apply to those who are simply carnally minded and slothful (pp. 381–82). Cf. Gerson's parallel evocation of the recitation of the hours and scupulosity (*De praeparatione ad missam*, in *Oeuvres complètes*, 6th consideration, 9:43). See Dyan Elliott, *Fallen Bodies: Pollution, Sexuality, and Demonology in the Middle Ages* (Philadelphia, 1999), 27–29.

[50] Gerson, *De remediis contra pusillanimitatem*, in *Oeuvres complètes*, 10:382, 385.

[51] Ibid., 10:381; cf. *Regulae mandatorum* no. 7, 9:96; no. 8, 9:97; no. 23, 9:100.

[52] Gerson, *De remediis contra pusillanimitatem*, in *Oeuvres complètes*, 10:381. Tentler points out that the tradition of consolation of the scrupulous is at least partially intended to build up the church's power against the overscrupulous who have doubts regarding sacerdotal power (*Sin and Confession*, 158).

[53] Thomas of Cantimpré, *The Life of Lutgard* 2.17, trans. King, 45–46; 3.2.14, 90, and 3.22, 101–2; cf. the way Margaret of Ypres was likewise obsessed with the saying of her hours (Thomas of Cantimpré, *The Life of Margaret of Ypres* c. 20, trans. Margot King, 3d ed. [Toronto, 1999], 35–36).

[54] Thomas of Cantimpré, *Life of Lutgard* 2.2.17, trans. King, 45; cf. idem, *De apibus* 2.52.4, 482–83.

with scrupulosity in women. In a confessional context, scrupulosity increases the contact between confessor and penitent, enhancing the chances of a gradual devolution from spiritual to carnal love.[55] But even more important, Gerson created a framework for stigmatizing and even pathologizing scrupulosity. Predictably, others would move in and gender this pathology as female. When reviewing the reasons for excessive scrupulosity in his *Consolation of a Timorous Conscience*, John Nider leads off with a discussion of complexions. Women, particularly old women and individuals with a melancholic complexion, are especially liable due to excessive coldness. In women especially, a certain constriction of the heart attends their fearfulness, and they frequently tremble, while the members attached to the heart are the more afflicted. The voice falters and the lips quaver, as is evident with respect to the woman with flux who fearfully approached Christ for healing (Mark 5:25), who is thus rendered as something of a type for scrupulosity. This association invites the resurfacing of a suppressed subtext for the entire issue of scrupulosity. For the original context of Gregory the Great's "habit of good minds" was over the question of whether a menstruating woman should be permitted to receive communion—a context withheld in Jacques de Vitry's later appropriation of this characterization. Although Nider does not invoke Gregory explicitly at this point, his analysis nevertheless unerringly rejoins scrupulosity with the flawed, bleeding, female body. Elsewhere, Nider will invoke Albert the Great, who alleges that the combination of woman's lack of heat and dominant moisture "into which terrible things are poured" render her naturally fearful. In addition to this complective propensity, other factors, such as retention of corrupt menstrual blood, inordinate vigils, fasting, care, solitude, or deep thought can also intrude to stimulate the disease of mania or melancholy (which is distinct from a naturally melancholic disposition)—the main symptom for which is excessive fearfulness. Certain individuals—referred to as *energuimini* or, more conveniently still, lunatics—are affected by the movement of the moon, which manipulates the moisture in their heads causing them to howl with fear. Demonic temptation can also wreak havoc with a healthy complexion, afflicting it with a black jaundice (*colera nigra*) likewise associated with fear.[56] When differentiating scrupulosity from the other passions, Nider makes the telling point that "it is that much more dangerous by the extent

[55] Cf. the comments regarding the scruples that arise in the course of meditation that appear in one manuscript of *De meditatione cordis*, in *Oeuvres complètes*, 8:83–84. Also see his account of a recently converted matron who, in her fervor, was directed by her intense attraction to various religious who might easily have taken advantage of her, had they not been stronger (*De simplificatione cordis*, 8:95). See his condemnation of priests whose carnal lust interferes with the performance of God's work—the example evoked being a confessor who prefers a beautiful over an ugly penitent, or young over old, or male over female penitent (*De signis bonis et malis* 9:166).

[56] John Nider, *Consolatorium timorate conscientie* (Paris, 1502?) 3.4–5 (unpaginated).

to which it is falsely reckoned a virtue."[57] He will accordingly trim Gregory's "habit of good minds" with Aquinas's interpretation of "good" in terms of the perfection of justice.[58]

The disinvestment in women as confessional exemplars, associated with Jean Gerson and sustained in the work of John Nider, interestingly corresponds with a parallel, but independent, Wycliffite critique of the sacrament. Gerson was a prime mover at the Council of Constance in 1415, during which views attributed to John Wyclif, including his rejection of auricular confession as a papal invention and a demonic snare, were condemned.[59] The same council consigned Hus, a continental exponent of Wycliffite views, to the flames. But their followers would continue to reject what had become the standard penitential package of the high middle ages. Thus a vernacular Wycliffite treatise on confession excoriates the practice, pointing out that Christ neither practiced confession nor taught it; that both Mary Magdalene and Peter were reconciled without confession, as was the woman taken in adultery. Nor was confession a practice of the early church. Confession as it came to be known in the later middle ages was nothing other than the invention of Innocent III and a device of the Antichrist.[60] Another Wycliffite treatise asks if it were at all likely that a God who values chastity "ordeyned sich a lawe to men, that prestis & wymmen shulde turne her faces to-gider, & speke lustful thoutes & dedis, which myght do harme to hem bothe; but this lawe gyueth occasioun to do synne as it fallith oft"?[61] In other words, both orthodox and heretical exponents were similarly apprised of how the sexual risks implicit in confession might far outstrip any possible spiritual benefits.

The Iron Glove: Confession and Inquisition

Nider's *Consolation of a Timorous Conscience* presents scrupulosity as a potentially lethal affliction, which could generate the life-threatening sin of despair.[62] His colorful *Formicarium*, moreover, adduces data in support of this point. A nun from Nuremberg named Kunegond was in constant fear that her confession was insufficient—a concern that Nider describes as natural in the fragile sex. The inordinate fear that she had committed a mortal sin, compounded by excessive fasts, not only caused her confessors to be concerned for her sanity but actually delivered her to death's door. Fortunately, God effected a timely removal of the fear of damnation a mere three

[57] Ibid., 3.2.
[58] Nider, *Consolatorium* 3.16; cf. 3.15.
[59] Session 15, arts. 9–11; Tanner, ed., *Decrees of the Ecumenical Council*, 1:422–23.
[60] F. D. Matthew, ed., *The English Works of Wyclif*, EETS o.s., 74 (London, 1880; rev. ed., 1902; reprint, Millwood, N.Y., 1973), 328–29.
[61] Ibid., 330.
[62] Nider, *Consolatorium* 3.2.

days before her death. The pious widow and prioress, Catherine de West-husen, afflicted by the identical concern, was likewise liberated under similar circumstances.[63]

Yet there were also instances in which the inward disposition of scrupulosity could lead to external dangers that, to the modern mind, might seem even more pressing than the fear of damnation. In particular, the propensity for confession and self-accusation could lead to the kind of self-incrimination that would facilitate the merging of the penitential forum with its harsher double: the inquisitional forum against heresy.[64] At this juncture, I should add that from a theological standpoint, even the confession of an unrepentant heretic is protected by the seal of confession. In theory, he cannot be denounced by his confessor. Canonical authorities, however, in particular, Raymond of Peñafort, believed that a heretic had relinquished the privilege of sacramental secrecy and that his confessor should denounce him to the inquisition—a view that, however contested, would remain in circulation due to the immense popularity of Raymond's manual for confessors.[65] We have also seen that at least one of Dorothea of Montau's confessors availed himself of Raymond's fiat.

But female scrupulosity often dispensed with the need for clerical denunciations. Indeed, following the basic contours of William of Auvergne's juristic analogy of the sacrament of penance, the perfect penitent was both culprit, accuser, arraigner, and prosecutor of him- or herself.[66] Even so, we should attempt to differentiate between two basic groups. First, there were those who, in the spirit of Gregory's "habit of good minds to recognize a sin where there is none," would accuse themselves without any real warrant. Stephen of Bourbon, a Dominican inquisitor who was active in France in the 1230s, tells of a noblewoman in a city where he was conducting heresy trials. "Holy and innocent, she approached me saying that she offered herself to me for burning as a heretic worse than all the others who were burned for infidelity, as she was thinking the worst things about the articles of the faith and the sacraments." When she acknowledged that she

---

[63] Nider, *Formicarium* 2.12 (Douai, 1602), 175–76. Cf. a similar instance, this time concerning a monk (176–77).

[64] On the parallels between these two confessional fora, see Annie Cazenave, "Aveu et contrition. Manuels de confesseurs et interrogatoires d'inquisition en Languedoc et en Catalogne (XIIIe–XIVe siècles)," in *La piété populaire au moyen âge*, Actes du 99e Congrès National des Sociétés savantes, Besançon, 1974 (Paris, 1977), 333–52.

[65] Raymond of Peñafort, *Summa de poenitentia* 3.34.60, 490–91.

[66] William of Auvergne, *De sacramentis* (*De sacramento poenitentiae*) c. 3, in *Opera omnia*, 1: 461; cf. 486; see also William's earlier *Tractatus novus de poenitentiae* of ca. 1223, where he outlines a similar plan (c. 1, in *Opera*, 1:571 [570–92]). Also see Nicole Beriou, "La Confession dans les écrits théologiques et pastoraux du XIIIe siècle: Médication de l'ame ou démarche judiciare?" in *L'Aveu: Antiquité et Moyen Age*, Actes de la table ronde organisée par l'Ecole française de Rome avec le concours du CNRS et de l'Université de Trieste, Rome 28–30 mars 1984 (Rome, 1986), 275–76.

never consented to these thoughts, he convinced her of her innocence and she left happy.[67] The scrupulosity of Aude, whose tortured doubts about the Eucharist soon brought her to the attention of Bishop Fournier's inquisition, seems to be of the same caliber.[68] Both women were fortunate in that inquisitional attention ultimately resulted in exculpation. But this was not invariably the case. For instance, Constance de Rabastens, one of the several female prophets who arose during the papal schism anticipating Joan of Arc, was sufficiently concerned about the orthodoxy of her revelations that she submitted them to the inquisitor of Languedoc. She was ultimately imprisoned for her scrupulosity.[69]

A second category might consist of women who were actually implicated in heresy, in which case the impulse to confess would be injurious to their personal safety, however salubrious for their souls. It is also worth noting that in the primarily female heresy of the Guglielmites, several women came forward without being summoned and confessed to the inquisition voluntarily, while none of the men did.[70] The testimony of the Olivite Na Prous Boneta, moreover, gives the impression of the kind of preparation for confession advocated by the clergy so that the penitent can easily "vomit forth her virus"—as Gerson would have it.[71] Her "confession," proffered without contrition or repentance, however, places her somewhere at the crossroads between the well-prepared penitent and the sacrificial witness at the center of a martyr's *passio*.[72]

But however we characterize the different kinds of confession, it is important not to be misled by the medieval emphasis that confessions be made *sponte*—voluntarily or even spontaneously. Medieval confessions were not "spontaneous" self-disclosures in the modern sense of the word. Rather, they were sponsored or elicited self-disclosures that are shaped within a patriarchal structure. The occasion and framework for any confession are institutional, as are the officers responsible for assessing the culpa-

---

[67] *Anecdotes historiques, légendes et apologues tirés du recueil inédit d'Etienne de Bourbon*, ed. A. Lecoy de la Marche (Paris, 1877), no. 227, 196.

[68] See Peter Dronke's discussion of her case in *Women Writers of the Middle Ages: A Critical Study of Texts from Perpetua (d. 203) to Marguerite of Porete (d. 1310)* (Cambridge, 1984), 213–14.

[69] See Renate Blumenfeld-Kosinski's "Constance de Rabastens: Politics and Visionary Experience in the Time of the Great Schism," *Mystics Quarterly* 25 (1999): 147–68.

[70] See, e.g., the testimony of Petra de Alzate and Katella de Gioziis, who sought out the inquisitors and confessed spontaneously without having been cited, in Marina Benedetti, ed., *Milano 1300: I processi inquisitoriali contro le devote e i devoti di santa Guglielma* (Milan, 1999), 116–20. They had been explicitly warned by the ringleader of the heresy, Mayfreda, not to reveal their heretical beliefs to their confessors. She further enjoined them to consult with her before seeing the inquisitors in the event that they were summoned. The inquisitors ordered that they reveal their errors in sacramental confession.

[71] See Gerson, *De confessione castitatis*, in *Oeuvres complètes*, 9:63.

[72] See the translation of her testimony by Elizabeth Petroff, in *Women's Visionary Literature* (Oxford, 1986), 284–90.

bility of penitent and defendant alike. However, these self-disclosures also emerge in the course of a relationship. Thus, according to Antoninus of Florence's *Confessionale*, "In truth, every confession occasions a revelation which cannot exist without the revelation of one and the perception of another."[73] The roles are determined in a fixed and gendered hierarchy. And yet, like all relationships, confession can be easily derailed and transformed by an imbalance in power.

The incident of Robert le Bougre and his nameless female victim can be read as a potential repository for social anxieties on the subject of confession—probing and possibly critiquing the essence of the confessional relationship. The occurrence lends itself to analysis as the monkish chronicler's encoded characterization of the mendicant orders and their auspicious (though resented) papal authorizations or even their lead in the newfangled learning of the schools. On a more figurative level, however, the episode can be read as a commentary on the relation of writing and monopolistic learning to coercive power. The fact that the central act of conjuring is effected by a cleric wielding an obscure piece of writing requires little commentary from a lay perspective: inquisitional registers were permanent records of individual and familial guilt. In a context where a relapse into heresy meant death at the stake and the detection of heretical ancestry meant confiscation of inheritance, these records were feared every bit as much as the inquisitors themselves.[74] The parchment further effaces the boundaries demarcating the penitential forum and the heretical forum and, ultimately, between the heretic's stake and the martyr's pyre, suggesting the illusory nature of such divisions.

But in addition to the overt magic of the parchment, there are more subtle forces at work. First, there is the female predisposition to confess, whether this is understood in terms of complexion or social construction. This predisposition has the effect of minimizing the distances between the dutiful confessee, the heretic, the blameless defendant, and the shameless seductress. And then there is the woman's beauty that, from a clerical perspective, is capable of working its own magic—transforming a preacher into a confessor, a confessor into a seducer, a seducer into an inquisitor, and an inquisitor into an agent of the devil. Like any relationship, confession was potentially transformative, frequently incalculable, and never safe.

[73] Antoninus of Florence, *Confessionale Anthonini*, fol. 32v.
[74] See James Given, *Inquisition and Medieval Society: Power, Discipline, and Resistance in Languedoc* (Ithaca, 1997), 25–51; Arnold, *Inquisition and Power*, 82–88.

CHAPTER THREE

"With the Heat of the Hungry Heart": Empowerment and *Ancrene Wisse*

Nicholas Watson

Introduction: Embodiments of the Inner Self

One of the spaces in which we experience ourselves as having, or lacking, power is the one we call the inner self: the space of interiority. Interiority is not the same, historically, as individuality. On the contrary, in Christian, as in Platonic and Stoic, thought, the inner self is in some respects less "individual" than the outer because closer to the image of God in which it was made. Even now, to experience the self as powerful means to experience it stereotypically, within known models. Yet an abiding strand of western thought still associates this space with the hidden, conceiving it as inaccessible to others or even to the self itself, and gazing at its imagined separateness with a mixture of wonder and fear. For Augustine, a thousand years later for Julian of Norwich, and five hundred years after that for Freud, the self remains exemplary and extraordinary at the same time. Whole literary and social institutions have formed around the need to expose this self to view, to help it achieve self-understanding, to conquer it from without, or to theorize the interpenetration of self and world or God. Elsewhere in this book, Dyan Elliott writes about one such institution, confession, and there are others, from the genres of *confessiones, meditationes,* and *soliloquia* (developed under the sign of the adage *nosce teipsum*) to psychoanalysis and Foucault's anatomizations of selfhood.[1]

---

[1] See David N. Bell, *The Image and Likeness: The Augustinian Spirituality of William of St. Thierry,* Cistercian Studies Series 78 (Kalamazoo, Mich., 1984); Charles Taylor, *Sources of the Self: The Making of Modern Identity* (Cambridge, Mass., 1989); Michel Foucault, *The Order of Things: An Archaeology of the Human Sciences* (New York, 1994).

The most anti-institutional of these institutions is the way of life of the hermit or anchorite. Whether as public prophets, private gurus, or potently silent signs, hermits are the nearest Christian culture has come to figuring interiority as a bodily mode of being. Martyring their social and sexual natures, hermits manifest to the world the essential integrity of the inner, lend fleshly clothing to the spiritual. Indeed, a certain glamour even today attaches to the word *hermit*, sustained by the reiteration of a cluster of metaphors, narratives, and paradoxes that are basic to eremitic identity. Rejecting community, including the monastery, hermits live "out" of the world in a space named the "desert," in which they challenge themselves, the society they have left behind them, and the forces of good and evil that struggle for jurisdiction over both. Heroic warriors, spiritual athletes, extremists whose existence both critiques and in their eyes embodies the meaning of the church as a whole, hermits remind us of the limits of the dichotomies that construct worldly living: soul and body, death and life, intent and act, ideal and institution, powerless and powerful, female and male. After a period of glory as the desert fathers and mothers of the early church, memorialized in the *Vitae patrum* and Cassian's *Collationes*, hermits achieved a second apogee in the reformation of the twelfth century,[2] but thereafter diminished in importance: the flexibility of their outward lives increasingly held suspect, their status increasingly subsumed by the friars and devout laity, the topoi that had seemed to guarantee their integrity increasingly invoked satirically, as signs of hypocrisy.[3] Since about the fifteenth century, hermits have had more purchase as images than as living practitioners. As such, however, they continue to wield authority as symbols of perfection or wisdom, as embodiments of the secrets of the heart. The spiritual director, the wise old woman, the romantic artist, the analyst, the social worker—all these ministers to selfhood have links to the figure of the hermit.

[2] For the desert fathers, see John Cassian, *Conferences*, trans. Colm Lubheid (New York, 1985); *Apophthegmata Patrum: The Desert Christian: Sayings of the Desert Fathers: The Alphabetical Collection*, trans. Benedicta Ward (New York, 1980). For the twelfth-century eremitic revival, see Henrietta Leyser, *Hermits and the New Monasticism: A Study of Religious Communities in Western Europe, 1000–1150* (New York, 1984); Giles Constable, *The Reformation of the Twelfth Century* (Cambridge, 1996).

[3] The last English hermit of international stature was Richard Rolle, the hermit of Hampole (d. 1349). William Langland's complex attitude to hermits at the end of the fourteenth century is a clear sign of their decline, given their earlier English prestige. In the prologue to *Piers Plowman* are "Eremites on an hep with hokede staues," who "Wenten to Walsyngham, and here wenches aftir" (a heap of hermits with hooked staffs went to Walsingham, their mistresses in tow). These are contrasted with "ankeres and eremites þat holdeth hem in here selles" (anchorites and hermits who keep to their cells). See Derek Pearsall, ed., *Piers Plowman by William Langland: An Edition of the C-text*, York Medieval Texts (London, 1978), Prologue 51–52, 30. For a study, see Ralph Hanna III, "Will's Work," in *Written Work: Langland, Labor, and Authorship*, ed. Steven Justice and Kathryn Kerby-Fulton (Philadelphia, 1997), 23–66. We await publication of Paulette L'Hermite-Leclercq's study of the history of anchoritism, but see "La Réclusion volontaire au moyen âge: Une institution religieuse spécialement féminine," in *La condición de la mujer en la Edad Media* (Madrid, 1986), 136–54.

This chapter reflects on ways in which the power associated with the hermit was and was not available to medieval women, by looking at perhaps the most influential eremitic text composed in England, the early Middle English *Ancrene Wisse. Ancrene Wisse*, probably a product of the first two decades after the Fourth Lateran Council of 1215, was written by an anonymous but highly educated cleric who may have been a Dominican, on behalf of a small group of women living as anchorites in the West Midlands.[4] As much a study of the ideals represented by its implied readers as the guide for them it purports to be—*ancrene wisse* means "information about anchoresses" as well as "instructions for anchoresses"—the work is as complex a product of the spiritual aspirations and tensions of its era as we have, especially as these relate to women. Not even Jacques de Vitry's pioneering attempt to modernize female sanctity, the *Vita* of Mary of Oignies, comes close.[5] On the one hand, *Ancrene Wisse* testifies to the decline of institutional opportunities for religious women from the late twelfth century on—addressed as it is not to nuns but to one of the informal groups Herbert Grundmann nicknamed "semi-religious"—and occasionally seems to share the antifeminist assumptions some scholars think were influential in that decline.[6] During the last fifteen years in particular, feminist readings of the text have often presented it in a negative light, as another example of the bad faith clerical writers are thought to have kept with their women readers, sometimes even as a frank expression of misogyny.[7] On the other hand, as we shall see, there is quite a bit that is genuinely radical about the work, from its refusal to make its readers submit to a vow of obedience, a specific habit, or a religious rule—a refusal that does as much to identify them with the eremitic tradition as the work's many references to the *Vitae patrum*—to its claims for the state of perfection they embody and will attain in eternity if they persist in their way of life.

Ancrene Wisse does describe its female readers as fragile vessels, who have to exert the utmost vigilance in guarding their lives from their carnal female natures: as *anchoresses*, like the recipient of Aelred's *De institutione*

[4] For an introduction, see Bella Millett, *"Ancrene Wisse," the Katherine Group, and the Wooing Group*, Annotated Bibliographies of Old and Middle English Literature 2 (Cambridge, 1996).

[5] See Jacques de Vitry, *Two Lives of Marie D'Oignies*, trans. Margot King, Peregrina Translations Series (Toronto, 1998); also Brenda Bolton, "Thirteenth-Century Religious Women: Further Reflections on the Low Countries' 'Special Case,'" in *New Trends in Feminine Spirituality: The Holy Women of Liège and Their Impact*, ed. Juliette Dor, Lesley Johnson, and Jocelyn Wogan-Browne, Medieval Women: Texts and Contexts 2 (Turnhout, 1999), 129–58.

[6] Herbert Grundmann, *Religious Movements in the Middle Ages: The Historical Links between Heresy, the Mendicant Orders, and the Women's Religious Movement in the Twelfth and Thirteenth Century with the Historical Foundations of German Mysticism*, trans. Steven Rowan (Notre Dame, 1995).

[7] An example of this vein of criticism is a scholarly howl of anguish by Sister Ritamary Bradley, chillingly entitled "In the Jaws of the Bear: Journeys of Transformation by Women Mystics," *Vox Benedictina* 8 (1991): 116–75. See also Elizabeth Robertson, *Early English Devotional Prose and the Female Audience* (Knoxville, 1990).

inclusarum (one of *Ancrene Wisse*'s main sources) who is expected to focus intently on guarding her virginity, a sealed state in need of the protection of the sealed cell that makes an anchorite an anchorite.[8] By reminding its readers of the "weakness" of their female flesh, which cannot endure much hardship, it repeatedly represents the heights of heroic asceticism as reserved for men only, deferring to the ascetic machismo of so much twelfth-century spirituality.[9] Although it gives them a limited role in instructing their servants and visitors, *Ancrene Wisse* further envisions the readers as recipients of teaching more than as teachers of others, explaining their usefulness as "anchors" of the church in terms of the effectiveness of their prayers and silent example. There is much talk of the exemplary silence of the Virgin, and almost no hint of the role of the hermit-as-prophet that educated male hermits, from Peter Damian to Richard Rolle, could play. More positively, the work presents the anchoresses with another, erotically charged image of their receptive femininity, by picturing Christ as their lover and spouse and stressing their need to choose him, as he has chosen them. But it tends to present even this choice in terms of worldly self-interest rather than spiritual idealism and omits much of the more elevated mystical language found in some of its sources.

Yet *Ancrene Wisse* also addresses its readers in a different way: as tough-minded, ambitious descendants of the heroic solitaries of the early church, attempting something the author himself cannot: as *hermits,* who are also women but whose gender is not of fundamental importance, and for whom enclosure is less a flight to safety than a stage on which the infinite desert of the inner self can be explored. The setting for parts III and IV of the work, on the inner self and its temptations, is specifically this desert, pictured as a refuge and place of prayer, but also as a place of persecution and combat, full of desert birds who represent aspects of the anchoritic life (the pelican, the sparrow, the nightingale) and desert animals who represent perversions of that life and the trials it encounters (the fox, the wolf, the lion, the pig, the unicorn, the bear, the serpent, the scorpion). In facing these animals as fiercely as her life demands, the anchoritic reader is imaged not so much as male (as in Barbara Newman's "virile woman") but rather as genderless, as an exemplary figure for all Christians, whose less rigorous lives still force them to battle temptation in their more muffled ways.[10] Thus part V of *Ancrene Wisse*, perhaps the first treatise on confes-

---

[8] Aelred of Rievaulx, *A Rule of Life for a Recluse*, trans. Mary Paul MacPherson, in *Treatises; the Pastoral Prayer*, Cistercian Fathers Series 2 (Spencer, Mass., 1971).

[9] Constable, *Reformation of the Twelfth Century*, 151–53, 193–94 points out that twelfth-century asceticism was moderate compared with that of earlier periods, pointing to a "humanizing" trend in attitudes to self-inflicted suffering, while citing examples of admiration for such suffering.

[10] Barbara Newman, *From Virile Woman to WomanChrist: Studies in Medieval Religion and Literature* (Philadelphia, 1995).

sion in Middle English, is explicitly addressed to a general audience—before part VI, on penance, which describes the anchoritic life as a crucifixion, reverts to the notion that the reader is uniquely burdened and privileged by suffering, and part VII, on love, which is full of spousal imagery, refeminizes her and reencloses her, this time not in a cell but a bower of spiritual bliss.

This chapter analyzes the implications of this shuttling in and out of gendered language, both for the text's first readers and for their late medieval descendants, in an exploration of the influence of the trope of the hermit on religious women's constructions of the inner self. I have two main areas to cover.

First, I revisit the question of the status of the anchoritic readers in the author's eyes, arguing that, despite the ambiguous institutional position he finds and leaves them in and despite his use of misogynistic rhetoric, he really does conceptualize them as the heroes he makes them out to be: women on the cutting edge of the spiritual movements of his time, whose lives are at once supremely elevated over others by their difficulty and supremely appropriate for others to know about and imitate. For the author, anchoresses are a harbinger of the breakdown of the hierarchical distinction between clerical and lay that his own status as (perhaps) a friar could also imply, and that was a long, slow outcome of the twelfth-century reformation: a conduit between the world of the professional religious, bound by their distinctive rules and habits, and the wider community to which anchoresses belonged, as laypeople and members of the secular communities that fed them; a conduit, equally, between these communities and the ascetic spirituality of the desert fathers.

Second, I suggest how *Ancrene Wisse* itself functioned as such a conduit, by looking at several late medieval derivatives of the text addressed to a more general readership, in some of which the anchoritic life has become portable, the cell internalized and made a figure for the heart. In these works, we see the translation of the eremitic mode into a structuring metaphor for devout gentry or bourgeois subjectivity, as the process of laicization announced by *Ancrene Wisse* and vigorously pursued by the late medieval English church reaches its climax, a century before the Reformation.[11]

Tender Flesh and Spiritual Athletics

Ancrene Wisse treats the anchoresses' lack of affiliation with a religious order—a matter the work suggests that they viewed with anxiety—by in-

[11] This chapter is a companion piece to another essay on which it draws extensively: "*Ancrene Wisse*, Religious Reform, and the Late Middle Ages," in *A Companion Guide to "Ancrene Wisse*," ed. Yoko Wada (Cambridge, 2003).

structing them, in its Introduction, to tell inquirers who want to know if they are black or white, Cistercians or Benedictines, that they belong to the "order of St. James" because they follow the second half of James's definition of *religio* (James 1:27b) and "from þe world witen him cleane and unwemmet" (keep themselves from the world, pure and unstained) (f. 3a.12–13/50).[12] This is a fascinatingly ambiguous move, on the one hand consigning the work's readers to a position on the institutional margins of the religious life, on the other making their very lack of formal institutional affiliation into a spiritual advantage, a sign of the dominance in their lives of what the work calls the "lady" rule of love over the "servant" one of mere practice:

> Pawel, þe earste ancre, Antonie and Arsenie, Makarie and te oþre, neren ha religiuse and of Sein Iames ordre? Alswa Seinte Sare and Seinte Siclecice, and monie oþre swucc, hewepmen ba and wummen, wið hare greate matten and hare hearde heren: neren ha of god ordre? And hweðer hwite oðer blake—as unwise ow easkeð, þe weneð þe ordre sitte i þe curtel—Godd wat noðeles ha weren wel baðe: nawt tah onont claðes, ah as Godes spuse singeð bi hire seoluen, *Nigra sum set formosa*, "Ich am blac and tah hwit," ha seið. (f. 3b.2–12)

> [Paul the first anchorite, Anthony and Arsenius, Macarius and the others, were they not religious, and of St. James's order? Also St. Sarah and St. Syncletica and many other such, both men and women, with their rough sleeping-mats and their harsh hair shirts: were they not of good order? And whether they were white or black—as the foolish ask you who believe that the order lies in the habit—God indeed knows that they were truly both: though not in their clothing, but in the sense God's spouse sings of herself, *Nigra sum set formosa* (Canticles 1:5): "I am black and yet white," she says.] (50)

The author cuts anchoritic readers off from active roles as preachers, associating those roles with the other half of James's definition of *religio* (James 1:27a)—how it consists of helping "widewen and federlese children" (widows and fatherless children), as do "prelaz and treowe preachurs" (prelates and true preachers) when they aid a soul "þe haueð forloren hire spus, þet is Jesu Crist, wið eni heaued sunne" (who has lost her husband, that is Jesus Christ, through any mortal sin) (f. 3.a.11–20/50). As Bella Millett argues in an article on "*Ancrene Wisse* and Books of Hours," in making these gestures, he aligns his text with the informal rules for an-

---

[12] Unless otherwise indicated, quotations from *Ancrene Wisse* are from *The English Text of the "Ancrene Riwle": Ancrene Wisse: Edited from MS. Corpus Christi College Cambridge 402*, ed. J. R. R. Tolkien, EETS o.s., 249 (1962). Here and elsewhere, punctuation and capitalization have been modernized. Translations are adapted from *Anchoritic Spirituality: "Ancrene Wisse" and Associated Works*, trans. Anne Savage and Nicholas Watson (New York, 1991), with separate page references.

chorites, Hospitallers, and Beguines that were coming into being all over Europe in the early thirteenth century. He does something similar when, in part I (on devotions), he advocates use of the Little Hours of the Virgin in preference to the full office, a clear sign of his laicizing tendencies.[13] Still, the passage also presents anchoresses as members of a mixed community of radical religious, whose emphasis on interiority is so firm that they understand questions about their clothing in a purely spiritual sense. At this moment of trial, moreover, as they defend the paradoxical and ungendered community to which they belong, the passage offers them voices: abrasive, riddling voices, intended to throw their interlocutors into confusion, by challenging their assumptions with "wundur and sullich" (strange and wonderful) (f. 3a.4/50) words. In the twelfth-century *Libellus de diversis ordinibus*, hermits are seen as holy for their very diversity and lack of "order," for their role as reminders of the limits of institutional religion.[14] Here, it seems, *Ancrene Wisse* is thinking in the same way about anchoresses.

It is not, of course, immediately clear how far anchoresses themselves could take advantage of this idealizing of their institutional marginality, although scholars who argue that English women tended to become anchoresses in fairly large numbers because there were so few regular places in convents need to take into account the extent to which the institutional tenuousness of the anchoritic life could be a reason for embracing it.[15] Nor is it immediately obvious how this heroizing of women solitaries is consistent with the antifeminist images the author directs at his readers in part II, on the custody of the senses: invoking Eve, Dinah, and Bathsheba as types of bad, curious, or "totilde" (peeping) anchoresses, and describing the face of "wummon þet schaweð hire to wepmones echne" (a woman who shows herself to the eyes of men") as a pit (69).[16] These passages, which seem to define the anchoritic ideal in exclusively negative terms, have contributed much to the work's reputation for misogyny in recent years (perhaps because they are so seductively easy to teach, confirming [as they seem to do] all the crudest assumptions students bring to their first encounters with medieval literature). But the crudity of these passages is the point. The author of *Ancrene Wisse* is doing something different here from revealing his attitude to women. He is deploying offensive language and offering delib-

---

[13] Bella Millett, "*Ancrene Wisse* and Books of Hours," in *Writing Religious Women: Female Spiritual and Textual Practices in Late Medieval England*, ed. Denis Renevey and Christiania Whitehead (Cardiff, 2000).

[14] *Libellus de diversis ordinibus et professionibus qui sunt in aecclesia*, ed. Giles Constable and Bernard Smith (Oxford, 1972), discussed in Constable, *Reformation of the Twelfth Century*, 47–55.

[15] For the lack of institutional opportunities for women, see Sally Thompson, *Women Religious: The Founding of English Nunneries after the Norman Conquest* (Oxford, 1990).

[16] Two leaves are missing from the Corpus manuscript here: text supplied from *The English Text of the "Ancrene Riwle": Edited from B.M. Cotton MS. Cleopatra C.vi.*, ed. E.J. Dobson, EETS o.s., 267 (1972), f. 24r. 6–7.

erately extreme advice in the way a modern coach scolds an athlete for weakness and sets high standards as a strategy for getting her to outperform.[17] If you accept the ascetic spirituality of the text on its own terms— and there, of course, is the rub—its misogynistic rhetoric is an important means of empowering its readers, by giving them the energy they need to repudiate easy patterns of behavior in favor of the virtuosically controlled lives they have chosen.

My athletic image is a careful one, not only because modern athleticism can plausibly be understood as a cultural translation of medieval asceticism, but because part II of *Ancrene Wisse* also images its readers as spiritual athletes, in a passage that casts more light on its treatment of gender. The context of the passage is an attack on grumbling anchoresses who have grown depressed by the arduousness of their life and the insults of others and have let their standards go. "Al fleschliche iwurðen: lahinde, lihte ilatet, ane hwile lihte iwordet, an oðer luðere iwurdet . . . grucchildes, meanildes . . . cursildes and chidildes, bittre and attrie wið heorte tobollen" (they have grown all fleshly: laughing, frivolous, speaking carelessly at one time, foully at another: grumblers and complainers, cursers and chiders, bitter and poisonous with swollen hearts) (f. 28b.29–29a.5/88). So the author begins, before giving a vignette of the virtuous alternative to this behavior, in which the anchoress speaks out only against the guilt of sin, and even then "setteð hire wordes swa efne þet ha ne þunche ouersturet, ne nawt ilead ouer skile, ah inwardliche and soðliche . . . in a softe steuene" (pronounces her words so levelly that she does not seem stirred up and is not led beyond reason, but speaks thoughtfully and truthfully in a soft voice) (f. 29a.10–12/88). There follows a richly metaphorical account of what the anchoress needs to do to maintain the second pose and avoid slipping into the first:

> *Filia fatua in deminoratione erit.* Þis is Salomones sahe. Þet hit limpe to ei of ow, godd ne leue neauer! "Cang dohter iwurð as mone i wununge." Þriueð as þe cangun, se lengre se wurse. Ȝe, as ȝe wulleð waxen and nawt wenden hindward, sikerliche ȝe moten rowen aȝein stream, wið muchel swinc breoken forð and gasteliche earmðes stealewurðliche sturien. And swa ȝe moten alle. For alle we beoð i þe worldes wode weater, þe bereð adun monie. Sone se we eauer wergið and resteð us i slawðe, ure bat geað hindward, and we beoð þe cang dohter þe gað woniende, þe wlecche þe Godd speoweð, as is iwriten herefter, þe bigunnen i gast, and i flesch endið. Nai, nai. Ah Iob seið, þe delueð efter gold hord, eauer se he mare nahheð hit, se his heortes gleadschipe makeð him mare lusti and mare fersch to diggin and deluen, deoppre and deoppre, aðet he hit finde. Ower heorte nis nawt on eorðe, forþi ne þurue ȝe ne nawt deluen dunewardes. Ah heouen uppart þe heorte. For þet

[17] Athletics still receives too little attention in feminist studies of the body, a point well made in the otherwise not very helpful collection *Sport, Men, and the Gender Order: Critical Feminist Perspectives*, ed. Michael A. Messner and Donald F. Sabo (Champaign, Ill., 1990), 1–15.

is þe uprowunge aȝein þis worldes stream: [Þa þe heorte walde lihtliche adun lihten mid the stream], driuen hire aȝeinward to deluen þe golthort þet is in heouene. And hwet is þet deluunge? ȝeornful sechinde þoht: hwer hit beo, hwuch hit beo, hu me hit mahe ifinden. Þis is þe deluunge: beon bisiliche and ȝeornfulliche eauer her abuten, wið anewil ȝirnunge, wið heate of hungri heorte; waden up of unþeawes; creopen ut of flesch; breo-ken up ouer hire; astihen up on owseolf wið heh þoht toward heouene—swa muchel þe neodeluker þet ower feble, tendre flesch heardes ne mei þolien. (f. 29a.12–29b.13)

[*Filia fatua in deminoratione erit* (Ecclesiasticus 22: 3)—this is Solomon's say-ing: may God never grant that it should apply to any of you! "The foolish daughter becomes like the moon in its waning." She prospers like a fool, the longer the worse. You, if you want to wax and not go backwards, must row confidently against the current, force your way ahead with much hard work and pull stalwartly with your spiritual arms. And so must you all. For we are all in this stream, in the world's wild water, which carries many under. As soon as ever we tire and rest ourselves in sloth, our boat goes backward and we are the foolish daughter who wanes as she goes (as is written later), who began in the spirit and end in the flesh. No, no. But as Job says, those who dig for a hoard of gold, the closer they get to it, the more ardent glad-ness of heart makes them, and the keener to dig and delve deeper and deeper until they find it. Your heart is not on earth, so you need not delve downward, but lift the heart upward. For that is this rowing against the world's current: even though the heart would readily flow down with the current, to drive against it, so as to delve the gold-hoard that is up in heaven. And what is that delving? Eager, seeking thought: where it is; what it is; how it can be found. This is the delving: to be busily and eagerly al-ways about it, with a constant yearning, with the heat of the hungry heart; to wade up out of sin; to creep out of the flesh; to break loose from her; to rise above her on your own with high thought toward heaven—and so much the more needfully, since your weak, tender flesh cannot bear harsh things.] (88–89)[18]

This remarkable piece of prose offers a good example of the author's ten-dency to slide in and out of gendered language. Beginning with a standard misogynistic topos of the woman as waning moon and ending with one of many references to women's supposed physical weakness, most of the pas-sage is a call to spiritual energy that collides three different metaphors (rowing upstream, digging for treasure, climbing out of and over the body) in a rhetorical mimesis of the restless and ruthless quest for holiness the passage is advocating. Despite the use of misogynistic topoi (which func-tion as spurs to action of the same kind as earlier allusions to Eve or

[18] The bracketed passage in the Middle English was supplied by E. J. Dobson on the basis of an early French translation of *Ancrene Wisse*. The two English manuscripts to contain this passage both omit the line, probably through eye-skip. I thank Bella Millett for supplying me with Dobson's translation and for other suggestions about the translation of this pas-sage.

Bathsheba), much of the power of the passage lies in its combination of vivid particularity and universal applicability, since the author needs to exercise his spiritual arms quite as vigorously as his readers, hence his alternation of "you" and "we." The closing reference to womanly weakness may seem to compromise this universality, but is actually part of *Ancrene Wisse*'s consistent attempt to acknowledge the role of bodily mortification in the ascetic life, while directing readerly attention toward inner and affective strategies of spiritual sustenance.

From our own point of view or from that of a fourteenth-century eremitic writer such as Rolle, the way of life depicted in *Ancrene Wisse* is harsh indeed, and it is hard at first to read the phrase "feble, tendre flesch" except as patronizing. However, once one compares this work's attitude to mortification to the scary regime of Aelred's *De institutione inclusarum*—which expects anchoresses to earn their livings on a pound of coarse bread, some vegetables, and the occasional milk dish; praises the spiritual benefits of sleep loss; and demands silence throughout Lent—things begin to look different.[19] Even Aelred's prescriptions do not include the requirement to perform self-flagellation, a practice our author elsewhere recommends as a last resort in dealing with sexual temptation, but seems to have associated with men.[20] In this passage, the author of *Ancrene Wisse* is substituting the exercise of mental vigor for the physical mortifications he might otherwise have prescribed, which he alludes to at the end of the passage in the word "heardes" ("harsh things"). The reference to women's lack of physical endurance functions not as a slur against them but as a justification for this substitution.

This substitution is a significant move, both inside the text, where it enables the author to offer a relatively moderate version of the ascetic life to readers, and outside it, as part of the larger history of asceticism. The most serious hindrance to the lay appropriation of the eremitic ideal that took place in the late middle ages was the association between hermits and harsh physical mortification, which in its extreme forms could only be endured by specialists. All ascetic works emphasize the virtue of *discretio* as a bulwark against excessive discipline, but what counts as discretion varies greatly from era to era.[21] In this passage of *Ancrene Wisse*, we see the ground being laid for a mode of asceticism that internalizes the notion of

[19] Aelred, *Rule of Life for a Recluse*, 45–61.

[20] *Anchoritic Spirituality*, 155–56, a discussion of "Benedict's remedy" for sexual temptation, carefully hedged around with warnings about the need not to go too far.

[21] Aelred is actually dismissive of *discretio* in relation to bodily suffering: "I do not say this in disparagement of discretion . . . [but] true discretion is to put the soul before the body, and where both are threatened and the health of the one can only be obtained at the price of the suffering of the other, to neglect the body for the sake of the soul" (*Rule of Life for a Recluse*, 23).

discipline, and in so doing makes a devout lifestyle more easily available to everyone, as the definition of *discretio* moves sharply away from the more rigorous forms of physical mortification (such as flagellation or wearing of hair shirts). Here, in a move that anticipates Rolle's elevation of "the fire of love" as the best instrument for dealing with sin in his own writings about the eremitic and anchoritic ideals, "heate of hungri heorte" is presented as a remedy for sloth as effective as the heat of physical pain.[22]

In an era where extreme physical mortification is being reinvented and theorized as S/M, we need to be cautious in judging how far this shift from physical to spiritual asceticism is, in and of itself, empowering; a queer reading of *Ancrene Wisse* and its relationship to Aelred, for example, might conclude the opposite. We can see the shift, however, as part of the larger project of *Ancrene Wisse*: to maintain the rigor and elevation of the eremitic ideal by which the work's readers live, while opening up the ideal to a larger number of potential practitioners. *Ancrene Wisse*, a vernacular work that refuses to identify itself as a "rule" (and thus limit its readership to members of an order), does in the first instance limit its address to women. But by treating these women as exemplary, as symbolic either of all Christians or of the "weak" who cannot aspire to the ascetic and intellectual heights attained by male practitioners, the work treats its audience as the pioneers of a movement of spiritual perfection that in theory encompasses everyone.

One of the fantasies that energized the early friars was the apocalyptic thought of Joachim of Fiore, who prophesied the imminence of a third "age of the Holy Spirit" in which the entire world would be enfolded in a single ideal of monastic perfection. However distanced it seems from apocalyptic thinking, there is at least a broad sense in which *Ancrene Wisse*, generous in its inclusiveness even as it is harsh in its specific directives, can be seen as an attempt to bring this world into being.[23]

The Figure of the Inner Hermit

This brings me to my second topic, which I discuss in detail in an essay parallel to this one (see note 11): the later history of *Ancrene Wisse* as a conduit between the anchoritic life and the devout laity, both women and men. In that essay, I analyze the Middle English works that can be shown to borrow from or rewrite portions of *Ancrene Wisse* and establish how widely in-

[22] Rolle's lack of interest in asceticism is a harbinger of late medieval attitudes in other English works. See Nicholas Watson, *Richard Rolle and the Invention of Authority* (Cambridge, 1991), chap. 2. See also the reflections in *Contemplations of the Dread and Love of God*, ed. Margaret Connolly, EETS, o. s., 303 (1993), written around 1400, which discusses the decline of asceticism over the preceding centuries.

[23] For twelfth-century apocalypticism, see Constable, *Reformation of the Twelfth Century*, chap. 4, "The Rhetoric of Reform."

fluential the work was. Just as, for its author, anchoresses often seem to symbolize a life of perfection uncluttered by learning or attention to religious forms, so the work itself later comes to symbolize the capacity of the English vernacular and its readership to aim as high as the work does aim. By the fourteenth century at the latest,[24] *Ancrene Wisse* figures the possibility of a life focused on the inner self and discreetly lived in public and in private, especially by women, but potentially by all. I also arrive at a conclusion that surprised me when I reached it: that, despite the prestige of the work among conservatives such as Walter Hilton and Nicholas Love and despite a modern reading of the work itself as conservative, the circles in which its influence was most direct were reformist, and in some cases associated with Lollardy. This means that *Ancrene Wisse* had its most important late medieval impact among the devout, somewhat puritanical gentry and later merchant Christians who were the principal lay audience for reformist writing and whose sense of religious self-worth and hostility to worldliness had a long history, both before and after the sixteenth-century Reformation.

For example, passages of *Ancrene Wisse*, as well as some of its larger claims and assumptions, are adapted in two late fourteenth-century treatises whose interrelationships suggest they are products of the same reformist milieu: *The Holy Book Gratia Dei* and *The Pater Noster of Richard Hermit*.[25] *Ancrene Wisse* may also have influenced a third work that circulates with the second of these, *Book to a Mother*.[26] All of these are addressed to or were read by lay women, and all of them share certain attitudes: contempt for the world, expressed as a sense of spiritual exclusivity harsher than anything in *Ancrene Wisse*; belief in the value of vernacular religious education and the Bible; and an implied antimonasticism. Unusual among Middle English works addressed to women, that is, all three construct the inner self along ascetic or penitential, more than affective, lines.

Ancrene Wisse has left a particular mark on how these works deal with the notion of a religious rule. Here, too, models of behavior are referred to as "rules" only with reluctant irony, as the works assert their own rele-

---

[24] Missing from my account is the situation in Anglo-Norman texts that derive material from *Ancrene Wisse*, such as the *Compileisun* partly edited by W. H. Trethewey, *The French Text of the "Ancrene Riwle": Edited from Trinity College Cambridge MS. R. 14. 7*, EETS, o. s., 240 (1958 for 1954).

[25] See Mary Luke Arntz, ed., *Richard Rolle and Þe Holy Boke Gratia Dei: An Edition With Commentary*, Salzburg Studies in English Literature: Elizabethan and Renaissance Studies 92, no. 2 (Salzburg, 1981); Florent G. A. M. Aarts, *Þe Pater Noster of Richard Ermyte: A Late Middle English Exposition of the Lord's Prayer* (Nijmegen, 1967).

[26] See Adrian James McCarthy, ed., *Book to a Mother: An Edition with Commentary*, Salzburg Studies in English Literature: Elizabethan and Renaissance Studies 92, no. 1 (Salzburg, 1981). My remarks on this work also make some use of my essay, "Fashioning the Puritan Gentry-Woman: Devotion and Dissent in *Book to a Mother*," in *Medieval Women: Texts and Contexts in Late Medieval Britain: Essays for Felicity Riddy*, ed. Jocelyn Wogan-Browne et al., Medieval Women: Texts and Contexts 3 (Turnhout, 2000).

vance for everyone, even as they question the ability of most people to live up to their high standards. *The Holy Book*, the most straightforward and least spiritually snobbish of the group, translates *Ancrene Wisse*'s injunctions about prayer and silence into instructions for "ilk a mane, of what state he be" (anyone, of whatever status), who must do "honeste werke, withowttene lettynge of his tyme" (conscientious work, without any time-wasting) and whose "uttire berynge, whareso he comes," must "so honeste be and faire þat louynge be to God, and stirryng of gude all þat hym seese" (whose appearance, wherever they go, must be so neat and proper that it brings praise to God, and an urge to be good in all who see them) (15). Here, *discretio* consists of frugality, not mortification, and the anchoritic virtue of stability becomes care in looking for a quiet inn when arriving in a new town (115). Despite being written in the first instance for nuns, *The Pater Noster* acknowledges only one rule, which all must follow but which does not of itself lead to salvation. This is the "new reule, swiþe hard to þole" (the new rule, most difficult to put up with) laid on Adam after the fall, which replaces the "ordre softe and ful of likyng" (lax and extremely pleasant order) he enjoyed in Eden, and which the work derives from God's curse: "in swoot of þi face þou schalt ete þi breed" (in sweat of your face you shall eat your bread), interpreting this as an injunction to avoid "idilnes, glotenye, and gelous kepynge and tendre ouer þe fleisch" (laziness, greed, and a cowardly and protective concern for the body) (13–14). *Book to a Mother* claims that the only rule worth following is "Cristes religioun" (Christ's religious rule), which consists in "Crist . . . with his conversacioun" (Christ and his way of living) (31). So far as other religious rules are concerned, "but thei acorde with Cristes religioun and helpe therto, thei ben noiouse, and better hit were to leve suche ordynaunces of men" (unless they are compatible with Christ's rule and help with it, they are a nuisance, and it would be better to renounce such merely human systems) (122). Of these works, only *Holy Book* is prepared to be treated as a rule in its own right. For the others, the word *rule* is even closer to implying hypocrisy than it is for the author of *Ancrene Wisse*. To live spiritually, following Christ or the law of love certainly involves rules; indeed, in all these works there are many, most of them fiercely puritanical. But not only are these rules seen as divine, mediated through the Bible, not through any human institution. Obedience to them is also seen as an expression of inner rectitude and spiritual responsibility rather than as a mere gesture of submission. The lay or vernacular reader has acquired the sturdy independence, the automatic suspicion for the hypocrisies of institutional religion, that *Ancrene Wisse* associates with eremitic living.

Similar attitudes to the rule also typify two more extended Middle English rewritings of *Ancrene Wisse*: a mid-fourteenth-century redaction of the work for an audience that apparently includes nuns and laypeople of both sexes, known as *The Pepys Rule*; and an early fifteenth-century treatise closely based on parts II and III of *Ancrene Wisse*, called *A Simple Tretis*.[27] Although neither of these works is opposed to monasticism as explicitly as contemporary Lollard writings, both use the eremitic nature of *Ancrene Wisse*, its emphasis on irregular religious living, as a platform from which to preach against formalism and hypocrisy. Christian living, according to these works, is ultimately not a communal but an individual thing, rooted in personal inner purity that expresses itself best by good living in the world and inner detachment from the world. The walls of a convent or cell do not act as barriers against sin, even leaky ones, but as the borders of dangerously secret spaces in which sin hides itself from inspection, which turn professional religious into mere simulacra of holiness. We are close, here, to the sneering Lollard term for monasticism, "private religion," with all its weight of disgust at improper kinds of "privity," and even closer to *Book to a Mother*'s characterization of the convent wall as a device that allows a nun to seem "a good womman" on the outside, but be "a schrewe" on the inside (124.11–12). Instead, the walls of the cell need to be built inside the self. So emerges the notion of the inner hermit or anchorite, who carries the cell within.[28]

The Pepys Rule characterizes the inner hermit in terms that derive directly from the opening of part II of *Ancrene Wisse*, reusing its delicate shifts between "windows" and "senses" for its own ends:

> Now vnderstondeþ þat a mannes body is cleped in holy wrytt sumtyme an hous, and sumtyme a citee, and sumtyme Goddes temple and Holy Chirche. Þan riȝth as ȝee see þat an ancre is bischett in an hous and may nouȝth out, riȝth so is vche mannes soule bischett in his body as an ancre. And þerfore vche man, lered and lewed, ȝif he wil queme God and be his deciple, helde hym in his hous, schete his dores and his wyndowes fast þat ben his fyue wyttes, þat he take no likyng to synne ne to werldelich þynges. And þan he is an ancre and wel better quemeþ God þan hij þat byschetten hem and taken hem to heiȝe lyf and ben werldelich. (44:2–12)

> [Now understand that in Scripture the human body is sometimes called a house, and sometimes a city, and sometimes God's temple and Holy Church. So, just as you see that an anchorite is shut in a house and cannot get out, so is every human soul shut into his body as an anchorite. And

---

[27] *The English Text of the "Ancrene Riwle": Edited from Magdalene College, Cambridge MS. Pepys 2498*, ed. A. Zettersten, EETS o.s., 274 (1976); *The English Text of the "Ancrene Riwle": Edited from British Museum MS. Royal 8.C.1*, ed. A. C. Baugh, EETS o.s., 232 (1956).

[28] The notion of the "inner hermit" or cell has some relation to that of the "inner cloister" popularized in the late fourteenth century by *The Abbey of the Holy Ghost* in particular; on this see, most recently, Christiania Whitehead, "Making a Cloister of the Soul in Medieval Religious Treatises," *Medium Aevum* 67 (1998): 1–29. Another obvious parallel is Walter Hilton's application of the old concept of the "mixed life" to the devout laity; see S. J. Ogilvie-Thomson, *Walter Hilton's "Mixed Life," Edited from Lambeth Palace MS 472*, Elizabethan and Renaissance Studies 92, no. 15 (Salzburg, 1986).

therefore, everybody, learned or unlearned, if he wishes to please God and be his disciple, let him shut his doors and windows that are his five senses tight, so that he takes no pleasure in sin nor in worldly things. And then he is an anchorite, and pleases God better than those who shut themselves in and set themselves to the life of perfection and remain worldly.]

In this passage, the laicization of the ascetic life proceeds apace, as the very desire for perfect living that motivated anchoritic enclosure is revealed as a dangerous spiritual pretentiousness: a desire for "heiʒe lyf," the life of perfection (a crucial phrase in *Ancrene Wisse*; e.g., at the opening of part IV) that all but inevitably, if paradoxically, reveals the anchorite to be secretly worldly. *Ancrene Wisse* is gradually morphing here into a work whose natural readership is the laity, the group who, by the late fourteenth century, are the heirs of the anti-institutional puritanism *Ancrene Wisse* derives from the eremitic tradition.

The implied audience for *Ancrene Wisse*, always a mix of women and men, is also becoming more male. Although *The Pepys Rule* survives in a manuscript likely compiled for nuns and addresses female religious as one of its main readerships, this text already contains much that is suitable for secular priests or for itinerant preachers and their patrons. Indeed, in addition to the metaphor of the inner cell, the work shows a marked interest in the apostolic life of preaching, a life most medieval texts by definition reserve for men, noting that the apostles "nere nouʒt bischett" (were not shut in) (44.29). There seems to be an unresolved tension here between two different ideals of perfection, both nonmonastic, but one clerical and male, the other lay and of mixed gender—even if the work does once suggest, most intriguingly, that holy women, too, can preach.[29]

A Simple Tretis, addressing the laity rather than the clergy, takes the masculinization of *Ancrene Wisse* in a different direction, and so avoids this tension. Justifying his decision to compile a treatise about the solitary life for laypeople, the author also claims that solitude is an inner quality:

Here wil sum men sey þat for to write or speke so mych of solitari lijf amang þe comen people of þe world is bot foly. Forwhy and all men were solitary, þen shold no men be marchantes, plughmen, ny men of craft, and so sholde þe world be confounded and at an end. . . . To þis wil I answer . . .

---

[29] "Þere ben two manere of wymmen þat ben trewe prelates and prechoures. Þise two hane þe heiʒest dale in heuene" (5.3–5)(There are two kinds of women who can be true prelates and preachers. These two have the highest reward in heaven). In context, it is hard to know what to make of this remark, part of a digression that seems either textually confused or to be a copy of a draft, and "wymmen" may, unfortunately, be an error. A later passage asserts that "womman ne owe nouʒth to prechen bot ʒif sche be þe ouer holyer . . . For seint Poule forbedeþ hem, bot man ne forbedeþ he nouʒth" (28.18–20)(a woman ought not to preach unless she is exceptionally holy . . . For Paul forbade them, but he did not forbid a man). Again, the thought here seems to be somewhat undigested, confirming the sense that *The Pepys Rule* is partly an experiment.

[that] . . . vnnethes may any man or woman be broght to such maner of ly-
fyng. Neiþelese, how al men and wymmen shold in party be solitary I wil
sey a few wordys. Seynt Gregory . . . spekes of two maner of peple. Þer ar
sum þat setten most her hert to haue worldly worship, worldly riches, and
lust of her flesh. . . . Anoþer peple þer is þat desiren noþing þat is in þis
warld, bot as to be a mene to b[r]yng þem to endles blis [. . .] For þouȝ þey
haue besines outeward—as gouernance of houshold, cure of paryshens as
parsones haue, gouernance of contres and cytees as sherefes, maires, and
baylees—ȝit her intent is euer set on "on þing": to do right and lawe of God,
kepyng clene her conscience. And many a tyme such men, when þey are by
hemselue, þey examyn her conscience, and if þey fynd anyþing amys, þey
amenden it by trew penance: þus þey are solitary in her intent, settyng her
hert [op]on "on þing," þat is on rightwisnes and Goddes plesance, wich ar
alon. And thus may every man, if he will, be in sum maner solitari and fer
from synful condicions of the world. . . . Neitheles, to forsake the world as
the aposteles did is a ded of perfeccion, and therfor not al men ar bounden
to that maner of forsakyng the world. Bot every man that wil be saved most
forsake the world on this wise. (43–44)

[At this point, someone will say that it is mere folly to write or speak so
much about the solitary life among the common people of the world. For if
everyone was solitary, then nobody would be merchants, ploughmen, nor
craftsmen, and so the world would be wrecked and finished. To this I wish
to reply that hardly any man or woman can be induced to undertake such a
manner of living. Even so, I wish to say a few words about how all men and
women should be solitary in part. St. Gregory talks about two kinds of people. There are some who fix their desires most strongly on having worldly
praise, worldly riches, and fleshly pleasure. There is another people who desire nothing that is in this world, except as a way to bring them to endless
bliss. For even if they have public employment—like administration of a
household, spiritual care of parishioners like parsons have, administration
of districts of communities like sheriffs, mayors, and bailiffs—their ambition
is always set on "one thing": to do justice and the law of God, keeping their
consciences clean. And such people examine their consciences many a time
when they are by themselves, and if they find anything wrong, they emend
it with sincere penance. And so they are solitary in ambition, setting their
hearts on "one thing," that is on righteousness and God's will, which are all
one. And in this way may every person, if he wants to, be in some sense solitary and far from the sinful practices of the world. It is true that to forsake
the world as the apostles did is a deed of perfection, and so all people are
not bound to that way of forsaking of the world. But everyone who wants to
be saved must forsake the world in this way.]

A Simple Tretis is written for women as well as men, but here it is public,
masculine living that has become the norm, as the notion of the inner anchorite effaces the special connection even *The Pepys Rule* retains between
enclosure and women. As a result, the dichotomy between silent solitaries
and preachers found in *The Pepys Rule* (as in *Ancrene Wisse* itself) implicitly
disappears, and we are left with an image of a community of public offi-

cials, conscious of their inner rectitude, spending their lives bringing "right and lawe of God" into the social and political realm. A hundred years after this text was written, Sir Thomas More, who wore a hair shirt all the time he was chancellor, was to become the most famous English exponent of this interiorized version of the eremitic ideal.

In most respects, I believe that *A Simple Tretis* and its colleagues form part of a project of selfhood-building that is more continuous with *Ancrene Wisse* than reactive against it. However, as *Ancrene Wisse* meets the secular world in these works, we have seen that its spirituality undergoes two major modifications, besides the shift in the implications of the term *discretio*. First, these later works repudiate *Ancrene Wisse*'s definition of the reader as living a "high life," a way of perfection, not merely salvation, preferring to stress the work's equally strong focus on meekness and humility. For them, everyone should live in the same, humble and ascetic way, and any claim to perfection is simply a sign of pride—as the word "high" (which can imply either "elevated" or "presumptuous") indeed suggests. As the longest work to borrow from *Ancrene Wisse*, *Book to a Simple and Devout Woman*, has it: "perlus hit is on hyȝ to clymbe, and siker wei to God hit is þat mon holde hym lowe" (it is perilous to climb up high, and it is a sure way to God that someone keep themselves low).[30] Second, partly because these works are for readers involved in the world as anchoresses are not and partly to compensate for the loss of distinction that follows from the universalization of the eremitic ideal, these later works tend to make more extended use of satire and polemic than does *Ancrene Wisse*.[31] Readers are expected to think humbly of their own efforts at Christian living, but they are also invited to judge the still more serious failures of Christian society at large, especially those with pretensions to holiness: monks, friars, nuns, and clerics. In a passage that implicitly suspends the general rule that women are not encouraged to internalize the prophetic dimension of the eremitic mode, the widow for whom *Book to a Mother* is written is told that judging others is Christlike: "Crist juggede and cursede muche in this world, and taughte forte jugge, to destruye sinne, ther as hit is opene agenus his hestis" (Christ judged and cursed a great deal in this world, and taught us to judge, in order to destroy sin, when it is obviously against his commandments) (72.23–5). Such a harsh attitude is necessary because of the way sin has infected "alle corsede popis, cardinallis, bishopis, prelatis, prestis, freris, monkes, chanouns, [nunnes]," creating a world fraught with hypocrisy (90.15–17). Not all *Ancrene Wisse*'s successors are as forthright as this, and some of them show anxiety about putting satirical weapons in the

[30] *Book for a Simple and Devout Woman*, ed. F. N. M. Diekstra, Medieavalia Groningana 24 (Groningen, 1998), 7635–36.

[31] This is not to say that satire is a foreign mode in *Ancrene Wisse*, which several times borrows satirical passages from Aelred's *De institutione* in praising the anchoresses' resolution to keep to their way of life. However, passages of satire are always brief and specific.

hands of women. For example, *Book for a Simple and Devout Woman* gives elaborate polemic descriptions of the sinfulness of the world, but ends by using *Ancrene Wisse*'s injunctions on womanly silence to imply strongly that it is not the reader's place to speak out by herself. Taken as a whole, though, these later works build powerfully on *Ancrene Wisse*'s separation of the inner from the outer, by offering their readers an attitude of disdain for worldliness and a confidence in being able to locate it in the heart of re-ligious and secular institutions, which gives the "inner self" an inextricably public dimension. Where the early readers of *Ancrene Wisse* can see them-selves as icons of holy living because of their very silence and notional sep-arateness from the world—"anchoring" the Church by representing Chris-tian heroism to their communities—their lay successors are closer to being sermons, sober presences in a sinful world whose clothing, bearing, and willingness to denounce sin is a living reproach to others. If Thomas More is a male embodiment of this attitude, his female counterpart is Margery Kempe.

Coda: Moral Power and Self-Containment

However uncomfortable *Ancrene Wisse* and the later works that draw on it can make us, their success depends on their ability to inculcate a sense of self-worth in those who try to live by them. One of their basic means of doing this is by invoking the trope of the hermit: a trope that allows quali-ties we tend to see as containing women—humility, silence, contempt for the flesh—to be understood as modes of power. Admittedly, this power is first and foremost an inner power. In differentiating so firmly between the outer and the inner, offering readers a fundamentally anti-institutional se-ries of self-images, *Ancrene Wisse* and its successors do nothing to combat the many kinds of institutional misogyny their readers had to live with. But the exaltation of literal or metaphorical solitude in these works does provide both a measure of ideological protection from misogyny and, par-adoxically, a sense of community. *Ancrene Wisse* surrounds the reader with evidences of her place in an eremitic tradition, going back as far as biblical figures such as Judith (interpreted as a solitary) and including holy women and men from many periods of history. The work's successors offer lay readers a similarly constructed community, partly by invoking *Ancrene Wisse* itself, as they struggle to cut the reader off from secular society by in-culcating a puritanical sense of her exclusivity: her obedience to a form of living that is now seen as necessary for everybody, but actually practiced by only a few.

Yet because hermits *embody* inner power, proclaiming the centrality of the interior from their places on the visible fringes of secular society, the eremitic trope does more than merely contain the women and men who in-ternalize it: even as it allows them to speak out against sin, it makes them figures of an ideal of self-containment. In this chapter, I have tried to show something of how *Ancrene Wisse* and its successors inculcate this ideal, and why the ideal is important to the history of women and power. Women often still figure self-containment, reflectiveness, and the mysteries of the inner self today, even in popular culture, and in ways that can either empower them or justify their continuing marginalization in the public sphere. *Ancrene Wisse* and its successors are part of the story of how this came to be so.

CHAPTER FOUR

Powers of Record, Powers of Example:
Hagiography and Women's History

Jocelyn Wogan-Browne

That hagiography can serve as empowering exemplary biography and that it can be creatively interpreted by individual medieval women for their own purposes is a phenomenon familiar in medieval England from the examples of Margery Kempe and Christina of Markyate. This chapter attempts to move away from such exceptional and nowadays well-known individual uses of hagiography to look at the genre's value in making visible what seems particularly elided from history's grand narratives—female communities.[1] Despite the once axiomatically accepted paucity of English nunnery records, there are many places where female communities can be seen to be creating and deploying narratives about themselves in a range of pragmatic and other ways. One might think of the fourteenth- and fifteenth-century abbesses at Barking Abbey and their re-arrangements of the house's commemorative traditions regarding their seventh-century foundress, St. Ethelburga, and their other predecessor saints and abbesses, or of the Syon nuns' seventeenth-century Spanish manuscript account of their history (commissioned by the abbess Barbara Wiseman [d. 1649] in the hope that the Infanta would intercede for Syon's return to England if she became Princess of Wales).[2] Nevertheless, conven-

[1] For an account of the occlusion of female community in English scholarship, see Jocelyn Wogan-Browne, " 'Reading is Good Prayer': Recent Research on Female Reading Communities," *New Medieval Literatures* 5 (2002): 229–97.

[2] For Barking's late medieval commemorations, much of the material is available in J. B. Tolhurst, ed., *The Barking Ordinale and Customary of the Benedictine Nuns of Barking Abbey*, 2 vols., HBS 65, 66 (London, 1927, 1928). On Syon see Christopher de Hamel, *Syon Abbey: The Library of the Bridgettine Nuns and Their Peregrinations after the Reformation: An Essay by*

tual women in England are often reckoned to be missing from the increased visibility *to us* of women's texts and literary culture that took place in, for instance, twelfth- and thirteenth-century German convents or the beguinages of the Low Countries.[3] Only with the increase in English texts and literacies in the fourteenth and fifteenth centuries, the story often runs, is there a women's literary history to reckon with in insular medieval culture.

Before the late fourteenth and fifteenth centuries (and with a continuing and significant afterlife during that later period), the most prominent text of women's religious lives in medieval England for modern scholarship is the *Ancrene Wisse* or *Guide for Anchoresses*, and its associated saints' lives, homilies, and exemplary meditations, known as the Katherine Group and the Wooing Group. Composed in English in the early thirteenth-century West Midlands for a household of three anchoresses and their servants by a cleric who was perhaps their relative or spiritual director, the *Guide* was twice translated into French and several times into Latin, used in monastic communities and among laypeople, and drawn on for many other texts in manuscript and in print into the early sixteenth century.[4]

The *Guide* fascinates us, and seems also to have fascinated audiences in medieval England, with its ambivalent and powerful imaging of a female

---

Christopher de Hamel, with the Manuscript at Arundel Castle (London, 1991), and on Syon's late medieval culture of record, see Mary C. Erler, "Syon Abbey's Care for Books: Its Sacristan's Account Rolls 1506/7–1535/6," *Scriptorium* 39 (1985): 293–307. See, for further examples, Nancy Bradley Warren, "Kings, Saints, and Nuns: Gender, Religion, and Authority in the Reign of Henry V," *Viator* 30 (1999): 307–22; idem, *Spiritual Economies: Female Monasticism in Later Medieval England* (Philadelphia, 2001).

[3] The classic account is Herbert Grundmann, *Religiösebewegungen im Mittelalter* (Berlin, 1935, 2d ed., Darmstadt 1961) but see further an important critique of Grundmann's thesis of spontaneous women's "movements," with its implicit occlusions of the continuities of female community by Carol Neel ("The Origins of the Beguines," in *Sisters and Workers in the Middle Ages*, ed. Judith M. Bennett et al. [Chicago, 1989], 240–60). Brenda Bolton's excellent studies of the *mulieres sanctae* of the Low Countries' early drew attention to the problem of whether or not England could be seen to have female communities comparable with Beguines; for her recent thinking (with summary of earlier scholarship), see her "Thirteenth-Century Religious Women: Further Reflections on the Low Countries' Special Case," in *New Trends in Feminine Spirituality: The Holy Women of Liège and Their Impact*, ed. Juliette Dor, Lesley Johnson, and Jocelyn Wogan-Browne (Turnhout, 1999), 129–57. On women's literacies in thirteenth-century England, see Bella Millett "Women in No Man's Land: English Recluses and the Development of Vernacular Literature in the Twelfth and Thirteenth Centuries," in *Women and Literature in Britain 1150–1500*, ed. Carol M. Meale (Cambridge, 1996), 86–103.

[4] The latest extant Latin manuscript of *Ancrene Wisse* is London, British Library MS Royal 7 C. x (early sixteenth century): see Bella Millett with the assistance of George B. Jack and Yoko Wada, "The Manuscripts," in *Ancrene Wisse, the Katherine Group and the Wooing Group*, Annotated Bibliographies of Old and Middle English Literature, II (Cambridge, 1996), 54. At the end of the fifteenth century, the English text contributes to the *Tretyse of Loue* printed by Wynkyn de Worde 1493 or 1494 (ed. John H. Fisher, EETS o.s., 223, London, 1951); between 1433 and 1441 a manuscript of a French version (London, BL Cotton Vitellius F. vii) was given to the Duchess of Gloucester by the Countess of Kent (Millett, *Ancrene Wisse, the Katherine Group and the Wooing Group*, 54).

self at once enclosed and autonomous in its anchorhold.[5] For my purposes here, the reception of the *Guide* and its associated texts in our narratives is the immediate point. The first modern editions of these works, *Seinte Katerine* in 1841 and the *Guide* in 1853, were made as the English Evangelical and other sororities were developing, when E. B. Pusey and others were writing *regulae* for women.[6] These medieval texts, however, were primarily received within the framework of a nationalizing English history, both within and outside the academy.[7] In the work of Tolkien and others, the *Guide* and its associated texts became testimony to the continuity (*pace* the Norman Conquest) of the robust, sane, masculine English language. Questions of audience and reception were dismissed in this era as womanish and sentimental.[8] The *Guide* helped further the nationalizing mission and credentials of the Early English Text Society (EETS, incepted in 1864), which in 1932 published as a separate volume R. W. Chambers's account of the *Guide*'s role in pedigrees of Englishness and which also, from 1944, published diplomatic editions of the *Guide*'s every manuscript and version (the last of these appearing in 2000).[9] Although not explicitly revalued as women's history until the early 1980s, the *Guide* and the associated saints' lives of the Katherine Group and the devotional meditations of the Wooing Group have thus had a long-sustained role in institutional narratives of the literary history of the English middle ages.

Against this reception history, I want to contrast a much less well-known manuscript collection, one I think quite as important as the *Guide* and its

[5] The best guide to both medieval and modern reception is Millett, *Ancrene Wisse, the Katherine Group and the Wooing Group*, 34–45 (modern scholarship on the *Guide*); 31–34, 49–61 (medieval dissemination). For reflection on current preoccupation with the *Guide*, see Sarah Beckwith, "Passionate Regulation: Enclosure, Ascesis, and the Feminist Imaginary," *South Atlantic Quarterly* 93 (1994): 803–24; Nicholas Watson, " 'With the Heat of the Hungry Heart': Empowerment and *Ancrene Wisse*," in this volume.

[6] James Morton, ed., *The Legend of St Katherine of Alexandria* (London, 1841); idem, ed. and tr., *The Ancren Riwle: A Treatise on the Rules and Duties of Monastic Life, Edited and Translated from a Semi-Saxon MS. of the Thirteenth Century* (London, 1853). For the sororities of the 1840s and 1850s, see Martha Vicinus, *Independent Women: Work and Community for Single Women 1850–1920* (Chicago, 1985), chap. 2.

[7] For a lucid overview, see Linda Georgianna, "Coming to Terms with the Norman Conquest: Nationalism and English Literary History," in *Literature and the Nation*, ed. Brook Thomas (Tübingen, 1998), 33–53. On the formation of professional English studies, see D. J. Palmer, *The Rise of English Studies: An Account of the Study of English Language and Literature from Its Origins to the Making of the Oxford English School* (London, 1965).

[8] Millett, *Ancrene Wisse, the Katherine Group and the Wooing Group*, 41–42.

[9] R. W. Chambers, "On the Continuity of English Prose from Alfred to More and His School," in *The Life and Death of Sir Thomas More by Nicholas Harpsfield*, ed. Elsie Vaughan Hitchcock, EETS o.s., 186 (London, 1932, repr. 1957 as EETS 191A). The most recent edition of a manuscript of the *Guide* is *The English Text of the Ancrene Riwle: The 'Vernon' Text*, ed. Arne Zettersten and Bernhard Diensberg, with an intro. by H. L. Spencer, EETS o.s., 310 (Oxford, 2000). For the EETS, see Derek Pearsall, "Frederick James Furnivall (1825–1910)," in *Medieval Scholarship: Biographical Studies on the Formation of a Discipline*, vol. 2, *Literature and Philology*, ed. Helen Damico (New York, 1998), 125–38.

associated texts. This is a manuscript exemplifying the complex interplay of factors that can mask women's histories. It also offers a very different sense from the Katherine Group lives of the ways in which hagiography might mean in women's literary culture.

London, British Library MS Additional 70513 is a manuscript collection consisting entirely of saints' lives in Anglo-Norman French. It is the largest single collection of Anglo-Norman saints' lives and the only one to contain saints' lives exclusively. Many of its texts appear to have no descendants, and eight of its thirteen lives are the only known copies of their texts. The manuscript has been known throughout the twentieth century to some specialists in Anglo-Norman, but known mainly as a resource for texts of individual lives and their contribution to philological study. Appearing in journals such as *Romania* and in the Anglo-Norman Text Society's editions, the lives have been largely known to Anglicist literary scholars as "French" texts.[10] For French scholars, their provenance makes such texts "English," unless they are included in the select pantheon of those works in Anglo-Norman, or works whose earliest manuscripts are Anglo-Norman, which are perceived as part of French literary history—works such as the *Chanson de Roland, Tristan, Saint Alexis*.[11] Against the combination of modern nationalisms, linguistic disciplinary boundaries, and national literary histories, it has been difficult for either francophone or anglophone scholars to see Anglo-Norman as a source of identity or power for their subject or themselves. Thus the collection of lives in Additional 70513 has barely figured in accounts of literary history in England, let alone in women's literary history in England as such.

---

[10] A. T. Baker began editing texts from the manuscript before the First World War (in the highly interventionist manner of the period) and continued to do so until his death in 1947. One study of the manuscript was never published because Baker's student at Sheffield University, J. Malone, did not survive the war to publish his Sheffield thesis. The last text in the manuscript without full edition (the life of Richard of Chichester) was edited in 1995. Alphabetically by saint, editions of the lives in the manuscript are: **Audrée** [Etheldreda]: *La vie sainte Audrée: Poème anglo-normand du XIIIe siècle*, ed. Östen Södergaard (Uppsala, 1955); **Catherine**: *The Life of Saint Catherine by Clemence of Barking*, ed. William MacBain, ANTS 18 (Oxford, 1964); **Elisabeth of Hungary**: "La vie de sainte Elisabeth d'Hongrie," ed. Ludwig Karl, *ZRPh* 24 (1910): 295–314; *Seven More Poems by Nicholas Bozon*, ed. Sr. Amelia Klenke, Franciscan Institute Publications Historical ser. 2 (New York, 1951); **Edmund of Canterbury**: "La vie de saint Edmond, archevêque de Cantorbéry," ed. A. T. Baker, *Romania* 55 (1929): 332–81; **Edward the Confessor**: *La Vie d'Edouard le confesseur, poème anglo-normand du XIIe siecle*, ed. Östen Södergaard (Uppsala, 1948); **Faith**: "Vie anglo-normande de sainte Foy par Simon de Walsingham," ed. A. T. Baker, *Romania* 66 (1940–41): 49–84; **Mary Magdalen**: "La vie de Madeleine," ed. R. Reinsch, *Archiv* 64 (1880): 85–94; also "Die Episode aus der Vie de Madeleine," ed. Ludwig Karl, *ZRPh* 34 (1910): 363–70; **Modwenna**: *Saint Modwenna*, ed. A. T. Baker and Alexander Bell, ANTS 7 (Oxford, 1947); **Osith**: "An Anglo-French Life of St. Osith," ed. A. T. Baker, *MLR* 6 (1911): 476–502; **Paphnutius**: "Vie de saint Panuce," ed. A. T. Baker, *Romania* 38 (1909): 418–24; **Paul the Hermit**: "An Anglo-French Life of Saint Paul the Hermit," ed. A. T. Baker, *MLR* 4 (1908–9): 491–504; **Richard of Chichester**: *La Vie seint Richard evesque de Cycestre*, ed. D. W. Russell, ANTS 51 (London, 1995); **Thomas Becket**: *La Vie de saint Thomas le Martyr par Guernes de Pont-Sainte-Maxence*, ed. E. Walberg (Lund, 1922).

[11] Andrew Taylor, "Was There a Song of Roland?" *Speculum* 76 (2001): 28–65.

The provenance of the manuscript, however, requires that it be considered in this context. The manuscript was owned by the Augustinian canonesses at Campsey in Suffolk and used, according to an early fourteenth-century inscription following the final text, for mealtime reading. Designed as a single collection of ten saints' lives in the late thirteenth century, the manuscript had three further lives by the Franciscan Nicholas Bozon (including the earliest vernacular life of Elisabeth of Hungary in England) added to it in the early fourteenth century.[12] It includes two lives of late twelfth-century female authorship from Barking Abbey (*Catherine*, see table 1, no. 13, and *Edouard*, no. 6), and a life of Thomas Becket of c. 1176 (no. 4), patronized by Barking and its abbess, who was at the time Becket's sister, Marie Becket.[13] The manuscript's life of St. Etheldreda of Ely (no. 8, the *Vie sainte Audrée*), is by a thirteenth-century woman writer also called Marie, but otherwise unknown (possibly a nun or vowess from Chatteris or Barking).[14] Thus all the hagiographic lives certainly by women in England are collected together here (in what, certainly in records from England, seems a relatively rare event—several women writers in one medieval manuscript).[15] Thus, too, a prestigious Augustinian female house reads, in the late thirteenth century, the late twelfth-century hagiographic compositions of a prestigious Benedictine nunnery, and adds to the collection in the early fourteenth century with

[12] The quiring, catchwords, and program of illustrated initials show that the original design embraced the last ten texts of the manuscript, to which the first three texts were subsequently added. The additions are on parchment, the rest of the manuscript is vellum, and the recto of f. 9 is stained and rubbed as if it had for a time been the outer leaf of the manuscript. The original ten lives have illustrated initials of the same rather distinctive type, with the exception of St. Faith. The rubric for her life begins on the bottom of f. 147rb while the life proper commences on f. 147va; it is conceivable therefore that the illustration was inadvertently omitted, and the value of the illustrations as a designed element of the original compilation remains unaffected. I have examined the manuscript myself and heard a paper by Delbert W. Russell on its codicology; further discussion awaits the publication of his paper and the results of Professor Russell's detailed work on the collection's scribes.

[13] This epilogue, addressed to "l'abeesse suer saint Thomas," is not present in the Campsey text, but is extant in a Picard manuscript (Paris, BN nouv. acq. fr. 13513, f. 98r-v, early thirteenth century), *La vie de seint Thomas le Martyr*, ed. Walberg, app., 210, and see xxiii–iv. A thirteenth-century abbess of Barking, Maud de Bosham (1215–47) was a relative of another of Becket's biographers, Herbert de Bosham (d. 1186): see E. A. Loftus and H. F. Chettle, *A History of Barking Abbey* (Barking, 1954), 31, n. 42.

[14] On Marie's identity, see further Virginia Blanton-Whetsall, "St Æthelthryth's Cult: Literary, Historical, and Pictorial Constructions of Gendered Sanctity," (Ph.D. diss., State University of New York, 1998), 311; Jocelyn Wogan-Browne, "Re-routing the Dower: The Anglo-Norman Life of St Etheldreda by Marie [?of Chatteris]," in *Power of the Weak: Studies on Medieval Women*, ed. Jennifer Carpenter and Sally-Beth MacLean (Urbana, Ill., 1995), 47–50.

[15] The significance of this co-presence of texts by women is unclear. Later receptions of women's work do not always recognize female authorship as such; the fifteenth- and early sixteenth-century transmission and adaptation of Christine de Pizan in England, for instance, rarely grants her authorial status and sometimes disguises her gender altogether. In her study of a well-known manuscript of later contemplative writing in England, Marleen Cré usefully challenges the notion that spiritual writings by women are ipso facto perceived as female spiritual writing ("Women in the Charterhouse? Julian of Norwich's *Revelations of*

Franciscan writings. The manuscript gives access potentially to well over a century of female communities and their literary culture.

The manuscript also names a lay patron, Isabella de Warenne, by marriage Countess of Arundel, for its life of Edmund, Archbishop of Canterbury (d. 1240, canonized 1246; see table 1, no. 7).[16] This life was composed by Matthew Paris in, as he says, "deux langages" (v. 1976) and translated "de latin en franceis apert" (vv. 32–33) for the countess. Isabella had also been the patron of the Latin source for the Campsey manuscript's Anglo-Norman life of Edmund's former chancellor, Richard of Chichester (a personal friend of the countess and a saint who posthumously cured her little nephew of an apparently fatal illness). It would be splendid to be able to show that the Countess of Arundel was also the patron of the Campsey collection, but the manuscript's latest text was composed in 1276, Isabella of Arundel died in 1279, and she would presumably have gifted such a collection to her own foundation, the Cistercian nunnery of Marham, if not to the female companion of her widowhood, Alice Tyrel.[17] In including Isabella's hagiographic texts, however, the manuscript does testify to the overlap of lay and religious women's reading that has been so crucial to the reinvigoration of our sense of nunnery culture and women's literary culture generally in fourteenth- and fifteenth-century England, and also offers a way into the spiritualities and patronages of thirteenth-century baronial women (often overlapping, but sometimes distinctive from, those of the royal women studied for this period by John Carmi Parsons and others).[18] The cultural and religious interests of elite women in thirteenth-century England are less well-known than the lives and texts of

---

Divine Love and Marguerite Porete's *Mirror of Simple Souls* in British Library, MS Additional 37790," in *Writing Religious Women: Female Spiritual and Textual Practice in Late Medieval England*, ed. Denis Renevey and Christiania Whitehead [Cardiff, 2000], 43–62). See also Kathryn Kerby-Fulton, "Hildegard and the Male Reader: A Study of Insular Reception," in *Prophets Abroad: The Reception of Continental Holy Women in Medieval England*, ed. Rosalynn Voaden (Cambridge, 1996), 1–18. The three texts by women in the Campsey manuscript may be there simply because their provenance made them readily known at Campsey; there may be no intent to anthologize female writing as such. Nevertheless the question of whether women's writing could be seen as a female tradition in contemporary manuscript forms is worth further exploration in complement to established scholarship on the influence of the hearing, reading, or seeing of particular texts for individual women.

[16] "La vie de saint Edmond," ed. Baker (henceforth referred to by line number in the text).

[17] I examine the evidence in "Lives of a Widow," chap. 5 of my *Saints' Lives and Women's Literary Culture: Virginity and Its Authorizations* (Oxford, 2001), but conclude that there is insufficient evidence to prove Isabella's patronage. On Alice Tyrel, see ibid., chap. 5, n. 31.

[18] On female literary subcultures, see Felicity Riddy, " 'Women Talking about the Things of God': A Late Medieval Subculture," in *Women and Literature in Britain, 1150–1500*, ed. Meale, 104–27. Particularly relevant among John Carmi Parsons's many studies of medieval queens is "Of Queens, Courts, and Books: Reflections on the Literary Patronage of Thirteenth-Century Plantagenet Queens," in *The Cultural Patronage of Medieval Women*, ed. June Hall McCash (Athens, Ga., 1996), 175–201. See also Margaret Howell, *Eleanor of Provence: Queenship in Thirteenth-Century England* (Oxford, 1998).

TABLE 1. Texts and authors in the Campsey manuscript

Saint	Author and date	Locations/associations
1. Elisabeth of Hungary	Bozon, end 13th–early 14th c.	Bozon probably from Nottingham, perhaps Steventon Priory
2. Paphnutius	Bozon	
3. Paul the hermit	Frere boioun (f. 8rb)	
4. Thomas Becket	Guernes (de Pont-Ste-Maxence, f. 48rb), 1172–6	Patronage from abbess of Barking 'suer saint Thomas' claimed in Paris MS BN f. fr. 13513
5. Magdalen	Will' (Guillaume le clerc, f. 55va) 1180 × 91-1238	G. associated with Kenilworth, Augustinian priory, known to Alexander Stavensby, bp. Coventry and Lichfield (1224–38)
6. Edward the Confessor	Nun of Barking* 1163 × 89	Barking: probable connections with Henry II's court
7. Edmund of Canterbury	Matthew Paris, 1247 × 59	Translaté de latin en romanz par la requeste la cuntesse de arundel (f. 85vb)†
8. Audrey of Ely	Marie (f. 134a)*	?Barking ?Chatteris ?Canonsleigh (Hugh de Northwold, abbot of Bury, then bp at Ely, translates shrine 1252)
9. Osith of Chich, Aylesbury, Hereford	Anon., late 12th c.	Alice de Vere (d. 1163), mother of Bp William de Vere of Hereford (author of a Latin version) becomes corrodian at Chich in her widowhood
10. Faith	Symon de Walsingham (f. 148ra) before 1214–5?	Horsham St. Faith cult site, Bury St. Edmunds (author's monastery), Fitzwalter patronage (intermarried with de Valoignes, late 12th c.)
11. Modwenna	Anon., early 13th c.	Based on Latin *vita* by Abbot Geoffrey of Burton (Richard of Bury becomes prior of Burton 1222)
12. Richard of Chichester	Pieres de fecham (f. 244va) 1276–7	Based on Bocking's *vita* of 1270, dedicated to Isabella of Arundel
13. Catherine of Alexandria	Clemence of Barking,* c. 1170 × c. 1200	Barking, ?Henry II's court

*Woman writer
†Woman patron

the men, such as Matthew Paris and Edmund of Canterbury, who wrote for them.

In the total ensemble of its saints, the Campsey manuscript includes three twelfth- and thirteenth-century bishops (table 2, nos. 4, 7, 12: Becket, Edmund, Richard), the last Anglo-Saxon king (no. 6, Edward the Confessor), three native British abbesses (nos. 8, 9, 11: all royal virgins, one a martyr, two married, one a widow—Audrée, Osith, Modwenna), two virgin martyrs (no. 13, Catherine of Alexandria, and no. 10, Faith of Agen and Conques), and the high-status penitent, Mary Magdalen (no. 5), all but Catherine, Faith, and the Magdalen native to Britain. In whatever way this selection is to be construed—for example, three native abbesses, three universal saints, three churchmen, one king; or one penitent harlot, one converted churchman, eight virgins (i.e., all the saints in the manuscript except the Magdalen and Becket)—the manuscript provides a plethora of role models for women. Here are precedents for anyone wanting to know how to found a monastic house (the three British princess abbesses); set up a less formal holy household (the Magdalen); defy a husband or father and/or woo a preferred bridegroom (Catherine, Faith, Osith); preach a sermon or make an eloquent speech (the Magdalen, Modwenna, Faith, and Catherine); arrange for female successors (Modwenna, Audrée); enjoy syneisactic *amicitia* and influence the compositions of clerical friends (Richard of Chichester); inspire and lead handmaidens (Audrée, Modwenna); be veiled in spite of uncooperative chaplains and also manage episcopal opposition (Osith); assert rights as a baronial landholder and claim the church's and the king's reciprocal obligations (Osith, Audrée, Modwenna); control estate reeves and stewards (Modwenna); exchange books cooperatively between nunneries (Osith, Modwenna); consult saints' lives for precedents (Audrée); take time out for a sabbatical (Modwenna's seven years of reclusion on Andresey in the Trent; Edward the confessor's Queen, Edith, and her self-cloistering in busy reading and embroidering in her chamber); see queenly patronage in action (the royal Audrée and Henry I's good queen Maud in Audrée's miracles); carry out female courtly mourning (Catherine, a king's daughter mourned by an empress's household); negotiate the claims of court and church, baronial and ecclesiastical spirituality and their perquisites (Becket, Richard, Edmund, Modwenna);[19] run the country without being a warleader *and* while remaining a virgin (Edward the Confessor). The manuscript has examples of all these and more and provides a very full guide to the concerns of elite women in or associated with religious lives.

[19] The manuscript's twelfth-century texts from Barking themselves represent similar overlaps of interest between an elite female community and the court, both in the reign of Henry II when they were composed and in their continuing thirteenth-century existence (especially as texts of royal and episcopal cults: even the legendary Catherine of Alexandria in the Barking *Catherine* is a royal princess converting an empress, with both saint and convert mourned by the women of court).

TABLE 2. Types of saints in the Campsey manuscript (in order of occurrence in the manuscript)

Saint	Activities and modern categorizations	Commemorations
Early 14th c. texts		
1. **Elisabeth** of Hungary	Biological mother, ascetic, charity worker (1207–31)	Canonized 1235, feast 17 (19) Nov.
2. **Panuce**, Paphnutius	Desert father (?4th c.)	None
3. **Paule le hermite**	First hermit, desert father (d. c. 345)	Feast 10 Jan.
Late 13th c. texts		
4. **Thomas de Cantorbéry**, Thomas Becket	Archbishop of Canterbury (1162–70)	Canonized 1173, feast 29 Dec., translation 7 July
5. **Marie Magdalene**	1st c., cult at Vézelay from 11th c.	Feast 22 July, translation 4 May
6. **Edward** the Confessor	Anglo-Saxon king (1003–66)	Feast 5 Jan., translation 13 Oct.
7. **Eadmund**, Edmund of Canterbury	Archbishop of Canterbury (1233–40)	Canonized 1246, feast 16 Nov., trans. 9 June
8. **Audree**, Etheldreda of Ely	Anglo-Saxon widowed princess abbess (d. 679)	Feast 23 June, translation 17 Oct.
9. **Osith** of Chich, Aylesbury, Hereford	Semi-legendary Anglo-Saxon married princess abbess (d. ?c. 700)	Feast 7 Oct., multiple translations
10. **Fey**, Faith of Agen and Conques	Semi-legendary young girl, culted from 11th c. at Horsham	Feast 6 Oct., translation 14 Jan.
11. **Modwenne**, Modwenna of Britain	Semi-legendary Irish princess abbess (?7th c.), culted at Burton, 12th c.	Feast 6 July
12. **Richard, evesque de Cycestre**	Bishop of Chichester (1244–53)	Canonized 1262, feast 3 April, translation 16 June
13. **Katerine**, Catherine of Alexandria	Semi-legendary virgin (?4th c.)	Feast 25 Nov.

By comparison, the Katherine Group mini-legendary associated with the *Guide* offers three virgin martyrs of the universal church, Katherine, Margaret, Juliana, each life customized and conformed to the same narrative morphology. These saints' lives are intensely spectacular accounts of virgin torture and eloquence designed for the inner theater of anchoritic contemplative reading, texts romancing and nuptializing enclosure and internalized ascetic heroism. The Katherine Group and the *Guide* image an ideal solitary self, persuasively embodied as an enclosed reader of romance scripts.[20] Where the *Guide* and *Seinte Katerine*, for instance, figure the heroine as a chamber reader of feminized nuptial romance, focused on her Christ bridegroom and trained in what Rosalynn Voaden has so splendidly called "the eroticization of waiting,"[21] the Campsey *Life of Catherine* by Clemence of Barking (whose own reading in Latin and the vernacular in her wealthy Benedictine nunnery must have been considerable), does not show Catherine as a solitary reader, and has her "taught letters and how to argue a case and defend her position" against any dialectician, emphasizing her as a public speaker, a *plaideresse*.[22]

The contrast between the West Midlands English and the East Anglian French collections can perhaps most quickly be imaged in their topographies. With only a few exceptions, the *Guide* locates its female subjects in a symbolic geography of other-worldly aspiration. The exceptions are that, in one passage, the anchoresses, multiplied to "twenty nuðe oðer ma [twenty now, or more]" from the original three and spreading toward "Englondes ende," are said to be living a common life *as if* they were a convent of Chester, Shrewsbury, Oxford, and London.[23] (This brief acknowledgment by analogy of what must have been extraordinary influence and prestige exercised by the original three recluses for whom the text was composed near the Welsh border recontains a whole female religious movement almost before we have had time to notice it.) The *Guide* also has one comparison between the hills of Armenia and the European Alps as symbolic heights of penitential achievement for the anchoresses: the humbler they are, the taller they are as hills raised toward heaven and hence the more readily the Christ bridegroom can come leaping and treading on them, imprinting his footsteps on them, as in the "swete luue boc" of the

[20] Linda Georgianna, *The Solitary Self: Individuality in the "Ancrene Wisse"* (Cambridge, Mass., 1981); Anne Savage, "The Solitary Heroine: Aspects of Meditation and Mysticism in *Ancrene Wisse*, the Katherine Group and the Wooing Group," in *Mysticism and Spirituality in Medieval England*, ed. William F. Pollard and Robert Boenig (Woodbridge, 1997), 63–84.

[21] In our joint paper, "An Eternity of Mills and Boon [Harlequin]?" (Liverpool John Moores University Conference on Women and Popular Culture, "Romance and Roses," 1995).

[22] *Vie sainte Catherine*, ed. MacBain, vv. 141–44, 335, 479. In Edmund of Canterbury's thirteenth-century *Mirour de l'eglyse* (a text of diffusion and influence closely paralleling *Ancrene Wisse*'s), it is also clear that hearing, discussing, and inquiring about texts, rather than solitary reading of them, is assumed as the basis of much female devotional learning (see Jocelyn Wogan-Browne, "Whose Bible Is It Anyway? Women and Holy Writings in Anglo-Norman England," forthcoming in *Proceedings of the Patristic, Medieval, and Renaissance Conference* (Villanova, Penn.).

[23] *The English Text of the "Ancrene Riwle": Ancrene Wisse: Edited from MS. Corpus Christi College Cambridge 402*, ed. J. R. R. Tolkien, intro. N. R. Ker, EETS o.s., 249 (1962), f. 69a/20–21, 27–8, and see further Watson, "With the Heat of the Hungry Heart," in this volume.

Song of Songs.[24] Otherwise, the places in which the anchoress is to reimagine her existence are the desert of the monastic founding fathers (and two desert mothers, Sarah and Syncletica, who are also mentioned), the cell, and Jerusalem.[25] The geography of the Katherine Group is, again, either biblical or largely symbolic, distant, romanced, even allowing for the effect of the crusades (of which the West Midlands were very well aware). Thus the place-names in the three texts comprise Paradise, an unspecified "Estlande," Asia, Chaldea, Babylon, Armenia, Nicomedia, Antioch, the Red Sea, Jordan (the river), Egypt, Sinai, Syon and Jerusalem, Alexandria, Rome, Illyria and Gaul ("franclonde," SK 1r, ll. 4 and 9, à propos the emperors Constantine and Maxentius and their wars with each other), and the Campagna ("champaine," SJ, 51v, ll. 753–4, à propos a translation of Juliana's relics).[26]

Communities are indissociable from the recorded existence of the solitaries whom they support, and traces of the communities, textual and historical, of the Katherine Group and *Ancrene Wisse* remain in these works, for all their presentation of solitary reading selves.[27] The way in which women's collective history is masked in the *Guide* and the Katherine Group is partly a matter of generic convention. This is hagiography as romance, the contained empowerment and simultaneous isolation of the individual. Campsey on the other hand provides a plethora of role models for individual enterprise, but they are set within what seems a historical rather than a romance collection and a much fuller sense of women in the collective. The *Guide* and its associated Groups are texts *for* women's reading; the Campsey manuscript collects texts *of* women's reading.[28]

The Campsey volume with its greater number of lives contains of course many more place-names than the Katherine Group and *Ancrene Wisse*. But my point here is the relation between the place-names and the women composing, reading, and hearing the texts in which they occur. Compared with the *Guide*'s and Katherine Group's concentration on the Christ bridegroom, the spiritual director, and the devil as the major relations of one's life, the networks in and implied by the Campsey manuscript are strikingly

[24] *Ancrene Wisse*, ed. Tolkien, f. 103a/5–11.

[25] For Sarah and Syncletica, see *Ancrene Wisse*, ed. Tolkien, f. 3b/5, 44a/10, 63b/14.

[26] References from Lorna Stevenson and Jocelyn Wogan-Browne, eds., *A Computer Concordance to the Katherine Group and the Wooing Group* (Cambridge, 2000). The Wooing Group similarly includes only Bethlehem and Syon as place-names.

[27] See Millett, " 'Women in No Man's Land.' "

[28] I can see no evidence to substantiate the possibility that the Wooing Group is by, rather than for the use of, women (though its meditative personae are certainly feminine). For further discussion see Susannah Mary Chewning, "Mysticism and the Anchoritic Community," in *Medieval Women in Their Communities*, ed. Diane Watt (Cardiff, 1997), 121–23. For a distinction between "transmissional" and "authorial" communities, see Ralph Hanna, "Reconsidering the Auchinleck Manuscript," in *New Directions in Later Medieval Manuscript Studies*, ed. Derek Pearsall (York, 2000), 102.

close to home, populous, and varied. Campsey, Barking, and Bozon's probable circuits of activity are all in East Anglia and the East Midlands (see map, fig. 1). Some of the saints culted in the manuscript evoke overseas territory. Of these, St. Catherine's Alexandria can probably be considered remote and exotic, but then there is the Magdalen and her "mesnee" (v. 710) at "Marceille" (vv. 27, 676)[29] and Pontigny near Soissons, the place of Becket's illness while in exile. It was thenceforth a politically important French site for English ecclesiastical courtier-saints (such as Isabella of Arundel's archbishop, Edmund, and her bishop, Richard) to be associated with in their *vitae*, and one to which Englishwomen made pilgrimages. Agen and Conques in the Garonne and Rouergues are also evoked through the life of St. Faith in the manuscript, but again this is not an evocation of the exotic. This life concerns French pilgrimage sites visited by English noblewomen, and in any case identifies itself as written in Benedictine Bury St. Edmunds, by Simon of Walsingham, a native of the major East Anglian cult site, Horsham St. Faith, itself founded by Sybil de Cheney and her husband on their return from Conques in 1105–7.[30] An important set of wall paintings of the foundation story was added to the Horsham priory in the thirteenth century.[31]

At the outer edges of the manuscript's English geography are Isabella of Arundel's own foundation, the Cistercian nunnery of Marham, in the north of the region, and in the south, Lewes castle, then belonging to her brother and the site of her nephew's cure through the posthumous powers of Richard, bishop of Chichester (at which the Countess herself is present in the Campsey life of this saint).[32] Beyond the immediate East Anglian center are contributions from further west: the two British virgin abbess lives of Osith and Modwenna. Osith's main cult center is in East Anglia, with con-

---

[29] "La vie de Madeleine," ed. R. Reinsch, *Archiv* 64 (1880): 85–94.

[30] On the foundation see William Dugdale, *Monasticon Anglicanum*, ed. J. Caley, H. Ellis, and B. Bandinel (London, 1817–30), iii, 636, nos. I and II, and for the gift of "nominatim terram de Rodeham quam Sibilla uxor praefati Robertis dedit," see *Cartulaire de l'Abbeye de Conques en Rouergue*, ed. Gustave Desjardins (Paris, 1879), no. 519. Sybil de Cheney was heiress to Ralph de Cheney (see Julian Eve, *A History of Horsham St Faith, Norfolk: The Story of a Village* [Norwich, 1992, rev. ed. 1994], 10). Conques itself was founded by Roger de Tosny, whose wife Gotheline also owned land in Norfolk. Adela of Blois gave to Conques in 1101 and 1108 (Desjardins, ed., *Cartulaire*, nos. 470, 486) and Walter Giffard and "mater ejus Agnes" visited Conques and donated to Horsham after 1107 (Desjardins, ed., *Cartulaire*, no. 497). I am grateful to Pamela Sheingorn for confirming (pers. comm.) that the cult of St. Faith in the British Isles was particularly strong among aristocratic women. (I know of no evidence as to whether the women of Campsey had any knowledge of Sybil de Cheney's role in the cult.)

[31] On the wall paintings see Dominic Purcell, "The Priory of Horsham St Faith and Its Wall Paintings," *Norfolk Archaeology* 35 (1970–73): 469–73; David Park, "Wall Painting," in *Age of Chivalry: Art in Plantagenet England 1200–1400*, ed. Jonathan Alexander and Paul Binski (London, 1987), 313, and plates 1 and 2.

[32] See *Vie seint Richard*, ed. Russell, 85–88, 140, n. to M89–98.

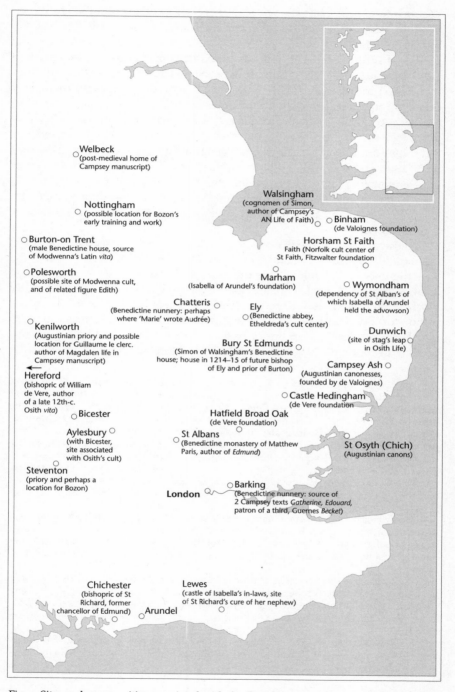

Welbeck
(post-medieval home of
Campsey manuscript)

Nottingham
(possible location for Bozon's
early training and work)

Walsingham
(cognomen of Simon,
author of Campsey's
AN Life of Faith)

Binham
(de Valoignes foundation)

Burton-on Trent
(male Benedictine house, source
of Modwenna's Latin *vita*)

Horsham St Faith
Faith (Norfolk cult center of
St Faith, Fitzwalter foundation

Polesworth
(possible site of Modwenna cult,
and of related figure Edith)

Marham
(Isabella of Arundel's foundation)

Wymondham
(dependency of St Alban's of
which Isabella of Arundel
held the advowson)

Chatteris
(Benedictine nunnery: perhaps
where 'Marie' wrote Audrée)

Ely
(Benedictine abbey,
Etheldreda's cult center)

Kenilworth
(Augustinian priory and possible
location for Guillaume le clerc,
author of Magdalen life in
Campsey manuscript)

Dunwich
(site of stag's leap
in Osith Life)

Bury St Edmunds
(Simon of Walsingham's Benedictine
house; house in 1214–15 of future bishop
of Ely and prior of Burton)

Campsey Ash
(Augustinian canonesses,
founded by de Valoignes)

Hereford
(bishopric of William
de Vere, author
of a late 12th-c.
Osith *vita*)

Bicester

Castle Hedingham
(de Vere foundation)

Hatfield Broad Oak
(de Vere foundation)

Aylesbury
(with Bicester,
site associated
with Osith's cult)

St Albans
(Benedictine monastery of Matthew
Paris, author of *Edmund*)

St Osyth (Chich)
(Augustinian canons)

Steventon
(priory and perhaps a
location for Bozon)

London

Barking
(Benedictine nunnery: source of
2 Campsey texts Gatherine, Edouard,
patron of a third, Guernes Becket)

Chichester
(bishopric of St
Richard, former
chancellor of Edmund)

Arundel

Lewes
(castle of Isabella's in-laws, site
of St Richard's cure of her nephew)

Fig. 1. Sites and communities associated with the Campsey manuscript. Reproduced (with minor modifications) by permission of Oxford University Press.

nections to London, but she has some central Midlands and Hereford connections (through Alice de Vere at Chich and her son William de Vere, bishop of Hereford, 1186–98).[33] Modwenna's cult was revived by the monks of Burton-on-Trent, but has probable connections to East Anglia.[34] Guillaume le Clerc's Magdalen life is probably from Kenilworth.[35] The sites mentioned in the lives of the three British abbesses—property owned by them, miracle and shrine sites, the homes of people cured at shrines, and so on—suggest further ways of focalizing, so to speak, the manuscript's viewpoint (see fig. 2). Less remote and exotic than *Ancrene Wisse*'s universe or the Katherine Group's hagiographic geography, Campsey's collection presents a knowable world, a world with contemporary possibilities of influence and with plenty of precedents for the exercise of female power in church, family, and collective forms, especially in the foundations made by its Anglo-Saxon and British princess–abbesses of their own and subsidiary communities.

In these mappings, the Benedictine monastery of Bury (see fig. 1) seems a potentially important transmission point in the networks that gather these lives together, just as much so as the individual patron and owner of saints' lives, Isabella of Arundel. As Virginia Blanton-Whetsall has stressed in her work on St. Etheldreda of Ely, Hugh de Northwold, abbot of Bury, became bishop of Ely (1229–54) and encouraged the thirteenth-century cult to which the Anglo-Norman life by Marie in the Campsey manuscript is important testimony.[36] Involved in Hugh de Northwold's notoriously dis-

[33] Alice became a corrodian at St. Osyth's, Chich; her son culted Osith while bishop at Hereford; the vernacular Osith life includes, uniquely, a miracle in which a Hereford woman is redirected from Bury to Chich. The ecclesiastical politics of the vernacular life focus on London, where, as a splendid recent study stresses, de Vere was brought up (at Henry I's court) and where St. Osith's landholdings at Chich were both promoted and later contested by Bishop Richard Belmeis I of London, object of one of Osith's vengeance miracles (Jane Zatta, "The *Vie Seinte Osith*: Hagiography and Politics in Anglo-Norman England," *Studies in Philology* 96 [1999]: 367–93). On de Vere, see Julia Barrow, "A Twelfth-Century Bishop and Literary Patron: William de Vere," *Viator* 18 (1987): 175–89; on Osith's cult and texts, Denis Bethell, "The Lives of St Osyth of Essex and St Osyth of Aylesbury," *Analecta Bollandiana* 88 (1970): 75–127.

[34] Modwenna's Anglo-Norman life is closely associated with that of Osith, whose cult sites are principally in East Anglia and London in the vernacular life (Modwenna is shown training Osith in this life and is also associated with Edith of Polesworth, a central Midlands house). For a further possible connection, see the discussion of Richard of Bury and n. 38 below.

[35] Guillaume (1180/1191–1238) was from Normandy but was employed by the Augustinian prior of Kenilworth on commissions and seems to have worked in the diocese of Coventry and Lichfield (M. Dominica Legge, *Anglo-Norman Literature in the Cloisters* [Edinburgh, 1950], 120), whose bishop, Alexander Stavensby (1224–38), responded to one of his poems in the 1230s.

[36] Blanton-Whetsall suggests that Hugh de Northwold, bishop of Ely and formerly abbot of Bury, encouraged Marie in the composition of *Audrée* in connection with his translation of the saint's shrine in 1252 (Virginia Blanton-Whetsall, "St Æthelthryth's Cult," 311, n. 16).

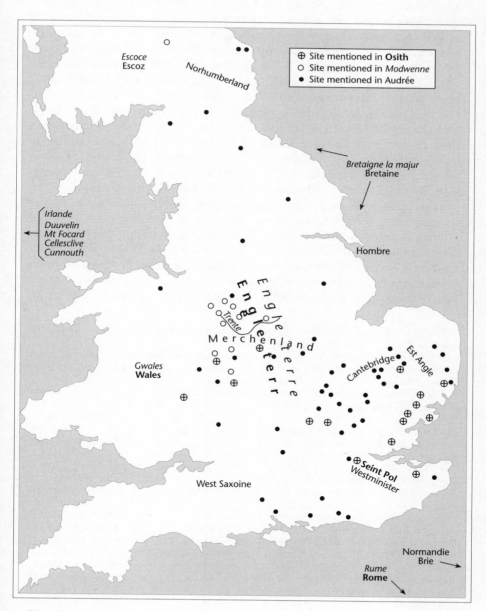

Legend:
⊕ Site mentioned in **Osith**
○ Site mentioned in *Modwenne*
● Site mentioned in Audrée

Escoce
Escoz

Norhumberland

Bretaigne la majur
Bretaine

Irlande
Duuvelin
Mt Focard
Cellesclive
Cunnouth

Hombre

Engleterre
Engleterre
Engleterre

Trente

Merchenland

Gwales
Wales

Cantebridge

Est Angle

West Saxoine

⊕ **Seint Pol**
Westminister

Normandie
Brie

Rume
Rome

Fig. 2. Sites associated with Osith, Modwenna, and Audrée.

puted election to the abbacy of Bury in 1214–15 were some of the region's major lay noblemen (Isabella of Arundel's father's generation of Bigods, Marshals, Fitzwalters, and Warennes for example)[37] and also monks subsequently connected with communities represented in the manuscript. Simon of Walsingham, author of the Campsey life of Faith, served on Hugh de Northwold's deputation to the pope as did Richard, the precentor of Bury who unsuccessfully contested the election and who became abbot of St. Modwenna's abbey of Burton on Trent in 1222; Bury's Nicholas of Dunstable is another Bury monk who subsequently went to Ely (as archdeacon) and then became bishop of Worcester, then of Winchester, and then chancellor to Henry III.[38] But there are also all the intrafamilial connections between these East Anglian houses and those who found, patronize, and staff them: de Veres, de Valoignes, de Cainetos, Bigods, Warennes, and Clares.[39] Bury is another node in the manuscript's networks to add to those of Barking, Campsey, and Isabella of Arundel and her ecclesiastic courtier-saints.

In so far as it charts and historicizes British identities and networks for its audiences, the Campsey manuscript can be seen in the traditions of women's historiographical as well as their hagiographical patronage. These traditions are relatively well known for early Latin patronage by women in Britain, but little explored for the huge riches of Anglo-Norman historiography other than for the queens of England.[40] One might think here of the royal and seigneurial genealogies carefully given for the Anglo-

[37] See *The Chronicle of the Election of Hugh, Abbot of Bury St Edmunds and Later Bishop of Ely*, ed. R. M. Thomson (Oxford, 1974), 83 n. 5, 168.

[38] Thomson, *Chronicle of the Election*, xvi, 193–94. A book from Bury's medieval library contains a letter from the niece of Hugh de Northwold, "Lucy of St Edmund's," to her brother Nicholas the archdeacon (ibid., 193, n. 5).

[39] A full study of the interconnections cannot be made here; I mention a few to give a sense of the possibilities. Joan de Valoignes (mentioned in 1211, 1220 x 1221) and Agnes de Valoignes (1234), probably sisters of the founder, Theobald de Valoignes, were first abbesses of Campsey (*VCH Suffolk* ii, 112, and Sally Thompson, *Women Religious: The Founding of English Nunneries after the Norman Conquest* [Oxford, 1991], app. A, 235); Christiania de Valoignes was abbess of Barking, 1200–13, and Anne de Vere abbess from 1295–1318 (Loftus and Chettle, *History of Barking*, 34, 36–38; *VCH Essex* ii, 121). For Lucy de Vere, prioress of Castle Hedingham, see Thompson, *Women Religious*, 220. Bishop William de Vere (see n. 33 above) was the son of Aubrey de Vere of Hedingham Castle, d. 1141 (whose son Aubrey became earl of Oxford, d. 1194) and Alice, daughter of Gilbert de Clare; she died c. 1163. William de Vere's sister Juliana married Hugh Bigod, first Earl of Norfolk. Alice de Vere's daughter Alice (sister of William de Vere) married Roger (d. 1177), son of Richard, Lord of Warkworth and nephew of Earl Hugh Bigod of Norfolk (Bethell, "The Lives of St Osyth," 97 and app. III, 122–23). Their son Henry of Essex forfeited his lands in 1163. Joan de Stutville may be the Joanna of the Bigod child's miracle in the life of Isabella of Arundel's saint, Richard of Chichester (W. Blaauw, *The Barons' War*, 181, n. 47). Joanna married Roger, Hugh Bigod's son, who inherited as Earl of Norfolk after his uncle Roger (d. 1297). For the de Caineto's (de Cheneys) see n. 30 above: Gunnora de Valoignes (d. before 1220) married into the Fitzwalters, as did Sibyl de Cheney.

[40] See Elisabeth M.C. van Houts, *Memory and Gender in Early Medieval Europe 900–1200* (Basingstoke, 1999). For a survey of francophone historiographical patronage, see Diana B.

Saxon princess saints in the Campsey manuscript, as well as of all the French and Middle English *Brut* and *Estoire* manuscripts yet to be fully studied as texts of women's as well as of men's historiography. There is need to do still more with women's history and lineage genres, whether the genealogies of Christ and the Virgin or regal, family, and household genealogies, or combinations of the two (such as the fifteenth-century Anglo-Norman Adam and Eve roll recently commented on by Diana Tyson in which Isabella of Arundel's mother and aunts and other women of the Marshal family are specially commemorated).[41] Not only lineages, but former elite female communities are imaged in the Campsey manuscript's account of Etheldreda's Ely, Modwenna's Burton, and Osith's Chich. Female holy kinships and families provide pedigrees, validations, and links with subsidiary communities and daughter houses as well as with the central cult sites, so that the history of women's collectivities and a collectively arrived-at history for women are both thinkable in the manuscript.

Both in the texts themselves and in the provenances and associations at work in the collection, then, a thickening sense of context for the Campsey manuscript accretes, even if we currently know nothing more definite about its compilation than we do of the *Guide* and the Katherine Group's. The *desideratum* of "thick" study of hagiography in its contexts has been persuasively put by Patrick Geary.[42] Hagiography, as he stresses, is "always occasional literature," not the single unvarying, apolitical "life" of the saints that often featured in earlier twentieth-century reception of saints' lives. We have to heed the variety of hagiographic collections and their associated texts, and the range of their occasions.[43]

But we need manuscript networks as well, for the Campsey manuscript defies any kind of compositional, hagiological, or other order and (partly because of its very richness and variousness) is resistant to thematic readings across the texts that would elucidate an ideal target reader, as the Katherine Group can be argued to do. Nor does there seem any monastic genre or occasion to which the Campsey collection conforms, or evidence of any clear formal principle for the inclusion and arrangement of texts, other than that the book, as per its inscription earlier referred to, provides mealtime reading at Campsey (which it does by no calendrical or other

---

Tyson, "Patronage of French Vernacular History Writers in the Twelfth and Thirteenth Centuries," *Romania* 100 (1979): 180–222; on Latin traditions, see Joan M. Ferrante, *To the Glory of Her Sex: Women's Roles in the Composition of Medieval Texts* (Bloomington, 1997), chap. 3, and idem, " 'Licet longinquis regionibus corpore separati': Letters as a Link in and to the Middle Ages," *Speculum* 76 (2001): 880–81.

[41] Diana B. Tyson, "The Adam and Eve Roll: Corpus Christi College Cambridge MS 98," *Scriptorium* 52 (1998): 301–16, esp. 305, 315–6.

[42] *Living with the Dead in the Middle Ages* (Ithaca, 1994), intro.

[43] Geary, *Living with the Dead*, 23, citing a *vita* written to defend the rights of nuns to draw water (rights claimed by the monks of the Welf monastery of Wingarten, 24–25).

conventional legendary scheme; see table 2, above, for the feasts of Campsey's saints). Nor can the collection be accounted for as the interests of an individual patron. The book could, rather, be seen as a contingent, specific expression of the interests not of one individual emblematizing her own position, but of a collectivity of elite women, combining monastic, ecclesiastic, and family threads.[44] This is geographically focused in the central eastern coast of England, but has networks stretching beyond, social networks moving through the barony, touching the court, passing through monastic family foundations and family networks up and down the Anglian coast. Isabella of Arundel, seductive though she is as a patroness, is presented in the manuscript as the patroness of the Edmund life (see table 1, no. 7 above), not of the collection. If the ten late-thirteenth-century texts were put together for her, it seems odd that she should be mentioned in the fourth of these, but not elsewhere. The placing of Isabella's name suggests more strongly that whoever was responsible for the manuscript knew her as the patron of the Edmund life than it suggests that she was the patron of the collection of ten lives.

The manuscript's concluding inscription should perhaps, then, be read in a collective sense. "Ce livre deviseie a la priorie de Kanpseie de lire a mengier" (This book given to/at the priory of Campsey for reading at meals) inscribed in a fourteenth-century hand at the end of the manuscript's final text might then mean "deviseie" not in the more common sense of "gifted [divided, shared out, bequeathed]" (i.e., donated in some way to/at the priory) but in the alternative sense of "designed," "devised," so that the book may have been "designed" (though not necessarily copied) at the priory of Campsey.[45] Monastic copyists were being replaced by professional scriveners in towns and universities in the thirteenth century,[46] and women's houses were experienced in getting their materials made out-of-house. (A good example is the elegant copy of Peter Comestor's *Historia*

[44] Network theory has been used in modern social sciences for some decades (see, e.g., Samuel Leinhardt, *Social Networks: A Developing Paradigm* [New York, 1977]), and for an influential account of women's relations and networks, see Carol Gilligan, *In a Different Voice: Psychological Theory and Women's Development* (Cambridge, Mass., 1982). Applications to medieval prosopography are rendered difficult, particularly in the case of medieval women, by absences of record and occlusions in the records that do exist. As a model, however, the paradigm of the network may allow us to envisage structures of relationship and modes of action even where we cannot fill in all the details (in Campsey's case, a complete trawl and reconstitution of networks passing through and centered in East Anglia would hardly be too much, and yet might not yield more than convergent, rather than conclusive information).

[45] The prospect that the manuscript was made by the clerics of the small chantry college established at Campsey in 1347 by Countess Maud de Ufford is tantalizing, but too late for the thirteenth-century section of the manuscript and late for the early fourteenth-century additions at the beginning of the manuscript, which must predate the inscription of ownership on the first leaf. (This, like the concluding inscription of function, is dated to the early fourteenth century.)

[46] As Andrew Taylor points out, even male monasteries were no longer major centers for copying in the thirteenth century. Professional scriveners were established in towns and

scholastica and Richard of St. Victor's *Allegories on the Old Testament* commissioned, according to the manuscript's inscription, for the wealthy, aristocratic, Benedictine nunnery of Elstow in Bedfordshire, by Cecily de Chanville, abbess from 1170–80, "in eruditionem et profectum conuentus sui." A further inscription at the end of the manuscript says that she died before it was completed [in 1191–2?] and that Robert of Bedford made it for her).[47] The Campsey canonesses could readily have had their manuscript made in Oxford, London, or perhaps Cambridge, and doubtless knew people in or going to these centers.[48]

We might therefore envision one of several scenarios of collective action. The one requiring least discussion at Campsey would involve the acquisition of the original late-thirteenth-century manuscript of ten lives (whether through Isabella of Arundel or someone who knew of her Anglo-Norman saints' lives), and the addition of the three early fourteenth-century lives. The more interesting prospect, and one that perhaps makes most sense of the nature of the manuscript's collection, is that the late thirteenth-century section of the manuscript was evolved at Campsey. Saints of the universal church of particular relevance to a prestigious community and a community including vowesses and lay corrodians were chosen (Catherine of Alexandria suggests, especially in the version of her life by Clemence of Barking in the Campsey collection, the learning and eloquence of elite female communities; the Magdalen is a high-status saint of special significance, as a repentant harlot, to biological mothers unable to produce children and remain virgin, yet desirous of a religious life).[49] But also chosen were saints who combined exemplary demonstrations of foundresshood, patronage, asceticism, leadership, and self-sacrifice (and, not least, getting their own way about their disposition in marriage) with being a part, geographically and institutionally, of the very topography and fabric of eastern England.

---

universities ("Authors, Scribes, Patrons and Books," in *The Idea of the Vernacular: An Anthology of Middle English Literary Theory, 1280–1520*, ed. Jocelyn Wogan-Browne, Nicholas Watson, Andrew Taylor, and Ruth Evans [University Park, Penn., 1999], 354). The situation described by Doyle for the fourteenth and fifteenth centuries (where "competent monastic scribes" were supplemented by "domestic employees and occasional outsiders") must have been anticipated among the nunneries, even fewer of whom had anything like an institutional scriptorium (A. I. Doyle, "Book Production by the Monastic Orders in England (c. 1375–1530): Assessing the Evidence," in *Medieval Book Production: Assessing the Evidence*, ed. Linda Brownrigg [Los Altos Hills, Calif., 1990], 1–19, esp. 15).

[47] David N. Bell, *What Nuns Read: Books and Libraries in Medieval English Nunneries* (Kalamazoo, Mich., 1995), s.v. Elstow, p.137. The complete inscription (not given in Bell), continues on f. 196v of London, BL Royal 7. F iii.

[48] The illustrated initials, with their distinctive full figures of the saints, may help narrow down the possibilities, but this point may be covered in the forthcoming study by Russell (n. 12 above).

[49] For the case that the Magdalen has as much to do with elite mothers, widows, and vowesses in thirteenth- and fourteenth-century England as with prostitutes, see my *Saints' Lives and Women's Literary Culture*, chap. 4.

The leading saint of the region, Bury's St. Edmund, Anglo-Saxon king and martyr to the Danes, was *not* included. It may simply be that Campsey had a separate manuscript of his life, or it may be a deliberate omission. One of the Campsey manuscript's abbess saints, Osith, is an Anglo-Saxon princess saint who was reinvented over the eleventh and twelfth centuries by the Augustinian canons at their new foundation of Chich as against the local Benedictines of Bury and the prestige of Edmund.[50] It may thus be that the manuscript maintains in regard to this choice a consciously Augustinian and female saintly profile (contrasting with the male Benedictine cult at Bury). Campsey's most authoritative native saint is certainly female: Audrée, the leading Benedictine Anglo-Saxon princess saint of eastern, and indeed of all, England. The Audrée life included in Campsey was written by a woman who was probably either in one of the East Anglian or Essex houses or known there, but it is also a life in which the unknown Marie reshapes institutional Benedictinism into a queenly figure whose powers and interests look remarkably like those of thirteenth-century elite women.[51]

If we read the manuscript as an expression of a collective interest, then, it seems that the women who owned and used it were interested (though not exclusively so) in their own region and topographies and in a range of religious and para-religious lives as well as in court, court styles, baronial families and ecclesiastical politics and influence, and a number of devotional and theological concerns.[52] They assembled the lives because they knew of or inquired for them among their networks, from abbess to abbess or prioress to prioress perhaps, or more probably with intermediate clerics, monks, and ecclesiastics, or their family connections (these two, of course, often being the same thing). They specially wanted both lives relevant to their region and lives of other women and communities like themselves, but were interested also in prestigious contemporary courtier churchmen (and such churchmen's role model, Becket), who were figures familiar in their own lives. They did not choose the unrelieved concentration on virgin martyrs compiled for women in the Katherine Group. Campsey's spectrum of exemplary biographies stresses a much wider age and role range in the lives of religious and para-religious women.

I think there are riches for the history of women in England here (all the more so for the embedding of Campsey texts in male as well as female ec-

---

[50] Wogan-Browne, *Saints' Lives*, chap. 2; on a London focus in the politics of the vernacular life, see Zatta, *"Vie Seinte Osith,"* n. 33 above. In the vernacular life, a shrine client finds no relief at Bury St. Edmunds and is redirected to Chich ("Osith," ed. Baker, vv. 1152–58).

[51] See further Wogan-Browne, *Saints' Lives*, chap. 6; Blanton-Whetsall, "St Æthelthryth's Cult."

[52] I have not addressed devotional and theological aspects of the manuscript's texts here, but for Clemence of Barking's Anselmian union of faith and reason in her late twelfth-century Catherine life, see my *Saints' Lives*, chap. 7. Jane Zatta has a study forthcoming on the theological claims of Campsey's life of Modwenna for (essentialized) female nature's special redemptive capacities.

clesiastical and family networks). All the Campsey lives need study by many more people, and more translations than the ones currently available or underway.[53] But they cannot be worked on in the grand, nationalizing way in which the *Guide* began its successful career in modern scholarship. Women's literary history, it still needs saying, can't be studied as part of grand narratives. The Campsey collection doesn't enter the nationalizing narrative of English scholarship at any stage of postmedieval antiquarian or scholarly inquiry. As a glance at what can be gleaned of the continuing literacies and audition of these communities suggests, these texts are texts of micro-literacies. Thus in the late fourteenth and fifteenth centuries, Campsey has well-kept French cellaresses' accounts and French-English psalters, Barking has English accounts, but theological manuscript collections in continental French as well as in English, while Isabella of Arundel's Marham has an elegant, fourteenth-century Latin list of the abbess's tenants (perhaps, one could speculate, prepared for the occasion of Eleanor of Castile's interest in Marham's being confirmed by Edward I after Isabella's death).[54] Women in England not only acquired French manuscripts in nunneries and elsewhere but continued to use Anglo-Norman texts into the fourteenth and fifteenth centuries.[55] Perhaps the best-known fifteenth-cen-

[53] The lives of Osith, Modwenna, and Audrée are forthcoming in a volume by Jane Zatta for the Boydell and Brewer Library of Medieval Women; the life of Audrée is translated by Christine Wille Garrison, "The Lives of St Ætheldreda: Representation of Female Sanctity from 700–1300" (Ph.D. diss., University of Rochester, 1990). For a translation of the Becket life in the manuscript, see Janet Shirley, *Guarnier's Becket* (London and Chichester, 1975); for St Catherine, see J. Wogan-Browne and Glyn S. Burgess in *Virgin Lives and Holy Deaths: Two Exemplary Biographies for Anglo-Norman Women* (London, 1996). Some extracts from the life of St. Faith are included in Brigitte Cazelles, *The Lady as Saint: A Collection of French Hagiographic Romances of the Thirteenth Century* (Philadelphia, 1991).

[54] Campsey's fifteenth-century French accounts are Ipswich, Suffolk County Record Office HD 1538/174; see Marilyn Oliva, ed., *Charters and Household Accounts of the Female Monasteries in the County of Suffolk* (Woodbridge, forthcoming). For the Barking cellaress's "Charthe" (BL, MS Cotton Julius D. viii) see Dugdale, *Monasticon* I, 442–45, and Eileen Power, *Medieval English Nunneries c. 1275–1535* (Cambridge, 1922), 563–68; for French theological collections acquired by Barking in the fourteenth and fifteenth centuries (Paris, BN fr. 1038; Oxford, Magdalen College, Lat. 41), see Bell, *s.v.* Barking, nos. 13, 15. Marham's flourished and decorated list of properties is Norwich, Norfolk Record Office, Hare 2213 (a later set of Latin accounts, mostly from the reign of Henry VI, is now NRO Hare 2201, 194x5–2212, 194x5; see Marilyn Oliva, *The Convent and the Community in Late Medieval England: Female Monasteries in the Diocese of Norwich, 1350–1540* [Woodbridge, 1998], 78, 100). Eleanor of Castile gave a gift of advowson to Marham in 1290, which Edward I confirmed to Marham for his soul and Eleanor's memory in February 1292 (John A. Nichols, ed., "The History and Cartulary of the Cistercian Nuns of Marham Abbey, 1249–1536" [Ph.D. diss., Kent State University, 1974], 28–29).

[55] The nunnery of Crabhouse in Norfolk, for instance, has its foundation story in French in the fourteenth century (Mary Bateson, ed., "The Register of Crabhouse Nunnery," *Norfolk Archaeology* 11 [1892]: 1–71); in 1535, the Augustinian canonesses at Lacock Abbey still had their Rule and other fundamental documents in French (*VCH Wilts*, vol. 3 [1956], 309). For a list of French texts in manuscripts securely provenanced to nunneries in England see Bell, *What Nuns Read*, Index II, Works in French.

tury book at Campsey is the sub-prioress Katherine Babington's copy of Capgrave's late Middle English life of Katherine, but Campsey's psalters continued to contain French prayers, and Reginald Rous and Anne Wingfield gave French book donations to the priory.[56]

As the obverse to hagiography's occasional nature, Patrick Geary laments what he sees as the loss of a master narrative for European hagiography entailed by the present necessity for detailed contextualization ("the broader meaning of medieval hagiography cannot be answered until we have dozens of . . . microstudies").[57] But Campsey's combination of specificity and exemplarity challenges the value of master narratives. The collection's ungeneralizability, its located and contingent nature, is a measure of its success as a record of and reflection on their personal and collective histories by a female community (a community, given the Barking texts of the manuscript, perhaps working in cooperation with other female houses). In this light, the relatively informal nature of so many conventual records starts to go with rather than against the grain of the genre, suggesting that a hagiography perceived as occasional may have much to offer for women's texts and histories.

The Campsey manuscript also suggests that rather than mapping literary history in conventional and institutionalized divisions of modern nation-states and of medieval political history, medieval literary territory should be defined on a more ad hoc basis and use family networks in establishing its parameters. The Campsey world is focused mainly in East Anglia, but with significant awareness of and contributions from the Continent, and the afterlife of some of its texts can be traced across the Channel (most notably the prose *remaniement* of the Barking life of Edward the Confessor for the Counts of St. Pol, a family that contributed Marie de St. Pol back across the Channel to become foundress of a Cambridge college).[58] Islands are less insular in an era where water-borne transport is swifter than road. There is a case for seeing not the English nation but East Anglia, northwest France, and the Flandrian coast as the topography of an important stretch of largely unwritten women's literary history in which the interchange of manuscripts in French and Latin through family as well as

[56] For Rous, see Oliva, *The Convent and the Community*, 69; Anne Wingfield, better known as the reader for whom BL, Harley 4012 was compiled, had affiliations with Syon, but her second husband, Sir Robert Wingfield (d. 1494), was from a local Suffolk family (see further Jacqueline Jenkins, "Lay Devotion and Women Readers of the Middle English Prose Life of St Katherine" in *The Cult of St Katherine in Medieval Europe*, ed. idem and Katherine J. Lewis [Brepols, forthcoming]).

[57] Geary, *Living with the Dead*, 28.

[58] For details of the manuscripts of the prose *remaniement*, see Ruth J. Dean and Maureen B. M. Boulton, *Anglo-Norman Literature: A Guide to Texts and Manuscripts*, ANTS OP 3 (London, 1999), 291, no. 523. The manuscript of Guernes' Becket life which cites Barking patronage (see n. 13 above) is itself a Picard manuscript and thus a further indication of such cross-channel connection.

ecclesiastical networks (and in the later Middle Ages in the importation of continental books) is as important as books in English.

Above all, the manuscript is a reminder that, even in England, even before Julian and Kempe in the fourteenth and fifteenth centuries, women are always there. The elision of the continuities of women's history has often been a feature of the very historiography making women visible, at least when it purports to be charting the sudden or spontaneous visibility of female communities (as in the perception of a twelfth- and thirteenth-century women's renaissance referred to at the beginning of this chapter). In registering the informal, quotidian, underrecognized, significant, and continuous presence of women in their own and others' religious and cultural history, thick and occasional hagiographic histories can play a part. But, as the English-French Campsey manuscript illustrates, this involves an interdisciplinarity of scholarship that still, even in medieval studies, can remain difficult to achieve in institutional forms, at least in the structures of university departments and careers. Medieval and modern grand narratives have to be simultaneously challenged and rewritten.

CHAPTER FIVE

Who Is the Master of This Narrative?
Maternal Patronage of the
Cult of St. Margaret

Wendy R. Larson

The fifteenth-century physician Anthonius Guainerius of Pavia offered the following advice for dealing with a woman in labor: "At the time of birth, it is good that the legend of blessed Margaret be read, that she have relics of the saints on her, and that you carry out briefly some familiar ceremonies in order to please your patient and the old women."[1] Guainerius's recommendation demonstrates St. Margaret of Antioch's role as the patroness of parturient women in the later middle ages. St. Margaret's protection for mother and child during birth might be invoked through prayers on an amulet or relics or belts for the mother to touch or wear.[2] As in the example of Guainerius, the saint's life might be read aloud or the text itself placed on the mother's belly in order to invoke St. Margaret's aid. Guainerius is clearly aware of the expectations of his patients and their female friends; they will want St. Margaret to be invoked as part of the childbirth ritual. This physician shows great sympathy for the suffering of women in the course of childbirth, as he refers to his patient as the "poor parturient

[1] ". . . et in presentis bonum est ut legenda beate margarite legatur sanctorum reliquias super se habeat et breviter quas sciveris cerimonias ut infirme tue ac vetulis applaudas facito." *Tractatus de matricibus*, fols. 2.3r—2.3v., cited with translation in Helen Lemay, "Women and the Literature of Obstetrics and Gynecology," in *Medieval Women and the Sources of Medieval History*, ed. Joel T. Rosenthal (Athens, Ga., 1990), 197.

[2] For examples of French parchment amulets, see Jean-Pierre Albert, "La legende de Sainte Marguerite un mythe maieutique?" *Razo* 8 (1988): 19–33, plate on 33; and M. Louis Carolus-Barre, "Un nouveau parchemin amulette et la legende de Sainte Marguerite patronne des femmes en couches," *Academie des Inscriptions et Belles-Lettres Comptes Rendus* (1979): 256–75, plates on 260, 272. For belts, see Jane Schulenburg, *Forgetful of Their Sex: Female Sanctity and Society ca. 500–1100* (Chicago, 1998), 230.

woman" (*pauperculam partentem*) and recognizes the comfort that calling on St. Margaret may bring to his patients. Although the physician himself may be less convinced of the efficacy of this practice—he does seem to be advocating the devotions to St. Margaret strictly as an emotional balm—his instructions make clear that St. Margaret is an integral part of the process of childbirth, and he makes no effort to eliminate her.

St. Margaret's association with childbirth was so ubiquitous in the late middle ages that we tend not to think about how the connection was established or maintained. In this chapter, I will explain briefly how I believe this connection developed, but I will concentrate primarily on how it was perpetuated. I will do this by tracing the use of the image of St. Margaret emerging from the belly of the dragon, the element of her iconography that was most firmly linked with childbirth. This image plays a significant part in the saint's cult, yet it was challenged and even excised by some medieval authors. The ways in which this image was handled in both texts and artifacts offers a thread with which to trace the role of patronage in the cult of St. Margaret. This chapter examines how the relationship between St. Margaret and mothers, embodied through the mothers' patronage, played a primary role in maintaining the image of the saint and the dragon despite clerical disapproval.

During the course of the middle ages, there were different opinions about what was properly part of the narrative content of the life of St. Margaret. These differences focused on the saint's battles with a dragon and demon. My argument that the patronage of women kept the dragon scene part of both the saint's life and her iconography means that the power of women explored in this essay is of a specific, limited sort. It is not a formal type of power, that is, one that makes overt claims to institutional authority, but is informal, in this case asserted by means of individual actions that ultimately had the effect of a collective force. The practices, or patronage, of women associated with the cult of St. Margaret, specifically with the saint as the protector of mothers during childbirth, affected the way St. Margaret was portrayed and venerated.

In this chapter, I define *patronage* in a saint's cult as the full range of practices and the artifacts those practices produced that were associated with promoting or drawing on the subject's sanctity and efficacy as an intercessor. This definition weighs equally artifacts such as the parchment amulets created to invoke the assistance of St. Margaret during childbirth and those texts of the saint's life in a martyrology or calendar. One consequence of labeling all artifacts, texts, and practices associated with a saint as types of patronage is that it places members of the ecclesiastical hierarchy and other religious and secular patrons on the same level. Thus patrons may be anchoresses who view St. Margaret as a model of chastity and read her life, parish priests who preach about her on her feast day, or laywomen of every social class who invoke the saint for protection during

childbirth.[3] Enlarging the definition of patronage to include all participants in cultic activity uncovers ways in which laypeople, and particularly women, helped shape the content of medieval religious spirituality.
This definition of patronage challenges models of medieval Christianity
that portray male experience as dominant, while female concerns are marginal and forced to operate subversively. Recognizing patronage in a variety of artifacts and practices also breaks down other familiar binaries of
sacred and secular or popular and elite accompanying theories that construct a top-down model of how religious concepts and values are trans-
mitted. The cult of St. Margaret shows how a broad definition of patronage can help provide a better understanding of how saints' cults operated
and were meaningful to those who participated in them.

The life of St. Margaret follows the familiar structure of a virgin martyr
legend. Margaret, the daughter of a pagan priest in Antioch, is sent to a nurse
outside the city after the death of her mother; there she is converted to Christianity. She catches the eye of Olibrius, a local Roman administrator, who
makes her an offer of marriage which she refuses, declaring herself a bride of
Christ. Margaret is tortured and imprisoned; a dragon appears in her cell
and swallows her; when she makes the sign of the cross, he splits open and
disappears. Another demon appears in her cell; she binds him and forces
him to confess to his evil schemes against people. Following more refusals
and torments, Margaret is finally beheaded. Her final prayer before her
death requests that those who invoke her name and memory may receive a
variety of benefits; among these are the protection for mothers and children.

The earliest extant *vitae* for St. Margaret come from the ninth century, in
both Greek and Latin.[4] The saint's primary efficacy was originally against
demons; in the Greek text she offers protection for cattle as well as against
lawsuits. In an early Latin text, she includes in her final prayer the petition
that "whoever builds a basilica in my name or from his labor furnishes a
manuscript of my passion, fill him with your Holy Spirit, the spirit of truth,
and in his home let there not be born an infant lame or blind or dumb."[5] A

---

[3] For a life of St. Margaret written for anchoresses, see *Seinte Marherete*, ed. Frances M.
Mack, EETS o.s., 193 (1934; reprint, 1958). For an example of St. Margaret in a medieval sermon, see John Mirk, *Mirk's Festial*, ed. Theodor Erbe, EETS extra ser., 96 (1905; reprint, 1987),
199–202.

[4] The Greek life is known as the *Passio a Theotimo*, ed. Hermann Usener, *Acta S. Marinae et
Christophori*, Festschrift zur Fünften Säcularfeier der Carl-Ruprechts Universität zu Heidel-
berg (Bonn, 1886), 15–47. This life is listed as number 1165 in the *Bibliotheca Hagiographica
Graeca*, ed. Francois Halkin, 3d ed. (Brussels, Société des Bollandists, 1957), 84–85. The Latin
life, written before 846, is listed as number 5303 in the *Bibliotheca Hagiographica Latina*, 2 vols.
(Brussels, Bollandist Society, 1900–1901), II, 787–88.

[5] "Et qui basilicam in nomine meo fecerit, uel qui de suo labore comparauit codicem pas-
sionis mee, reple illum Spiritu Sancto tuo, spiritu ueritatis, et in domo illius non nascatur infans claudus aut cecus neque mutus." Latin text and translation in Mary Clayton and Hugh
Magennis, eds., *The Old English Lives of St. Margaret* (Cambridge, 1994), 214–15.

similar formula is repeated in the two Old English accounts of her *passio* in which the saint also promises that children will be protected from demon-possession or madness.[6]

The first mention of protection for mothers occurs in the twelfth-century (c. 1153) French legend by Wace, and this becomes a standard element.[7] A thirteenth-century Middle English life of Margaret shows the concern for mothers and children in its most fully developed form.[8] In this account, the demon confesses to harming mothers and their children during childbirth: "There indeed I would come, during childbirth to do her harm. If the child were unblessed, I'd break its foot or arm, or the woman herself in some way I would harm."[9]

The mother's welfare finally pushes aside concern for the child in John Lydgate's fifteenth-century Middle English life of the saint, which stresses St. Margaret's protection for mothers but does not mention the child at all.[10] The association of St. Margaret with childbirth was not evident from the beginning, nor necessarily derived from her iconography, but rather stemmed from her efficacy against demons.[11] The maladies against which she promises protection—blindness, dumbness, lameness, and madness—are all associated with demonic activity. Margaret was an active deliverer, not a passive object to be delivered. As the legend was modified and the connection with childbirth made more explicit, the image of the saint being delivered whole from the belly of the beast came to represent a mother's hope for a similar fate for her child. Once established, the connection between the image of St. Margaret's delivery from the dragon and her patronage of mothers became a ubiquitous combination. A prayer to St. Margaret illustrates the way in which a mother might turn to the saint for assistance:

> Madame, Saint Margaret . . . when a woman / big with child who turns her devout heart towards you / and humbly begs you / that God may save her from peril, / and may not delay His help to her, / this is when I pray to you

[6] BL Cotton Tiberius A iii and Cambridge, Corpus Christi College 303, both in Clayton and Magennis, *Old English Lives*.

[7] *La vie de sainte Marguérite/Wace; édition, avec introduction et glossaire par Hans-Erich Keller, commentaire des enluminures du ms. Troyes 1905 par Margaret Alison Stones*, ed. Hans-Erich Keller, Beihefte zur Zeitschrift für romanische Philologie, Band 229 (Tübingen, 1990).

[8] Cambridge University Library Additional 4122. The manuscript is from the fifteenth century, although the anonymous text dates to about 1250, a contemporary to the *South English Legendary*. The text is cited from *Middle English Legends of Women Saints*, ed. Sherry Reames, assisted by Martha Blalock and Wendy R. Larson (Kalamazoo, 2002).

[9] "Thedyr wolde I come belyve, in childyng to do her harme. / If it were unblessed, I brake it foote or arme, / Or the woman herselfe in some wyse I dydde harme" (220–22).

[10] John Lydgate, "The Legend of Seynt Margarete," from *The Minor Poems of John Lydgate*, ed. Henry Noble McCracken, EETS o.s., 107 (1910), 173–92.

[11] "Margaret's miraculous escape out of the dragon's belly had long since earned her the role of patron saint of childbirth." Eamon Duffy, "Holy Maydens, Holy Wyfes: The Cult of Women Saints in Fifteenth- and Sixteenth-Century England," *Studies in Church History* 27 (1990): 196.

honored virgin / noble and blessed martyr / through your blessed passion, / through your saintly petition / may you pray to God for me / and sweetly ask Him / that He may comfort me through His pity / in the pain which I have to undergo / and that He—without danger to soul or body—make my child come out / safe and sound, so I can see him / baptized joyously.[12]

While mothers and those concerned for their welfare (in fact, in the early Latin and Old English lives, the beneficiaries of St. Margaret's promises are grammatically male) were interested in the saint's ingestion and emergence from the dragon, scholars raised questions about the dragon and demon scenes in the saint's life.

The ninth-century *Old English Martyrology* simply left out both these scenes, although they are the most distinctive elements of her legend. In the tenth century, the Greek hagiographer Simeon Metaphrastes complained about accounts of the life of St. Marina (as St. Margaret is known in the eastern church) that featured her encounter with both the dragon and a demon, calling them "malicious interpolations."[13]

A similar interest in removing what one writer called "superstitious" material from the lives of the saints caused Jacopo da Voragine in his collection *The Golden Legend* (1260) to suggest that when Margaret saw the dragon in her cell, she simply made the sign of the cross and the dragon disappeared. Then he offers the more popular version: that the saint was swallowed by the dragon, made the sign of the cross inside him, and then burst out unharmed. However, Voragine declares this account "apocryphal" and "frivolous."[14] Voragine's rhetorical strategy is intriguing; he denies the veracity of the dragon ingestion account, yet does not drop it from his text altogether. (He also notes St. Margaret's efficacy for women in childbirth.) In comparison, in the Casinensis recension of the Latin *passio* and the *Old English Martyrology*, the swallowing is simply excised.[15] Clearly this was an option for Voragine too, yet he leaves the scene in despite his obvious disapproval.

[12] "Madame saincte Marguerite . . . que femme / grosse d'enfant qui a toy, dame, / de cuer devot retourneroit, / et humblement te requerroit, / que Dieu de peril la gardast / et luy aider point ne tardast, / si te prie, vierge honoree, / noble martire et bieneuree, / par ta benoiste passion, / par ta sainte peticion, / que Dieu vueilles pour moy prier / et doulcement luy supplier que par pitié il me conforte / es douleurs qu'i fault que je porte, / et sans peril d'ame et de corps / face mon enfant yssir hors / sain et sauf, si que je le voye / baptizé a bien et a joye." In Pierre Rézeau, *Les Prières aux saints à la fin du moyen âge*, 2 vols. (Geneva, 1982), 2:323–25. Text and translation in Renate Blumenfeld-Kosinski, *Not of Woman Born: Representations of Caesarean Birth in Medieval and Renaissance Culture* (Ithaca, 1990), 7–8.
[13] Metaphrastes's writing has only been preserved in an early modern translation by Lawrence Surius, *Vitae Sanctorum ex probatis auctoribus et mss. codicibus primo quidem per R. P. Fr. Laurentium Surium Carthusianum editae, nunc vero multis sanctorum vitiis auctae, emendatae et notis marginalibus illustratae*, 4 vols. (Cologne, 1617–18), 3:248.
[14] Jacobi de Voragine, *Legenda Aurea vulgo Historia Lombardica Dicta*, ed. Theodor Graesse (Lipsiae, 1850), 401.
[15] Clayton and Magennis, *Old English Lives*, 34.

An illustration from a tenth-century manuscript of the life of St. Margaret portrays the scenario that Voragine favors. The saint confronts the dragon and raises her hand to make the sign of the cross, driving the beast away.[16] It is interesting therefore to note an illumination from a manuscript of *The Golden Legend* that shows the dragon with Margaret's dress hanging out of his mouth.[17] This popular motif may be seen as a visual argument against the noningestion theorists. It is, of course, possible that a medieval illuminator might not be aware of the exact content of the text being illuminated and thus might use an ingestion image in a text that argues against this idea. However, the gap between text and image reminds us again of the variety of patrons and needs composing the cult. That Princeton University Press used the image for the cover of a 1993 translation of *The Golden Legend* underlines the futility of attempting to dispose of such a dramatic and well-loved image.

In the thirteenth-century *South English Legendary*, the narrator also exhibits concern about the veracity of the swallowing of the saint. He nimbly skirts the issue by giving the standard account of Margaret's ingestion and deliverance and then commenting: "But I cannot say if this is true for it is not written as truth; but whether it is true or not, no man knows" (165–66).[18] He goes on to explain that it is problematic to believe that a demon could be destroyed even by a very powerful saint. At the end of the text the narrator recommends that women read the life of Margaret when they are going to give birth: "When women bear a child, in the company of other women, it is good that they read her life, for certainly it is the truth"(317–18).[19] The text claims to be concerned with "truth," even as it seems to struggle with what that truth is. The technical demonological issue forces a questioning of the tale's veracity, yet the story must also be true for the women who hear the story as part of the ritual of childbirth. Despite a lack of endorsement or even denunciation from patrons whom we might conventionally label as "dominant," the account of St. Margaret's swallowing and the image of her emergence from the dragon's belly persisted. The definitions of "truth" for different audiences of this text are not the same, yet they are simultaneously, if not seamlessly, present. The hege-

[16] Known as the Fulda manuscript, Hannover Library, I 189, fol. 20r. For a facsimile and thorough commentary see *Passio Kiliani*, ed. Hans Immel, commentary by Cynthia J. Hahn (on this image, see 111–14) (Graz, Austria, 1988).

[17] The illumination is in Huntington Library, San Marino, Calif., HM 3027, fol. 19v. It appears on the cover of vol. 2 of *The Golden Legend: Readings on the Saints*, trans. William Granger Ryan (Princeton, 1993). The publisher's choice of illustration is even more odd because St. Margaret's *vita* appears in vol. 1.

[18] Ac þis ne telle ich noʒt to soþe for it nis noʒt to soþe iwrite / Ac weþer it is soþ oþer it nis inot noman þat wite," *The South English Legendary*, vol. I, ed. Charlotte D'Evelyn and Anna J. Mill, EETS o.s., 235 (1956), 297.

[19] "Wymmen þat wiþ oþer were wanne hi child bere / Hit were god þat hi radde hure lyf þe sikerore ʒe seoþ it were," ibid., 302.

monic control often claimed for one group, the writers of texts, was mediated or modified by others who held onto the ingestion story and image. In other words, the question of who is the master of this narrative is not easily answered.

While the dragon scene was debated and even excised from textual accounts, its popularity as an image continued. One obvious explanation for this discrepancy between the textual and visual traditions is simply that the saint emerging from the dragon is such a wonderfully dramatic image that no artist could bear to lose the opportunity to re-create it. Recalling the audience and patrons for this image, however, also reminds us that it was sponsored by women interested in this image for its efficacy in childbirth. Whether she sponsored a window, statue, or manuscript, or simply offered a few pennies for some candle wax, for a woman who turned to St. Margaret for protection during childbirth, the loss of the image of the saint with the dragon would be unthinkable.

Earlier, in the illumination from *The Golden Legend*, we saw how Margaret's dress hanging from the dragon's mouth was a sign of Margaret's ingestion and might be understood as a visual assertion that she was swallowed. The motif of Margaret's protruding dress is common, and may represent the interests of a patron for whom Margaret's emergence from within the dragon gave a sign of the saint's power and efficacy in connection with childbirth. The image's proliferation on an enormous variety of objects underlines its popularity and persistence, and testifies to the concerns of the mostly female patrons who sponsored these artifacts. Let's look at a series of these items.

The image of St. Margaret emerging from the dragon appears on a fourteenth-century French parchment amulet with prayers for use in childbed.[20] An amulet like it might have been kept in a small hinged metal box with loops to be hung at the waist or neck, much like an example from the Boston Museum of Fine Arts (fig. 1). Its use is not specifically indicated, although the combination of St. Margaret and St. Catherine, patroness of nurses, may link it to childbirth as well.[21] The text around Margaret says "Hail, Holy Face of Christ," which refers to an image that would have been in the frame inside the box; the names of the Three Kings (who are frequently invoked in charms) are placed around St. Catherine on the other side.

Jacopo da Voragine might have pointed to an object like the late fourteenth-century embossed leather casket now at the Metropolitan Museum

[20] Plate in Albert, "La Legende de Sainte Marguerite," 33. The amulet was introduced in A. Aymar, "Le sachet accoucher et ses mystères" *Annales du Midi* 38 (1926): 273–347. For more on the use of parchment amulets by royal French women, see Joly, *La vie sainte Marguerite*, 29.

[21] Box 46.1249, Museum of Fine Arts, Boston. *Catalogue of Medieval Objects: Metalwork*, ed. Nancy Netzer (Boston, 1991), 107–8.

Fig. 1. The hem of St. Margaret's dress clearly protrudes from the dragon's mouth in this image on a metal amulet holder. Silver box. Northern Europe, mid-fourteenth century. Accession number 46.1249. Arthur Mason Knapp Fund. Courtesy Museum of Fine Arts, Boston. Reproduced with permission. © 2002 Museum of Fine Arts, Boston. All rights reserved.

of Art as an example of the problems brought about by fantastic or superstitious associations with St. Margaret. An image of St. Margaret emerging from the dragon with her dress hem dangling from his mouth appears on the upper-left corner of the lid. The remaining panels include two scenes from the romance *Chatelaine de Vergi* and others described by the museum's catalogue as "scenes of gallantry and grotesque monsters."[22] It is a peculiar combination of images: human heads appear on beastly bodies in some panels, while embracing couples may be discerned on others. The casket's decorative program may have been considered appropriate for a woman, possibly as a wedding gift, because it portrays lovers and the presence of St. Margaret implies the safe arrival of future children. The context of St. Margaret's appearance on the casket is similar to her image in Jan van Eyck's "Arnolfini Betrothal" (1434), where she functions as one sign of a

[22] Metropolitan Museum of Art, accession number 23.229.1.

fruitful marriage.[23] While such a combination of sacred and secular might be distasteful or even blasphemous to someone like Voragine, for those who regarded the image of St. Margaret and the dragon as an emblem of safety along with fecundity, a gift like the leather casket would be received gratefully.

A fourteenth-century Italian illuminated life of Margaret was also designed to suit the specific needs of a mother.[24] The series of illuminations includes her encounter with the dragon (she is definitely swallowed according to both the image and the text), the demon (whom she binds and beats), and a scene of pilgrims coming to her shrine for cures. At the end of the *passio* appears an image of a midwife bringing out an infant to the mother in bed, which functions as an emblem of the safe childbirth for both mother and child that St. Margaret has just promised in the text (fig. 2).[25] Above the childbed scene is written a prayer that invokes the Trinity as well as the miraculous mothers of the New Testament and Apocrypha: Elizabeth, Anna, and Mary. The manuscript ends with the texts of the seven penitential psalms. Clearly this example reflects the needs of the women who were sponsoring text production, following the promise of St. Margaret who pledged to intercede on behalf of those who owned a copy of her life or had it read aloud to them. This example, however, goes beyond mere reflection by incorporating an image of the audience into the text itself.

The image of the new mother and her healthy infant acts as a useful reminder that ultimately the version of St. Margaret's legend that served the needs of a larger and apparently more influential set of patrons prevailed. The overwhelming number of extant artifacts produced for a wide range of patrons, including manuscripts, amulets, wall paintings, icons, reliquaries, and embroideries, all focus on the very scene that a smaller, although more institutionally powerful group, attempted to excise from the legend. The case of St. Margaret offers a counter-example to the more common model of the dominant clergy exercising hegemonic control over lay believers, especially women. However, instead of simply reversing that model and claiming a subversive role for women, this essay has sought to portray women's patronage of St. Margaret as actively and openly promoting those aspects of the cult that best addressed their needs and concerns.

Unfortunately, much evidence of women's activities has been lost or obscured because of its ephemeral nature. Books that were laid on a woman's

---

[23] St. Margaret appears on the left finial of the bed in the painting. National Gallery, London.

[24] The manuscript is BL, Egerton 877. The childbed scene is on f.12 verso.

[25] In a late thirteenth-century French wall painting, St. Margaret herself appears at a woman's bedside, although there is no clear sign that the woman is an expectant mother. Church of St. Cerneuf de Billom (Puy-de-Dôme). See Paul Deschamps and Marc Thibout, *La peinture murale en France au début de l'époque gothique* (Paris, 1963), 144–5, plate LXXVI-1.

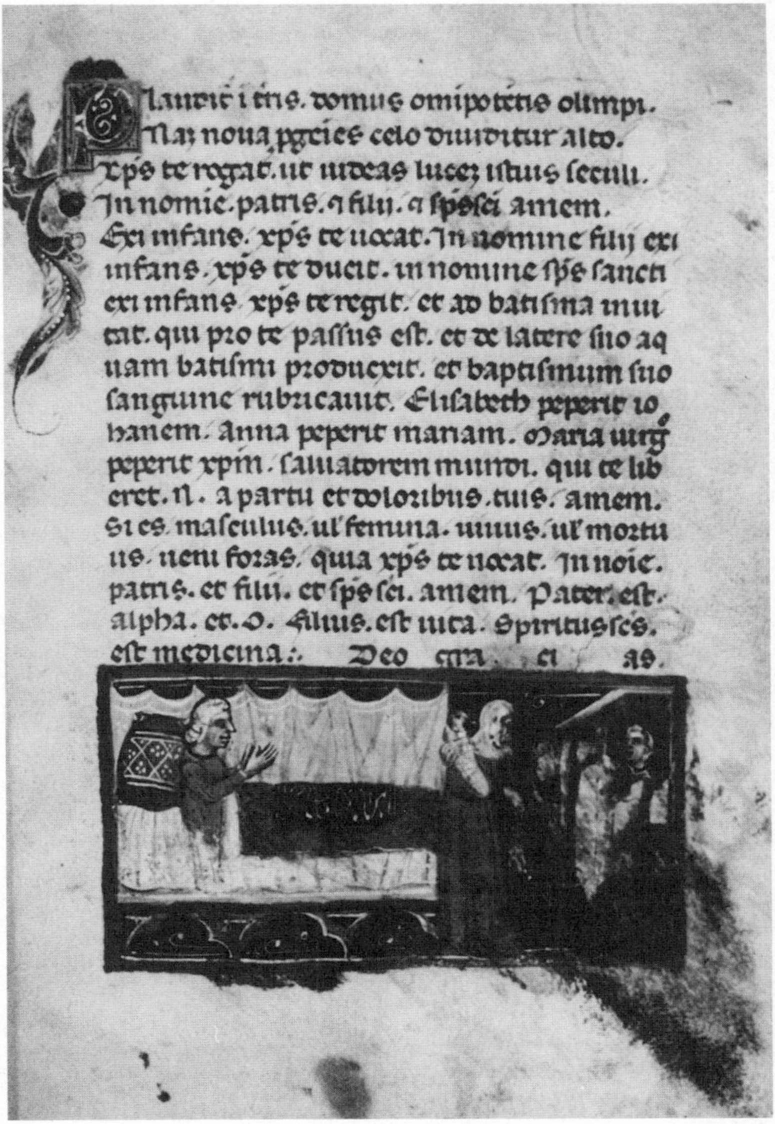
Plaudit i tris. domus omipotetis olimpi.
Nam noua pgcies celo diuiditur alto.
xps te rogat. ut uideas luce; istius seculi.
In nomie. patris. et filij. et sps sci amen.
Exi infans. xps te uocat. In nomine filij exi
infans. xps te ducit. in nomine sps sancti
exi infans. xps te regit. et ad batisma inui
tat. qui pro te passus est. et de latere suo aq
uam batismi produxit. et baptismum suo
sanguine rubricauit. Elisabeth peperit io
hanem. Anna peperit mariam. Maria uirg
peperit xpm. saluatorem mundi. qui te lib
eret. n. a partu et doloribus tuis. amen.
Si es masculus. ul femina. uiuus. ul mortu
us. ueni foras. quia xps te uocat. In noie.
patris. et filij. et sps sci. amen. Pater. est.
alpha. et. O. Filius. est uita. Spiritus scs.
est medicina. Deo gra. et as.

Fig. 2. A newborn is presented to his mother by the midwife. Above, the text of a prayer for mothers follows the story of the life of St. Margaret. Italian, fifteenth century. By permission of the British Library, Egerton MSS 877, fol. 12v.

belly during labor (instead of carefully tended in a library) were worn out with use, candles burned away, and only a few parchment amulets have survived out of the assuredly countless numbers that were made. Writing about childbirth practices involving the life of St. Margaret as a site of text dissemination, Jocelyn Wogan-Browne has noted, "It is a sobering thought that, apart from a few chance remains, an entire world of hagiographic textual practice centered on an important audience constituted by pregnant women has virtually disappeared, in part because of that audience's need for transmission of the saint's life in a particularly perishable form."[26] The types of patronage with which women may be most typically associated, particularly if we consider women of all economic levels, are thus more vulnerable to passing without formal record or adequate attention from historians.

This examination of women's role as patrons in the cult of St. Margaret has focused on a very narrow aspect of women's influence in this particular cult as well as women's work in the development and maintenance of saints' cults generally. The differing readings and presentations of St. Margaret's life and iconography indicate the need for a broad, interdisciplinary approach to understanding how cults function, particularly in the case of a cult in which women played such a critical part. Simply reading texts or viewing images of this saint would have failed to convey how the two primary means of presenting the saint to her medieval audience were at variance in some important respects. In the adoption of St. Margaret as a protector in childbirth, some of the texts condemn, while the surviving material objects endorse—and it is the objects that testify to women's interest. The texts that warn against this devotion are the product of male clerical culture; they contrast with the elements of material culture such as the metal or leather boxes described above. Of course material culture is not exclusively female, yet since women participated rarely in male learned culture, it is often such physical remains that speak to us of female needs and desires. Bringing together these two elements has permitted an opportunity to reconsider who was the master of this narrative of St. Margaret and the dragon, and thus, in part, has helped us to reconfigure the shape of the larger master narrative regarding the nature of the relationship between women and power in the middle ages.

[26] Jocelyn Wogan-Browne, "The Apple's Message: Some Post-Conquest Hagiographic Accounts of Textual Transmission," in *Late-Medieval Religious Texts and Their Transmission*, ed. A. J. Minnis (London, 1994), 53.

CHAPTER SIX

"The Wise Mother": The Image of St. Anne Teaching the Virgin Mary

Pamela Sheingorn

In her *Book of the Three Virtues*, Christine de Pizan wrote, "the wise mother will give great attention to the upbringing and instruction of her daughters," and she clearly included literacy among the areas of instruction.[1] This chapter argues that although in the late middle ages Christine's statement was virtually a truism, modern scholarship, by focusing on the education of male children, has neglected this aspect of medieval culture.[2] Yet there is significant evidence for female literacy, especially visual evidence, in the

This chapter was presented at the conference, "Parents and Children in the Middle Ages," sponsored by the Medieval Club of New York, on March 2, 1990. It first appeared in *Gesta* 32, 1 (1993): 69–80. The author is grateful to the journal's editor for permission to reprint. My research was facilitated both by the files and by the knowledgeable and generous staff of the Index of Christian Art, Princeton University.

[1] In this passage, Christine is specifically concerned with the responsibilities of a princess for the education of her daughters. For a critical edition see *Christine de Pizan: Le Livre des Trois Vertus*, ed. Charity Cannon Willard (Paris, 1989). For an English translation see Christine de Pisan, *The Treasure of the City of Ladies or the Book of the Three Virtues*, trans. Sarah Lawson (London, 1985). For a biography of Christine see Charity Cannon Willard, *Christine de Pizan: Her Life and Works* (New York, 1984). For a discussion of her attitudes toward education, see Astrik L. Gabriel, "The Educational Ideas of Christine de Pisan," *Journal of the History of Ideas* 16 (January 1955): 3–22.

[2] For example, in the widely cited collection of essays *The Flowering of the Middle Ages* edited by Joan Evans (London, 1966; reprint 1985), the chapter on education, "The Sum of Knowledge," by Richard Hunt, subtitled "Universities and Learning," does not mention women. They were, of course, excluded from the universities. Among the extensive illustrations to the chapter, the only women to appear are personifications, objects of charity, and Heloise taught by Abelard, an implicitly negative example. Current scholarship has begun to address questions of female literacy.

scene of St. Anne teaching her daughter from a book, a scene quite popular in the art of northern Europe from the early fourteenth century to the Reformation, and in Catholic countries until modern times. I explore several readings of the scene, and in particular I argue that it promulgated the notion of mothers as teachers and daughters as apt and willing pupils, just as it celebrated literacy, especially among upper- and middle-class women.

Though well-known in the middle ages, St. Anne's story does not appear in the canonical Gospels. She is, however, an important figure in the apocryphal *Protevangelium of James* and texts deriving from it, for example, the *Pseudo-Matthew*.[3] Written in about 150 c.e., the *Protevangelium* tells the story, familiar from Giotto's frescoes in the Arena Chapel, of Joachim's sacrifice, rejected because he and his wife Anne had no children, of their sorrow turned to joy by angelic visitation, and of the angel's message that they would become parents.[4] Anne responded at once to the angel, saying, "As the Lord my God lives, if I bear a child, whether a male or female, I will bring it as a gift to the Lord my God, and it shall serve him all the days of its life" (4.1). Of course Anne did bear a child, a female child. According to the *Protevangelium*, when Mary was two years of age, Joachim wanted to "bring her up to the temple of the Lord, that we may fulfill the promise which we made" (7.1), but Anne persuaded him to wait until her daughter was three. The scene of the tiny child ascending the steep, formidable steps of the Temple while the anxious parents look on became a favorite in the pictorial arts.[5] According to later versions of the story—for example, *The Mary Play from the N.town Manuscript*—Mary recited a psalm for each of the fifteen steps.[6]

After the Presentation in the Temple, the *Protevangelium* shifts to Mary's twelfth year, the year of her marriage to Joseph. The only mention of her accomplishments is a comment that she could spin and weave. She was occupied with these activities when the angel of the Annunciation appeared to her, and was so represented in art until the eleventh century. At about

[3] For a discussion of the *vita* of Saint Anne, along with further bibliography, see "Introduction," in *Interpreting Cultural Symbols: Saint Anne in Late Medieval Society*, ed. Kathleen Ashley and Pamela Sheingorn (Athens, Ga., 1990), 1–68.

[4] For the portion of the *Protevangelium* that tells Anne's story (secs. 1.1–8.1), see Edgar Hennecke, *New Testament Apocrypha*, vol. 1, *Gospels and Related Writings*, ed. William Schneemelcher; English trans. J. B. Higgins et al., ed. R. McL. Wilson (Philadelphia, 1963), 374–78; reprinted as Appendix to Ashley and Sheingorn, "Introduction," *Interpreting Cultural Symbols*, 53–57.

[5] See Gertrud Schiller, *Ikonographie der christlichen Kunst* (Gütersloh, 1980), 4.2, 67–72. For the impact on liturgy in the West, see William E. Coleman, *Philippe de Mézières' Campaign for the Feast of Mary's Presentation* (Toronto, 1981).

[6] *The Mary Play from the N.town Manuscript*, ed. Peter Meredith (London, 1987). See also *The N-Town Play: Cotton MS Vespasian D.8*, ed. Stephen Spector, vol. 1, *Introduction and Text*, EETS, supplementary ser., 11 (1991), 81–94.

this time, concomitant with the growth of Mary's cult, the idea developed that because she was mother of God, Mary must have been both spiritually and intellectually gifted. Byzantine sermons from the eighth to tenth centuries described her as possessing the wisdom of Athena, and one version of the *Pseudo-Matthew* claims: "No one could be found who was better instructed than she (Mary) in wisdom and in the law of God, who was more skilled in singing the songs of David (Psalms)."[7] In the thirteenth century Albert the Great taught that Mary had been a master in the seven liberal arts.[8] It is not surprising, therefore, to find that in Annunciation scenes Mary's spindle was replaced by a book.[9] In some renditions the book is open to Isaiah 7:14—"Behold a virgin shall conceive and bear a son." The idea that Mary was reading this especially appropriate text was spread, for example, by Nicholas Love's translation into English of the popular devotional text, the *Meditationes vitae Christi*. Love wrote that Gabriel appeared "before þe virgine Marie, þat was in hire pryue chaumbure þat tyme closed & in hir prayeres, or in hire meditaciones perauentur redyng þe prophecie of ysaie, touchyng þe Incarnacion."[10]

It was, of course, possible that Mary was literate when she was born, but a natural assumption in the middle ages was that she was taught in the Temple, just as children were taught in contemporary monastic schools. Thus stained glass from the beginning of the thirteenth century in Chartres Cathedral shows a schoolroom scene in which Mary and four other pupils sit before their teacher, and fourteenth-century glass in the Frauenkirche at Esslingen depicts Mary after her Presentation as a solitary student in the Temple, beginning to learn her Psalter with verse one of the First Psalm. A

---

7 Quoted in Gertrud Schiller, *Iconography of Christian Art*, trans. Janet Seligman (Greenwich, Conn., 1971), 1:42. It should be noted that the idea of Mary as a book in which God wrote the Incarnation was articulated as early as the fourth century and employed frequently thereafter. See Klaus Schreiner, " '. . . wie Maria geleicht einem puch': Beiträge zur Buchmetaphorik des hohen und späten Mittelalters," *Archiv für Geschichte des Buchwesens* 11 (1971): cols. 1437–64.

8 Wolfgang Braunfels, *Die Verkündigung* (Düsseldorf, 1949), xiv–xv. For assertions by writers beginning as early as the ninth century that Mary was reading the Psalter when Gabriel appeared to her, see Schreiner, " '. . . wie Maria," 1443.

9 David M. Robb, "The Iconography of the Annunciation in the Fourteenth and Fifteenth Century," *Art Bulletin* 18 (1936): 480–526. For a thorough discussion of Mary as reader at the Annunciation see Klaus Schreiner, "Marienverehrung, Lesekultur, Schriftlichkeit: Bildungs- und frömmigkeitsgeschichtliche Studien zur Auslegung und Darstellung von 'Maria Verkündigung,' " *Frühmittelalterliche Studien* 24 (1990): 314–68.

10 *Nicholas Love's Mirror of the Blessed Life of Jesus Christ: A Critical Edition*, ed. Michael Sargent, Garland Medieval Texts 18 (New York, 1992), 21–22. Sargent indicates that the specification of the content of Mary's reading is an addition by Love to the text that he was translating. See his extensive note to this passage. I am grateful to Professor Sargent for allowing me to see relevant portions of his book before its publication. Schreiner, "Marienverehung," traces the association of Mary with Isaiah from the early Christian period into the late middle ages.

historiated initial showing Mary as a member of a class of girls taught by a schoolmaster decorates a book of sermons made for a house of Cistercian nuns in the diocese of Constance between 1325 and 1350 (fig. 1). The choice of subject suggests the possibility that the designer of the book saw some parallel between Mary's experience and that of the nuns.

In the face of expansion of the Marian narrative consistent with the apocryphal accounts, it is particularly striking to find development in another direction, namely that of Mary's mother Anne as her teacher. Such scenes occur first in England, early in the fourteenth century, in wall paintings, stained glass, sculpture, embroidery, and manuscript illumination.[11] An embroidered altar frontal of about 1320 to 1340 presents one typical format with both figures standing (fig. 2). The directed gazes, open book, and Anne's gesture all indicate that here the mother acts as teacher. In the sequence of scenes on the frontal, the Virgin's presentation in the Temple comes before her education by her mother, an inconsistency that seems not to have troubled the embroiderers. The same illogical sequence can be found in the early fourteenth-century English wall paintings at Croughton, which implies that Anne continued to teach her daughter up to the moment that her father Joachim led her off to be married.[12] In an apparently unique solution, fourteenth-century stained glass from the choir of Orvieto

[11] Christopher Norton, David Park, and Paul Binski, *Dominican Painting in East Anglia: The Thornton Parva Retable and the Musée de Cluny Frontal* (Woodbridge, 1987). See the roughly chronological list of examples compiled by David Park on pp. 51–52. Veronica Sekules suggests that the earliest example may be in a manuscript: "A new illustration of the Virgin's life appears in England in the early fourteenth century in the Alphonso Psalter, the education of the Virgin by her mother, St Anne." See Veronica Sekules, "Women in Art in England in the Thirteenth and Fourteenth Centuries," in *Age of Chivalry: Art in Plantagenet England 1200–1400*, ed. Jonathan Alexander and Paul Binski (London, 1987), 43. The Alphonso Psalter, BL MS Add. 24686, is catalogue no. 357 in that volume. For an illustration of the scene of Anne teaching the Virgin see fol. 2v, illustrated in Lucy Freeman Sandler, *Gothic Manuscripts 1285–1385*, 2 vols., A Survey of the Manuscripts Illuminated in the British Isles 5 (London, 1986), I, fig. 2.

[12] On Croughton see E. W. Tristram and M. R. James, "Wall-paintings in Croughton Church, Northamptonshire," *Archaeologia* 76 (1927): 179–204. M. D. Anderson points out a similar inconsistency in the Marian section of the Middle English dramatic cycle she calls *Ludus Coventriae*, now usually referred to as the N-Town cycle. This cycle includes the Presentation of the Virgin (see note 6 above for references). Anderson observes,

in the *Ludus* the play of the "Betrothment of Mary" opens with the Bishop's command that all maidens of thirteen years old shall come to the Temple to be betrothed. Joseph then consults Anna, apparently in their own home, and they take Mary once more to the Temple. At Croughton the painting of the presentation is followed by a scene in which Joachim takes Mary by the hand and leads her away from Anna who is shown sitting with an open book in her hand (Plate 5a). There is no stage direction in the *Ludus* that Anna shall be teaching her daughter to read when the play opens, but such a grouping would have been suggested to any medieval producer by the popularity of this subject in church imagery.

M. D. Anderson, *Drama and Imagery in English Medieval Churches* (Cambridge, 1963), 113.

Fig. 1. *Nativity and Virgin Mary at School*, c. 1325–50. Courtesy of the Bodleian Library, University of Oxford, MS Douce 185, fol. 35v.

Fig. 2. *St. Anne Teaching the Virgin Mary* from an *opus anglicanum* altar frontal, c. 1320–40, Victoria and Albert Museum, 8128–63. Courtesy of the Board of Trustees of the V&A.

Cathedral places the scene of Anne's teaching Mary inside the Temple; as a result its position after the Presentation is not so jarring.

There are not many other attempts to integrate the scene of Anne's teaching into pictorial treatments of the Marian narrative, which usually move directly from the Presentation in the Temple to the events surrounding the Wedding of Mary and Joseph. But in *devotional* contexts the scene not only survives but flourishes (fig. 3). In fact, it serves as the major devotional image of Anne, who is virtually never represented alone, but rather with her daughter and her book. This grouping implies that Anne's act of teaching carries singular importance, as does the fact that the book is virtually always open. Though a book appears with great frequency as an attribute of sacred figures, it is more often closed.

The devotional image of Anne teaching the Virgin Mary flourishes in spite of a virtual if not total absence of textual sources. In medieval iconography this is quite unusual, for it is common practice to trace an image to authorized sources and to explain its details through references to exegesis and commentary. The very existence of such a scene, floating free of a textual anchor and surfacing in a variety of contexts, suggests that it performed important symbolic functions in late medieval cultural practices. It is these contexts and functions that we need to understand.

One such context is Incarnation history. In his book on the garb and attributes of saints in German art, Joseph Braun explains that St. Anne's book

Fig. 3. *St. Anne Teaching the Virgin Mary*. Westminster Abbey, Chapel of Henry VII, c. 1502–12. Courtesy of the Royal Commission on the Historical Monuments of England.

"is to be understood here as the book of the Old Testament, in which the Messiah was promised to humankind."[13] E. W. Tristram observes that, "In wall-painting, the subject of St. Anne teaching the Virgin may sometimes form part of a 'history', but more frequently appears either singly or beside an Annunciation."[14] The Annunciation and Education of the Virgin scenes are paired on a rare surviving English panel painting of about 1335 now in the Cluny Museum. David Park comments: "Iconographically, these subjects form a perfect foil, both emphasising the special role of the Virgin in God's design."[15] On the altar frontal, the book is open to the passage: "*Audi filia et vide et inclina aurem tuam, quia concupuit rex speciem tuam*" (Listen, daughter, and see, and incline your ear, for the king desires your beauty), a variant of the Vulgate text of Psalm 44:11–12. Christian exegesis has placed these words in the mouth of Christ as bridegroom and has understood them as addressed most generally to the Christian soul, more specifically to virgins, and most specifically, as here, to Mary. As David Park observes, "the Vulgate text has been altered so as to place the emphasis directly on the divine choice of Mary to be the bride of Christ. St Anne points deliberately at the word *rex*. . . . The text thus prefigures the moment of the Annunciation which was depicted at the other end of the panel, when Mary, through her submission to the divine word, enabled God's redemptive plan to be brought to fulfilment."[16]

The specific understanding of the scene of Anne teaching the Virgin Mary in terms of Incarnation history can also be generalized, as Gertrud Schiller suggests. She sees the book in these scenes as a symbol for Christ, the Logos, the Word.[17] And this reading is substantiated by the rise of another subject in the late middle ages, that of the St. Anne Trinity; that is, the grouping of Anne, her daughter Mary, and her grandson, Jesus, as an infant (fig. 4). The two subjects, Anne teaching the Virgin Mary and the St. Anne Trinity, can be seen as two somewhat different embodiments of the same idea—that of the Incarnation. I have argued elsewhere that, whereas the traditional Trinity of Father, Son, and Holy Ghost emphasizes Christ's divinity and immortality, the St. Anne Trinity, especially in the composi-

[13] Joseph Braun, *Tracht und Attribute der Heiligen in der deutschen Kunst* (Stuttgart, 1943), col. 79, my translation. Frank Olaf Büttner makes a more general argument that representations of reading in late medieval manuscripts refer to salvation history: "An verschiedenen Inhalten kehrt ein Motiv denselben Gehalt hervor. Für das Motiv des Lesens hiess dieser Gehalt: Erwartung und Vergegenwärtigung des göttlichen Heilsplans"; " 'Mens divina liber grandis est': Zu einigen Darstellungen des Lesens in spätmittelalterlichen Handschriften," *Philobiblion* 16 (1972): 99.

[14] E. W. Tristram, *English Wall Painting of the Fourteenth Century* (London, 1955), 23.

[15] Park in *Dominican Painting in East Anglia*, ed. Norton, Park, and Binski, 44; see plate 2 for a color reproduction of the frontal in its present state, plate 11 for a color reproduction of *St. Anne Teaching the Virgin*, and plate 44 for a detail of the book.

[16] Park in *Dominican Painting in East Anglia*, ed. Norton, Park, and Binski, 50.

[17] Schiller, *Ikonographie der christlichen Kunst* (Gütersloh, 1980), 4.2, 76.

tional arrangement where it replicates a popular way of representing the traditional Trinity (fig. 5), emphasizes the lineage of Christ's physical body.[18] The matrilineal Trinity is the Trinity of the Incarnation.

But St. Anne and the Virgin Mary had roles in contemporary medieval society in addition to their places in Incarnation history, a fact that some scholars have tended to ignore or misunderstand. Stephan Beissel, for example, states that when the group of Anne teaching the Virgin does not include the Christ Child, it "reveals in this omission a sharp decline from the older and deeper meaning, in which Jesus was always the purpose and goal."[19] According to Beissel, with the exclusion of the Child Jesus, the group comes very close to a genre scene. By setting up a false dichotomy between high theological meaning and genre scene, Beissel suppresses the cultural functions of hagiography in the late middle ages. From the perspective of Incarnation history as understood by the twentieth-century scholar, Anne's role may be limited to grandmother of Christ, mother of the Virgin, and she may have existed only to fill a place in a genealogical chart, the end goal of which was the Incarnation. But in late medieval culture, Anne was not confined to the historical past—she was a powerful presence. As Kathleen Ashley and I wrote in the introduction to *Interpreting Cultural Symbols: Saint Anne in Late Medieval Society*, the essays gathered in that book

> show that the figure of Saint Anne functioned symbolically for a wide range
> of social groups in their cultural practices. She represented the cult of the
> family to gentry and aristocracy. She was called on by individual women as
> a sympathetic intercessor in childbearing. She bore a metaphorical relation
> to a number of crafts, such as woodworking, and was therefore their appro-
> priate patron. She exemplified affective behaviors to nuns in a convent.[20]

Nor does this exhaust the list of her functions, for we need to add the cultural function of the grouping of Anne, Mary, and book.

First I will demonstrate the hitherto unrecognized function of this grouping as the core around which other scenes were built. Though I have organized this material in terms of increasingly complex composition, this is for the sake of convenience and is not meant to be an implicit argument for a specific line of development.

The question of Anne's attributes is a good place to begin. Joseph Braun, who categorizes St. Anne's attributes in terms of her postures, lists four

[18] Pamela Sheingorn, "Appropriating the Holy Kinship: Gender and Family History," in *Interpreting Cultural Symbols: Saint Anne in Late Medieval Society*, ed. Ashley and Sheingorn, 169–98. On the painting by the Master of Frankfurt see John Oliver Hand, "*Saint Anne with the Virgin and the Christ Child* by the Master of Frankfurt," *Studies in the History of Art* 12 (1982): 43–52.
[19] Stephan Beissel, *Geschichte der Verehrung Marias in Deutschland während des Mittelalter* (Freiburg-im-Breisgau, 1909), 582; my translation.
[20] Ashley and Sheingorn, eds., *Interpreting Cultural Symbols*, 2.

The Image of St. Anne Teaching the Virgin Mary

Fig. 4. *St. Anne, Virgin, and Child,* South German, late fifteenth to early sixteenth century. Courtesy of Philadelphia Museum of Art, 1964-140-1. Given by Mrs. Hedy V. Fishman.

Fig. 5. Master of Frankfurt, *St. Anne with the Virgin and the Christ Child*. Photograph © 2002 Board of Trustees, National Gallery of Art, Washington, D.C. Gift of Mr. and Mrs. Sidney K. Lafoon, 1976.67.1 (2071).

possibilities.[21] The first is a book, although I know of no examples in which Anne is shown alone with a book. Second, according to Braun, Anne may have a figure of the child Mary on her arm. The earliest known image of Anne in the West, that painted on the west wall of the presbytery in the Roman church of Santa Maria Antiqua in about 650, presents Anne in this way, as does the early thirteenth-century trumeau at Chartres. But these are among the rare examples of Anne and Mary without a book. Third, says Braun, Anne may be accompanied by Mary holding Jesus on her lap, and fourth, Anne may hold Mary on one arm and Jesus on the other. Braun is firmly convinced that "The third and fourth attributes, which ruled the field at that time, rendered the book superfluous."[22] If the interpretation of the scene is restricted to a statement about the Incarnation, then, strictly speaking, Braun is correct; the book and the Christ Child both refer to the Word, the Logos, the second person of the Trinity, and the presence of both creates a redundancy. But the numerous examples of St. Anne with Mary who holds her child Jesus in which one or more books feature prominently (fig. 6) suggest that the book had another function in the minds of artists and their patrons. More recent scholars than Braun have found the category of St. Anne Trinity sufficient for such works of art and have tended not to explore, or even mention, the presence of a book. Yet the book itself often seems a focal point in the composition. In one type, Anne appears to neglect her grandson in order to pursue her reading, as in an English manuscript of about 1400 (fig. 7), and in another, Mary is engrossed enough in her reading lesson to ignore her son's bid for her attention (fig. 8).[23] Braun is so little attuned to the significance of the book in the St. Anne Trinity that he goes on to argue that in the type of composition in which Anne holds Mary on one arm and Jesus on the other, a book could not possibly appear since both of Anne's hands are already engaged. Again his logical argument is contradicted by surviving evidence, for both Veit Stoss and Tilman Riemenschneider found satisfying solutions to this compositional conundrum (fig. 9).[24] As Hanswernfried Muth notes, in Riemenschneider's sculpture Mary is "ganz in das Studium ihres Buches versunken" (entirely engrossed in studying her book).[25] Of course there are examples of the St.

[21] Braun, *Tracht und Attribute*, cols. 79–82.

[22] Braun, *Tracht und Attribute*, col. 80, my translation.

[23] MS Metz B. M. 620 is catalogue no. 24 in *Metz enluminée: Autour de la Bible de Charles le Chauve; Trésors manuscrits des églises messines* (Metz, 1989), 164. It is a composite fourteenth-century manuscript from the convent of the Celestines in Metz. I wish to thank Adelaide Bennett for bringing this manuscript to my attention.

[24] For an illustration of Veit Stoss's sculpture for Saint Anne's Church in Vienna see Beda Kleinschmidt, *Die heilige Anna: Ihre Verehrung in Geschichte, Kunst und Volkstum* (Düsseldorf, 1930), fig. 171.

[25] Hanswernfried Muth, *Tilman Riemenschneider. Die Werke des Bildschnitzers und Bildhauers, seiner Werkstatt und seines Umkreises im Mainfränkischen Museum, Würzburg* (Würzburg, 1982), 82.

Fig. 6. *St. Anne Trinity*, Lower Rhine, early sixteenth century. Courtesy of Suermondt-Ludwig-Museum, Aachen.

Fig. 7. *St. Anne Trinity*, c. 1400. Courtesy of the Bodleian Library, University of Oxford, MS Aubrey 31, fol. 31r.

Fig. 8. *St. Anne Teaching the Virgin Mary in the Presence of the Christ Child.* Courtesy of Bibliothèque municipale, Metz, MS B.M. 620, fol. 1v.

Fig. 9. Tilman Riemenschneider, *St. Anne Trinity*, after 1510, Mainfränkischen Museum, Würzburg. Courtesy of Foto Zwicker Berberich Atelierbetriebe.

Anne Trinity that do not include a book, but scholarly emphasis has fallen on one extreme to such an extent that it has not adequately dealt with the kind of image in the painting of the St. Anne Trinity by Cornelisz van Oostsanen, in which the figures of Mary and Christ shrink in significance beside the book to which Anne directs her gaze (fig. 10).

The Holy Kinship, the grouping of Anne with her three daughters, their fathers, husbands, and sons, is usually described as deriving compositionally from the subject of the St. Anne Trinity.[26] Thus it is no surprise that frequently, though not always, books are present, not only as attributes of Anne and/or Mary but also in the hands of many members of this apparently scholarly clan.

Two further examples indicate the variety of contexts in which the combination of Anne, Mary, and book can appear. The first is a late fifteenth-century plague broadsheet, showing the St. Anne Trinity and a kneeling man who seeks Anne's help against the plague.[27] The other is a complex composition that combines the core scene of Anne teaching the Virgin with the St. Anne Trinity, the Holy Kinship, and a woman with her patron saint—the Duchess of Bedford, Anne of Burgundy—kneeling before an opened book in the presence of her patron saint Anne (fig. 11). Marcel Thomas's commentary on this page from the Bedford Hours mentions neither St. Anne's book nor that of Anne of Burgundy, and finds that the imagery "stress[es] the notion of marriage."[28] Although Janet Backhouse gives a fuller, more balanced description, she also does not note Anne of Burgundy's book and uses the marginal figures from the Holy Kinship to argue for a "stress on family relationships . . . peculiarly appropriate to Anne [of Burgundy] given the long catalogue of diplomatically significant marriages within her immediate family circle."[29] Yet the main stress is surely on Anne of Burgundy's relationship with the grouping Anne/Mary/book, and it is time to investigate the meaning of that grouping.

First, in manuscripts, of which the Bedford Hours is a good example, there seems to be some connection between the presence of this image and patronage or ownership by women, a connection first observed by Nigel Morgan. Although the fact that Anne is the duchess's name saint is sufficient to explain her presence here, it is surely significant that the duchess mirrors not only St. Anne's name but also her activity—both have open books before them.

[26] Pamela Sheingorn, "The Holy Kinship: The Ascendancy of Matriliny in Sacred Genealogy of the Fifteenth Century," *Thought: A Review of Culture and Idea* 64, no. 254 (September 1989): 268–86.

[27] For illustration see Kleinschmidt, fig. 399.

[28] Marcel Thomas, *The Golden Age: Manuscript Painting at the Time of Jean, Duke of Berry* (New York, 1979), 83.

[29] Janet Backhouse, *The Bedford Hours* (New York, 1990), 37. Büttner ("Mens divina," 101–2) discusses the acts of reading in this miniature.

Fig. 10. Cornelisz van Oostsanen, *St. Anne Trinity*, 1525. Courtesy of Gemäldegalerie, Staatliche Museen Preussischer Kulturbesitz, Berlin.

A similar relationship occurs in the first of sixteen full-page miniatures following the calendar in the Fitzwarin Psalter, an English manuscript of the mid-1340s. As Veronica Sekules comments, "the female donor of the manuscript is included in the scene kneeling before St Anne as she teaches the Virgin to read, as if she too is anxious to benefit from [Anne's] instruction."[30]

[30] Sekules, "Women in Art," 43. For an illustration of this miniature (fol. 7 in MS. lat. 765, Paris, Bibliothèque nationale), see *Age of Chivalry*, ed. Alexander and Binski, 501. For a discussion of the manuscript see Sandler, *Gothic Manuscripts*, II, catalogue no. 120.

Fig. 11. *Duchess of Bedford before St. Anne Teaching the Virgin Mary*, Bedford Hours. By permission of the British Library, MS Add. 18850, fol. 257v, c. 1423.

Nicholas Rogers has identified the patroness and owner of the manuscript as Amice de Haddon.[31] In a fifteenth-century Book of Hours of Sarum Use made in France (fig. 12), both St. Anne and the Virgin carry books, and some of the prayers in the manuscript suggest that it had a female owner.

Certainly the evidence of the image itself, as well as the limited information regarding specifically female patronage, should be considered part of the growing body of knowledge about female literacy in the later middle ages.[32] Works of art in which women hold open books strongly suggest a culture in which women read. Rather than interpret the presence of a book as a general indication of female piety, as is often done, we should take it as evidence of a literate woman, an owner of books, and possibly even a patroness, for there is extensive evidence that women owned books and commissioned vernacular literature or translations from Latin into a vernacular.[33] Among these is the only known illustrated example of the *Manuel des péchés*, whose opening initial shows Joan Tateshal, its patroness "stand[ing] imperiously" and "appear[ing] to command her scribe to begin writing the text."[34]

But the scene of Anne teaching the Virgin Mary to read, which appeared in the fourteenth century and became so popular throughout western Europe, surely does more than record evidence of historical circumstances, for its originating purpose can scarcely have been to illustrate the fact that women in a particular time and place could read. That is, rather than simply mirroring the society of which it is a part, art functions to shape that society; it plays an active role. It is no accident or coincidence that the image of Anne teaching the Virgin Mary appeared when it did. At the beginning of the fourteenth century there was a new urgency regarding literacy. M. T. Clanchy argues for a "shift from sacred script to practical literacy" in the twelfth and thirteenth centuries. "Practical business was the foundation of the new literacy."[35] He speaks of "the growth of a literate mentality,"[36] which was a cultural fact by the beginning of the fourteenth

---

[31] Nicholas Rogers, "The Original Owner of the Fitzwarin Psalter," *Antiquaries' Journal* 69 (1989): 257–60.

[32] For examples of recent studies on literacy see Rosamond McKitterick, *The Uses of Literacy in Early Medieval Europe* (Cambridge, 1990), and Katherine O'Brien O'Keeffe, *Visible Song: Transitional Literacy in Old English Verse*, Cambridge Studies in Anglo-Saxon England 4 (Cambridge, 1990). There is also a recent interest in medieval female literacy; for examples, see Susan-Marie Harrington, *Women, Literacy, and Intellectual Culture in Anglo-Saxon England* (Ph.D. diss., University of Michigan, 1990), and Margaret P. Hannay, ed., *Silent But for the Word: Tudor Women as Patrons, Translators, and Writers of Religious Works* (Kent, Ohio, 1985).

[33] Susan Groag Bell, "Medieval Women Book Owners: Arbiters of Lay Piety and Ambassadors of Culture," *Signs* 7 (1982): 742–68.

[34] Adelaide Bennett, "A Book Designed for a Noblewoman: An Illustrated *Manuel des Péchés* of the Thirteenth Century," in *Medieval Book Production: Assessing the Evidence*, ed. Linda L. Brownrigg (Los Altos Hills, Calif., 1990), 173. For a color illustration of fol. 1 of this manuscript (Princeton University Library, Taylor Medieval MS I), see ibid., color plate E.

[35] M. T. Clanchy, *From Memory to Written Record: England 1066–1307* (London, 1979), 263.

[36] Ibid., 2.

Fig. 12. *St. Anne and the Virgin Mary with Books*, c. 1430–40. Courtesy of the Bodleian Library, University of Oxford, MS Auct. D. inf. 2.11, fol. 51v.

century, the time when the image of Anne teaching the Virgin begins to appear. In other words, in order to function in their own "modern world," people found it increasingly necessary to be literate. And, in regard to the broad geographical area in which our image can be found, it is important to note Clanchy's words: "The shift from memory to written record . . . was not restricted to England although it is most evident there. It was a western European phenomenon."[37]

Nor was this new literacy restricted to the vernacular. In a French vocabulary written by an Essex knight for a Lady Denise de Montchensy to use as a tool in improving her children's French, the knight, Walter of Bibbesworth, assumes that she has already taught them from the Latin primer.[38] As Clanchy argues, "A little *clergie* [i.e., the knowledge found in a primer] had the advantage of keeping children's options open. From inclination or necessity, boys or girls could subsequently join the 'religious', provided they had a grounding in Latin and some local influence."[39] And in England there was an even more compelling reason for teaching children some Latin for, "[f]rom the fourteenth century, . . . a little Latin, 'benefit of clergy', was also an insurance against being hanged. Thus by 1300 parents of all social classes had strong motives for seeing that their children were *clerici* and *literati* in the new minimal sense of being capable of reading a verse from the Bible."[40] One reading, then, of the new scene of St. Anne teaching the Virgin would find it to be an advertisement for a life insurance policy that parents, specifically mothers, could "purchase" for their children.

Some or all of these functions may inform a full-page miniature in a Sarum Book of Hours of about 1325–30, in which the Virgin, sheltered in Anne's fur-lined cloak, holds an alphabet book (fig. 13).[41] The book contains six capital letters, separated by ruled lines, which spell the word "Domine." In a similar vein, a fourteenth-century wall painting at Mentmore, Buckinghamshire, now destroyed, showed the Virgin in the Education scene holding a scroll with the letters *A B C*.[42]

Only slightly earlier Walter of Bibbesworth had written a rhyming vocabulary in French with some interlineations in English for the Lady Denise de Montchensey to use in teaching her children not elementary

[37] Ibid., 5.

[38] A. Owen, ed., *Le Traité de Walter de Bibbesworth sur la langue française* (Paris, 1929).

[39] Clanchy, *From Memory*, 196.

[40] Ibid., 196. Ralph V. Turner notes the irony that "[t]he possibility of gaining benefit of clergy in late medieval England by reading a verse of Scripture has doubtless contributed to the modern myth of the illiteracy of the laity throughout the middle ages." See "The *Miles Literatus* in Twelfth- and Thirteenth-Century England: How Rare a Phenomenon?" *American Historical Review* 83 (1978): 930.

[41] For a description of this manuscript see *Age of Chivalry*, ed. Alexander and Binski, 151, 154–55.

[42] Park in *Dominican Painting in East Anglia*, ed. Norton, Park, and Binski, 53.

Fig. 13. *St. Anne and the Virgin Mary*, c. 1325–30. Courtesy of the Bodleian Library, University of Oxford, MS Douce 231, fol. 3r.

French, which, Walter says, everyone knew how to speak, but the specialized vocabulary that would allow them to function in the adult world of estate management and of the court. Denise was widowed and her children might well have been in danger of losing their social status if they could not function in educated French.

A late example of a child's first book, a primer, reinforces the conclusion that children's literacy was a mother's responsibility, and that the imagery of St. Anne and her daughter served as the vehicle for communicating that responsibility. The key images are on pages one and fourteen, the first and last pages of the Primer of Claude of France, made around 1505–10 (figs. 14 and 15). On the first page, St. Anne presents the Virgin Mary and Claude of France to Claude's name saint, Claude of Besançon. Claude holds a closed book and seems to seek St. Claude's support and assistance as she begins her reading lessons. On the last page Claude kneels before her own open book, following along as St. Anne teaches the Virgin. Having reached the last page of her primer, she can now read. But the primer insists more directly that Claude's literacy is her mother's responsibility, for Claude's mother was named Anne.

It is perhaps the concern for the early education of children by their mothers that explains why even in scenes where the Infant Jesus is present, the Virgin Mary is shown as a girl learning her letters from her mother. And of course one purpose of literacy that cannot go unmentioned was to provide the ability to read a Book of Hours. That is surely one reason that often on the books in these scenes we find the words, *Domine labia mea aperies*, the opening versicle of Matins in the Hours of the Virgin.

Once we approach this image in terms of its cultural functions, it can open for us aspects of medieval culture that have resisted traditional approaches. For example, with few exceptions, such as the excellent work of Judith M. Bennett and Barbara Hanawalt,[43] we have no studies that illuminate domestic life in general and specifically that of any but the upper class. Thus, although we have a variety of sources attesting to widespread literacy among upper-class women, it is much more difficult to say anything about the middle class, other than to note that apparently Margery Kempe could not write. But St. Anne's popularity was not confined to the upper classes. In seeking to understand "the importance of St. Anne plays and altars and guilds in late medieval East Anglia,"[44] Gail McMurray Gibson examines a poem about Anne in the fifteenth-century commonplace book compiled by a Norfolk man named Robert Reynes. She finds that the poem presents Anne as "a model East Anglian matron, tending to her

[43] Judith M. Bennett, *Women in the Medieval English Countryside: Gender and Household in Brigstock Before the Plague* (Oxford, 1987); Barbara Hanawalt, *The Ties That Bound: Peasant Families in Medieval England* (Oxford, 1986).

[44] Gail McMurray Gibson, *The Theater of Devotion: East Anglian Drama and Society in the Late Middle Ages* (Chicago, 1989), 83.

Fig. 14. Primer of Claude of France, 1505–10. Courtesy of the Fitzwilliam Museum, Cambridge, MS 159, p. 1.

Fig. 15. Primer of Claude of France, 1505–10. Courtesy of the Fitzwilliam Museum, Cambridge, MS 159, p. 14.

tithes, her almsbasket, and her prayerbook. She lives a busy, comfortable, and pious life." "It is difficult," Gibson concludes, "to imagine a saint with more obvious bourgeois appeal."[45] And women modeling themselves on Anne found her image—a mother teaching her daughter—readily available, for she appeared not only on manuscripts whose expensive illuminations largely restricted ownership to the upper class but also painted on the walls of parish churches and standing near their altars. Relatively inexpensive alabaster figures and panels were distributed not only throughout England but, as products of an export industry, reached many churches in western Europe.[46]

This image also gives us access to the neglected area of domestic life in the middle ages and, in particular, forces us to see that this culture considered the mother's role as her children's first teacher to be important, even crucial.[47] This message may also be encoded in the personification of Grammatica as a woman teaching boys their ABCs, as in a fifteenth-century German manuscript now in Vienna, though the common medieval practice of using female figures to personify abstractions, such as the Virtues and Vices, complicates this reading.[48] Nevertheless, studies of medieval education generally neglect even to mention the mother as teacher. In a particularly egregious example, an article on the education of women in the middle ages offers the following conclusion: "Aristocratic women received some education at court or castle. Upper-class women learned at the manor, from private clergy. In the later middle ages poor university students may have acted as tutors. But girls had to learn at home from fathers, brothers, clergy."[49] Yet surely "girls who learned at home" became mothers who could teach their daughters at home. In fact a group of treatises in the voice of a mother addressed to her daughter, written in the same centuries in which our image flourished, indicate that mothers did exactly that. A Middle English poem found in a number of fourteenth- and fifteenth-century manuscripts and entitled "How the Good Wife Taught her Daughter" celebrates the continuity of this private, domestic education when, near the

[45] Ibid., 84.

[46] On English alabasters see Francis W. Cheetham, *English Medieval Alabasters* (Oxford, 1984).

[47] This aspect of the mother's role is not explored in Clarissa W. Atkinson, *The Oldest Vocation: Christian Motherhood in the Middle Ages* (Ithaca, 1991). In Atkinson's view, late medieval motherhood "was comprehended in terms of physical suffering and service" (167).

[48] The image is on folio 1 of a composite manuscript of texts in Middle High German, Vienna, Oesterreichische Nationalbibliothek, Cod. 2975. See *Martin Luther und die Reformation in Deutschland* (Frankfurt am Main, 1983), no. 86. For an analysis of female personifications see Marina Warner, *Monuments and Maidens: The Allegory of the Female Form* (New York, 1985).

[49] Sara Lehrman, "The Education of Women in the Middle Ages," in *The Roles and Images of Women in the Middle Ages and Renaissance*, ed. Douglas Radcliff-Umstead (Pittsburgh, 1975), 141.

end of the poem the mother says, "Now have I taught thee, daughter, as did my mother me."[50]

Finally, if the image of Anne teaching the Virgin is so widespread in the late middle ages, how have we failed to notice its importance? Among a number of possible reasons, I would like to point to three. First, we have interpreted late medieval culture as dominated by affective piety, an affective piety focused on the relationship of Mary and Jesus, mother and son, emotionally heightened by the tension between its absolute uniqueness and its human qualities. I think it would probably be fair to say that we are attracted by the extreme emotional tones that characterize this relationship as well as by the erotic undercurrents always present in Christ's dual role as son and bridegroom. In our interpretations of the late middle ages, we have allowed this extraordinary, multidimensional parent-child relationship to overshadow another that speaks to a more balanced though less dramatic medieval understanding of parenting, namely that of Anne and Mary, mother and daughter, a domestic, human relationship.

This image has also been neglected because, despite some protestations to the contrary, we have not sufficiently recognized that the middle ages was a visual culture.[51] We have not developed ways of integrating into our understanding images that stand outside of the textual matrix, although the recent development of pictorial hagiography by such scholars as Cynthia Hahn, Barbara Abou-el-Haj, and Magdalena Carrasco heralds a welcome change.

And third, as with so many other aspects of women's history, the iconography of this image was willfully distorted by Victorian ideologies of femininity in the nineteenth century, and we have not entirely succeeded in discarding that pernicious legacy. In her feminist study of embroidery, Rozsika Parker offers a telling juxtaposition of two images. The earlier is a medieval embroidery of St. Anne teaching the Virgin Mary, a typical example in which both females gesture toward the pages of an open book. The later is a painting by Dante Gabriel Rossetti dated 1848–49 and entitled *The Girlhood of Mary Virgin*. The arrangement of figures is similar, but in this visualization of "the concept of femininity as purity and submissiveness," Mary bends over an embroidery frame as Anne instructs her in the fine points of rendering a lily in split-stitch.[52]

Finally, we must recognize that in promoting literacy this image could

---

[50] Tauno F. Mustanoja, ed., *The Good Wife Taught Her Daughter. The Good Wyfe Wold a Pylgremage. The Thewis of Goud Women* (Helsinki, 1948).

[51] For important exceptions see the first two chapters of V. A. Kolve, *Chaucer and the Imagery of Narrative: The First Five Canterbury Tales* (Stanford, 1984), and Susan K. Hagen, *Allegorical Remembrance: A Study of the "Pilgrimage of the Life of Man" as a Medieval Treatise on Seeing and Remembering* (Athens, Ga., 1990).

[52] Rozsika Parker, *The Subversive Stitch: Embroidery and the Making of the Feminine* (New York, 1984), figs. 18, p. 30, and 19, p. 31; the quotation is from the caption to fig. 18.

suggest, but not control, the uses to which female literacy would be put. The position of one of the leading scholars of the theory of literacy, Jack Goody, has evolved significantly on this point. R. W. Niezen summarizes Goody's position in the 1970s: "Alphabetic literacy, he suggests, is responsible for the growth of knowledge because it makes permanent the relationship between the word and its referent, making it possible to scrutinize language and subject the ideas it communicates to criticism and revision."[53] But Goody refined this position in stating "two opposed consequences of the permanency of ideas that writing brings about: 'criticism and commentary on the one hand and the orthodoxy of the book on the other.'"[54] And more recently Goody has moved to the consideration of "a wide range of social implications of literacy."[55] We are left with a situation in which "[t]he link between literacy and the development of a critical approach to ideological messages is therefore more problematic."[56]

Some scholars would see no possibility at all of "a critical approach to ideological messages" in the material we have been examining. Surely medieval women put literacy to a wide range of social uses. Many, undoubtedly most, used it to articulate orthodox ideologies more clearly. Nikki Stiller argues that the relationship between Anne and the Virgin as presented in medieval literature, specifically in the N-Town cycle, serves the dominant ideology by inculcating passivity in women. She points specifically to Anne's willingness to give up her three-year-old daughter and Mary's acquiescence in entering the Temple as paradigms of proper behavior for medieval women. "What better model for mothers and daughters than Our Lady and Her mother, Anne?" Stiller asks in her despair at their willing passivity.[57] It is undoubtedly true that most of what women were urged to read in the late middle ages reinforced the ideology of patriarchy and instructed women as to their proper place within it. Reading may most frequently have been part of an image of submissive behavior, as in the N-Town play of the Marriage of Mary and Joseph. When Joseph leaves, Mary indicates that she will simply wait and read until he returns:

And I xal here abyde your agencomynge
And on my Sawtere-book I xal rede. (10/423–4)[58]

And though Mary's reading is mentioned several times in the cycle, it seems always confined to the Psalter. In fact, Martin Stevens suggests that

[53] R. W. Niezen, "Hot Literacy in Cold Societies: A Comparative Study of the Sacred Value of Writing," *Comparative Studies in Society and History* 33.2 (April 1991): 226.

[54] Ibid., 226.

[55] Ibid., 227.

[56] Ibid., 251.

[57] Nikki Stiller, *Eve's Orphans: Mothers and Daughters in Medieval English Literature* (Westport, Conn., 1980), 52.

[58] Spector, *N-Town*, 109.

the cycle contrasts the knowledge of the "Doctors" in the play—"all the science of their day as taught in the trivium and the quadrivium"[59]—with Mary's "true learning"—"what man learns from the Psalms, Mary tells us, is how to be virtuous and how to love. As the paradigmatic human being committed to a life of learning, that is what she has gathered from her own assiduous reading of the Psalter."[60] How could we expect that one of the most central constructions of medieval culture, the Virgin Mary, would not forward the dominant ideologies of that culture?

Yet we should not forget that another possible consequence of literacy is to foster criticism and commentary, and that there were literate women in the late middle ages, most notably Christine de Pizan, who employed her literacy to construct a devastating critique of the ideology of patriarchy. Although we cannot predict the end to which it will be used, we can agree that literacy is power. Through the pictorial arts, Anne empowers her daughter and encourages other mothers to follow her example.[61]

[59] Martin Stevens, *Four Middle English Mystery Cycles: Textual, Contextual, and Critical Interpretations* (Princeton, 1987), 216.

[60] Ibid., 217. Schreiner is convinced that reading, as encouraged by Mary's example, served primarily to deepen feelings of piety: "Im Auge zu behalten ist allerdings dies: Lesen, das durch mariologische Bild- und Textzeugnisse veranlasst und gestützt wurde, diente weder der Unterhaltung noch der beruflichen Ausbildung oder geistigen Selbstvervollkommnung. Lektüre war auch nicht eine Form des Glücks, sondern ein Mittel moralischer Besserung und vertiefter Religiosität. Nur als Quelle einer persönlichen und verinnerlichten Frömmigkeit stärkte Lesen das Selbstgefühl und die Subjektivität mittelalterlicher Frauen" ("Marienverehrung," 318).

[61] I was not able to consult a forthcoming essay by Wendy Scase, "St Anne and the Education of the Virgin: Literary and Artistic Traditions and Their Implications," in *England in the Fourteenth Century: Proceedings of the 1991 Harlaxton Symposium*, ed. Nicholas Rogers, Harlaxton Medieval Studies 3 (Stamford, 1994), 81–96.

CHAPTER SEVEN

Did Goddesses Empower Women?
The Case of Dame Nature

Barbara Newman

Around 1975, when the number of feminists studying medieval literature could be counted on the fingers of both hands, textbook accounts routinely linked the vogue for idealized female figures, such as romance heroines and allegorical goddesses, with a supposed rise in the status of women. By 1990, feminists were legion and this consensus had largely reversed itself. More exacting studies of change in women's social and economic status had failed to demonstrate any clear gains and, in fact, were more likely to show a decline. In literature, with the increasing popularity of the "madonna-whore complex" as an interpretive construct, idealized and demonized female figures came to be seen as two inseparable poles in a broad strategy to objectify and dehumanize women. But this picture in turn has been challenged. Intensive studies of women writers, especially mystics, have shown that many of them did find goddess figures empowering and frequently spoke in the name of such divine alter egos as Sapientia and Dame Amour. In my book, *God and the Goddesses*, I examined selected medieval goddesses in a wide range of texts by male and female writers both religious and secular, exploring the cultural and theological work that such figures do.[1] In many instances, I have found, gender ideology seems only tangential to a writer's investment in a particular goddess. But this is emphatically not the case with texts that feature Natura, the "daughter of God" whose sphere of influence concerned sex, gender, and procreation.

Lady Nature, a goddess invented by Bernard Silvestris and Alan of Lille

---

[1] Barbara Newman, *God and the Goddesses: Vision, Poetry, and Belief in the Middle Ages* (Philadelphia, 2003). This chapter is condensed and adapted from chap. 3.

in the twelfth century, is among the bugbears of contemporary theorists, who have devoted considerable energy to deconstructing the whole concept of "nature" along with the gendered dichotomy of nature and culture.[2] So, prima facie, we might expect the writings where this goddess figures prominently to enforce the most repressive available gender norms. In this essay I will test that hypothesis through readings of three medieval French writers: Jean de Meun, Heldris of Cornwall, and Christine de Pizan. Nature's allegiances do not remain stable from one text to another, and the values she represents are not always the same. In the *Roman de la Rose*, for example, Nature stands for active heterosexuality as opposed to sodomy on the one hand and chastity on the other, while in the *Roman de Silence* and *Le Livre de la mutacion de Fortune*, she signifies anatomical vis-à-vis cultural gender. But Nature's is not the sole authoritative voice in these texts. In fact, her very presence signals her participation in a debate whose conclusion is not foregone. For Christine de Pizan as for the mysterious Heldris of Cornwall, that debate concerns the still-controversial question as to whether, or under what circumstances, "becoming male" is a viable and empowering strategy for women.

The immensely popular *Romance of the Rose* must be our starting point for any investigation of Dame Nature in French literature. When Jean de Meun took up the unfinished romance of Guillaume de Lorris circa 1275, he made its delicate plot the foundation of a vast, sprawling edifice that both dwarfs and deconstructs the original. Dame Nature and her sidekick, the so-called priest Genius, are the last of six prolix authority figures introduced by Jean to vie for the allegiance of his protagonist, the callow Amant, who is seeking by fair means and foul to lure his Rose into bed. When Nature first appears, we see her as a blacksmith hard at work in her forge, hammering out new individuals to replace those killed by Death.

> Touz jors martele, touz jors forge,
> Touz jors ses pieces renovele
> Par generacion novele.[3]

> [She is always hammering and forging,
> Always renewing her creation
> By new acts of generation.]

---

[2] See, e.g., Carolyn Merchant, *The Death of Nature: Women, Ecology, and the Scientific Revolution* (San Francisco, 1980); Carol MacCormack and Marilyn Strathern, eds., *Nature, Culture and Gender* (Cambridge, 1980); Judith Butler, *Gender Trouble: Feminism and the Subversion of Identity* (New York, 1990); Donna Haraway, *Simians, Cyborgs, and Women: The Reinvention of Nature* (New York, 1991).

[3] Jean de Meun, *Roman de la Rose*, lines 16,010–12. I cite the edition of Daniel Poirion, *Le Roman de la Rose* (Paris, 1974).

Jean borrowed this figure from Alan of Lille's *De planctu Naturae*, where the unlikely smith is Nature's protégée Venus, and her hammer and anvil are transparent metaphors for sexual organs.[4] In keeping with this image, most illuminated *Rose* manuscripts include a standard miniature of "Nature at her forge." Standing before her anvil with hammer in hand, the goddess uplifts her mighty arm to forge a bird, a beast, or most often, a baby.[5] This symbolic portrayal of lovemaking also provides a sinister object lesson in hermeneutics, since anyone foolish enough to neglect the allegory and read the image "literally" would see in Nature the most unnatural of mothers, a veritable Medea, poised to smash the vulnerable infant lying on her anvil.

Like Alan of Lille's Natura, Jean de Meun's goddess is deputized by God to oversee all procreation, and she can discourse impressively on natural science and philosophy. But Jean radically departs from Alan in positing a breach between Nature and God's other daughter, Lady Reason, since in his view, only Reason enables humans to contemplate the divine order which, by definition, transcends Nature. Thus Dame Raison, the first of Jean's authoritative speakers, upholds Christian sexual ethics. She is an implacable foe of the God of Love and deploys all her arguments, in vain, to dissuade Amant from his quest of the Rose. Dame Nature, on the other hand, supports the cause of Cupid and Venus because her own interest in procreation dovetails with their pursuit of sexual pleasure. Compared with Alan's Natura, Jean's Nature is logically more consistent, though rhetorically even more sly. *De planctu Naturae* famously ends with a solemn anathema in which Natura's priest, Genius, excommunicates all sodomites. Jean de Meun adapts this motif with a cunning and controversial twist, which has dismayed readers from Christine de Pizan through the mid-twentieth century. Acting on Nature's authority, his Genius anathematizes not only homosexuals but also celibates and virgins: for if same-sex love is *contra naturam*, that is to say nonprocreative, so too is lifelong abstinence. Nor do Genius and Nature have any vested interest in marriage; heterosexual promiscuity suits their interest—and the Lover's—as well as or better than wedlock. In his preaching to Love's barons, Genius tells them exactly what they wish to hear:

> Arés, por Dieu, baron, arés,
> Et vos linages reparés.
> Se ne pensés forment d'arer,
> N'est rienz qui les puist reparer.

---

[4] Natura speaks: "To assure that faithful instruments would preclude the corruption of shoddy workmanship, I assigned [Venus] two prescription hammers with which to undo the snares of the Fates and prepare many kinds of things for existence. I also gave her noble workshops with anvils suited for this craft, instructing her to apply the same hammers to the anvils and devote herself faithfully to the formation of creatures. By no means should she let the hammers stray from the anvils in any deviation." Alan of Lille, *De planctu Naturae* 10, ed. N. M. Häring, *Studi Medievali*, terza serie, 19.2 (1978), 845.

[5] Rosemond Tuve, *Allegorical Imagery: Some Mediaeval Books and Their Posterity* (Princeton, 1966), 324.

Rescorciés vous bien par devant,
Aussi cum por coillir le vent,
Ou, s'il vous plaist, tuit nu soiés,
Mes trop froit ne trop chaut n'aiés.

[Plow, for God's sake, barons, plow,
And renew your lineages!
If you don't think of plowing vigorously,
Nothing can restore them.
Tuck up your clothes in front,
As if to wanton with the wind,
Or if you wish, go completely naked,
But don't get chilled or overheated.]

(19,701–8)

Ne vous lessiés pas desconfire,
Grefes avés, pensés d'escrire.
N'aiés pas les bras emmouflés:
Martelés, forgiés et souflés.

[Don't let yourselves be vanquished!
You have a stylus; think of writing.
Don't let your arms be muffled:
Hammer away, use forge and bellows!]

(19,793–96)

In the event, Nature proves to be on the "winning" side of the *Rose*, insofar as the Lover follows her counsel rather than Reason's. This does not, of
course, make her an authorial mouthpiece.[6] Chaucer, I believe, read the
Roman de la Rose correctly in the prologue to his *Legend of Good Women*,
where he presents himself as the object of Cupid's wrath for having translated the *Rose* into English. The God of Love comically accuses the poet of
sacrilege because the *Rose* "is an heresye ayeins my lawe, / And [thou]
makest wise folk fro me withdrawe."[7] In other words, Cupid—and presumably Chaucer—understood Jean de Meun to be a partisan of Lady Reason, not Lady Nature. Chaucer's assigned penance for his poetic sin
against Love is to compile a new martyrology, whose alternate title is *The
Seintes Legende of Cupide*. But if this new text at least theoretically refur-
bishes the reputations of women, it certainly does not empower them, for
what the poet presents is a long litany of victims and suicides.

[6] For Jean de Meun as a partisan of Nature, see the massive work of Alan Gunn, *The Mirror of Love: A Reinterpretation of "The Romance of the Rose"* (Lubbock, 1952). For the partisans
of Reason see D. W. Robertson Jr., *A Preface to Chaucer: Studies in Medieval Perspectives*
(Princeton, 1962), 196–203 et passim; John Fleming, *The "Roman de la Rose": A Study in Allegory and Iconography* (Princeton, 1969); and idem, *Reason and the Lover* (Princeton, 1984). My
own reading is in substantial agreement with Fleming's.
[7] Geoffrey Chaucer, *Legend of Good Women*, F prologue, lines 330–31. In *The Riverside
Chaucer*, ed. Larry Benson et al. (Boston, 1987), 597.

Does Nature in the *Rose* empower women? Hardly. If Chaucer well understood Jean de Meun's irony, Christine de Pizan well understood his misogyny. Jean's characterization of Nature is antifeminist in two distinct but compatible ways. First, she collaborates with the God of Love to enable Amant's conquest of the Rose—and a conquest it most decidedly is. If the Rose is "the first important pregnant heroine in European literature," as a critic once quipped,[8] she is hardly the first to be seduced and abandoned, nor the last to be objectified. After Amant has overridden the protests of Fair Welcome, opened the petals of the Rose, and scattered his bit of seed, he goes on to wonder idly whether others have since followed him into the narrow passage—but that is no longer his concern, nor is it Nature's. Had the Rose been an actual woman, or at least a speaking subject in the poem that bears her name, she could easily have ended up with Chaucer's hapless martyrs of love in *The Seintes Legende of Cupide*.

Dame Nature also serves Jean de Meun's satirical ends in another respect that has little to do with her role in the plot. The scene of her "confession" to Genius provides the occasion for a vicious antifeminist rant by the priest, culminating in his command to "flee, flee, flee, flee, flee" the dreadful beast called Woman.[9] Genius not only proves himself a hardened misogynist but even persuades Nature to agree with his assertion that "nothing swears or lies more boldly than a woman." Worse still, she calls him "courteous and wise" for making such remarks,[10] and admits that she herself must reveal her mysteries because "a woman can keep nothing secret."[11] But the confession scene is not just antifeminist in a generic way. It has a more precise target, for Jean's satire is aimed sharply and scathingly at Beguine spirituality. Indeed, the situation has all the hallmarks of "abuse" that opponents of the Beguine movement held up for ridicule.[12] A loquacious, high-minded woman with pretensions to learning summons "her" priest for confession; he jumps at her bidding, yet does not trouble to hide his contempt for her sex; she in turn uses confession as a pretext to instruct the priest, rambling interminably about high theological matters and boasting of her intimate relationship with God.

8 Charles W. Dunn, intro. to *The Romance of the Rose*, trans. Harry Robbins (New York, 1962), xxv; cited polemically in Fleming, *Roman de la Rose*, 243–44.

9 "Biau seignor, gardés vous des fames, / Se vos cors amés et vos ames, / . . . Fuiés, fuiés, fuiés, fuiés / Fuiés, enfant, fuiés tel beste." *Roman de la Rose*, 16,577–83.

10 "Car riens ne jure ne ne ment / De fame plus hardiement."—"Certes, sire prestres, bien dites / Comme preus et cortois et sages. / Trop ont fames en lor corage / Et soutillités et malices." *Roman de la Rose*, 18,127–33.

11 "Fame sui, si ne me puis taire, / Ains vuel des ja tout reveler, / Car fame ne puet rienz celer." *Roman de la Rose*, 19,218–20.

12 On this tradition see Renate Blumenfeld-Kosinski, "Satirical Views of the Beguines in Northern French Literature," in *New Trends in Feminine Spirituality: The Holy Women of Liège and Their Impact*, ed. Juliette Dor, Lesley Johnson, and Jocelyn Wogan-Browne (Turnhout, 1999), 237–49. Jean's satire is more explicit in his portrayal of Constrained Abstinence, a Beguine who accompanies the friar Fausemblant (False Seeming).

Nul autre droit je n'i reclaime,
Ains l'en merci quant il tant m'aime
Que si tres povre damoisele
A si grant maison et si bele;
Icis granz sires tant me prise
Qu'il m'i a por chambriere prise.
Por sa chambriere? Certes vere,
Por connestable et por viquere,
Dont je ne fusse mie digne,
Fors par sa volenté benigne.

[I claim no other right from him,
But thank him that he loves me so much
That he has given me, such a poor damsel,
Such a great and beautiful mansion.
This great lord values me so much
That he has taken me to be his maid.
His chambermaid? Surely, in fact,
His vicar and his châtelaine—
A post which I by no means deserve
Except through his gracious will.]
(16,775–84)

For a moment Nature sounds like a mystical Beguine exulting that so great a Sovereign has brought so lowly a maiden to his court.[13] Genius for his part absolves Nature and gives her a penance that is "good and pleasing," just as excessively lax friars were said to do.[14] To crown the irony, her penance consists in resuming her labors in the forge—the very activity she has just confessed as sinful.

It is safe to say that this particular goddess, as Jean de Meun constructed her, is no friend to women. But the Nature tradition she represents, which we can trace in a straight line of development from Bernard Silvestris to Alan to Jean de Meun to Chaucer,[15] is not the only one. There is an alternative, less familiar version of the goddess who differs in her iconography as well as her sphere of influence. If the Nature of Alan and Jean is "about" sex, the Nature of Heldris of Cornwall and Christine de Pizan is "about" gender. And if the phallic goddess of the *Rose* is a blacksmith, the more womanly goddess of *Silence* and *Lavision-Christine* is a baker.

The *Roman de Silence*, written in the second half of the thirteenth century

[13] Cf. Mechthild of Magdeburg, *The Flowing Light of the Godhead* I.4, trans. Frank Tobin (New York, 1998), 43. Of course Jean de Meun could not have known Mechthild's German text, but such imagery was a commonplace of Beguine spirituality.

[14] "Si tost cum ot esté confesse / Dame Nature, la deesse, / Si cum la loy vuet et li us, / Li vaillans prestres Genius / Tantost l'assot et si li donne / Penitance avenant et bonne." *Roman de la Rose*, 19,411–16. On the inadequacies of Genius as a confessor see Tuve, *Allegorical Imagery*, 268–69, and Fleming, *Roman de la Rose*, 207.

[15] George Economou, *The Goddess Natura in Medieval Literature* (Cambridge, Mass., 1972).

but not published until the 1960s, was belatedly "discovered" by critics in the 1980s and now seems fetchingly postmodern.[16] Its transvestite hero/ine is called "Silence," and its authorship, fittingly enough, remains shrouded in mystery. "Master Heldris of Cornwall," the self-identified poet, is otherwise unknown. Linguistic features indicate that the text originated in Picardy, not Cornwall, and the poet's name is almost certainly a pseudonym, possibly that of a woman.[17] *Silence* can be read as an elaborate, ambivalent gloss on a speech Jean de Meun puts in the mouth of la Vieille:

Touz jors Nature retorra,
Ja por habit ne demorra.
Que vaut ce? Toute creature
Vuet retorner a sa nature,
Ja nou lera por violence
De force ne de convenance.
. . . .
Trop est fors chose de Nature:
Nature passe norreture.

[Nature always comes running back:
No habit will ever chase her out.
What is that worth? Every creature
Wishes to return to its nature;
It will never forsake it through the violence
Of force, promise, or convenience.
. . . .
Too mighty a force is Nature:
Nature surpasses Nurture.]

(14,025–38)

The maxim that "Nature passe norreture" was proverbial,[18] but no text prior to *Silence* constructs "Noreture" as an allegorical character. In

---

[16] *Silence: A Thirteenth-Century French Romance*, ed. and trans. Sarah Roche-Mahdi (East Lansing, 1992). All citations are from this text. Translations designated "RM" are Roche-Mahdi's; the rest are my own.

[17] Kathleen Brahney, "When *Silence* Was Golden: Female Personae in the *Roman de Silence*," in Glyn Burgess and Robert Taylor, eds., *The Spirit of the Court* (Cambridge, 1985), 61; Roche-Mahdi, *Silence*, xi; Suzanne Akbari, "Nature's Forge Recast in the *Roman de Silence*," in *Literary Aspects of Courtly Culture*, ed. Donald Maddox and Sara Sturm-Maddox (Cambridge, 1994), 46; Lorraine Stock, "The Importance of Being Gender 'Stable': Masculinity and Feminine Empowerment in *Le Roman de Silence*," *Arthuriana* 7 (1997): 28–29. Akbari notes that "the misogyny undoubtedly present in the work is no evidence against female authorship, for misogyny was and is not unique to men."

[18] Simon Gaunt, "The Significance of Silence," *Paragraph* 13 (1990): 203–4; Roche-Mahdi, *Silence*, xviii–xix; Akbari, "Nature's Forge Recast," 41; Adolf Tobler and Erhard Lommatzsch, *Altfranzösisches Wörterbuch* (rpt. Wiesbaden, 1965), VI, 808.

Heldris's romance, Nature and Nurture come onstage in person to argue about the protagonist's gender.

But first the plot. Born a girl, the aptly named Silence is dressed and raised as a boy because her parents are trying to circumvent the law of King Ebain, who has impulsively disinherited all women. Silence receives a chivalric education and soon demonstrates great skill in jousting and other knightly sports. Upon reaching puberty, s/he ponders the wisdom of remaining disguised, but quickly realizes that "a man's ways are worth more than a woman's" (2637–38). Nevertheless, Silence runs away with a pair of traveling minstrels in order to learn skills that will stand him in good stead if he is ever unmasked.[19] In minstrelsy he quickly surpasses his masters and, fleeing from their murderous envy, strikes out on his own. Our hero eventually makes his way to the court of Ebain, where he has the misfortune to become the love-object of the king's wife, Eufeme. As Silence does not reciprocate her passion but pleads feudal honor, the queen—unaware that she herself loves a woman—accuses Silence of being a homosexual and even a male prostitute.[20] Eufeme tries to avenge herself on the unwilling boy by accusing him falsely of rape and, when this scheme fails, sending him to the King of France with a forged letter demanding the bearer's execution. But the canny French king defies the order and grants Silence knighthood instead. Summoned back to England, the new knight heroically saves the king's life in a battle against rebellious counts. Now in high favor with Ebain, Silence is victimized once again by the wrathful Eufeme. This time she tries to get rid of him by sending him on a quest to capture Merlin, knowing that only a woman can succeed in that task. Silence does catch the sly master of disguise, with Merlin's own help, but his success inevitably leads to his exposure. In the final scene, a laughing Merlin appears at court and unmasks not only Silence but also Eufeme—who turns out to have been keeping a male lover disguised as a nun for many years. Enraged, Ebain has his queen and her lover put to death, repeals the law against female inheritance, and marries the newly regendered heiress, Silence.

This tantalizing tale has been diversely interpreted. Some critics read the ending as a victory, others as a defeat for Silence, while Heldris has been variously hailed as a proto-feminist, denounced as a misogynist, and post-

[19] In my pronoun usage I follow the lead of the narrator, who collaborates with Silence's gender masquerade by referring to the hero as "he" throughout the period of his disguise. Surprisingly, even the most Butlerian critics tend to undercut their insistence on the performative quality of gender by referring to the hero/ine as "she." See, e.g., Roberta Krueger, "Women Readers and the Politics of Gender in Le Roman de Silence," in Women Readers and the Ideology of Gender in Old French Verse Romance (Cambridge, 1993), 101–27; Peggy McCracken, " 'The Boy Who Was a Girl': Reading Gender in the Roman de Silence," Romanic Review 85 (1994): 517–36.
[20] On this theme see Kathleen Blumreich, "Lesbian Desire in the Old French Roman de Silence," Arthuriana 7 (1997): 47–62.

modernized as a champion of ambiguity and indeterminacy.[21] More deeply than any medieval poet except Alan of Lille, Heldris probes the dilemmas posed by the goddess Nature: How far does her power extend and what are its limits? How much that goes by the name of "nature" is actually due to nurture, or to human choice, custom, or chance? If it is possible to tamper with Nature's will, is it ever desirable? If indeed "Nature / Signorist desor Noreture" ("Nature has lordship over Nurture," 2423–24), is her sovereignty benign or despotic? The goddess's contested terrain in *Silence* turns out to involve not only gender but also class, morality, and even species.

Nature makes her first appearance in the scene of Silence's birth. Proud of her art, she announces her intention to create a masterpiece (*ouvre forcible*). She is tired of crude, vulgar work and resolves to use only her finest white flour and her most exquisite mold. With her own hand she inscribes the girl's delicate features and paints her face with lilies and roses, asserting that "once in a while I must show what I can do" (RM 1885). Having invested so much in Silence, Nature sees the child as her own little girl ("sa puciele," 1868; "ma mescine," 1873; "ma fille," 1927). Thus she is furious when the parents deface her art by "changing her daughter into a son" (RM 2263). What seems to irritate her most is that Silence's lovely complexion will be damaged, for as a boy he must be tanned by the sun and hardened by rough winds. This concern recurs throughout the text, most notably at the end. After Silence is revealed to be a woman, Nature takes three days to "repolish" her entire body, removing every trace of suntan, before she can marry the king. The obsession with surfaces suggests that gender itself is a superficial matter: Silence's core identity cannot or does not change, but a new dress and a makeover suffice to restore her womanhood.

The scene set in Nature's bakery serves Heldris for an extended commentary not on gender but on class. The narrator explains that Nature has many grades of dough or flour: "She always makes quality folk from the refined clay, and riff-raff from the coarse" (RM 1833–34). Deviations from the expected norm—aristocrats aren't always noble, nor peasants base— are explained by defects in the baking process. If a little coarse matter is mixed in with the fine, it goes straight to the heart and sullies the whole creation. Conversely, some men of low birth possess a noble character be-

[21] For *Silence* as a proto-feminist romance see Brahney, "When *Silence* Was Golden"; Regina Psaki, trans., *Le Roman de Silence* (New York, 1991), intro.; Stock, "The Importance of Being Gender 'Stable.' " For Heldris as a misogynist see Gaunt, "The Significance of *Silence*"; Krueger, "Women Readers"; Blumreich, "Lesbian Desire." Deconstructive readings that stress the indeterminacy of the text include Kate Mason Cooper, "Elle and L: Sexualized Textuality in *Le Roman de Silence*," *Romance Notes* 25 (1985): 341–60; R. Howard Bloch, "Silence and Holes: The *Roman de Silence* and the Art of the Trouvère," *Yale French Studies* 70 (1986): 81–99; and Peter Allen, "The Ambiguity of Silence: Gender, Writing, and *Le Roman de Silence*," in *Sign, Sentence, Discourse: Language in Medieval Thought and Literature*, ed. Julian Wasserman and Lois Roney (Syracuse, 1989), 98–112.

cause they have, by accident as it were, a bit of fine clay in their makeup. In Silence's case, character and status are perfectly congruent because she is made from only the purest material. After Nature has sifted her flour and kneaded her dough, she proceeds to mold, inscribe, and paint it. Heldris seems here to be making a distinction analogous to the Aristotelian dichotomy of form and matter, though with antithetical meaning. Silence's matter—the fine white flour—represents her noble character, while her gender is signified by the inscription and coloring, or superficial form, stamped on that matter. This unusual privileging of matter over form explains why gender is more mutable than character.

But Nature, a goddess scorned, does not like her work to be altered in either respect. After Silence's fateful baptism as a boy, she vows to prove that she is stronger than Nurture.

> "Il ont en mon desdaing cho fait
> Quanses que miols valt Noreture
> Que face m'uevre!" dist Nature.
> "Par Deu! par Deu! or monte bien!
> Il n'a en tiere nule rien,
> Ki par nature ait a durer,
> Ki puist al loing desnaturer."

> ["They have done this to spite me,
> As if the work of Nurture
> Were worth more than mine!" said Nature.
> "For God's sake! A fine state of affairs!
> There is nothing on earth
> Living in Nature's realm
> That can be denatured for long."]
>
> (2266–72)

The goddess stakes her all on her masterpiece, the child in whom she means to show the full extent of her power, but she brooks a forceful challenge from her adversary and loses the first several rounds. The question at stake in Nurture's challenge is indeed whether anyone can or should be "denatured," temporarily or permanently. When Silence reaches puberty, Nature reappears and visits the boy-girl with sharp reproaches. She is wasting her fabulous beauty and deceiving the "thousand women" who have allegedly fallen in love with her; she should abandon her freewheeling forest life and "go to a chamber and learn to sew" (RM 2528) because, after all, she is not really the boy "Scilentius"—it is all a fraud. But Silence is puzzled by this charge: "Donques sui jo Scilentius, / Cho m'est avis, u jo sui *nus*" (2537–38). It is a brilliantly punning line: "Either I am Scilentius, so I think, or else I am no one / or else I am nude." Without his carefully nurtured masculine identity, Silence is either a social nobody or a naked female body—which may after all amount to the same thing.[22] This sober reflection enables Nurture to frame her counterargument: She commands Nature to "leave [her] nursling alone" because Silence has been completely "denatured" and will always resist her. Both ladies have become fiercely possessive of the youth; as Nature had once called her "my daughter," Nurture now calls him "my foster-child" (*noreçon*, 2593). Punning in turn, Nurture boasts that she can succeed perfectly in turning a *noble enfant* into a *malvais home* (2602). The vaunt is both true and false: Silence may indeed be a "defective male" but s/he is hardly a "bad man."[23] Further slippage arises from the context. Nurture claims that she can make "a thousand people" work against Nature, just as Silence does, but since we do not know if the natures they were born with are good or bad, we cannot decide whether her power is beneficial or harmful. Nurture, like Nature, is a morally ambiguous force.

When the two adversaries have argued to a standstill, the debate is resolved by Reason, who—here as in the *Roman de la Rose*—sides against Nature. Heldris's Reason is no celestial daughter of God; she represents something more like shrewd pragmatism. Nevertheless, her victorious arguments should preclude any simplistic reading of Nature as the poet's mouthpiece. Reason's case reinforces Nurture's on three counts. First, Silence at twelve already understands that in his society, a man's life is valued far more than a woman's: "miols valt li us d'ome / Que l'us de feme, c'est la some" (2637–38). Since he is now on top, why should he willingly step down? "Deseure sui, s'irai desos?" (2641). In addition, he remembers the law that initially prompted his disguise: he does not want to lose his inheritance or prove his father a liar. Finally, as a youth governed by Reason, Silence has no taste for the games of Cupid: his "mouth [is] too hard for kisses, / and arms too rough for embraces" (RM 2646–47). This declaration can be read as a rejection of female sexuality, for Silence insists that he is really a boy, not a girl ("vallés sui et nient mescine," 2650). Yet Nature's promptings never go so far as to awaken desire for *any* partner in the young hero. The opposite of Jean de Meun's Amant, he heeds Reason and resolves to renounce sexuality altogether: "C'onques ne fu tels abstinence" ("Never was there such abstinence," 2659).

The final Nature–Nurture debate concerns not Silence but Merlin, who has challenged the "nature of man" even more fundamentally because he straddles the boundary between human and animal. "Ne sai s'il est u hom

---

[22] For more elaborate readings of this passage see Cooper, "Elle and *L*," 341–42; E. Jane Burns, *Bodytalk: When Women Speak in Old French Literature* (Philadelphia, 1993), 243.

[23] "Bad man" is Psaki's translation; "defective male" is Roche-Mahdi's. The latter recalls the Aristotelian and Thomist definition of woman as *mas occasionatus*, a defective or misbegotten male.

u bieste" (5908), says Silence.[24] Nature has made Merlin a man (human and male), so he has the same carnivorous instincts as any other man. But Nurture—that is, his own predilection—has taught him to live like a beast in the forest, subsisting on a vegetarian diet. Silence, tutored by Merlin himself in the guise of an old graybeard, lures Merlin the Wild Man with roast meat, which he cannot resist. But the salted meat induces a great thirst the wizard tries to assuage with the honey, milk, and wine that Silence has laid out in succession, until he collapses in a dyspeptic, drunken stupor. Seeing Merlin thus turn away from the *noreture* (food/training) to which he had long been accustomed, Nature gloats in triumph. But what we actually see in the episode is not so much a one-sided victory for Nature as a Lévi-Straussian synthesis. The foods that Silence uses to ensnare the wizard are coded both masculine and feminine: roast meat and wine evoke the warriors' banquet hall, milk and honey the female body. Likewise, cooked meat and wine are processed foods, raw honey and milk unprocessed, symbolizing the spheres of Culture and Nature respectively.[25] But to confound any simple resolution, Heldris has tied Merlin's human "nature" to culture—the world of the court, to which he must now return—and his "nurture" to the wilderness of a self-imposed exile. In effect, Silence and Merlin trap one another (6457–58), so it would not be amiss to read Merlin's ending as a mirror image of Silence's. Nature humiliates both of them, seizing Merlin by the scruff of his neck to thrust him toward the meat and compelling Silence to bear the shame of a public disrobing. But the goddess, though vindicated, does not have the final word, for by dint of their nurture and their wits, both Silence and Merlin manage to remain "on top" despite their apparent undoing.

If, as many critics have noted, the romance retreats in the end from its radical premise, it does not retreat nearly as far as some have claimed. Much discussion of the text has been bedeviled by a confusion of the nature/nurture question with the problem of misogyny. It is true that *Silence* does not ultimately challenge the medieval gender hierarchy. Heldris and most of her characters, including the protagonist, remain convinced that men's lives, opportunities, and achievements are more valuable than women's. Within that framework, however, *Silence* does demonstrate that the best man for the job might be a woman, given sufficient scope—that is,

[24] "I don't know whether he's man or beast." Merlin's role as wild man of the woods overlaps with another tradition that makes him half human, half demonic. Eufeme describes Merlin to Ebain as "fil al diäble" (5792); Geoffrey of Monmouth, who invented the character, makes him the son of an incubus and a royal nun.

[25] "Not only does cooking mark the transition from nature to culture, but through it and by means of it, the human state can be defined with all its attributes, even those that, like mortality, might seem to be the most unquestionably natural." Claude Lévi-Strauss, *The Raw and the Cooked*, trans. John and Doreen Weightman (New York, 1969), 164. See also Elisabeth Moltmann-Wendel, *A Land Flowing with Milk and Honey: Perspectives on Feminist Theology*, trans. John Bowden (New York, 1986), 1–4.

nurture—to exercise her talents. In a problematic disclaimer at the end of the poem, Heldris praises the woman who "works well against Nature," adding formulaically that no "good woman" should be offended by the disgrace of bad women like Eufeme.

> Maistre Heldris dist chi endroit
> C'on doit plus bone feme amer
> Que haïr malvaise u blasmer.
> Si mosterroie bien raison:
> Car feme a menor oquoison,
> Por que ele ait le liu ne l'aise,
> De l'estre bone que malvaise.
> S'ele ouevre bien contre nature,
> Bien mosterroie par droiture
> C'on en doit faire gregnor plait
> Que de celi qui le mal fait.

> [Master Heldris says right here
> That one should love a good woman more
> Than one hates or blames a bad one.
> I will show you exactly why:
> For a woman has less occasion
> (If she has the opportunity at all)
> To be good than to be wicked.
> If she works well against Nature,
> I will show as a matter of right
> That one should take more account of her
> Than of the one who does evil.]
>
> (6684–94)

Freed from the confusion created by an early editorial mistake,[26] this oft-reviled passage actually softens and nuances the apparent triumph of Nature. Silence, Heldris suggests, qualifies as a "good woman" precisely *because* she "works well against Nature," that is, against the devalued *us de feme* that Nurture and Reason had taught her to reject. This is necessary not because "female nature" is intrinsically evil, but rather because female *nurture*—misinterpreted as nature—gives women like Eufeme so many occasions to do harm and so few to perform acts of conspicuous valor and virtue. Thus Silence finds that "becoming male" allows her to reveal the sterling stuff of her *human* nature in the public sphere, the only space that counts. If in the end she reverts to her "natural" womanhood, it is only after her gender masquerade has deconstructed the forced reduction of a noble and aspiring nature to a limited and constricting nurture. So, even

---

[26] The editions of Lewis Thorpe, *Le Roman de Silence* (Cambridge, 1972), and Sarah Roche-Mahdi both have a comma after v. 6690 and a period at the end of 6691. I have adopted the valuable emendation of Simon Gaunt, "Significance of Silence," 211. This reading makes good sense out of a passage that is garbled in both the Psaki and Roche-Mahdi translations.

though Nature claims the victory over her foe, mollifying any conservatives in the audience, the romance as a whole embodies a more ambivalent version of the medieval proverb: "Nature passe nourriture / Et nourriture survainc nature" ("Nature surpasses Nurture, and Nurture vanquishes Nature").[27]

To the best of our knowledge, the *Roman de Silence* itself soon fell silent; it seems to have left no trace on subsequent texts. Yet it is hard not to wonder whether Christine de Pizan could have known Heldris's offbeat romance, for she was keenly interested in its themes. The sole surviving manuscript of *Silence* was still in France during her lifetime, and presumably others once existed.[28] The fact that Christine never cites *Silence* need not imply that she was unfamiliar with the tale because, like most scholarly authors, she did not choose to mention "popular" writings but only learned authorities (preferably Greek or Latin) who would bolster her own reputation. In any case, though we can find no conclusive evidence for Christine's knowledge of *Silence*, it is curious that both the works in which she herself deploys the goddess Nature should bear such significant affinities with the romance. In *The Book of the Mutation of Fortune*, Christine represents herself as a transgender heroine like Silence: born a woman, but transformed by circumstance into a man. And in *Lavision-Christine* (*Christine's Vision*), she depicts Nature as a bakerwoman in an allegory of gestation and birth. This image was far from conventional, although one or both writers might have derived it from a folk tradition: to this day a pregnant woman is said to "have a bun in the oven."

But Christine certainly did know the *Rose*, and she attacked it both frontally and obliquely throughout her career.[29] The obverse of her famous assault in the *Querelle de la Rose* was a strategy of writing her own allegories to undo the damage she believed Jean de Meun had done in his. In particular, she took pains to reinvent his allegorical figures so as to make them serve feminist ends. Thus, in her *Epistle of the God of Love* (1399), she turns the tables by making Cupid himself "excommunicate" misogynists such as Jean de Meun and seducers such as Amant; in *The City of Ladies* (1405) she rehabilitates Jean's Lady Reason, whom she found all too irrational in her defense of obscenity; and in *The Mutation of Fortune* (1403) and *Christine's Vision* (1405), she takes up the cause of Nature. Much like

[27] *Le Livre des Proverbes Français*, ed. M. Le Roux de Lincy, 2d ed. (Paris, 1859), 2:352; cited in Akbari, "Nature's Forge Recast," 41.
[28] On the history of the manuscript (now University of Nottingham, MS. Mi.LM.6), see Thorpe, ed., *Le Roman de Silence*, 1–12.
[29] See Eric Hicks, ed., *Le Débat sur le Roman de la Rose* (Paris, 1977); Joseph Baird and John Kane, ed. and trans., *La Querelle de la Rose: Letters and Documents* (Chapel Hill, 1978); Kevin Brownlee, "Discourses of the Self: Christine de Pizan and the *Romance of the Rose*," in *Rethinking the Romance of the Rose: Text, Image, Reception*, ed. Kevin Brownlee and Sylvia Huot (Philadelphia, 1992), 234–61.

Heldris of Cornwall, Christine feminizes the iconography of the goddess and repositions her as a means to discuss gender and culture rather than sexuality.

In *The Mutation of Fortune* the author presents her own life as a tug of war between two goddesses. Lady Nature is introduced as a potent maternal figure; supplanting Christine's biological mother, she surpasses even her beloved father in knowledge and power.

> My mother who was great and grand and more valorous than Penthesilea (God had made her well!) surpassed my father in knowledge, power, and value, despite the fact that he had learned so much. She was a crowned queen from the moment that she was born. Everyone knows of her power and strength. It is clear that she is never idle, and, without being overbearing, she is always occupied with many, diverse tasks: her impressive works are found everywhere; every day she creates many beautiful ones. Whoever wanted to count all that she has done and continues to do would never finish. She is old without being aged, and her life cannot end before Judgment Day. God gave her the task of maintaining and increasing the world as He had made it, in order to sustain human life: she is called Lady Nature. She is the mother of every person: God thus calls us all brothers and sisters.[30]

The goddess is described as an awesome virago, more valiant than the Amazon queen whom Christine would extol in *The City of Ladies* (I.19), while still playing her traditional role as God's partner in creation. In reaction against Jean de Meun, however, Christine desexualizes Nature's work, suppressing the blacksmith image, and she cites Scripture (Mark 3:35) to invest the goddess's universal motherhood with a moral rather than merely biological character. Thomas de Pizan, writes his daughter, strongly desired a son who could inherit his wealth (that is, his learning), but it was not to be:

> He failed in his intention, for my mother [Nature], who had much more power than he, wanted to have for herself a female child resembling her, thus I was in fact born a girl; but my mother did so much for him that I fully resembled my father in all things, only excepting my gender. . . . But because I was born a girl, it was not at all ordained that I should benefit in any way from my father's wealth, and I could not inherit, more because of custom than justice, the possessions that are found in the very worthy fountain [of the Muses].[31]

It is Nature who shapes Christine to be her father's daughter in mind and spirit, but Nature too who creates her a woman in her own image and like-

---

[30] Christine de Pizan, *Le Livre de la mutacion de Fortune* 1.5, lines 339–68, ed. Suzanne Solente (Paris, 1959), 1:18–19. Trans. Kevin Brownlee in *Selected Writings of Christine de Pizan*, ed. Renate Blumenfeld-Kosinski (New York, 1997), 93–94.

[31] *Mutacion de Fortune* I.6, lines 388–96, 413–19, ed. Solente, 1:20–21. Trans. Brownlee, *Selected Writings*, 94.

ness. Thus the writer carefully avoids blaming the goddess for her gender or suggesting that femaleness is a defect. Instead, she vigorously denounces the injustice that bars women from the learned professions.

While Christine clearly viewed sexism as unnatural, just what she considered to be "natural" is no easy question. Alan of Lille's Natura had acknowledged her ignorance of theology, while Jean de Meun's Nature not only opposed the counsel of Reason but explained that rationality was a divine gift beyond her purview.[32] Christine seems at first to oppose Jean's position outright. She recounts that her mother Nature gave her a golden crown set with four precious jewels—not as precious as her father's learned arts, yet more freely available. These gems are Discretion, Consideration, Recollection, and Memory, all endowments pertaining to reason. As if anticipating objections, however, Christine corrects herself with a more theologically precise explanation. Such qualities in fact belong to the soul, which is God's direct creation, for Nature fashions only bodies. Yet they are indeed her gifts insofar as the body's composition gives some people a greater receptiveness to intellectual gifts, while others have a diminished capacity for them. Thus, Christine concludes, "Nature allows or denies to us the opening of the body to the goods of the soul, according to the diverse capacities of the body to receive them, although God sends the soul into the body."[33] In this way she accounts for the natural inequality of human endowments while denying that gender is responsible for it, except insofar as "custom" or Culture distorts the intentions of Nature.

Yet Fortune giveth what Custom taketh away. When Christine reaches marriageable age, her "beautiful mother Nature" places her "in the service of a lady of high birth, who was slightly related to her, although they did not look at all like each other, and they were not cut from the same cloth."[34] This lady is Fortune, a goddess of dubious provenance. Christine's master Boethius had thoroughly deconstructed her, as had Alan of Lille in the *Anticlaudianus*, in a passage echoed by Jean de Meun's Reason and later by Christine herself. By pointing out the distant kinship and lack of affinity between the two queens, Christine could only be disparaging Lady Fortune. Nevertheless, it is Fortune who comes to Christine's rescue when she

32 "Sanz faille, de l'entendement / Connois je bien que voirement / Celi ne li donnai je mie. / La ne s'estent pas ma baillie, / Ne sui pas sage ne poissant / De faire riens si connoissant. / Je ne fis onc riens pardurables; / Quant que je fais est corrumpable." *Roman de la Rose*, 19,055–62.

33 "Si ay bien ma cause prouvee / Que Nature octroye ou nous vee / Les biens de l'ame ouvrer ou corps, / Selon que les divers accors / De l'instrument si les avoye, / Combien que Dieu ou corps l'envoye." *Mutacion de Fortune* I.9, lines 703–8, ed. Solente, 1:31. Trans. Brownlee, *Selected Writings*, 98.

34 "Ma mere Nature la belle / . . . me volt mettre servir / Une dame de hault parage, / Qui. I. poy lui tient de lignage, / Mais ne s'entre ressemblent pas, / Ne sont pas faites d'un compas." *Mutacion de Fortune* I.7, lines 469, 476–80, ed. Solente, 1:23. Trans. Brownlee, *Selected Writings*, 95.

sinks into paralyzing grief after the shipwreck of her husband's death. A physical sex change at the hands of Fortune supplies the metaphor for a change of vocation and gender roles, as through the vicissitudes of fate— emotional loss and financial need—Christine gains what her sex had initially denied her, the right and obligation to chart the course of her own voyage.

> Wearied by long crying, I remained, on one particular occasion, completely overcome; as if unconscious, I fell asleep early one evening. Then my mistress came to me, she who gives joy to many, and she touched me all over my body; she palpated and took in her hands each bodily part, I remember it well; then she departed . . . I awakened and things were such that, immediately and with certainty, I felt myself completely transformed. I felt my limbs to be stronger than before, and the great pain and lamentation which had earlier dominated me, I felt to be somewhat lessened. Then I touched myself all over my body, like one completely bewildered. Fortune had thus not hated me, she who had transformed me, for she had instantly changed the great fear and doubt in which I had been completely lost. Then I felt myself much lighter than usual and I felt that my flesh was changed and strengthened, and my voice much lowered, and my body harder and faster. However, the ring that Hymen had given me had fallen from my finger, which troubled me, as well it should have, for I loved it dearly.[35]

In ascribing her mythic transformation to Lady Fortune, Christine opposes a powerful counterforce to Lady Nature. Like Heldris in *Silence*, she demonstrates that identity is shaped not only by birth but just as much by random chance and political circumstance.

In her own case, the trope of "becoming a man" means much the same as it did in early Christian hagiography. The martyr Perpetua dreamed that she had become a man on the eve of her battle with wild beasts in the arena, while the transvestite monks Marina and Euphrosyna (commemorated in *The City of Ladies*) lived out their entire religious lives in male garb.[36] In this context the virile woman is one who possesses the intelligence, courage, and integrity that cultural norms denied to women as such.[37] Yet why would Christine, with her insistence on the natural worth and equality of women, have felt the need to describe her transformation

---

[35] *Mutacion de Fortune* I.12, lines 1321–55, ed. Solente, 1:51–52. Trans. Brownlee, *Selected Writings*, 106.

[36] *Book of the City of Ladies* III.12–13. E. J. Richards, ed., in *La Città delle Dame* (Milan, 1997); trans. E. J. Richards, *The Book of the City of Ladies* (New York, 1982), 241–45. Perpetua is not mentioned in *The City of Ladies*, but Christine may have been familiar with her story. See Lori Walters, "Fortune's Double Face: Gender and the Transformations of Christine de Pizan, Augustine, and Perpetua," *Fifteenth-Century Studies* 25 (1999): 97–114.

[37] On this tradition see Kerstin Aspegren, *The Male Woman: A Feminine Ideal in the Early Church* (Uppsala, 1990); Gillian Cloke, *This Female Man of God: Women and Spiritual Power in the Patristic Age, AD 350–450* (London, 1995), especially 212–21.

in such terms? The answer seems to be twofold. First, she had represented her period of mourning as a near-suicidal depression, curable only by radical surgery; only by ceasing to be a woman at all could she cease to be a helpless widow and thus acquire control of her life. She needed to be released not from womanhood as such, but from what contemporary moralists stigmatized as "womanish grief." Second and more obviously, the new social roles she would undertake—as poet, scholar, political adviser, and primary wage-earner for her family—were in all eyes the roles proper to a man.

But Christine ends her account on a wistful note:

> As you have heard, I am still a man and I have been for a total of more than thirteen full years, but it would please me much more to be a woman, as I used to be when I used to talk with Hymen, but since Fortune has transformed me so that I shall never again be lodged in a woman's body, I shall remain a man, and with my Lady Fortune I shall stay.[38]

Does the lady protest too much? Even though she notes that the jewels in her mother Nature's crown (i.e., her rational faculties) "grew much bigger" when she became a man, the protagonist Christine feels nostalgia for her original gender and still uses feminine adjectives (*estrangiee, logiee*) to modify her "virile" persona. Meanwhile, the author Christine is still casting about for a feminine—and feminist—poetics. In her two great works of 1405, *The City of Ladies* and *Christine's Vision*, she will find one.[39] So her metamorphosis, like that of Silence, proves to be transient after all: Lady Fortune will be cast out as Lady Nature returns triumphant.

Lavision-Christine deals primarily with French politics, but it begins with an original and puzzling allegory of Nature. Midway through the pilgrimage of life, Christine writes in homage to Dante, she has a marvelous dream, in which she beholds a Cosmic Man whose head pierces the clouds, while his feet span the abyss and his belly is wide as the earth. His eyes radiate brightness and his mighty breaths fill the world with freshness. With his insatiable mouth he takes in "material and corruptible bodies" as nourishment, and from his lower orifice he purges himself. The Cosmic Man is dressed in a beautiful, subtly colored robe of silk and on his forehead are stamped five letters spelling the name C*H*A*O*Z. Beside him stands "a great crowned shade in the form of a woman" who resembles a powerful

---

[38] "Com vous ouëz, encor suis homme / Et ay esté ja bien la somme / De plus de .XIII. ans tous entiers, / Mais mieulx me plairoit plus du tiers / Estre femme, com je souloie, / Quant a Ymeneüs parloie, / Mais puisque Fortune estrangiee / M'en a, si jamais plus logiee / N'y seray, homme remaindray / Et o ma dame me tendray." *Mutacion de Fortune* I.12, lines 1395–1404, ed. Solente, 1:53. Trans. Brownlee, *Selected Writings*, 107. Christine completed *La Mutacion* in November 1403; her husband had died in 1390.

[39] Sylvia Huot, "Seduction and Sublimation: Christine de Pizan, Jean de Meun, and Dante," *Romance Notes* 25 (1985): 372–73.

queen.[40] Although this lady is never named, she is obviously Nature. Her duty is to attend to the continual feeding of Chaos, and for that purpose she is surrounded by cooking utensils, which Christine compares to the waffle irons one sees in Parisian shops. In her cosmic kitchen she compounds a "mortar" of bitter, sweet, heavy, and light ("fiel, miel, plomb, et plume") and pours it ceaselessly into her molds, which she then bakes in the enormous, furnacelike mouth of Chaos. As soon as she takes them out, little bodies spring from the molds—but immediately Chaos swallows them alive into his vast belly. Day and night the lady continues to feed him. As Christine's spirit draws nearer to witness the marvel, it falls into the hands of Nature, and she too is molded and baked like the others. At the lady's express wish "and not because of the mold," Christine is given a female body.[41] After she has been swallowed up by Chaos, the lady's chambermaid comes and gives her a sweet liqueur to drink. Nourished within the body of Chaos, she matures and begins to learn about "the diversity within the figure's belly," that is, the world.

Christine's new myth of Nature and Chaos may have been distantly influenced by Plato's *Timaeus*, but it stands self-consciously aside from the tradition of Alan of Lille and Jean de Meun. The figure of Chaos is the first surprise, for male mythic figures of this type are much rarer than goddesses in medieval literature.[42] Chaos is an insistently material deity; his ovenlike mouth represents the womb and his belly the world. The male, not the female, is thus made to signify corporeality, insatiable appetite, and inexhaustible plenitude. In a delightful inversion of the scatology such a myth might lead us to expect, the "excrement" of Chaos is pure spirit, for only departing souls can leave the world-system in which all matter is endlessly recycled. Strangely, however, Nature herself has become incorporeal: Christine calls her a "shade" (*ombre*) and emphasizes that she had "no visible or tangible body." The materiality of Chaos and the spirituality of Nature go some distance toward reversing traditional gender stereotypes. But in other respects, Nature seems more feminine than in the myth elaborated by Jean de Meun. No longer a hammer-wielding smith, she is now charged with the typically female tasks of cooking and feeding a man. As Sylvia Huot has perceptively observed, the use of this metaphor for Nature's creative work subordinates the act of sexual intercourse to the gestation of the fetus in the womb. "From the male perspective, procreation is centered on the moment

[40] "Delez le dit ymage avoit assistant une grant ombre coronnee de fourme femmenine comme se fust la semblance dune tres poissant royne naturelment fourmee sanz corps visible ne palpable." Christine de Pizan, *Lavision-Christine* I.2, ed. Mary Louis Towner (Washington, D.C., 1932), 74. A new edition by Christine Reno and Liliane Dulac is in preparation.

[41] "Mais comme le voulsist ainsi celle qui la destrempe avoit faitte a la quel cause ce tient et non au moulle iaportay sexe femenin." *Lavision* I.3, ed. Towner, 75.

[42] The closest analogue to Christine's Chaos may be the Cosmic Man who dominates Hildegard of Bingen's *Liber vite meritorum*. But Hildegard's figure signifies God, while Christine's emphatically does not.

of sexual conquest . . . From the female perspective, however, procreation is a process of growth which begins with fertilization . . . and ends with fruition, itself a new beginning."[43] In the *Rose*, the phallic Nature with her hammer and anvil had informed a poetics of male desire; in *Lavision-Christine*, Nature in her kitchen assimilates the work of reproduction to everyday female labor.

Once again Christine stresses the intentionality of Nature in assigning gender to bodies. As in *The Mutation of Fortune*, she is born female because Lady Nature wills it so, not because of any defect or irregularity in the "mold." Here Christine implicitly rejects the Aristotelian view of women as deficient males, an idea sanctioned by Thomas Aquinas and refuted by Reason in *The City of Ladies*.[44] The unnamed "chambermaid" of Nature, a "wise woman" who feeds the newborn babe with a "sweet and very mild liquid," must be Christine's biological mother, now given a modest role to complete the myth's validation of maternity above virile potency.[45]

Much later in the text, Nature makes one more brief but telling appearance. Christine is recounting the first stages of her career as a scholar and writer, and as she begins to deepen her knowledge of poetry,

> Nature rejoiced in me and said: "Daughter, be happy when you have fulfilled the desire I have given you, continue to apply yourself to study, understanding the writings better and better." All this reading was not enough to satisfy my thoughts and intelligence; rather, Nature wanted that new books should be born from me, engendered by study and by the things I had seen. Then she said to me: "Take your tools and hammer on the anvil the matter I will give you, as durable as iron: neither fire nor anything else can destroy it; from this you should forge delightful things. When you carried your children in your womb, you felt great pain when giving birth. Now I desire that new books should be born from you, which you will give birth to from your memory in joy and delight; they will for all time to come keep your memory alive before the princes and the whole world. Just [as] a woman who has given birth forgets the pain and labor as soon as she hears her child cry [John 16:21], you will forget the hard work when you hear the voices of your books."[46]

This is Nature's first appearance as a literary muse. With remarkable economy Christine links a number of her central insights about vocation and

[43] Huot, "Seduction and Sublimation," 367.

[44] *Book of the City of Ladies* I.9.2. Cf. E. J. Richards, "Virile Woman *and* WomanChrist: The Meaning of Gender Metamorphosis in Christine," in *"Riens ne m'est seur que la chose incertaine": Études sur l'art d'écrire au Moyen Âge offertes à Eric Hicks*, ed. Jean-Claude Mühlethaler and Denis Billotte (Geneva, 2001), 239–52.

[45] "Adonc present vint la chamberiere de la ditte dame qui buretes tenoit pleines dune liqueur doulce et tres souefve de laquelle a abruver doulcement me pris par quel vertu et continuacion mon corps de plus en plus prenoit croissence force et vigueur. Et ycelle sage croissoit et engroissoit la pasture au feur de ma force . . ." *Lavision* I.3, ed. Towner, 75.

[46] *Lavision* III.10, ed. Towner, 163–64; trans. Blumenfeld-Kosinski, *Selected Writings*, 193–94.

gender. In the first place she stresses, as in *The Mutation of Fortune*, that it is Nature herself who endowed her with an aptitude for learning: the goddess's old covenant with Reason, broken by Jean de Meun, is back in force. By identifying her intellectual ability as Nature's gift, this time without qualifications, Christine defuses the objection that scholarship and writing are unnatural activities for a woman. No longer does she have to become a man in order to write. What need is there to "father" books when she can mother them? So, in the second place, she revises the ancient analogy between creation and procreation. Alan of Lille had used writing as a metaphor for sex; Christine reverses tenor and vehicle to make childbirth a metaphor for writing. Even as she adapts the hammer-and-anvil image from the *Rose*, she desexualizes it and strips away the salacious innuendoes with which Jean de Meun had invested the writing process. Unlike Jean's goddess Nature at her forge, forever toiling to produce ephemeral bodies, Christine as Nature's protégée will forge something indestructible and "durable as iron"— namely her books—to attain the same immortality sought by her male precursors. Her labor pangs as a writer are to issue in transcendence and eternal memory, in a sublimation of maternity that proceeds from the same feminine Nature who gave her a female body in the first place.

The will and power of goddesses, it seems, depend very much on the dispositions of their votaries. If it is fair to say that Heldris of Cornwall challenged the canonical "thealogy" of Nature, as it appears in the *Rose*, then Christine de Pizan launched nothing less than a full-scale reformation. Nature in *The Mutation of Fortune* signifies biological as opposed to social gender, just as she does in *Silence*, and Christine's fictive sex change, like that of Heldris's woman warrior, proves that anatomy does not have to be destiny. By the time she wrote *Lavision*, however, Christine had changed her strategy and turned Nature into an all-purpose figure of female creativity, whether expressed through motherhood, through domestic labor (Nature's kitchen), or through intellectual work (her own writing). In this highly atypical text, all opposition between Nature and Culture ceases. Instead, Nature becomes a promoter of culture and specifically of women's cultural achievements—a role she shares with her old friend Reason in *The City of Ladies*, a book completed in the same year. This revisionist view of Nature was a vital plank in Christine's feminist platform and marks her as the first thinker to understand how readily dichotomies between Nature and Culture tend to marginalize Nature's "own" sex.[47] While goddesses did not empower women always and everywhere, Christine de Pizan showed that she at least knew how to empower all goddesses.

[47] See the classic anthropological study by Sherry Ortner, "Is Female to Male as Nature Is to Culture?" in *Woman, Culture, and Society*, ed. Michelle Rosaldo and Louise Lamphere (Stanford, 1974), 67–87, and Carol MacCormack, "Nature, Culture, and Gender: A Critique," in *Nature, Culture, and Gender*, ed. MacCormack and Strathern, 1–24.

CHAPTER EIGHT

Women in the Late Medieval English Parish

Katherine L. French

In medieval and early modern England, the basic unit of public worship was the parish. Although women comprised half of the membership, their activities, religious or secular, have not received much attention in the historical literature. Scholars have focused on what they consider to be the more visible activities of men and have thereby gendered the collective behavior of parishioners male or mostly male.[1] By adhering to this position, scholars have overlooked the importance of the parish as an institution that assisted female visibility. This visibility came to include collective action taken in all-women's groups. Indeed the parish became a major forum for women's group activities[2] that provided them with opportuni-

I would like to thank Sandy Bardsley, Gareth Bestor, Becky Krugg and the editors of this volume for their help on this chapter.

[1] Andrew Brown states after two-hundred-some pages of discussion of "popular piety" that he could have discussed women, but that this was not a book about gender. Brown is assuming that gender has no place in a discussion of collective action or lay religious behavior. Parish life and lay activity are gendered male, and gendering it male is taken as gender-neutral. Andrew Brown, *Popular Piety in Late Medieval England: The Diocese of Salisbury, 1250–1550* (Oxford, 1995), 256–58. Eamon Duffy, *The Stripping of the Altars* (New Haven, 1992), has a short discussion of women's parochial activities, but he does not believe that gender made any difference in religious practice. He writes, "[W]ithin the diversity of medieval religious options there was a remarkable degree of religious and imaginative homogeneity across the social spectrum" (p. 3; see also 131–54, 265, esp. 153).

[2] See Clive Burgess in " 'A Fond Thing Vainly Invented': An Essay on Purgatory and Pious Motive in Late Medieval England," in *Parish Church and People: Local Studies in Lay Religion, 1350–1750*, ed. Susan Wright (London, 1988), 56–84. He argues that rather than seeing the financial obligations to the parish as one more set of burdens placed on an already resentful and overtaxed laity, there was an excess of voluntary support directed at the parish

ties unavailable outside the parish. Thus the expected limits of gender-related behavior expanded with respect to the parish. What was the significance of women's greater visibility and activity within the parish, and what did these expanded opportunities mean to women and their communities?

Although scholars have largely ignored the issue of women's parochial involvement, it did not go unnoticed by contemporaries, who were often disturbed by it.[3] Women's parish involvement and their increasing visibility created a tension in parish life that the clergy and the laity tried to relieve by using this participation to affirm expected female behavior. Women themselves, however, were also a part of the process; their interests, while different from men's, were not always distinct from the patriarchal norms that governed them. Although women's visibility made their voices louder and their concerns more apparent to the parish, it did not turn the late medieval English parish into a female utopia.[4] The maintenance of approved models of behavior was not without its subversive component, and women's participation in the parish both reinforced traditional gender roles and challenged women's secondary status. In this chapter, I will survey the range of women's participation in the parish, looking at how it drew on expected behavior for women and also created new opportunities for action and self-expression.

Canon law made the laity responsible for their parish churches, particularly the maintenance of the nave. To meet these needs, the laity appointed churchwardens to oversee the process.[5] This obligation to maintain the nave provided women of all classes with a variety of ways to support their parishes. Women attended mass, provided labor and money for maintaining and furnishing the nave, and contributed their organizational skills and pious interests in support of the veneration of the saints. A woman's social status and stage of life also shaped her parish involvement. Wealthy women typically contributed more than less well-off women, and married

---

and its endowments, which was a manifestation of the laity's interest in their own salvation. The collective needs of the parishioners combined with their responsibilities to the parish to create a forum for salvation "self-help." Additionally R. A. Houlbrooke states "Yet certain economic and social functions were largely reserved to them [women], and some of these brought them together in sizeable groups, arguably facilitating the development of independent common opinions." R. A. Houlbrooke, "Women's Social Life and Common Action in England from the Fifteenth Century to the Eve of the Civil War," *Continuity and Change* 1 (1986): 171. The combination of these two approaches opens the way for a discussion both of specific religious concerns for women and their active participation in the parish.

[3] A good discussion of this concern can be found in Felicity Riddy, "Mother Knows Best: Reading Social Change in a Courtesy Text," *Speculum* 71 (1996): 66–86, and Karen Winstead, *Virgin Martyrs: Legends of Sainthood in Late Medieval England* (Ithaca, 1997).

[4] Judith M. Bennett, "Medieval Women, Modern Women: Across the Great Divide," in *Culture and History: 1350–1600*, ed. David Aers (Detroit, 1992), 147–75.

[5] Charles Drew, *Early Parochial Organisation in England: The Origins of the Office of Churchwarden*, St. Anthony Hall Publications 7 (York, 1954).

women's participation differed from single women's. We must also understand women's parish participation as taking place under the legal and economic systems of late medieval England because the parish owned property and hired workers.

The work women performed for the parish was similar to the work they did for their households or in the larger community. The connection between domestic and familial concerns was a theme that ran through women's parish participation. Outside the parish, a married woman usually worked part time at many different jobs; in addition to helping her husband with his work, whether it was agriculture, manufacturing, or lordship, she also provisioned the house, arranged the meals, oversaw the kitchen garden, and attended to children and servants if there were any.[6] Some women also ran their own businesses, although these tended to be small and temporary.[7] Although there are examples of women artisans supplying parishes with goods and services, women generally played a subordinate role in maintaining the parish.[8] Laundry and mending were predominantly women's jobs.[9] John Mirk tried to valorize this work in his *Instructions for Parish Priests* by explaining that the altar cloths and the surplices must be clean for mass, but it was nevertheless still low paying and

[6] This is a huge field; for more on women, work, and legal status see Kay E. Lacey, "Women and Work in Fourteenth- and Fifteenth-Century London," in *Women and Work in Pre-Industrial England*, ed. Lindsey Charles and Lorna Duffin (London, 1985), 24–82; Maryanne Kowaleski, "Women's Work in a Market Town: Exeter in the Late Fourteenth Century," in *Women and Work in Preindustrial Europe*, ed. Barbara Hanawalt (Bloomington, 1986), 145–64; Judith Bennett, "The Village Ale-Wife: Women and Brewing in Fourteenth-Century England," in *Women and Work in Preindustrial Europe*, 20–36; Barbara Hanawalt, *The Ties That Bound: Peasant Families in Medieval England* (Oxford, 1986); P. J. P. Goldberg, *Women, Work, and Life Cycle in a Medieval Economy: Women in York and Yorkshire, c. 1300–1520* (Oxford, 1992); Judith M. Bennett, *Ale, Beer and Brewsters in England: Women's Work in a Changing World, 1300–1600* (Oxford, 1996).

[7] Kowaleski, "Women's Work."

[8] For example, the Salisbury parish of St. Edmund's hired goldsmith Margery Ingram to mend (but not manufacture) liturgical items. *Churchwardens' Accounts of St. Edmund's and St. Thomas, Sarum: 1443–1702*, ed. Henry James Fowle Swayne, Wiltshire Record Society 1 (1896), 13. The churchwardens of Yatton in Somerset hired "a silk woman" to make them a cope. Somerset Record Office, D/P/yat 4/1/1 (Yatton CWA), fol. 264.

[9] For a sample of whom parishes hired to do their laundry and mending, see Somerset Record Office, D/P/yat 4/1/1 (Yatton CWA), fols. 82, 86, 89, 92, 101, 104; D/P/ban 4/1/1 (Banwell CWA), fols. 11, 79; D/P/pilt 4/1/1 (Pilton CWA), fol. 53; Essex Record Office, D/P 11/5/1 (Great Dunmow CWA), fols. 6v, 11v, 19, 20, 21; London, Guildhall Library, 1239/1 part 2 (St. Mary at Hill CWA); 1279/1 (St. Andrew Hubbard CWA), fols. 19v, 51, 86; Suffolk Record Office, FC 185/E1/1 (Walberswick CWA). *The Early Churchwarden's Accounts of Bishops Stortford*, ed. Stephen G. Doree, Hertfordshire Record Society 10 (1994), 79, 86; "Accounts of the Churchwardens of St. Dunstan's, Canterbury," ed. J. M. Cowper, *Archaeologia Cantiana* 17 (1887): 82; "Churchwardens' Accounts of the Parish of St. Andrew, Canterbury," ed. Charles Cotton, *Archaeologia Cantiana: Transactions of the Kent Archaeological Society* 33 (1920): 5, 18; *The Transcript of the Churchwardens' Accounts of the Parish of Tilney, All Saints, Norfolk: 1443–1589*, ed. A. D. Stallard (London, 1922), 18, 45, 47, 51, 97, 99.

menial.[10] When a parish brought in artisans to work on the church, women tended to look after them. When the parish of All Saints, Tilney in Norfolk needed to repair the church windows, Robert Nobile's wife lodged and fed the workers.[11] Although women did most of the mending without overt male supervision, far fewer oversaw new sewing for copes, chasubles, altar clothes, and hangings that required embroidery or expensive, colored cloth. As with other occupations involving women, they worked under the supervision of men.[12] In 1524, the small market town of Stogursey in Somerset employed a vestment maker and his wife to make new vestments for the church. The parish fed both of them in partial payment for their work.[13]

Like the rest of the medieval economy, the church did not place the same value on women's work as men's, considering it to be less important and valuable. In the thirteenth-century diocesan statutes for Worcester, the bishop identified four saints' days—the feasts of Agnes, Margaret, Lucy, and Agatha—when men were to work but women were not.[14] In the anonymous fifteenth-century collection of sermons called the *Speculum Sacerdotale*, the author states that for three days after Easter, no one was to work. "But in the iiij daye it is lawefull to men for to tyle and use werkys of the erþe, but wymmen oweþ for to cese fro here werkys. And why? Rurale workis ben more nedeful þen other."[15] Although the assumption that all men were rural workers is anachronistic by the fifteenth century, this sermon articulated a commonly held belief about the relative worth of men's and women's economic contributions. These values would have translated to women's work for the parish, and the jobs that parishes hired women to do reflected their larger socioeconomic roles. Even though women's level of involvement inside the parish was the same as outside the parish, it incorporated their concerns for the maintenance of the nave and provided the parish with needed labor.

Parishes depended on a variety of fund-raising strategies to hire artisans and to furnish the nave.[16] Urban parishes tended to rely on rents from parish-owned property, whereas rural parishes hosted a variety of ales, festivals, and revels to raise money. All parishes relied on bequests and gifts. In these cir-

[10] John Mirk, *Instructions for a Parish Priest*, ed. Edward Peacock, EETS o.s., 31 (London, 1902), 58, 60.

[11] *Churchwardens' Accounts of Tilney*, 134.

[12] Kay Staniland, *Embroiderers* (Toronto, 1991).

[13] Somerset Record Office, D/P/stogs 4/1/1 (Stogursey CWA), fol. 26v.

[14] Christopher Cheney, "Rules for the Observance of Feast Days in Medieval England," *Bulletin for the Institute of Historical Research* 34, no. 90 (1961): 137. This mandate also served further to associate women with these particular virgin martyrs. See also Barbara Harvey, "Work and *Festa Ferianda* in Medieval England," *Journal of Ecclesiastical History* 23, no. 4 (1972): 291.

[15] *Speculum Sacerdotale*, ed. Edward Weatherly, EETS o.s., 200 (London, 1936), 128.

[16] Katherine L. French, *The People of the Parish: Community Life in a Late Medieval English Diocese* (Philadelphia, 2001), 99–141.

cumstances women's specific contributions are difficult to identify and assess. We know women attended ales and festivals and occasionally even organized them. For example, in 1537, Elizabeth Whochyng was one of the ale wardens for the midsummer ale in the parish of Trull in Bath and Wells.[17] Women also frequently rented property from the parish, but overall their financial support was less than that of men because they typically earned less.

Gifts and testamentary bequests constituted the most common means of supporting the parish. Although wealth and personal interest could affect the level of parish support, there were also differences between men's and women's giving practices that reveal how legal and economic constraints further defined women's involvement.[18] When we consider the material goods testators left to parishes in their wills, we can also see how both men and women demonstrated their pious concerns. The differences between men's and women's giving practices suggest that women used their notions of home economy and domesticity to act out their piety. Women's gifts to the parish reflected the relationships they had to their material goods and household possessions. For much of their lives, they could not count on being able to liquidate their material assets, and, consequently, their identification with objects—both as signs of their domestic skills and their gender—seems stronger than men's.

Because of the law of coverture, a married woman could not make a will without her husband's permission. As a result the majority of women's wills were written by widows. Some of the differences in the items left as bequests by men and women can be explained by the fact that widows were usually breaking up households, whereas men often had a family that still needed provisioning, which meant leaving the household intact. Women also gave what they controlled, usually items from their dowry, which often included household items. Despite these circumstances surrounding will making, we find that both women and men gave those items that had the most meaning to them and reflected a lifetime of interaction with their beneficiaries, such as the parish. In a survey of wills from Bath and Wells and Lincoln, the most common categories of gifts to parishes in men's wills were vestments; liturgical items, such as chalices, paxes, and candlesticks; and household items, such as tools and furniture. The three most common types of gifts that women gave to the parish were household items, such as sheets, table clothes, and dishes; clothing, such as dresses or kerchiefs; and jewelry, usually wedding rings, but also beaded necklaces.[19] Men also gave more books than women.

17 Somerset Record Office DD/CT 77 (CWA Trull), fol. 44.

18 Katherine L. French, " 'I Leave My Best Gown as a Vestment': Women's Spiritual Interests in the Late Medieval English Parish," *Magistra* 4 (1998): 57–77.

19 Data for this finding come from *Somerset Medieval Wills: 1383–1500*, vols. 1–3, ed. F. W. Weaver, Somerset Record Society, 16, 19, 21 (1901, 1903, 1905); *Medieval Wills from Wells*, ed. Dorothy O. Shilton and Richard Holworthy, Somerset Record Society 40 (1925), 1–87; *Lincoln Wills: 1427–1532*, vols. 1–3, ed. C. W. Foster, Lincoln Record Society, 5, 10, 24 (1914, 1918,

The differences between men's and women's bequests reflect some of the different concerns that they had for the parish. In particular, women were more likely to specify exactly how the parish should use their gifts, whereas men generally left this to the discretion of the churchwardens; they could use the bequests for the church or sell them and use the money as they saw fit. For example, when Henry Stephyns of Castle Cary in Bath and Wells made out his will, he left everything to his parish and made the churchwardens his executors. His will states that his goods were to be "fully spent about such necessary building as shall be thought most convenient by the most honest men of the parish for the maintenance of the church."[20] Women, however, were less likely to leave this decision in the hands of parish administrators. The work in the household or the economy often required them to piece together limited resources, and their wills often explained how the goods should be adapted for parish needs. Avice de Crosseby of St. Cuthbert's parish in Lincoln left a wooden board to the parish clerk "suitable for making wax tapers," "j carpet . . . to cover the bodies of the dead," and "j very little leaden vessel to mend the eaves or gutter of the church."[21] Lifelong habits of frugality and adaptability became expressions of piety and a means of influencing in small ways local religious observances.

Although adapting household goods to parish use was a pious act, it could also be construed as bossy and controlling. Women may have had less to give, but their directions as to how the parish should use their gifts required churchwardens to address their concerns. By offering suggestions, women became posthumously involved in parish administrative decision making—from which they had generally been excluded during their lives. Some women could be quite inventive in how they expected the parish to use their goods. Agnes Bruton, a well-to-do woman in Taunton in the diocese of Bath and Wells, left her "red damaske mantell and [her] mantell lyned with silk" to become costumes for the parish's Mary Magdalene play.[22] Agnes Cakson of Addlethorpe in the same diocese asked that "a basyn, a laver, and a towell" be given to the font "to weshe folkes handes with when they crysten chylder."[23] Denise Marlere, a brewster in Bridgwater in Bath and Wells, gave vats from her brewing business to the vicar, the parish chaplain, the parish, the chapel of St. Katherine, and the local hospital and Franciscan friary. She explained that they would be useful for wax making.[24] More common, however, were women's instructions

---

1930); *The Courts of the Archdeaconry of Buckingham: 1483–1523*, ed. E. M. Elvey, Buckingham Record Society 19 (1975).

[20] *Medieval Wills from Wells*, 59–60.

[21] *Lincoln Wills*, 1:5–7.

[22] *Somerset Medieval Wills*, 2:52–57.

[23] *Lincoln Wills*, 3:157.

[24] *Bridgwater Borough Archives*, vol. 3, ed. Thomas Bruce Dilkes, Somerset Record Society 58 (1945), 9–11.

for how to turn their clothing and housewares into items of liturgical significance. Sheets became altar cloths, gowns and dresses became copes and vestments, and kerchiefs became corporaxes to cover the host. Agnes Sygrave of Stowe in Lincoln left to "the high altare of Stowe my best shete to be an altare clothe, and my best kyrchyff to be a corporax."[25] Dame Margaret Chocke of Ashton, in Bath and Wells went so far as to specify that when her "gown of blew feluett, [her] kyrtll of blew damaske, . . . and a coverlet of tapstry werek with eglis [eagles]," which were to "ley before the hyght auter in principal festes and other tymes," were not in use they were to "be occupied on a bedde in the chauntry house to kepe it from mothes."[26] Even towels of diaper cloth, plain white linen without any embroidery or other identifying marks, were able to be close to the host. The donor's name might be forgotten, but this type of gift still elevated or sacralized the mundane items of her everyday life. Other women in the congregation would see the possibility that their own goods could be put in touch with God.[27] Adapting household items to the liturgy connected women's work to the worship of God, but their instructions showed that they were attempting to hold onto what little economic power they had and not relinquish it completely to the men who ran the parish.

Another feature of women's bequests was that they left goods to individual saints much more frequently than men did.[28] Wedding rings and kerchiefs were the most common items, but veils and girdles were also popular. Joan Mudford of Glastonbury, Somerset, left to the image of St. Mary one gold ring and a kerchief and to the statue of St. Katherine a gold ring.[29] The saints received items that had physically marked the donor as a woman and were intended to adorn these female saints in similar ways: kerchiefs on the head, decorative girdles around the waist, and necklaces around the neck.

Parish fund-raising gave women further access to the liturgy and an opportunity to express their concerns through the sale of seats. With the introduction of pews in the fifteenth century, some parish administrations began to sell seats. Financing the parish by selling seats had the side effect of sanctioning the relationships and priorities that grew out of the seating arrangements. Women and men were expected to attend three services on Sundays, and they could also attend the daily mass and other canonical

[25] *Lincoln Wills*, 3:143.

[26] *Somerset Medieval Wills*, 1:244–45.

[27] This would be important, as the host played such a prominent role in late medieval religious observances. For more see Miri Rubin, *Corpus Christi: The Eucharist in Late Medieval Culture* (Cambridge, 1991).

[28] In the two dioceses of Bath and Wells and Lincoln, no men left bequests to adorn a saint statue. For more on this see French, " 'I Leave My Best Gown.' "

[29] *Somerset Medieval Wills*, 1:250.

hours said by the parish and stipendiary priests.[30] During services, men and women did not sit together. Women generally sat on the north side of the nave and men on the south, although some churches placed women in the back (or west) and men in the front (or east) of the nave.[31] Once the laity began to install permanent seats, seating arrangements began to play a role in the social dynamics of the community because they visibly identified the sex and status of the occupant. Seating men and women separately gave women greater visibility. They became an identifiable group in a specific part of the nave, not intermingled with men.

Purchasing a seat appears to have been predominantly a women's concern.[32] For example, between 1460 and 1530 in the parish of St. Margaret's, Westminster, 737 women bought seats compared to only 275 men.[33] Women in this parish also changed their seats more often then men; 22 percent of women changed their seats compared to only 13 percent of men. This suggests a range of concerns regarding seat location that interested men less. A new seat might move one closer to the front to a better position for seeing the priest elevate the host, or it might put one closer to an image or chapel of special significance. Seating arrangements also marked rites of passage. In many parishes, such as St. Mary's in Dover, there was a pew for women to sit in while they were churched.[34] Not only did the service mark a woman's successful childbirth, but her special place in the nave emphasized this accomplishment as well. Some parishes had separate seats for married and unmarried women.[35] Similar arrangements occur in other town parishes such as St. Edmund's in Salisbury or Ashton-Under-Lyne in Cheshire, although the records are less detailed.[36]

Seating arrangements involved women in a host of social negotiations.

[30] Christopher Wordsworth and Henry Littlehales, *The Old Service-books of the English Church* (London, 1904), 15.

[31] Margaret Aston, "Segregation in Church," in *Women in the Church*, ed. W. J. Sheils and Diana Wood, Studies in Church History 27 (Oxford, 1990), 238–42.

[32] J. Charles Cox also notes, with great unease, that women bought more seats. He suggests this was so because more women attended mass, an observation others have made as well. J. Charles Cox, *Bench-ends in English Churches* (Oxford, 1916), 20–25.

[33] WCA, E1, E2 (St. Margaret's Westminster, CWA). In a parish of two thousand, this meant that only a portion of the parish—the more financially well-off—was involved in seating concerns in any given year. Most still brought their own stools or stood in the back.

[34] BL, Egerton MS 1912 (St. Mary's, Dover CWA), fols. 6a, 10.

[35] WCA, E2 (St. Margaret's Westminster, CWA) (1518), no folio numbers.

[36] Although there are examples of rural churches selling seats, it seems to have been primarily an urban practice. *Churchwardens' Accounts of St. Edmund's and St. Thomas, Sarum*; "Rental and Custumal" quoted in full by Winifred M. Bowman, *England in Ashton-Under-Lyne* (Cheshire, 1960), 167–8. Not all parishes sold seats, however. Some parishes installed seats but left the negotiation over who sat where to oral culture and local custom. In rural areas, the right to hold a seat was often based on land holding. See French, *People of the Parish*, 162–70.

They bought seats near friends (as Alice Lucas did when she purchased a seat with Margaret Eldersham in St. Margaret's Westminster)[37] or far from rivals. Seating arrangements could also be a manifestation of self-aggrandizement as is suggested by Agnes Tebbe's desire to move from a seat she had used for ten years to a seat vacated by the death of Mistress Stevenson.[38] Any place where there was competition and self-promotion, there was risk of tension and sometimes even violence, as Margaret Dobell discovered when Walter Soly claimed her and her husband Giles's seats in the parish church of Minehead, Somerset. During mass one day, Walter and his associates pulled Margaret out of her pew, beat her up, and destroyed the pew![39]

Seating arrangements also allowed women to show off the material trappings of devotion, such as prayer books and rosaries, and the fittings of status and wealth, such as clothing, jewelry, and a pretty face. As signs of vanity, the clergy sought to eliminate this behavior. One fifteenth-century confession manual assumes that vanity was a female vice and instructs the cleric to ask women "have ye mayd youe more gayer in kerchufs or any other rayment att any tyme ffore plesure of young men then off god?" and "have ye weschett your face wt any maid waters off herrbs to make youe fayr?"[40] Mirk's *Instructions for Parish Priests* showed similar concerns when explaining how a priest should administer confession to women—God was to be their focus not the women's looks or social status.[41] Behavior during mass was not just fodder for didactic literature, and clerical authorities in charge of enforcing morality paid close attention to the laity's behavior in the nave. In 1517, Johanna and Alice Marcrofte of Trawden parish in Lancashire were charged with talking during divine office,[42] and Margaret Crosslie of another parish in the same region was accused of being "a notorious chatterbox [who] impedes divine office."[43]

Both men and women used seat location to display their own hierarchies, although their concerns were not the same. To be sure, women's status was usually predicated on their husbands' or fathers' status, but that does not lessen its importance to women, however acquired. Women could act out concerns and priorities in the nave of the church, one of the few places where they could legitimately gather in all-women's groups. The ex-

---

[37] WCA, E2 (St. Margaret's, Westminster CWA) (1518), no folio numbers.

[38] WCA, E2 (St. Margaret's, Westminster CWA) (1515), no folio numbers; E1 fol. 508 (purchase of seat).

[39] Public Record Office, STAC 2/12/224–226.

[40] BL, Sloane MS 1584. These are the questions asked of a single woman; of a married woman the cleric asks a variation: "Have you weschyd your face wt ony styllyd waters ore owyntements to make youe fayrer in the syght off pepull?" "Have you schewyd your brests open to tempt any to syne?" "Have you had any envy agayns any womane that sche has bene fayrer then youe or better lovyd than youe?"

[41] Mirk, *Instructions for a Parish Priest*, 27–28, 43.

[42] *Ecclesiastical Court Book of Walley*, ed. Alice Cooke, Chetham Society 44 (1901), 54.

[43] Ibid., 55.

istence of a women's subculture is something that most men seem to have taken for granted, even if they found it threatening.[44] Thus the requirement of church attendance brought a great deal of anxiety to the clergy because it gave women a chance to congregate, converse, compare, and compete with each other.

Women also often organized on a temporary basis to help raise money for large-scale renovations and major building projects. In so doing they arranged themselves in groups, often according to age or marital status, to collect money. During the three-year rebuilding of St. Petrock's Church in Bodmin, Cornwall, the unmarried women raised over two pounds for construction.[45] Although the sum is not large, the women acted as a group to express their interest in this particular project. In some communities this interest found further expression in the formation of all-women's groups, either the more formally constituted guilds or the less formal stores. However permanent or elaborate the structure of these groups, they were organized to support side altars, chapels, or lights dedicated to a variety of saints.[46]

Parish guilds and stores were a ubiquitous feature of medieval religious life. They provided common forums for shared devotional interests, conviviality, and social and political networks.[47] Membership in single-sex groups was defined around a number of factors, the most common being marital status. For women, there were guilds for maidens or wives and Hocktide festivities for married women. For men, there were guilds for single and married men, but also Plow Monday celebrations (the first Monday after Epiphany when men celebrated the return of the growing season) and hoggling (a revel at Christmas, New Year, or the Feast of the Circumcision).[48] Membership could also be determined by residency or occupation. In Wimborne Minster, Dorset, there was one guild for the "wives of the town" and another for the "wives of the country or land."[49] In the parish of St. Martin-in-the-Fields in Westminster, the midwives maintained a light.[50]

[44] Steve Hindle, "The Shaming of Margaret Knowsley: Gossip, Gender and the Experience of Authority in Early Modern England," *Continuity and Change* 9 (1994): 391–419.

[45] "Accounts for the Building of Bodmin Church: 1469–1472," ed. John J. Wilkinson, *Camden Miscellany VII*, Camden Society, old ser., 14 (London, 1874), 5, 10, 33.

[46] I discussed this issue in "Maidens' Lights and Wives' Stores: Women's Parish Guilds in Late Medieval England," *Sixteenth Century Journal* 29 (1998): 399–425.

[47] Gervase Rosser, "Going to the Fraternity Feast: Commensality and Social Relations in Late Medieval England," *Journal of British Studies* 33 (1994): 430–46; Caroline M. Barron, "The Parish Fraternities of Medieval London," in *The Church in Pre-Reformation Society: Essays in Honour of F. R. H. du Boulay*, ed. Caroline M. Barron and Christopher Harper-Bill (Woodbridge, 1985), 13–37; H. F. Westlake, *The Parish Gilds of Mediaeval England* (London, 1919).

[48] W. Carew Hazlitt, *Faiths and Folklore of the British Isles*, 2 (1905; reprint, New York, 1965), 495–96; Ronald Hutton, *The Rise and Fall of Merry England: The Ritual Year, 1400–1700* (Oxford, 1994), 12–13, 16–17, 87–89.

[49] Dorset Record Office, PE/WM CW1/40 (Wimborne Minster CWA).

[50] *St. Martin-in-the-Fields: The Accounts of the Churchwardens, 1525–1603*, ed. John V. Kitto (London, 1901), 70. (The originals were destroyed in World War II.)

Often a woman's guild had a male counterpart. In Horley, Surrey, the women ran the guild of St. Katherine and the men the guild of St. Nicholas.[51]

Although all guilds and stores accepted gifts and legacies, women's guilds raised money in other ways that drew on members' skills and interests. In St. Edmund's parish in Salisbury and St. Ewen's in Bristol, the women held dances.[52] Women's guilds also raised money by hosting collections. In St. Margaret's, Westminster, the maidens held their collection on the feast of St. Margaret, and St. Thomas's in Salisbury and Holy Trinity in Exeter had their Whitsun collections run by the women.[53] The women's guilds in Woodland and Chagford in Devon had more sophisticated finances; they earned their income from rental property, brewing, and the sale of wool.[54]

Celebrations of Hocktide gave married women another opportunity to participate in all-women groups to raise money for their parish. Hocktide falls on the second Monday and Tuesday after Easter.[55] Although Hocktide was a recognized feature of the parish calendar, it was not celebrated in every community. From its earliest appearances in the fifteenth century to its abolition in the Reformation, Hocktide appears most often in parishes in or near towns rather than in rural communities.[56] On Hock-Monday the women set about capturing and tying up the men, releasing them upon payment of a forfeit. On Tuesday the roles were reversed.

The money women raised in Hocktide celebrations and through their guilds supported a variety of parish concerns that reflect some of the religious interests of late medieval women. The money usually went to maintain a light or an altar dedicated to a particular saint, although existing accounts are often vague and simply refer to the light as "the wives' light," "the dames' light," or "the maidens' or virgins' light."[57] When we examine known dedications, however, the most common patron saints were the Vir-

---

[51] BL, Additional MS 6173 (Horley CWA).

[52] *Churchwardens' Accounts of St. Edmund's*, 73, 76, 79, 83, 85, 365; *The Church Book of St. Ewen's, Bristol: 1454–1485*, ed. Betty Masters and Elizabeth Ralph, Bristol and Gloucestershire Archaeological Society 6 (1967), 30, 68, 77, 78, 261.

[53] WCA, E1 (St. Margaret's, Westminster CWA), fol. 370; *Churchwardens' Accounts of St. Thomas, Sarum*, 273–75; Devon Record Office 1718 ADD/PW3 (Holy Trinity, Exeter CWA).

[54] Devon Record Office 2260 A/PW1(Woodland CWA); 1429A/PW2 (Chagford CWA).

[55] Katherine L. French, " 'To Free Them from Binding': Women in the Late Medieval English Parish," *Journal of Interdisciplinary History* 27 (1996): 387–412.

[56] Ibid.; Hutton, *Rise and Fall*, 26, 56–60.

[57] Devon Record Office DD70914 & DD70915 (St. Mary Steps CWA); *St. Edmund's, Salisbury*, 79; *St. Thomas', Salisbury*, 274–75; "Croscombe Church-Wardens' Accounts," in *Church-Wardens' Accounts of Croscombe, Pilton, Yatton, Tintinhull, Morebath, and St. Michael's Bath*, ed. Edmund Hobhouse, Somerset Record Society 4 (1890), 6, 21.

gin Mary and the virgin martyrs.[58] At St. Mary the Great in Cambridge, part of the Hocktide money supported a light dedicated to the Virgin Mary.[59] The women's interests in the Virgin were not confined to Hocktide; in 1518, they held a separate collection to build a new tabernacle for the St. Mary statue.[60] In 1491, John Brigge of St. Edmund's in Salisbury asked to be buried in the north altar, called the wives' altar, under the image of the Blessed Virgin Mary. He left twenty shillings for the maintenance of this altar.[61] In Ashburton, Devon, the St. Mary's altar received support from both the men's and women's guilds. In 1491, when the carved panel behind the altar (the reredos) needed repainting and gilding, the women put out a coffer before the altar to collect donations.[62] Income levels from both guilds suggest that of the two groups, the wives' guild was more active; they contributed comparatively more money and appear more regularly in the churchwardens' accounts.

In addition to supporting the cult of the saints, both Hocktide and guild money provided needed parish furnishings. In 1497 the women of St. Edmund's, Salisbury, spent the Hocktide income on new windows for the church.[63] In 1532, the women of St. Martin in the Fields in Westminster spent their Hocktide money on a satin altar cloth and two curtains.[64] In the parish of St. Margaret's in Westminster, the maidens' collection helped support and renovate the parish's chapel of St. Margaret.[65]

Women's pious concerns reflected their domestic spheres of action. Within their families, women spun wool, washed and mended the clothes, and dressed the children. Buying altar clothes and banners for side altars dedicated to women saints is a similar gesture. Furthermore, altars to Mary, Margaret, or the other virgin martyrs comforted women facing the uncertainty of childbirth or the fear of infertility.[66] Activities conducted in all-women's groups, whether at Hocktide, with its clear-cut gender roles and its focus on male and female sexual contact, or in women's guilds, with their emphasis on marital status, provided ways of incorporating women's concerns about marriage and their interactions with men into local religious life and parish participation.

No membership rolls survive for any of the women's guilds—which leaves unanswered the question of what sort of women joined these guilds

---

[58] French, "Maidens' Lights and Wives' Stores," 421–2.
[59] *Churchwardens' Accounts of St. Mary the Great, Cambridge, from 1504–1635*, ed. J. E. Foster, Cambridge Antiquarian Society 35 (1905), 34.
[60] Ibid.
[61] Public Record Office, PROB11/9 fols. 5r–5v.
[62] *Churchwardens' Accounts of Ashburton*, 18, 49.
[63] *St. Edmund's, Salisbury*, 365, 47.
[64] *St. Martin-in-the Fields*, 31.
[65] WCA, E1 (St. Margaret's, Westminster CWA), fol. 370.
[66] Winstead, *Virgin Martyrs*.

and who ran them. Examining the lay subsidy records for 1524 in conjunction with a list of wardens for women's guilds in Chagford and Morebath in Devon, Horley in Surrey, and St. Mary the Great in Cambridge indicates that the leadership came from a relatively broad range of the upper-middling parish women. As with other voluntary associations of the time, membership in these guilds was probably equally broad.[67] Although women from the better-off families in the parish served as wardens, economic status was not always the determining factor in attaining office; women from the poorer families were also represented. In fact, the parish's wealthiest women, the local gentry, do not appear to have been very interested in serving as wardens for these local guilds, nor did their husbands or fathers generally serve as churchwardens.[68] As with guild wardens, the women in charge of Hocktide were typically members of prominent parish families and often the wives of either current or past churchwardens.[69] Although England's economic and legal systems constrained women's financial and material contributions and reaffirmed their secondary status, the foundation of guilds, stores, and the celebration of Hocktide moved women out of their traditional roles into positions of both visibility and leadership. Their leadership implied responsibility for organization, management of money, and the political acumen to spend it properly and allowed them to draw on their domestic and economic experiences and their influence within their family and social networks.

The social aspects of guilds are another area where women's visibility in the parish affirmed traditional gender expectations. Women's guilds in general provided women with support, affirmation, and probably sympathy, but they also filled needs specific to the life stage of their members. English women's later age of marriage in the fifteenth and sixteenth centuries prolonged the time between childhood and marriage.[70] During this stage, many women worked as servants or with their families. Maidens' guilds would have offered these women comfort and support and given them visibility that would help them attract husbands.[71] Working with a young men's guild allowed women to show off their piety and economic sense and to meet a variety of eligible men. In 1534, the maidens' and young men's guilds of Morebath joined together to replace a stolen chalice.

---

[67] French, "Maidens' Lights and Wives' Stores," 413–18.

[68] This would fit in with the findings of those who have argued that the gentry were retreating to their manor houses and private chapels, leaving parish maintenance and administration to the non-elites. There has been much debate on this subject. For a summary see Beat Kümin, *The Shaping of a Community: The Rise and Reformation of the English Parish c. 1400–1560* (Aldershot, Hants., 1996), 32–40.

[69] French, " 'To Free Them From Binding,' " 408–9.

[70] Hanawalt, *The Ties That Bound*, 188–204; Goldberg, *Women, Work, and Life Cycle*.

[71] In 1480, the churchwardens' accounts for Croscombe specifically state that the female warden for the maiden's guild was Roger Mor's servant. "Croscombe Church-Wardens Accounts," 8.

The churchwardens' accounts explain that "a pon *ys ye* yong men & may-
dyns of *ys parrysse* dru themselffe to gethers & wt there geftis & *provysyon*
the bofthyn a nother challis wt out an chargis of *ye parrysse*."[72] The effort to
replace the chalice not only developed the organizational skills of both
groups but also put marriageable men and women into close proximity.
Wives' guilds also offered a venue for women to share common concerns.
Men had collective political, judicial, and economic associations. Women's
guilds offered an alternative to these exclusively male institutions. It is
likely that the members of wives' guilds attended each other's childbirths,
churchings, and funerals. Like the maiden's guilds, they provided a forum
for displaying piety and working for the parish.

Parish guilds and stores in England are unique in that they gave women
the opportunity to join single-sex organizations that were openly sanctioned by the parish community.[73] These guilds allowed women to support
the parish in substantial, positive, and socially approved ways. In no other
medieval institution did women enjoy the opportunity to serve in leadership positions. Guilds and stores also provided a guarded and religiously
sanctioned organization for what were probably large numbers of unmarried young women, and wives' organizations assisted women through different stages of the life cycle, such as childbirth and perhaps widowhood
and remarriage. These opportunities created tension in parish life because
they empowered women on the one hand and enforced what was considered the "proper" behavior on the other. The collective nature of women's
guilds allowed members greater mobility. Women could go out and solicit
money for the parish without compromising their virtue and reputation;
on their own, such actions would have been unacceptable.

Perhaps the greatest source of anxiety about women's visibility came
from the Hocktide celebrations.[74] Hocktide activities first playfully dissolved and then rebuilt the often invisible or assumed gender roles. This
holiday became important to parishes because it enabled them to address
the tension between affirming women's traditional roles and their growing
visibility. The controlled rituals of inversion allowed women to organize,
but only in ways that ultimately affirmed their secondary status within the
parish. The division of Hocktide into male and female halves need not be

[72] "Accounts of the Wardens of the Parish of Morebath, Devon: 1520–1573," ed. Erskine
Binney, *Devon Notes and Queries* supp. vol., 1903–4 (1904): 64.

[73] There do not seem to have been any all-women's confraternities in Italy, and women's
activities in confraternities of men and women were systematically restricted over the
course of the fifteenth century. James R. Banker, *Death in the Community: Memorialization and
Confraternities in an Italian Commune in the Late Middle Ages* (Athens, Ga., 1988), 68–71, 149;
Giovanna Casegrande, "Women in Confraternities between the Middle Ages and the Mod-
ern Age: Research in Umbria," *Confraternities: The Newsletter of the Society for Confraternity
Studies* 5 (1994): 8–9; Nicholas Terpstra, *Lay Confraternities and Civic Religion in Renaissance
Bologna* (Cambridge, 1995), 116–31.

[74] French, " 'To Free Them From Binding.' "

understood as simply conflict between the sexes. Parishes sponsored gen-der-related activities for married couples because conviviality, gender identification, and life stage—all themes in the Hocktide celebrations—were also important concerns for the parish community. The holiday had no single meaning within parish culture, instead it offered a way to find the intersection of a number of issues relating to local religious participation. As Natalie Zemon Davis has argued, games involving sexual role-reversal and separate male and female activities expressed a variety of communal concerns: they "gave a more positive license to the unruly women,"[75] they affirmed traditional sexual relationships during times of change in the "distribution of power in family and political life,"[76] and they helped parishioners to negotiate the outside world by interpreting it through local concerns.[77]

The cessation of Hocktide suppers for women was one manifestation of anxiety surrounding women's activities. When parishes initially celebrated Hocktide there was usually a supper for the women, although it never became a permanent feature, and there was never a dinner for the men. When St. Mary at Hill in London first celebrated Hocktide in 1498, the parish contributed sixteen pence "for iij ribbes of bieff to the wyven on hokmonday & for ale & bred for them that gaderyd."[78] In the next year, there were only two ribs of beef, and in 1500 only bread and ale.[79] After 1500, the women continued to celebrate Hocktide, but the parish no longer provided a dinner for them. Similarly, for early celebrations in Kingston-upon-Thames, St. Edmund's in Salisbury, and St. Giles in Reading, the parishes paid for "mete and drynke at Hocktyde,"[80] but these expenses disappeared shortly thereafter. The initial inclusion of a feast suggests that parishes reacted to the women's activities in much the same way as to a parish guild. Gervase Rosser has written that "[f]easting and drinking were in the Middle Ages regarded as defining activities of the guilds."[81] Annual guild dinners allowed members to form new social relationships by integrating members from potentially disparate social backgrounds into the guild community and allowing for the development and expansion of common ideas and attitudes.[82]

The disappearance of Hocktide suppers suggests that the holiday and its activities challenged assumptions about community involvement. The activities of capturing and binding united women as they reenacted in comic

[75] Natalie Zemon Davis, "Women on Top," in *Society in Culture in Early Modern France* (Stanford, 1965), 143–7.

[76] Ibid., 150.

[77] Davis, "The Reasons of Misrule," in *Society and Culture in Early Modern France*, 103, 109.

[78] London, Guildhall Library MS 1239/1 part 1 (St. Mary at Hill CWA), fol. 159.

[79] London, Guildhall Library MS 1239/1 part 1 (St. Mary at Hill CWA), fols. 164, 179.

[80] Kingston Borough Archives, KG2/2/1 (Kingston-Upon-Thames CWA), fol. 24.

[81] Rosser, "Going to the Fraternity Feast," 431.

[82] Ibid., 432–3.

form their shared experiences with men. A subsequent feast would further unite them and strengthen their conviviality and solidarity, possibly creating an atmosphere of defiance.[83] Such a situation would permanently undermine the very relations between men and women that the church needed to uphold. The feast was such a potent forum for women that parishes could not allow it to become permanent, lest they lose control of it. Solidarity among women had to be channeled in ways that would reestablish their behavior within traditional limits.

Hocktide's bawdy and unruly behavior also earned much criticism from the authorities. Between 1406 and 1419, the mayor of London repeatedly forbade an activity called "hokking" carried out on the Monday and Tuesday after Easter.[84] Later proclamations linked hokking with gambling and other games that the authorities considered too violent to permit.[85] In 1450 John Carpenter, Bishop of Worcester, roundly condemned the holiday, considering it to be a "noxious corruption" and a sign of "spiritual illness."[86] The sexual license of the holiday especially drew his anger, and he writes:

> alas, when the solemn feast of Easter has ended women feign to bind men, and on another (or the next) day men feign to bind women, and to do other things—would that they were not dishonorable or worse!—in full view of passers-by, even pretending to increase church profit but earning loss (literally damnation) for the soul under false pretenses. Many scandals arise from the occasion of these activities, and adulteries and other outrageous crimes are committed as a clear offense to God, a very serious danger to the souls of those committing them, and a pernicious example to others.[87]

Visitations also found Hocktide problematic. The episcopal visitation of the diocese of Canterbury cited widow Johanna Hornys of the Kent parish of Little Mongeham for failure to turn over money gathered at Hocktide.[88] We do not know if this was embezzlement on Johanna's part or due to a desire by the women to determine how the proceeds should be spent. Much like the condemnations of women's behavior while sitting in church, these passages reflect the visibility women gained from parish participation. Furthermore, they hint at women's concerns about sex, status, and self-pro-

---

[83] Houlbrooke, "Women's Social Life and Common Action," 171–5.

[84] *Calendar of Letter-Books of the City of London at the Guildhall: Letter-Book I (c. 1400–1422)*, ed. Reginald R. Sharpe (London, 1909), 48, 72, 85, 124, 161, 194, 211; Henry Thomas Riley, *Memorials of London and London Life in the Thirteenth, Fourteenth and Fifteenth Centuries* (London, 1868), 561.

[85] *Letter-Book I*, 72; *Memorials*, 571.

[86] *Records of Early English Drama: Herefordshire and Worcestershire*, ed. David N. Klausner (Toronto, 1990), 349–50; 553–4.

[87] Ibid.

[88] *Kentish Visitations of Archbishop William Warham and His Deputies, 1511–1512*, ed. K. L. Wood-Legh, Kent Records 24 (1984), 101.

motion, all issues that drew their attention away from God and made clerical authorities anxious.

Hocktide celebrations were a controlled way to examine and reaffirm traditional gender roles in the face of the changing social dynamics that accompanied the growing influence of the parish in late medieval England. It was a carnivalesque holiday that disrupted male-female relationships.[89] Games and rituals of inversion, such as Hocktide, called attention to, defined, and preserved the status quo.[90] Nonetheless, women derived status from participating in Hocktide. Under its auspices they organized themselves, raised money, and purchased items that the community needed.

The opportunities for all-women's gatherings provided forums for the expression and articulation of a women's subculture that the clergy would have feared. Although many of these parish activities reasserted women's secondary status and upheld traditional gender definitions, they simultaneously challenged them by providing women with unprecedented leadership roles and sanctioned opportunities for social comment. Women's involvement in the parish therefore had a subversive quality because it allowed them to express their own desires and their concerns about the parish and its activities. By raising money and directing their bequests, women challenged the predominantly male parish administration and its control over parish resources. Although women used these opportunities primarily to support the parish, the means by which they did this made the clergy nervous—which is itself a testament to the power of a women's subculture. Women's activity in the parish is significant because it was a part of local religious life and not separate from or in addition to it. Despite the misogyny of much clerical discourse, Christianity at the parish level provided women with ways to construct meaning and value around their family and social lives, and, in turn, their concerns and values shaped parish life.

The changes in local religion that resulted from women's growing visibility ended with the Reformation. The abolition of Hocktide marks the loss of an opportunity for critiquing the social order. As another example of what Peter Burke termed the "triumph of Lent," the reformers stressed social conformity and deference to authority, replacing what they saw as disorderly, exuberant displays.[91] The abolition of saintly images from the parishes removed the purpose of the guilds and stores and the need for Hocktide fund-raising activities. With the Reformation also came changes to many churches' interiors. Some communities re-pewed their churches, and increasingly women began sitting with their families instead of each

---

[89] Peter Burke, *Popular Culture in Early Modern Europe* (New York, 1978), 192–4; Sally-Beth MacLean, "Hocktide: A Reassessment of a Popular Pre-Reformation Festival," in *Festive Drama*, ed. Meg Twycross (Cambridge, 1996), 233–41.

[90] Burke, *Popular Culture*, 200.

[91] Ibid., 207.

other. The family, overseen by the father or husband, increasingly became the unit of piety.[92] Although churches still needed to be cleaned, there were no longer saints to be dressed and adorned with the handiwork of parish women, and the vestments and altar cloths they created out of their own clothes and housewares were gone. When this happened, women lost an outlet for pious expression and collective organization. Their responsibilities to their households had previously given them the means to venerate the saints and ask for God's intercession, but in the reformed religion of the 1550s, these were no longer acceptable practices.

[92] For the impact of Protestant ideologies on women and the family see Lyndal Roper, *The Holy Household: Religion, Morals, and Order in Reformation Augsburg* (Oxford, 1989).

CHAPTER NINE

Public Exposure? Consorts and Ritual in Late Medieval Europe: The Example of the Entrance of the Dogaresse of Venice

Holly S. Hurlburt

Even the most powerful late medieval consorts[1] participated infrequently in the fundamental power-building activities of states and therefore appear rarely in the historical sources generated by these activities, such as chronicles and governmental documents.[2] Scholars of early modern queenship and those interested in the influence of consorts must look elsewhere for evidence of their participation in the shaping of state and society. Although recent scholarship has begun to elucidate consorts' nuanced relationship with power in various forms, a survey of this literature reveals little attention to royal ritual.[3] Occasions such as religious and state festivals, diplomatic visits, and rites of passage such as births, corona-

---

I thank John Carmi Parsons for his interest in my research on the dogaresse and for suggesting comparison with other royal women, and Mitch Hammond for reading and critiquing drafts of this work.

[1] For the purposes of this chapter, a *consort* is the wife of a royal or political figure.

[2] John Carmi Parsons observes the limits of queenly influence in "Family, Sex and Power: The Rhythms of Medieval Queenship," in Parsons, ed., *Medieval Queenship* (New York, 1993), 8.

[3] Parsons has observed that "the topic needs investigation: as the king's wife was neither warrior nor lawgiver, ritual had an especially crucial role in the construction of queenship, beginning with the fundamental queen-making act of coronation," ibid. Recent works on queenship include *Medieval Queenship*, ed. Parsons; *Women and Sovereignty*, ed. Louise Olga Fradenburg (Edinburgh, 1992); *Power of the Weak: Studies on Medieval Women*, ed. Jennifer Carpenter and Sally-Beth MacLean (Urbana, 1995); *Queens and Queenship in Medieval Europe*, ed. Anne Duggan (Woodbridge, 1997); Elizabeth A. Lehfeldt, "Ruling Sexuality: The Political Legitimacy of Isabel of Castile," *Renaissance Quarterly* 53 (2000): 31–56; Theresa Earenfight, "Maria of Castile, Ruler or Figurehead? A Preliminary Study in Aragonese Queenship," *Mediterranean Studies* 4 (1994): 45–61.

tions, and deaths placed not only consorts but also masses of elaborately dressed ladies-in-waiting in the public eye. These public appearances by such an assembly of women, whose threatening and threatened sexuality necessitated that their day-to-day visibility be limited, created a live-action tableau of female community and reminded viewers of women's multiple roles as wives, mothers, and consumers. These occasions served not so much to glorify individual women as to draw attention to their gender's role in the creation and maintenance of political and dynastic ties. Hence these appearances have been generally understood to present women as symbolic objects, safely enclosed within the confines of patriarchal male ideology.[4] However, rituals often do not offer a single perspective and frequently embody tensions between the real and the symbolic. Using the example of the entrance ceremony of the fifteenth-century dogaresse of Venice, this essay will suggest that ritual occasions also created visual reminders of the consort's physical proximity to the locus of political power, presented the rare vision of a community of women, and implied that consorts and royal women possessed potential influence, not just as wives and mothers but as intercessors and political actors in their own right.

The dogaressa was the wife of the Venetian doge, the often aged, life-term elected head of the republic. The office of the doge evolved over centuries from a position of great power to one constrained by a series of constitutional limitations. Because of her husband's elective position, the dogaressa must be seen as fundamentally different from most queens or consorts. She was subject to the same strict constitutional limitations as her husband and also swore to the oath of office (called the *promissione ducale*) prepared for each doge. The oath prohibited the ducal family from many common activities such as investing in international trade, intervening in city factions, accepting gifts, or lobbying with the government for family members.[5] Because she was the wife of an elected official, the dogaressa did not have the same dynastic function as a queen because her sons could not only not inherit her husband's position but were constitutionally barred from holding the most powerful offices during his reign. Hence Venetian law strictly controlled motherhood—traditionally a consort's most fundamental role—as a means to exercising influence. Further, since age and experience were valued characteristics for ducal candidates in the late middle ages, many dogaresse were generally past the age of fertility at

[4] For example, Edward Muir observes, "The ceremonial representation of womankind occurred largely in a political and courtly context; women as well had been elevated to an ideal status, and thus reduced to passive subjects of the all-embracing aristocratic republic." *Civic Ritual in Renaissance Venice* (Princeton, 1981), 304.

[5] On the *promissione*, see Gisela Graziato, ed., *Le promissioni del Doge di Venezia dalle origini alla fine del duecento* (Venice, 1986), and my doctoral dissertation, "'La Serenissima Domina Ducissa': The Dogaresse of Venice, 1250–1500" (Ph.D. diss., Syracuse University, 2000), 76–105.

their entrances, so their sexuality offered fewer opportunities and posed fewer threats. As a result, the public ceremonies in which the dogaressa took part were, for the most part, devoid of the fertility references common to many consort's appearances.[6] Despite these constitutional differences in the offices of queens and dogaresse, both positions gave women unusual proximity to the male-dominated loci of political power in medieval Europe. As was frequently the case with medieval queens, the dogaresse played a featured role in the celebrations surrounding their husbands' accession to office.

Immediately after his election, the new doge greeted the assembled populace in the Piazza San Marco, the political center of the city. He entered the church of San Marco, received a blessing, and from the adjacent ducal palace, he swore to uphold the dictates of the *promissione ducale* and the honor of the city.[7] This series of events took place within the closed geography of the city center, and its participants were all male. After his election, the doge sponsored a series of tournaments, jousts, and popular feasts that often lasted several weeks. One such celebratory event was the entrance of his wife into the Doge's Palace.[8]

According to the various books of ceremony and chronicles that described the entrances of fifteenth-century dogaresse such as Dogaressa Dea Morosini Tron (1472), the event typically took place a few weeks to months after the doge's election and had three distinct elements: a private oath-taking, a procession by land and canal through the city to the Piazza San Marco, and the dogaressa's entrance first into the church and then the ducal palace, where she was seated on the ducal throne.[9] The processional

[6] On procreative ability and queens, see Claire Richter Sherman, "Taking a Second Look: Observations on the Iconography of a French Queen," in *Feminism and Art History: Questioning the Litany*, ed. Norma Broude and Mary Garrard (New York, 1982), 104; Richard Jackson, *Vive le Roi!: A History of the French Coronation from Charles V to Charles X* (Chapel Hill, 1984), 30–31; Parsons, "Medieval Queenship," 4–7. On the age and childbearing status of dogaresse, see Hurlburt, "Ducissa," 58–65.

[7] On the doge's election, see Muir, *Civic Ritual*, 281–89; Federica Ambrosini, "Ceremonie, feste, lusso," in *Storia di Venezia*, vol. 5, *Il rinascimento: Società ed economia*, ed. Alberto Tenenti and Ugo Tucci (Rome, 1996), 441–84.

[8] According to fifteenth-century chronicler Marino Sanudo, the entrance of the dogaressa was the ultimate event in the 1423 election celebrations of Doge Francesco Foscari. Marino Sanudo, *Vitae Ducum Venetorum*, in *Rerum Italicarum Scriptores (RIS)*, ed. Ludovico Muratori (Milan, 1733), XXII, col. 968.

[9] My discussion of the dogaressa's entrance is drawn primarily from a description of the entrance of Dogaressa Dea Morosini Tron in 1472 that appears in similar form in several sources, including Archivio di Stato di Venezia (ASV), Collegio, *Libro Ceremoniale*, I, fol. 7r; and ASV, Collegio Secreta, *Liber Promissionum*, I, fol. 40r. On the evolution of the ceremony, see Hurlburt, "Ducissa," 109–25. The dogaressa's entrance is the one element of her position that has been well-studied by recent scholars; see also Muir, *Civic Ritual*, 291–6; Matteo Casini, *I gesti del principe: La festa politica à Firenze e Venezia in età rinascimentale* (Venice, 1996), 37–38; Maximilian Tondro, "Memory and Tradition: The Ephemeral Architecture for the Triumphal Entries of the Dogaresse of Venice in 1557 and 1597" (Ph.D. diss., Cambridge University, 2002), 17–30.

entrance of the dogaressa differed from the election-day celebrations for the doge in both geography and personnel. The ducal festivities featured no formal procession along the canals and streets of the city. Rather, his ceremonies focused solely on the political center. The largest city-wide procession associated with the doge's election instead featured the dogaressa and traversed various regions of the city, incorporating more viewers and uniting the city. In addition, the dogaressa's entrance was more socially inclusive; her procession prominently featured two groups excluded from both the political franchise and the doge's election ceremony—guildsmen and women.[10]

Sources place the greatest emphasis on the processional element of the dogaressa's entrance, describing the participants and their order of appearance in painstaking detail. Servants, musicians, family, and a court of ladies opened the procession. The dogaressa appeared in the middle, representing the center or heart, placing her as the focus. In addition, many of the most powerful Venetian officeholders, including members of the ducal council and the Senate followed the dogaressa, ranked in descending order of importance.[11] The slow progression of this group, elaborately and officially dressed, through the streets and canals of Venice flanking the dogaressa and her ladies gave various citizens and visitors ample opportunity to view the unusual gathering of women in this ritual. Further, visual association with the doge's servants, musicians, and governmental elite politicized the dogaressa.

The most remarkable feature of the dogaressa's caravan, which most distinguished it from other Venetian ducal, civic, or religious celebrations, was the sheer number and identity of women—relatives of the doge and dogaressa, wives of Venetian political officials, and matrons of Venice, both young and old—who participated. The lack of an active presence by women in Venetian public events and ceremonies has been well documented; this

[10] In the celebrations surrounding the election of Doge Lorenzo Tiepolo (1268), the guilds paid homage to both doge and dogaressa. However, by the fourteenth century the guilds participated in the dogaressa's celebration only. On Tiepolo's election celebrations, see Martino Da Canal, *Les Estoires de Venise*, ed. Alberto Limentani (Florence, 1972), 283–99. On the guilds and the dogaressa, see Richard Mackenney, *Tradesmen and Traders: The World of the Guilds in Venice and Europe, c. 1250–c.1650* (Totowa, N.J., 1987), 141–42.

[11] ASV, *Ceremoniale*, I, fol. 7r. In many ways, the dogaressa's processional order mimicked that used for the ducal *andate* or outings to commemorate religious and political festivals, which have been thoroughly discussed by Edward Muir. Muir describes the three sections into which the doge's procession was divided: (1) musicians, servants, standard-bearers, church officials, and non-noble bureaucrats; (2) the doge, the ballot-bearer, ambassadors, and some men bearing the symbols of the doge's power; and (3) the nobility, organized by the hierarchy of their offices. Muir, *Civic Ritual*, 193. The dogaressa's procession featured this basic tripartite organization, but the personnel differed in number and identity. Musicians, servants, and family members preceded the dogaressa, the middle section consisted of the dogaressa, her escorts, and ducal councilors, and the third portion consisted of officeholders, but apparently fewer than in the doge's procession.

ritual was a notable exception.[12] Humanists such as Venetian Francesco Barbaro commented on the necessary limits placed on the public appearances of patrician females: "I would have wives be seen in public with their husbands, but when their husbands are away wives should stay at home." This maxim makes all the more remarkable the dogaressa's procession, in which she and countless of the city's most elite women appeared without their husbands, complicating the patriarchal vision of the Venetian republic.[13]

However, even in this procession dedicated to a woman and populated with a multitude of women, no female appeared unchaperoned; male family members and governmental representatives accompanied the matrons and the dogaressa herself. In this respect, the dogaressa and her ladies represented every woman whose purity had to be shielded from the threats of public exposure for her own sake, but more importantly for the honor of her husband and family. The councilors, procurators, and relatives did not safeguard just the honor of these women; they symbolically safeguarded the Venetian social system of patriarchy and the honor of their state.[14]

[12] Works by painter Gentile Bellini (*Procession in St. Mark's Square*, 1496) and engraver Jost Amman (*Feast of the Sensa*, 1560) illustrate women as ritual spectators. In addition to Muir's observations on women's limited role in civic ritual (see above, note 4), Dennis Romano also discussed the restrictions placed on women in public and related these restrictions to issues of honor in "Gender and Urban Geography," *Journal of Social History* 23 (1989): 339–53. Other scholars suggest that in some circumstances, both everyday and ceremonial, women of various classes and careers did occasionally occupy public space. See Monica Chojnacka, *Working Women in Early Modern Venice* (Baltimore, 2001); Robert C. Davis, "The Geography of Gender," in *Gender and Society in Renaissance Italy*, ed. Judith C. Brown and Robert C. Davis (London, 1998), 19–38; Deanna Shemek, "Circular Definitions: Configuring Gender in Italian Renaissance Festival," *Renaissance Quarterly* 48 (1995): 1–40; Linda Guzzetti, "Le donne a Venezia nel XIV secolo: Uno studio sulla loro presenza nella società e nella famiglia," *Studi Veneziani* n.s. 35 (1998): 15–88. Women did participate in the spectacles to greet foreign guests, especially female dignitaries; see, e.g., the arrivals of Caterina Cornaro (1489) and Anne of Foix (1502) as discussed by Patricia Fortini Brown, "Measured Friendship, Calculated Pomp: The Ceremonial Welcomes of the Venetian Republic," in "*All the World's a Stage*": *Pageantry in the Renaissance and Baroque*, ed. Barbara Wisch and Susan Scott Munshower (University Park, Pa., 1990), 136–87. At least one dogaressa, Marina Nani Foscari, participated in the greeting of female dignitaries in Venice; Hurlburt, "*Ducissa*," 217–33.

[13] Francesco Barbaro, *De Re Uxoria*, in *The Earthly Republic: Italian Humanists on Government and Society*, ed. Benjamin G. Kohl and Ronald G. Witt (Philadelphia, 1978), 204. However, Barbaro's pronouncement is somewhat ambiguous because elsewhere he observed that women "should not be shut up in their bedrooms as a prison, but should be permitted to go out, and this privilege should be taken as evidence of their virtue and propriety." Ibid. Venice was gendered feminine, being called "La Serenissima," the most serene one, and allegorical figures of the city were common. See David Rosand, "Venezia Figurata," in *Interpretazioni Veneziane: Studi di Storia dell'Arte in onore di Michelangelo Muraro*, ed. Rosand (Venice, 1984), 177–96. On the dogaressa's role in this gendering, see Bronwen Wilson, " 'Il bel sesso, e l'austero Senato': The Coronation of Dogaressa Morosina Morosini Grimani," *Renaissance Quarterly* 52 (1999): 73–139.

[14] Sherry Ortner suggests that women's sexual purity is a concern among developing states because "[it] is seen as adaptive for the social coherence, economic viability or cultural reputation of the group." In other words, the chastity of Venetian noblewomen sug-

Chroniclers who describe the fifteenth-century entrances of the dogaresse and their other public activities emphasize the number and dress of
their court of ladies, highlighting this rarely seen feminine montage. Several types of women processed with the dogaressa, forming her court. First
came a group of young married noblewomen, then older married noblewomen, in pairs. Following these women came the wife of the grand chancellor, the non-noble counterpart of the doge. Finally came the daughters
and daughters-in-law of the dogaressa. In addition, two servants carried
the train of the dogaressa's gown. Most of these women, not just the dogaressa and wife of the grand chancellor, were born into and married into the
most politically and economically powerful families in Venice.[15] Through
their presence, these women called to mind the crucial sociopolitical networks created via patrician marriage in the city.[16]

The entrance ceremony created a rare moment of public interaction and
participation for many noblewomen. Not only did it afford them the opportunity to meet and socialize outside homes and churches, but it also
provided a moment of limelight. These women and their elaborate gar-
ments surely became the center of attention in the procession. Frequently
the stringent Venetian sumptuary laws were suspended for such events,
giving women an opportunity to don their finest and temporarily assume a
persona separate (although always related) from that of their husbands
who usually accompanied them in public.[17] The entrance of the dogaressa
offered these women an instant of self-expression and sisterhood in a
uniquely female community and allowed them to make a rare contribution
to the corpus of Venetian ritual as more than spectators.

---

gested the power of the patriarchal state to protect its own. Ortner, "The Virgin and the
State," *Feminist Studies* 4 (1978): 22. The concern with protecting the virtue of the dogaresse
is evident in two pieces of fifteenth-century Venetian legislation; see Hurlburt, "Ducissa,"
170–72.

[15] For example, in his description of the visit of German empress in 1452, Sanudo noted
that two hundred women, dressed in jewels and silk, accompanied the dogaressa. Sanudo,
Vitae, col. 1143. A similar court of women consisting of a hierarchy of the wives of the most
important court officials was common in the Byzantine empire. Alexander P. Kazhdan and
Michael McCormick, "The Social World of the Byzantine Court," in *Byzantine Court Culture
from 829 to 1204*, ed. Henry Maguire (Washington, D.C., 1997), 182–85; and Pseudo-Kodinos,
Traité des Offices, ed. Jean Verpeaux (Paris, 1976), 287.

[16] Themes of women and family networks have been developed by Stanley Chojnacki in
several essays in his *Women and Men in Renaissance Venice* (Baltimore, 2000). For the networks established by ducal marriages, see Hurlburt, "Ducissa," 34–58.

[17] On the suspension of sumptuary laws for various ceremonies, see Guilio Bistort, *Il
magistrato alle pompe nella republica di Venezia* (Bologna, 1912), 33–36, and Diane Owen
Hughes, "Sumptuary Law and Social Relations in Renaissance Italy," in *Disputes and Settlements: Law and Human Relations in the West*, ed. John Bossy (Cambridge, 1983), 90–91. On
fashion as a mode of self-expression, see Stanley Chojnacki, "La posizione della donna a
Venezia nel Cinquecento," in *Tiziano e Venezia: Convegno internazionale di studi, Venezia, 1976*
(Vicenza, 1980), 65–70; and the comments of Nicolosa Sanuti of Bologna in Hughes, "Sumptuary Law," 86–87.

Since only married women formed this court (with the possible exception of the maidens who carried the dogaressa's train), the procession, as well as the dogaressa herself, represented the fundamental function of Venetian patrician women and symbolized the importance of marriage to state and society. The young matrons who marched ahead of the dogaressa, recently married and prepared to bear children and therefore maintain noble family size and honor, represented the middle stage of the female life cycle. The older matrons stood for the female life cycle in its twilight, after they had birthed, raised, and married off countless children. This generational suggestion was made abundantly clear by the presence of the dogaressa's married daughters and daughters-in-law. The average age of dogaresse at their husband's election in the late fifteenth century was at least fifty-nine. The advanced age of the dogaressa and her court of matrons called to mind the successful system of gerontocracy at work in Venice.[18] Like the elderly men who ruled in Venice, elderly women represented the wisdom of old age and a life lived in service of family and state. Further, the vision of an aged dogaressa, surrounded by her female progeny and distanced from her husband and sons, downplayed the threatening implications of dynasty but still allowed a celebration of marriage and family, the building blocks of the political elite of Venice, building blocks cemented by these very women and their procreative ability.[19]

The dogaressa's entrance ceremony emphasized the influence Venetian women exercised through marriage; in addition, it closely resembled the ritual of marriage both in general formulae and in the specifics peculiar to Venice, thus creating a ceremony in which the dogaressa emblematically married the state. The three general phases of a late medieval Italian wedding were the dowry negotiations, carried out by male relatives; the celebration of the wedding at the house of the bride's father; and the procession of the bride and trousseau through the city to the house of the husband, after which the newlyweds consummated their union.[20] In the

[18] Matteo Casini has called this assemblage of women "an exaltation of femininity within the family." *Gesti*, 43. On male gerontocracy, see Robert Finlay, "The Venetian Republic as a Gerontocracy: Age and Politics in the Renaissance," *Journal of Medieval and Renaissance Studies* 8 (1978): 157–78. Dea Morosini married Nicolo Tron in 1424, at which time she was most likely around sixteen. Hence, in 1474 she was sixty-four or older; Hurlburt, "*Ducissa*," 64.

[19] The various texts that describe Dea Morosini Tron's entrance make no specific mention of the participation of her son but do make reference to a group of blood relatives of the doge and dogaressa that could have included him. However, this group, possibly including sons and other male family members, was visually separated from the dogaressa by the court of matrons. See sources discussed in note 9. In the sixteenth century the dogaressa's entrance cortege was larger; Sansovino's list of participants in the 1557 entrance of Dogaressa Zilia Dandolo Priuli included her son and sons-in-law; still her progeny did not appear directly *with* the dogaressa. Francesco Sansovino, *Venetia: Città nobilissima et singolare* (Farnborough, England, 1968).

[20] Christiane Klapisch-Zuber, "Zacharias, or the Ousted Father: Nuptial Rites in Tuscany between Giotto and the Council of Trent," in *Women, Family, and Ritual in Renaissance Italy,*

case of the dogaressa, the phase of dowry negotiations corresponded to the oath-taking ceremony that preceded her entrance. Sources use the same Italian word—*giuramento*—to describe both the agreement between families over the dowry and the dogaressa's oath to uphold the *promissione*. Important officials of her governmental "family" witnessed this event, as in a typical marriage ceremony. Further, the event sometimes took place at the house of the dogaressa's father or brother, and the dogaressa presented the governmental representatives a symbolic dowry in the form of purses that contained coins.[21] Even as husbands frequently provided their brides with elaborate trousseaux to demonstrate their wealth and honor, after 1457 the state required the dogaressa to wear an official ducal cloak in all her public appearances for the honor of state, a legislative act that ensured that she appeared not just as a woman but as a depersonalized representative of the government.[22] In the most overtly politicized aspect of the dogaressa's entrance, she processed first to the church of San Marco and then to the Doge's Palace, a building that encompassed *both* public and private as ducal residence and city hall. The seating of the dogaressa on the ducal throne represented the consummation of this political arrangement.[23]

The entrance of the dogaressa and its marriage symbolism shared many details with actual weddings—everyday occurrences in Venice. In describing a typical patrician wedding, Francesco Sansovino stressed that the guests included many important government officers; "in sum, all the no-

---

trans. Lydia G. Cochrane (Chicago, 1985), 181–9; Patricia Labalme and Laura Sanguinetti White, "How to (and How Not to) Get Married in Sixteenth-Century Venice (Selections from the Diary of Marin Sanudo)," *Renaissance Quarterly* 52 (1999): 43–44; James Grubb, *Provincial Families of the Renaissance: Private and Public Life in the Veneto* (Baltimore, 1996), 8–11.

[21] Language provides a further link between these two ceremonies. Klapisch-Zuber noted that the common verb used to describe the last phase of this process meant "to bring one's wife under one's roof." The same sentence construction implying an action by the doge in bringing his consort to the palace appeared in more than one description of the dogaressa's entrance. Klapisch-Zuber, "Zacharias," 189. On the oath-taking element of the dogaressa's entrance, see *Ceremoniale*, I, fol. 7r; Hurlburt, "*Ducissa*," 81–83. On dowries, Labalme and White observed that "dowries were more than private exchanges of wealth. They were meant for public display and were actually publicly displayed in a demonstration of wealth which served the self-satisfaction of the city and its propaganda," "Married," 48. On the marriage procession as a time of exhibition by the husband and family, see Klapisch-Zuber, "The Griselda Complex: Dowry and Marriage Gifts in the Quattrocento," in *Women, Family, and Ritual*, 213–46.

[22] The law of 1457 prescribed an official uniform for both doge and dogaressa. See ASV, Maggior Consiglio, Deliberazioni, *Regina*, fol. 15r. Other members of the government such as senators and ducal councilors also had particular costumes. See Margaret Newett, "The Sumptuary Laws of Venice in the Fourteenth and Fifteenth Centuries," in *Historical Essays by Members of the Owens College, Manchester*, ed. T. F. Tout and J. Tout (New York, 1902), 245–78.

[23] Asa Boholm addresses but does not fully develop the metaphor of the dogaressa's entrance as a wedding. Boholm, "The Coronation of Female Death: The Dogaressas of Venice," *Man* 27 (1992): 91–104.

bility." Sansovino also noted the pageantry involved in a patrician wedding, from the participation of musicians, to the large number of guests, to the particular sugary confections prepared for the event—all items that weddings shared in common with the dogaressa's entrance. Further, he made the association between patrician marriage and the state by noting that at one time, brides had been presented to the doge.[24] Evidence from Venetian sumptuary law reveals concern for the appearance of the bride, who was allowed certain adornments prohibited to other women (such as pearls) during her wedding. In addition, this legislation revealed particular concern with the women who attended the bride, frequently decreeing the precise number of women and their marital status. As in the entrance of the dogaressa, a variety of women accompanied the bride on her procession. Sumptuary legislation frequently included a blanket exemption for the dogaressa, suggesting that every time she appeared in public, this matron became a symbolic bride.[25]

Not only was the entrance of the dogaressa similar to a wedding in its external trappings, but it also typified the same blend of familial and civic issues.[26] The family of both doge and dogaressa, including brothers of both and daughters and daughters-in-law, occupied important spaces in her procession. The dogaressa, located centrally between family and government representatives, stood for the crucial role of all patrician women in Venice who increased social and political mobility of their natal family through marriage and who within marriage produced heirs that perpetuated the system. Patrician daughters cemented another generation of advantageous marriages, and noble sons assumed their places within the government.[27] Venetian marriages united families, created political factions and economic partnerships, facilitated dynastic continuity, and therefore commanded a good deal of ritual importance. A tension existed in this ritual, which simultaneously created the dogaressa as a woman restricted from acting in the interests of her own children and as a symbol for the role

[24] Sansovino, *Venetia*, 401–2. Certain weddings, like that of Giacomo Foscari, son of Doge Francesco, and Lucrezia Contarini in 1442, created the same festive atmosphere across the city as the entrance of a dogaressa and even followed the same processional pattern.

[25] Bistort, *Magistrato*, 90–96; and Newett, "Laws," 261–67.

[26] "Venetian patrician marriages in this period exemplified the blending of familial and civic concerns," Labalme and White, "Married," 45.

[27] Giovanni Caldiera suggested that the family was a microcosm of the government; although he did not glorify women's role in this model, he did acknowledge their procreative power. Margaret King, "Personal, Domestic and Republican Virtues in the Moral Philosophy of Giovanni Caldiera," *Renaissance Quarterly* 28 (1975): 554–57. On women's roles as social conduits and perpetuators of the patrician class in Renaissance Venice, see Chojnacki, *Women and Men*. See also Labalme and White, "Married," 43–72. Boholm ("Coronation," 102–3) suggests that the dogaressa simultaneously represented every patrician woman and none because she was married to a man whose identity was subsumed by the office he occupied.

of women in the (pro)creation and stability of the Venetian sociopolitical system.

The ritual and imagery of weddings carried still further import in Venice. Many important civic festivals were expressed in terms of marriage. For instance, a key annual festival in Venice occurred on Ascension Day when the doge "married" the sea by dropping a blessed ring into the lagoon. On this day the sea became the bride and through this ritual the doge proclaimed Venice's patriarchal authority and dominion over it. In this way, the state became a typical patriarchal family. In another ritual, the doge married each new abbess of the convent of Santa Maria delle Vergini.[28] Hence, the marital language of the dogaressa's entrance was one familiar to Venetians and placed the event in the same category as other important civic events that occurred more frequently.

It should not surprise us that a woman's procession should be seen in terms of a nuptial ritual. Women who were not nuns rarely acted in city rituals *with the exception of* weddings, which ritualized a woman's passage from father to husband. The dogaressa's entrance symbolized this same passage from father to husband, as well as passage from husband to government. The conscious use of wedding symbolism encased a potentially disturbing vision of women's public interaction within the accepted ritual vocabulary of a ceremony that defined women in patriarchal society.

However, wedding ritual should not just be seen as an expression of patriarchal constraints, particularly in the case of the dogaresse. The notable absence of the dogaressa's actual husband the doge in his wife's entrance ceremony suggested her (temporary) autonomy. In particular, the restrictions placed on the dogaressa by the ducal oath and the seating of the dogaressa on the vacant ducal throne in the Hall of the Great Council at the completion of her procession implied the dogaressa's place as a potential independent political actor.[29] The mere appearance of this noblewoman in a public ritual without her male counterpart further signified the position of the dogaressa, clearly an unusual woman, and one of unusual political and cultural importance to the state.

How does the entrance of the dogaressa compare with those of other regal consorts and female rulers of the late medieval era? I would like to

[28] In addition, the Venetian festival of the Purification of the Virgin incorporated the legend of tenth-century kidnapped brides to highlight marital themes. Like the entrance of the dogaressa, this annual ritual offered roles to the city's women and celebrated their social contributions. However, women's prominent place in this ritual was curtailed after 1379. Muir, *Civic Ritual*, 135–56. See also Jutta Gisela Sperling, *Convents and the Body Politic in Late Renaissance Venice* (Chicago, 1999), 206–15; Ambrosini, "Ceremonie, feste, lusso," 444. On the state as patriarchal family, see the writings of Caldiera as discussed by Margaret King, "Caldiera," 535–74. Bronwen Wilson also discusses the relationship between the dogaressa and the ritual language of marriage; "Grimani," 87–88.

[29] On dogaressal restrictions in the *promissione*, see Hurlburt, "*Ducissa*," 76–105.

conclude with some introductory observations on this question. Although scholars have traced the development of coronation ritual for early medieval queens, systematic analysis of women's political ritual in the fourteenth and fifteenth centuries is frustratingly absent.[30] The women of the principalities of northern Italy sadly are not exceptions to this rule. Many Italian city–states achieved political stability in the fifteenth century, at which time they became increasingly concerned with ceremony and its implications. Yet scant attention has been paid by modern scholars to occasions such as Bona of Savoy's entrance into Milan (1468) or celebrations surrounding Caterina Sforza's entrance into Forlì with Girolamo Riario (1481), her assumption of power there after her husband's murder (1488), or how these and other events seen together nuance our understanding of Renaissance pageantry.[31]

Despite the relative paucity of studies focusing directly on royal coronation ritual of the late middle ages, it is clear that the entrance ceremonies of consorts, regents, and queens of the late middle ages were important ceremonies full of religious and civic pomp. One rare example of a well-studied medieval female coronation is that of Queen Jeanne, wife of Charles V of France, whose entrance was preserved in a coronation book, probably commissioned by her husband, that has been the subject of much illuminating study by Claire Richter Sherman. The coronation rites of medieval Byzantine empresses have also received some attention.[32] A cursory

[30] Early coronation ritual is discussed by Janet Nelson, "Early Rites of Queen-Making and the Shaping of Medieval Queenship," in *Queens and Queenship in Medieval Europe*, ed. Duggan, 301–16. See also Richard Jackson on the ninth-century coronation of Judith, daughter of Charles the Bald, *Ordines Coronationis Franciae: Texts and Ordines for the Coronation of Frankish and French Kings and Queens in the Middle Ages* (Philadelphia, 1995), 1:73–86.

[31] In his study of the court of Galeazzo Maria Sforza, Gregory Lubkin notes that most of the celebrations for Bona of Savoy's arrival in Milan were canceled due to plague and weather. He does not indicate what was planned. Lubkin, *A Renaissance Court: Milan under Galeazzo Maria Sforza* (Berkeley, 1994), 52–55. Ernst Breisach notes that on her first entrance to Forlì, Caterina rode in a military procession with her husband and attended a ball. Breisach, *Caterina Sforza: A Renaissance Virago* (Chicago, 1967), 52–53. Both these authors got most of their information on these occasions from archival sources I have been unable to consult. For the legend of Caterina and her victory over conspirators, see Julia Hairston, "Skirting the Issue: Machiavelli's Caterina Sforza," *Renaissance Quarterly* 53 (2000): 687–712.

[32] For the purposes of this short comparison, I have distinguished between queens who ruled in their own right, such as Giovanna I of Naples (r.1343–81), not discussed here, and royal consorts, such as Jeanne of France and most Byzantine empresses. I am particularly interested in the comparison between Venice and Constantinople because of Venice's close relationship with the east. On Byzantium, the Pseudo-Kodinos's *Traité des Offices*, written in the mid-fourteenth century, gives an outline of the coronation of the empress in conjunction with her husband, 252–74; see also Donald Nicol, *The Byzantine Lady: Ten Portraits, 1250–1500* (Cambridge, 1994); Lynda Garland, "The Life and Ideology of Byzantine Women: A Further Note on Conventions of Behavior and Social Reality as Reflected in Eleventh- and Twelfth-Century Historical Sources," *Byzantion* 58 (1988): 361–89. Given Venice's historical relationship with the Byzantine empire, I believe comparison between empress and dogaressa could be fruitful. On Jeanne and the Coronation Book of 1365, see Claire Richter Sher-

comparison of the coronation rites for Jeanne and Byzantine empresses with the entrance of the fifteenth-century dogaressa reveals that female entrances shared certain salient characteristics but also had some crucial differences. These differences tell us much about the peculiar nature of political ceremony in republican Venice and the dogaressa's crucial role in that context. First, and most obviously, the dogaressa's ceremony cannot be called a coronation because she received no crown, ceremonial headgear, or other trappings of royalty.[33] Second, the most important elements of a queen's coronation generally took place within a church, although civic processions sometimes preceded or followed events. The liturgy of these events linked queens with their pious biblical predecessors. Although she visited the sacred relics in San Marco as part of her entrance, the dogaressa's ritual contained no such explicitly religious role.

The meaning of these rituals differed in one particularly notable way. Most queens, consorts, and empresses entered office as young, fertile women on whom rested the dynastic future of the family and crown. In the ceremonies for the queens of France, great emphasis was placed on the queen's procreative ability, from stressing the legal succession of her children and her right to act as regent, to comparisons with famous biblical mothers. In many cases, this maternal emphasis shaped the coronation of Byzantine empresses as well.[34]

With the responsibility of childbearing in these monarchical regimes came the possibility of regency or outright rule by women. Hence the women's coronations carried direct political import. By contrast, the dogaressa possessed no potential for regency or rule. Further, no part of the dogaressa's entrance into the republican political realm of Venice stressed fertility for the sake of dynastic continuity. Her generally advanced age and the absence of her husband downplayed any suggestion of dynastic

---

man, "The Queen in Charles V's 'Coronation Book': Jeanne de Bourbon and the 'Ordo ad Reginam Benedicendam,'" *Viator* 8 (1977): 255–98; "Iconography," 100–117.

[33] According to the Pseudo-Kodinos, the new empress was crowned and given a jewel-encrusted staff that was considered to be her emblem; her husband's was a cross; *Traité*, 261. In France, Queen Jeanne received a crown (albeit smaller than the king's) and a scepter. Sherman, "Ordo," 270. The doge received his crown (*corno*) in the final part of his ceremony, but no such crowning ritual took place in the dogaressa's entrance. Muir, *Civic Ritual*, 288; Tondro, "Memory," 97. A portrait of Dogaressa Giovanna Dandolo Malipiero on the reverse of a ceremonial medal of her husband, Pasquale Malipiero (1457–62) displays headgear that is definitely not the ducal corno. However, in the sixteenth century, dogaresse were frequently depicted wearing a smaller version of the ducal corno. See, e.g., the overleaf of ASV, Collegio, *Ceremoniale*, I; or the illustrations of Giacomo Franco in his *Habiti l'huomeni et donne Venetiane* (Venice, 1610).

[34] Sherman notes that this emphasis was particularly evident in the ceremony for Charles V and Jeanne of Bourbon because they had been married for fourteen years before he succeeded to the throne and had no children. Sherman, "Ordo," 269, 292–93. Empress Irene, the former Yolanda of Monferrat, received the empress's crown from her husband only after she gave birth, again linking coronation with procreation. See Nicol, *Portraits*, 49.

imperatives. Even though republican rhetoric nullified any fertility symbolism or references in the entrance of the dogaressa, the presence of her
family members, and specifically her married daughters and daughters-in-
law, still highlighted the crucial networks between families created by
queens, consorts, and women everywhere. The presence of the grown
progeny of the dogaressa situated her at a different point in the female life
cycle than young, nubile queens. Dogaresse had usually passed through
their youthful, threatening sexuality, but many were still mothers and had
thus completed medieval woman's most fundamental duty.

Finally, unlike other European and Mediterranean female consorts, the
dogaressa proceeded through her coronation alone, without her consort. In
the Byzantine Empire, the emperor usually crowned his consort himself,
confirming their relationship. Although King Charles V is not present in
any of the miniatures of the 1365 Coronation Book that depict elements of
the coronation ceremony dedicated to Jeanne, they were crowned on the
same day and at the same location, the cathedral of Reims.[35] Even when
French kings and queens could not be crowned jointly, the intent was a collective one, and the king almost certainly attended the later ceremony of
his wife. By contrast, the doge was always and intentionally absent from
the dogaressa's entrance—a nonappearance that consciously lessened the
similarity of ducal rites to those of monarchical regimes and eliminated
comparisons between the elected doge and dynastic kings.[36] Further, unlike Jeanne, who was seated on her own diminutive throne and in no way
replaced the king, the dogaressa took her place on the doge's chair at the
completion of her ceremony, symbolically occupying his space.[37] Although
the patriarchal presence of physical husband was replaced by patriarchal
state in the dogaressa's ceremony, the absence of a male authority figure

[35] On the crowning of Byzantine empresses, see the Pseudo-Kodinos, *Traité*, 260–63. In
the case of France, Sherman has observed that tradition dictated that the king and queen be
crowned together when "circumstances permitted." Otherwise the queen was crowned
alone at St. Denis, rather than at the cathedral in Reims. Apparently circumstances were less
permissive in the fifteenth century than in previous eras because Jeanne of Bourbon (1364)
was the last queen to be crowned at Reims. Sherman, "Ordo," 268–70.

[36] One of the earliest descriptions of a dogaressa's entrance ceremony is that of Marchesina Tiepolo, wife of the thirteenth-century Doge Lorenzo Tiepolo (1268–75). Marchesina
was of royal blood, the daughter of a Mediterranean prince. She did not have an "entrance"
like later dogaresse—she participated in her husband's celebration in the Piazza San Marco.
Later the guilds visited first the doge at the ducal palace and then the dogaressa at the couple's private home to pay homage. By the fourteenth century the dogaressa's celebration
was completely separate from that of the doge. See Martino da Canal, *Estoires*, 283–99; Hurlburt, "Ducissa," 116–22.

[37] On Jeanne's royal symbols, all of which were smaller or less pronounced than those of
Charles, see Sherman, "Iconography," 105–6. Interestingly, the ducal throne was the only
ducal symbol present in the dogaressa's entrance—the use of other vital items such as the
ducal umbrella is not mentioned. On ducal symbols, see Muir, *Civic Ritual*, 103–19.

from the ceremony created for her on some levels an identity independent from any male.

Despite these crucial differences, a few general similarities in these women's entrances are equally telling. In the French and Byzantine ceremonies, the entrance of a female ruling figure frequently involved a procession, a gathering of the most important religious and political figures in the realm, and the religious blessing of the woman in question. In each case the woman was the object of pomp and ceremony, marking her as an emblem of royalty. The symbolism of these ceremonies suggested that the female in question had less political significance than her male counterpart, but perhaps as much ceremonial import as he had.[38]

In each case, the coronation or entrance of a female consort was an occasion that featured multitudes of women. In his description of the arrival of the future Byzantine empress, the Pseudo-Kodinos noted that the wives of various imperial officials accompanied the emperor to meet the royal arrival. Several of the miniatures of the Coronation Book of King Charles V dedicated to Queen Jeanne's coronation depict her accompanied by several women.[39] Again, as in the dogaressa's entrance, these ceremonies showcased the merits of women both as ritual actors and as citizens of the realm.

[38] Sherman observes that the ordo (written "rule" or description) of the queen's coronation called for her throne to be smaller than the king's, and the miniatures that accompany the ordo reveal that the queen entered Reims Cathedral by a side door unlike the king who came through the main portal. Sherman, "Ordo," 274–75. In Byzantium it was customary for the emperor to crown the empress himself, suggesting her subjugation to him. Nicol, *Portraits*, 74. The Pseudo-Kodinos wrote, "After the crown was placed upon her head by the hand of the emperor, her husband, she prostrated herself in front of him, as if to say that she is his subject and depends upon him." *Traité*, 261. A twelfth-century Byzantine commentary on rulers observed that the role of emperors included "the enlightening and strengthening both of soul and body . . . likewise the care and thought given to subjects by the empress is simply directed to the welfare of the body and only to that (for women are devoid of the power of giving spiritual succor)," Garland, "Byzantine Women," 388–89. A similar observation about the lack of a liturgical role for the empress appears in George Majeska, "The Emperor in His Church: Imperial Ritual in the Church of St. Sophia," in *Byzantine Court Culture*, ed. Maguire, 4. On processions and queens, see lists compiled by Lawrence M. Bryant, "The Medieval Entry Ceremony at Paris," in *Coronations*, ed. J. M. Bak (Berkeley, 1990), 89–90.

[39] See especially the scenes, "The Preparation for the Unction of Jeanne de Bourbon" and "Jeanne de Bourbon Receives the Ring," in Sherman, "Ordo," figs. 7, 10. On the Byzantine court of women, which apparently became less segregated from men and more active in ceremony in the late middle ages, see the Pseudo-Kodinos, 287; Alexander P. Kazhdan and Michael McCormick, "The Social World of the Byzantine Court," in *Byzantine Court Culture*, ed. Maguire, 182–85. There is remarkable similarity between the female-dominated dogaressal procession and the procession of the newly elected mayoress of the English city of Coventry. There the retiring mayoress went with a retinue of the leading ladies of the city to meet and escort the new mayoress to her inauguration at St. Michael's church. As in the case of the dogaresse, the mayoress of Coventry did not take part in her husband's inauguration, but had a separate ceremony. Anthony Fletcher, *Gender, Sex, and Subordination in England, 1500–1800* (New Haven, 1995), 90–91. Thanks to Cissie Fairchilds for this reference.

The differences in the entrance ceremonies of queen, empress, and doga-ressa in part stem from the constitutional differences in these offices, as well as local custom. Despite the variations discussed above, these gen-dered rituals sent similar messages to their audiences about the multiva-lent roles and responsibilities of royal women through their use of the com-mon and expandable language of marriage symbolism and customs. Scholars have noted various similarities between coronations and wed-dings—the use of similar prayers and the use of a ring as a signifier are but two examples.[40] It should not surprise us to find the repeated use of these symbols in civic as well as religious ritual; marriage was not only a com-mon occurrence in the lives of most Europeans but also a fundamentally political act.[41] In addition, many of the early medieval coronation cere-monies that established precedent for the rituals of the fourteenth and fif-teenth centuries *also served as* wedding ceremonies for the king and his bride. Further, marital rhetoric appeared in medieval political philosophy. The male ruler was frequently depicted as the father of his people, and even occasionally as the bridegroom of the state.[42] Hence the entrances of political consorts were extraordinary gendered events encapsulated in an everyday language with several levels of meaning.

Finally, as previously noted, the use of wedding symbolism made more comfortable the presence of a woman in the political sphere.[43] Although wedding imagery could be constricting for women by making visible the system of patriarchy, it is also true that women of the late middle ages gained much of their influence—be it economic, familial, or social—through marriage. Hence, marriages and the rituals that employed the marriage paradigm certainly enclosed women in a safe patriarchal vision, but these events also created female communities of authority. The unusual appearance and progress of a mass of women through a city to its political or religious center challenged the traditional masculinity of civic ritual

[40] On prayers, see Parsons, "Medieval Queenship," 8. On the use of a ring, see Sherman, "Ordo," 269.

[41] "The political marketplace for state and family in sixteenth-century France is mar-riage." Carla Frecero, "Marguerite de Navarre and the Politics of Maternal Sovereignty," in *Women and Sovereignty*, ed. Fradenburg, 133.

[42] Richard Jackson comments extensively on marriage imagery and coronations; he notes that the first overt marriage metaphor occurs in the coronation of Queen Anne of Brittany in 1504; see Jackson, *French Coronation*, 86–90, and Ernst Kantorowicz, *The King's Two Bodies: A Study in Mediaeval Political Theology* (Princeton, 1957), 207–23.

[43] Sherman, "Ordo," 268. Although Sherman and others have noted that royal weddings and coronations were more often separate after 1200, the combination of marriage and en-trance ceremony occurred frequently in the principalities of northern Italy in the fifteenth century and in the Byzantine empire. This was the case with the entrance of Bona of Savoy into Milan in 1468 and the entrance of Eleonora of Aragon into Ferrara in 1473. Werner Gun-dersheimer, "Women, Learning, and Power: Eleonora of Aragon and the Court of Ferrara," in *Beyond Their Sex: Learned Women of the European Past*, ed. Patricia Labalme (New York, 1980), 42–43. See also the Pseudo-Kodinos, *Traité*.

and, at least temporarily, gendered that city female. In other words, unlike the unfortunate Griselda, whose public exposure was one of humiliation and patriarchal control, these entrance rituals both contained *and* empowered their female participants.[44] Further studies of female consort ritual will do much to elucidate the duality of ritual as limiting and empowering for women and will also contribute to a more nuanced understanding of gendered spaces and women in the public eye.

[44] In the story of Griselda, most famously told by Boccaccio, the poor bride is literally exposed by her groom when he tests her fidelity by returning her, humiliated, to her father. Giovanni Boccaccio, *The Decameron*, trans. Mark Musa and Peter Bondanella (New York, 1982), 672–81. The rituals described in this chapter resemble those described by Natalie Davis in an article on sexual inversion. Davis observes that ritual participation frequently confirmed the patriarchal model but also had the potential to challenge or undermine it. Davis, "Women on Top," in *Society and Culture in Early Modern France* (Stanford, 1965), 130–1.

CHAPTER TEN

Women's Influence on the
Design of Urban Homes

Sarah Rees Jones

The Gendering of Domestic Space

This chapter addresses the issue of how far women, and attitudes toward women, influenced the design of urban homes in later medieval England.[1] The relationship between women and the built environment was not considered in Erler and Kowaleski's 1988 collection of essays on medieval women and power, but six years later Roberta Gilchrist's book, *The Archaeology of Religious Women*, persuasively demonstrated the distinctive contribution that the study of the built environment can make to our understanding of the construction of gender identities.[2] Scholarly debates about the extent to which space was gendered have also surfaced. Barbara Hanawalt, for instance, has suggested that space was "very gendered" in the middle ages with respectable female activity being confined to such areas as the home or the cloister.[3] By contrast, Jeremy Goldberg has argued that spatial distinctions were less gendered before the second half of the fifteenth century when craft workshops became "increasingly masculinised and mercantile households increasingly feminised" as social practices changed in the later middle

---

[1] All the primary research in this article is based on the city of York between 1300 and 1500. The author wishes to thank Maryanne Kowaleski for her many editorial suggestions and criticisms, so generously given.

[2] Roberta Gilchrist, *Gender and Material Culture: The Archaeology of Religious Women* (London, 1994).

[3] Barbara Hanawalt, "At the Margins of Women's Space in Medieval Europe," in idem, *"Of Good and Ill Repute": Gender and Social Control in Medieval England* (Oxford, 1998), 70–87.

ages.[4] Evidence drawn from records of property ownership and management and from the archaeology of urban buildings can illuminate these issues.

The relationship between gender and domestic buildings is complicated by several issues, particularly the difficulty of distinguishing spaces that were specifically designed for, or used by, one sex rather than another.[5] Homes were also often workplaces, and the same room might be used for a variety of domestic and productive purposes. Smaller houses had to be especially flexible in how their space was used. The design of the timber-framed constructions so typical of the later medieval English town could also be easily and frequently changed through relatively modest building work. The constant alterations, divisions, amalgamations, and extensions of houses to suit the changing needs of their occupants means, moreover, that what now survives from the fabric of these buildings cannot give us a full insight into this past history of flexible use.

Nevertheless, archaeologists and historians have amassed a considerable body of information about changes in the design of urban houses and have ventured several hypotheses with implications for the relationship between gender and buildings.[6] The proliferation of rooms in the largest town houses, especially after c. 1400, is seen as evidence for an increase in privacy, as different rooms became increasingly specialized in use. John Schofield has suggested that this proliferation of rooms in the larger London houses enabled the clearer separation of working from domestic spaces within the home.[7] He identifies three spheres of activity: workshops and retail space, service areas (such as kitchens and pantries), and living accommodation (such as halls, chambers, and parlors), and argues that the segregation of working from domestic space anticipated, by at least a century or more, this separation of workplaces from the home that has previously been thought to be typical of early modern (or "capitalist")

[4] P. J. P. Goldberg, "Household and the Organisation of Labour in Late Medieval Towns: Some English Evidence," in *The Household in Late Medieval Cities, Italy and Northwestern Europe Compared*, ed. Myriam Carlier and Tim Soens (Louvain-Apeldoorn, 2001), 61.

[5] Jane Grenville, "Houses and Households in Late Medieval England: An Archaeological Perspective," in *Medieval Women: Texts and Contexts in Late Medieval Britain: Essays for Felicity Riddy*, ed. Jocelyn Wogan-Browne et al. (Turnhout, 2000), 309–28.

[6] Scholars have established a working typology in the design of urban buildings for the broad period, c. 1250–1600. Two trends stand out: the proliferation, by 1300, of small single- or double-roomed "cottages" as population densities in towns increased; and the growing complexity of the larger timber-framed "hall" houses constructed after c. 1250, especially after c. 1400. See Derek Keene, *Survey of Medieval Winchester*, Winchester Studies 2 (Oxford, 1985), 1:155–76; John Schofield and Alan Vince, *Medieval Towns* (London, 1994), 63–98; Jane Grenville, *Medieval Housing* (London, 1997), 157–93; Royal Commission of Historical Monuments England, *An Inventory of Historical Monuments in the City of York*, vol. 3 (Oxford, 1972), lxi–lxxviii; vol. 5 (1981), lviii–lxxiv.

[7] John Schofield, *Medieval London Houses* (New Haven, 1995), 61–93; idem, "Urban Housing in England, 1400–1600," in *The Age of Transition. The Archaeology of English Culture 1400–1600*, ed. David Gaimster and Paul Stamper (Oxford, 1997), 127–44.

modes of production.[8] We can extend this analysis to mid-sized hall houses, where it was common practice for the main residence to be located at the rear of urban plots away from the street, while the street frontage would typically be developed with a small number of shops, or workshops, or cottages for renting out to tenants. This arrangement afforded some separation of work and residence, at least for the occupants of the larger "hall" house.

Yet the separation of working from living space was subtle and gradated because some productive work, such as carding and spinning, was clearly conducted in the living space of the main house, and inventories from craftsmen's houses suggest that a wide variety of working implements and stores might be left in rooms described as parlors or chambers.[9] Moreover, the reasons for the separation were often more practical than gendered because some workplaces—such as smelting furnaces, bake houses, and even kitchens with large ovens—posed a fire risk to the home and thus were located away from the main living accommodation.[10] Thus this spatial segregation facilitated a conceptual separation not so much between domestic and working accommodation, as between the kind of work that could safely and quietly be done in the house as part of domestic life and the heavy, noisy, and dangerous work that could not. A similar polarity was also used to structure the working day. Civic and guild regulations permitted only quiet work (including office work) to be done outside set working hours, for various reasons, including the disturbance caused by heavier and noisier industrial processes.[11] In conduct literature this emphasis on

---

[8] According to Schofield these three spheres of activity might be evident both in the horizontal plan of houses, with workshops occupying one side of a courtyard and living space the other, or in the vertical plan, with workshops on the ground floor and living space above.

[9] For example, carding and spinning often took place in the halls of such houses: Goldberg, "Household and the Organisation of Labour," 66; P. M. Stell and Louise Hampson, *Probate Inventories of the York Diocese, 1350–1500* (unpublished typescript, University of York, 1999), passim.

[10] This separation was evident in middling sized and larger town houses, especially in the thirteenth and early fourteenth centuries, although these working spaces often had other rooms above that were used as living accommodation by servants and tenants. Keene, *Survey of Medieval Winchester*, 1:159; Schofield, *Medieval London Houses*, 69–71; Grenville, *Medieval Housing*, 171–74, 181–89; Sarah Rees Jones, "The Household and English Urban Government," in *The Household in Late Medieval Cities*, ed. Carlier and Soens, 87; idem, "Historical Introduction," in *Medieval Urbanism in Coppergate: Refining a Townscape*, ed. R. A. Hall and K. Hunterman, The Archaeology of York, 10/6 (London: Council for British Archaeology, 2002), 684–98. This separation also reflected the ideal spatial arrangement that was found in aristocratic houses and imitated in prestigious public town buildings such as guildhalls; see Kate Giles, "Framing Labour: The Archaeology of York's Medieval Guildhalls," in *The Problem of Labour in Fourteenth-Century England*, ed. J. Bothwell, P. J. P. Goldberg, and W. M. Ormrod (Woodbridge, 2000), 75–76.

[11] Maud Sellers, ed., *York Memorandum Book, A/Y, part 1*, Surtees Society 120, 1912 for 1911, 49, 102, 180–81; R. R. Sharpe, ed., *Calendar of Letter Books of the City of London, Letter Book K* (London, 1911), 199.

physical safety in the home was translated into an emphasis on moral safety, thus casting an implication of moral impropriety on female employment and activities located outside the home.[12]

This notional zoning of houses into safe and dangerous working areas may therefore have had some influence on popular perceptions of the gendered nature of work. The kinds of occupations most safely located in the domestic part of the house, such as spinning, carding, and some brewing, are also those most commonly associated with female employment in written sources by the second half of the fourteenth century.[13] In contrast, occupations least likely to be pursued in the domestic zone, such as heavy metal trades and baking, were less frequently practiced by women.[14] To date, however, the debate about the degree to which the physical space of the house was gendered has tended to consider only how social conduct and mores affected the design of buildings, not how the buildings shaped those mores.[15]

Yet the evidence of the buildings might indeed provide a fresh perspective on the debate as to how far gender norms were reproduced in women's and men's daily lives.[16] The ideal separation of dangerous from safe spaces was not always easily maintained in the crowded conditions of the later medieval town, especially in homes of up to about six rooms. Kitchens in particular were often integrated into the main building and sometimes located on the first floor, perhaps indicating the obvious point that of all the "dangerous" spaces, kitchens were most associated with domesticity.[17] Living quarters also extended above workshops, and work-related activities might be located in a variety of rooms in the house.[18] For all but the wealthiest sections of the urban population, therefore, the segregation of dangerous from safe working spaces may often have been difficult to achieve in practice. Yet it was still an influential ideal, and the degree to which dangerous activities had become gendered seems to have been a stronger influence still. The kitchen, for example, was the most likely of all

[12] Hanawalt, "At the Margins of Women's Space," 70–87.

[13] Simon A. C. Penn, "Female Wage-Earners in Late Fourteenth-Century England," *The Agricultural History Review* 35 (1987): 5; P. J. P. Goldberg, *Women, Work and Life-Cycle in a Medieval Economy: Women in York and Yorkshire c. 1300–1520* (Oxford, 1992), 104–37; Maryanne Kowaleski, *Local Markets and Regional Trade in Medieval Exeter* (Cambridge, 1995), 120–75. It is interesting that brewing, which done on a large scale is perhaps not so "safe," was progressively taken over by men in the later middle ages: Judith M. Bennett, *Ale, Beer, and Brewsters in a Changing World, 1300–1600* (Oxford, 1996).

[14] Ibid. Some women, however, were employed in all of these trades.

[15] Grenville, "Housing and Households," 320.

[16] Hanawalt, "At the Margins of Women's Space," 76–83; P. J. P. Goldberg, "The Public and the Private: Women in the Pre-Plague Economy," in *Thirteenth-Century England, III,* ed. P. R. Coss and S. D. Lloyd (Woodbridge, 1991), 75–89.

[17] We have evidence of this in several towns from at least the mid-fourteenth century: Keene, *Survey of Medieval Winchester,* 1:159; Schofield, *Medieval London Houses,* 69–71.

[18] See notes 9 and 10 above.

the "dangerous" spaces to be associated with the living accommodation, the smelting furnace the least likely.

The social construction of gendered space in the urban home was also a reflection of other kinds of status apart from gender. Accommodation for poorer urban dwellers—typically cottages containing no more than two rooms and built either in rows along street frontages or in crowded court-yards off the street—offered no place for specialist workshops.[19] Referred to as "rents" in York and elsewhere, these accommodations also included single rooms, often above a landlord's shops. The absence of designated workshop space in these homes also reflected the expectations of many guild masters, who not only discouraged their employees from owning their own workshops but also limited and controlled the circumstances under which male employees, both apprentices and journeymen, might marry and establish households of their own.[20] Thus the marital status of many urban employees was determined by their place in the hierarchy of labor and further reflected in and reinforced by the design of "rents." Indeed it is in these kinds of "rents" in fourteenth-century York that clusters of female tenants lived, along with the elderly of both sexes, male tenants who sold their labor to others (such as builders), men who worked in "light" trades such as barbers, and scribes, clerks, and priests. For example, in 1342 one row of cottages was tenanted by William Symes, Margaret Scrivener, Agnes de Strensall, and Elisabeth de Malton, while another was tenanted by Alice de Derlington, John Parow, Thomas de Miton, Mathilda de Bolton, Stephen the tiler, Robert the carpenter, and Robert the plasterer, and a third row by Alexander the mason, Elias the plasterer, and Sir Geoffrey Langhald, a priest.[21]

The design of both larger and smaller town houses thus influenced, and was influenced by, prevailing ideas about the social nature of labor and its relationship to gender and marital status. Men's domestic status, in terms of their ability to marry and establish a household, was as much related to their economic status as was that of women, and it influenced the style of housing provided for them. These small "rents" were, by design, a form of dormitory-style housing whose occupants were not expected to own workshops and other facilities such as kitchens.[22] As employees, and possi-

[19] See works cited in note 6 above; see also S. Rees Jones, "Property, Tenure and Rents: Some Aspects of the Topography and Economy of Medieval York" (D.Phil. diss., University of York, 1987), I, 200–6, 241–3; D. Keene, "Landlords, the Property Market and Urban Development in England," in *Power, Profit and Urban Land: Landownership in Medieval and Early Modern Northern European Towns*, ed. Finn-Einar Eliassen and Geir Atle Ersland (Aldershot, Hants., 1996), 103–6.

[20] Rees Jones, "Household and English Urban Government," 71–87.

[21] York Minster Library (YML), VC 4/1/7. However, whenever housing pressure eased or means allowed, tenants often seized the opportunity of renting more than one cottage and so enlarging their home.

[22] Martha Carlin, "Fast Food and Urban Living Standards in Medieval England," in *Food*

bly also as tenants, they were subject to the government of the master householder, who circumscribed their prospects of formal marriage.[23] The domestic status of such tenants, both male and female, thus shared many common characteristics in which their sex was less important than their place in hierarchies of labor and property ownership.[24] As the built environment facilitated the construction of normative social hierarchies, so its design could also be used to reinforce cultural aspects of gender, such as the regulation of marriage, that were not easily or simply related to biological sex.

Such overlapping gender identities could be found even in the largest houses, for not all "safe" work was associated with women. Many men also worked in the "residential" parts of the house. Office work in particular was done at home, and some middling to larger houses of the later fourteenth and fifteenth centuries contained a special room, sometimes called the "counting house," for such work.[25] Office work was undertaken by both sexes. It was expected that wives should help their husbands with the financial side of their business, as well as manage businesses on their own.[26] In normative texts, however, this work was gendered male. In Chaucer's "Shipman's Tale" it is the husband who withdraws upstairs to his counting house, just as in the household inventory of the London grocer Richard Toky in 1391 the counting house was gendered male by the full

---

and Eating in Medieval Europe, ed. M. Carlin and Joel T. Rosenthal (London, 1998), 42–44. Again, although the original design did not provide for purpose-built workshops or kitchens, it was quite possible for existing buildings to be adapted or extended to provide such facilities. A row of small cottages constructed in Aldwark, York, c. 1300 was not provided with kitchens, although some of the rooms had hearths. Larger hearths, for both domestic and "semi-industrial" purposes were inserted in the later fourteenth or fifteenth centuries: R. A. Hall et al., *Medieval Tenements in Aldwark, and Other Sites,* The Archaeology of York 10/2 (York: Council of British Archaeology, 1988), 105, 108–9.

[23] Sarah Rees Jones, "Household, Work and the Problem of Mobile Labour: The Regulation of Labour in Medieval English Towns," in *Problem of Labour in the Fourteenth Century,* ed. Bothwell, Goldberg, and Ormrod, 140–44, 152–53; idem, "Household and English Urban Government," 71–73, 80–83.

[24] Michael Rocke has further argued that similar social hierarchies in fifteenth-century Florence even influenced sexual mores. Socially dominant males were expected to be sexually dominant in both homo- and heterosexual relationships. Subservient male partners were thus, according to Rocke, "feminized" and their cultural gender was determined by social status as much as by sex; see Michael Rocke, "Gender and Sexual Culture in Renaissance Italy," in *Gender and Society in Renaissance Italy,* ed. J. Brown and Robert C. Davis (London, 1998), 150–70.

[25] Schofield, *Medieval London Houses,* 74, 233, 235.

[26] "How the Good Wife Taught Her Daughter," in F. J. Furnivall, ed., *The Babees Book,* EETS o.s., 32 (1868), 41–42; Kowaleski, *Medieval Exeter,* 124, 139, 154. For recent summaries of the debate about married women's work see S. H. Rigby, *English Society in the Late Middle Ages: Class, Society, and Gender* (London, 1995), 271–73; Mavis Mate, *Women in Medieval English Society* (Cambridge, 1999), 51–54; Caroline M. Barron, "London 1300–1540," in D. M. Palliser, ed., *The Cambridge Urban History of Britain, I, 600–1540* (Cambridge, 2000), 427–8 and works cited there.

set of armor and weapons kept there.[27] Yet the location of such work in the home rendered this a rather ambiguous and second-rate kind of masculinity, less impressive than more adventurous, outdoor, physical pursuits.[28] As Isabel Davis and Felicity Riddy have suggested, the urban home may therefore have been a location where normative gender identities were challenged and new kinds of masculinity and femininity created.[29]

Hanawalt and Goldberg's differing opinions on the extent to which the demographic and economic circumstances of the fifteenth century provoked a stronger gendering of residential and working space than earlier could thus also benefit from recognizing that simple categories of masculine and feminine are not adequate.[30] The organization of domestic space into safe and dangerous zones seems to have had a marginal influence on women's patterns of employment. Instead, the complexities of urban work (which encompassed business as well as manual skills), the cramped and crowded interiors of all but the minority of urban houses, and the hierarchical nature of the organization of labor all combined to modify simple stereotypes. Goldberg also posits that a decline in demand for urban property in the fifteenth century facilitated a reassertion of traditional values in the clearer demarcation of working and residential space. But his chronology of change in the gendering of work involves a sequence of specific changes over relatively short periods of time between 1350 and 1500, and such historical specificity is not easily related to the more static idioms of rhetoric.[31] This is as true of our consideration of the rhetoric evident in the design of buildings as of normative texts. In particular our knowledge of the date of surviving buildings is still not sufficiently specific to permit an easy correlation between changes in building type and short-term changes in social practice.[32] Before we can examine

[27] Chaucer, "The Shipman's Tale," in *The Canterbury Tales*, in *The Riverside Chaucer*, 3d ed., ed. Larry D. Benson (Boston, 1987), ll. 75–88; A. H. Thomas, ed., *Calendar of Plea and Memoranda Rolls of the City of London 1381–1412* (Cambridge, 1932), 212–3.

[28] Which may suggest why Richard Toky kept his armor in his office: to provide it with a more appropriately masculine ambience.

[29] For femininity see Felicity Riddy, "Looking Closely: Authority and Intimacy in the Late Medieval Urban Home," chap. 11 in this volume. For masculinity see Isabel Davis, "John Gower's Fear of Flying: Transitional Masculinities in the *Confessio Amantis*," paper delivered at the Conference on "Rites of Passage," York, 2001, and to be published in P. J. P. Goldberg et al., eds., *Rites of Passage* (Woodbridge: Boydell, forthcoming). I am grateful to Isabel for permission to cite her unpublished work.

[30] Hanawalt, "At the Margins of Women's Space," 76–83; Goldberg, "Public and the Private."

[31] S. H. Rigby, "Gendering the Black Death: Women in Later Medieval England," *Gender and History* 12, no. 3 (2000): 746.

[32] Much of Schofield's evidence for the use of rooms, for example, comes from surveys of London houses in the seventeenth century, while the dating of buildings by style of construction can offer only a very broad chronology that is hard to reconcile with the more precise dates used by historians. Schofield, *Medieval London Houses*, 150, 152; Grenville, "Houses and Households," 315.

the relationship between the developing form and function of urban domestic buildings further, we urgently need a program of more scientific dating, such as dendrochronology, to provide more specific dates of construction and alteration for all surviving medieval town buildings. We also need to consider more carefully the evidence not only for how buildings were designed but also for how they were actually used and developed over time.

Women and Property

So far this chapter has reviewed evidence from studies based on archaeology, on literature, and on the role of labor in the construction of households and gender identities. The remainder of this chapter offers an alternative framework for thinking about the gendering of domestic space using records of property ownership and management. Although much work has been done on the property market in late medieval English towns, almost none of it has considered patterns of housing ownership, management, and occupation from a gendered perspective. This chapter will suggest three main areas where further research might be useful in relation to the study of women in particular: home ownership, the value of the house as a medium for conveying status and identity, and the management of urban estates.

WOMEN AS HOME OWNERS

We know a great deal about the conventions of English common law concerning townswomen's ownership of property, but relatively little about the ways in which social practice conformed to the norms of the law. In theory, property taken into a marriage by a wife became part of the conjugal estate controlled by her husband, but when he died it reverted to her and to her descendants.[33] Widows' rights varied in detail from one town to another, but in many they enjoyed a right of residence in the conjugal home for life, a right to one third of their husband's property for life, and one third of their wealth in moveable goods (or one half if there were no children).[34] These conventions ensured that women who owned property could be powerful entities in the urban property market. They might be much sought after as marriage partners and could be

---

[33] S. J. Payling, "The Politics of Family: Late Medieval Marriage Contracts," in *The McFarlane Legacy: Studies in Late Medieval Politics and Society*, ed. R. H. Britnell and A. J. Pollard (Stroud, 1995), 25–26; Jennifer Ward, ed. and trans., *Women of the English Gentry and Nobility* (Manchester, 1995), 16–18, 85–90; Peter Fleming, *Family and Household in Medieval England* (Basingstoke, 2000), 36–42, 83–121. All provide lucid accounts of the legal framework of property ownership and of innovations in legal practice from the thirteenth century.

[34] Keene, *Survey of Medieval Winchester*, 1:216; Caroline Barron, "Introduction: The Widow's World," in *Medieval London Widows 1300–1500*, ed. Caroline M. Barron and Anne F. Sutton (London, 1994), xvii–xxi.

in a position to dispose of relatively large quantities of property both during their life and at their death, enjoying the patronage that went with that power.

Such bald statements of either local custom or common law paint a very deceptive picture of the actual legal position of women in relation to property in the later middle ages. For, by the early fourteenth century, many legal devices (such as entails or conditional gifts, uses, trusts, wills, and leaseholds) were developing whereby families could make much more flexible choices about the ownership and inheritance of property than the bare requirements of common or customary law would suggest.[35] In order to understand women's property interests, we therefore need to study the ways in which families exploited these choices. In England, to date, more detailed work has been done on the social use of the law among the gentry, nobility, and peasantry than among townspeople.[36] Studies of the aristocracy, in particular, suggest a severe curtailment of female property rights from the end of the fifteenth century and particularly after 1536. As yet there is nothing comparable, for an urban context, to Martha Howell's work on fifteenth- and sixteenth-century Douai in Flanders, which also traced a significant reduction of female property rights and the increasing concentration of wealth in male-dominated lineages.[37]

How were women treated in the urban property market in England? No clear trends have yet been established for urban practice, partly because records of lay property ownership in towns tend to be much more dispersed, and thus incomplete, than surviving noble or manorial archives.[38] Sufficient specific examples survive from English towns, however, to suggest that it was commonplace in England after 1300 for urban families to use the new legal devices available to alter female rights to property. In the period 1300–1450 these changes did not necessarily exclude women from the own-

[35] See note 33 above.

[36] L. Bonfield, *Marriage Settlements, 1601–1740: The Adoption of the Strict Settlement* (Cambridge, 1983); R. E. Archer, "Rich Old Ladies: The Problem of Late Medieval English Dowagers," in *Property and Politics: Essays in Later Medieval English History*, ed. A. J. Pollard (Gloucester, 1984), 15–35; R. M. Smith, "Women's Property Rights Under Customary Law: Some Developments in the Thirteenth and Fourteenth Centuries," *Transactions of the Royal Historical Society* 5th ser., 36 (1986): 165–94; idem, "Coping with Uncertainty: Women's Tenure of Customary Land in England c. 1370–1430," in *Enterprise and Individuals in Fifteenth-Century England*, ed. J. Kermode (Stroud, 1991), 43–67; Ward, *Women of the English Gentry and Nobility*, 16–18, 85–90; S. J. Payling, "Social Mobility, Demographic Change, and Landed Society in Late Medieval England," *Economic History Review* 2d ser., 45 (1992): 51–73; S. J. Payling, "The Economics of Marriage in Late Medieval England: the Marriage of Heiresses," *Economic History Review* 2d ser., 54 (2001): 413–29.

[37] Martha C. Howell, *The Marriage Exchange: Property, Social Place and Gender in Cities of the Low Countries, 1300–1550* (Chicago, 1998).

[38] However, relatively full surviving series of wills, such as those from London and York, would sustain a coherent study of patterns of bequests of property among family members, especially when (as in London) these could be combined with a full series of registered property transactions.

ership of property altogether, but may have emphasized the relationship between a woman and particular kinds of property, especially her home. The following examples from later-medieval York indicate some of the varieties of choice available to property owners in towns. They also illustrate how legal arrangements for the inheritance of property enabled people to give some concrete expression to affective relationships within the family.

In 1330 Richard Tunnock, a goldsmith, left his dwelling house in Stonegate to his wife for her life, and after her death to her son John. He left a different property to his own son, and divided the rest of his city properties between a third son and his daughter, Katherine.[39]

In 1334 John Gatenby died, but prior to his death he and his wife Agnes had used a conveyance through feofees [trustees] to ensure that the property in York brought to the marriage by Agnes was transferred into a new title owned by both of them jointly. On John's death he bequeathed this property to her, allowing inheritance by her heirs (so respecting the fact that the property was inherited from her family), but this was on the fresh condition that if Agnes were to share the tenements, having a certain couple called Alan Helk de Killum and Mathilda his wife to live with her, she was to pay John's son, William, an annual rent of twenty shillings from the property. In fact the property eventually passed to Katherine, daughter of Alan de Killum, and her husband, though we do not know how.[40]

Adam Skipwith, a skinner, bequeathed his house in Petergate to his wife, Isolde, for her life in 1337. After her death the tenement was to revert to their son Adam on condition that within two years he gave five pounds to each of his younger brothers. Further conditions described what was to happen to the estate if Adam (or the other brothers) died before their mother, the very last resort being to endow an obit for the family. Just over thirty years later, in 1370, Robert Skipwith, the youngest and only surviving son, did indeed use the property to endow an obit for his parents and two older brothers in the nearby chapel of St. Leonard's Hospital.[41]

In 1392 William Strensall, a butcher, used feofees to ensure that his wife shared his title to his houses and shops in Stonegate and Micklegate, reserving inheritance first to their joint heirs and second to his heirs alone.[42]

In 1427 William Selby, a former mayor of York, left a house each to his wife, his sister, and his niece, but the rest of his large and valuable estate to his nephew since he did not have a son.[43]

[39] YML, L2/4f, fol. 8.
[40] YML, L2/4f, fol. 16; M2/4, fol. 3; VC 3/Vi 97, 317, 427, Vo 47.
[41] BL, Cotton MS Nero D iii, fols. 183, 184v; *Calendar of Patent Rolls, 1367–70*, 399.
[42] J. W. Percy, ed., *York Memorandum Book B/Y*, Surtees Society, 186, 1973, 24–25.
[43] YML, L2/4f, fols. 227–8. Selby was dealing with a common problem in the disease-ridden later middle ages, namely the high failure rate of families to produce immediate surviving heirs: Sylvia L. Thrupp, *The Merchant Class of Medieval London* (Ann Arbor, 1948), 199–206; Payling, "Economics of Marriage," 414.

In 1465 William Vescy, a merchant, also used feofees to ensure that his house in Coney Street would be inherited after his death by his niece, her husband, and their children.[44]

These examples, together with others from London and Winchester, offer us some insight into common, though not universal, social practices that modified the more rigid provisions of common law.[45] First, they suggest that it was common for couples to establish a joint title to property that either husband or wife had brought into the marriage. The reasons for such jointures and their consequences have been much disputed,[46] but they certainly aided in the second common feature of these property arrangements, which was the tendency for couples to practice a form of partible inheritance, either dividing their properties between different children from one or more marriages (as in the case of Richard Tunnock) or providing cash settlements for younger children from the main (and perhaps only) family property (as in the case of the Skipwith family). In the example of William Strensall the jointure not only protected his new wife's claim to dower in his estate but also the rights of inheritance of the children of their marriage against the interests of children from any of Strensall's earlier or subsequent wives.[47] Without such explicit provision the claims of city orphans to their inheritance could be easily abused.

Women both gained and lost from these arrangements. Some women, such as William Vescy's niece in 1465, inherited more property than they would have done otherwise. Yet many widows lost the power to choose how to dispose of their property if its inheritance had already been agreed.[48] Presumably many mothers understood such an act of placing their children's interests before their own as an act of love. Indeed John

[44] York Memorandum Book A/Y, part 2, 231–2.

[45] Keene, Survey of Medieval Winchester, 1:190–1; D. J. Keene and V. Harding, Historical Gazetteer of London before the Great Fire. Part 1. Cheapside (Cambridge, 1987), 57 microfiches.

[46] Such jointures were often made at the time of marriage and used to safeguard a wife's right to dower in her husbands' estates: Ward, Women of the English Gentry and Nobility, 16–18; Fleming, Family and Household in Medieval England, 36–42; Keene, Survey of Medieval Winchester, 1:190; Derek Keene, "Tanners' Widows, 1300–1350," in Medieval London Widows, ed. Barron and Sutton, 6; Payling, "Politics of Family," 29–31. As Payling argues, jointures also safeguarded the inheritance of the children of a marriage and allowed the paternal grandparents to contribute to their maintenance. In urban contexts such jointures were sometimes made after marriage and seem to have involved the wife's inheritance just as often as the husband's. Thus jointures were a way in which both maternal and paternal families could provide for a couple's children.

[47] Children from any other marriages were probably provided for in separate agreements.

[48] Almost certainly, however, such arrangements were usually made with the woman's technical agreement, since without her cooperation any "conditional gift" of the property, which had created a new pattern of inheritance without her consent, could have been easily undermined by a challenge in the courts.

Lawney and his wife Margaret described their settlement of properties on the children of their marriage as a sign of "our grete love to you oure eyris."[49]

Above all, the surviving agreements suggest that great importance was attached to providing widows, but also other women, with homes. William Selby's bequests are a good example of a man providing homes for close, unmarried female relatives in addition to his wife. In this respect popular usage reinforced, and even extended, common rights of widow's bench.[50] Indeed, one obvious conclusion to draw from these property arrangements is that the first priority of landowners was to use their property in a functional way to provide their relatives, and perhaps especially their female relatives, whether married or unmarried, with a secure residence, either within or outside the main family home.[51] Families therefore invested significant amounts of money and time in transforming the abstract concepts of property law into the more social concept of a home.

CHANGES IN THE HOUSE AS AN OBJECT OF STATUS

This emphasis on the house as a home, rather than simply an investment, can be placed within a wider context of the changing social use of housing in the later medieval English town. In England a house could not be owned separately from the land on which it was built, and all titles under common law related to the ownership of the land rather than any buildings constructed on it.[52] However, in the later middle ages at least two developments in legal and social practice increasingly enabled people to value individual houses separately from the land, or burgage tenement, on which they stood. These developments focused more attention on the individual house and accelerated investment in the notion of the house as "home."

One process is of particular significance: namely, the changing relationship between families, households, and houses.[53] In thirteenth-century

---

[49] Margaret's son from an earlier marriage was separately provided for: Thrupp, *Merchant Class of Medieval London*, 123–24.

[50] See also Keene, "Tanners' Widows," 14, 16–17.

[51] The arrangements we find at death mirrored those made during life. For examples from York of unmarried women living alone or with other female relatives, see Cordelia Beattie, "A Room of One's Own? The Legal Evidence for the Residential Arrangements of Women Without Husbands in Late Fourteenth- and Early Fifteenth-Century York," in *Medieval Women and the Law*, ed. N. J. Menuge (Woodbridge, 2000), 51–55. The York evidence suggests that some unmarried men, particularly clergy, were similarly provided with accommodation by families wealthy enough to do so.

[52] S. F. C. Milsom, *Historical Foundations of the Common Law* (London, 1969), 88–126.

[53] Although we might often assume a one-to-one relationship between a single conjugal household and their house, detailed studies of patterns of occupation in continental cities have revealed different sets of relationships between families and buildings, suggesting household formation in the central middle ages differed from the late middle ages. See

English towns, the main units of land ownership in a town were *burgage tenements*: large plots of land that were developed with more than one house. The main house commonly occupied the rear portion of such a site, while the street frontage was developed with separate shops or cottages, which could be let out to provide a rental income. The relationship between the main householder and the tenants of these smaller properties, however, was not always purely commercial. In the later thirteenth century, the main burgage holder might sublet the smaller units on the plot to relatives, friends, "employees," and business associates.[54] So, for example, a father might sublet subsidiary buildings to his children, both married and single. Hence a burgage might support a small cluster of related households, each occupying separate buildings (or separate elements of a larger building) on the same site, but with shared access to some common facilities, such as the yard or court and perhaps some other facilities such as latrines or ovens. Such extended or stem-family groups may even have feasted together in the hall of the main house.

By the fourteenth century, however, such stem-family housing clusters were disappearing as familial relationships between burgage owners and their tenants became less common.[55] The reasons for the fragmentation of stem-family groups were complex, but three developments can be singled out. First were changes in the pattern of urban landownership as corporate landlords, such as the church, acquired and directly managed more freehold property and let it to any available tenant, thus disrupting familial relationships. Second, the higher death rate and higher rates of immigration to towns after the Black Death also disrupted families and promoted a higher turnover among tenants. Third, the political status attached to the ownership of burgage tenements was gradually being replaced by other forms of citizenship more likely to be associated with membership in a trade or craft, rendering the ownership of burgage plots less essential to the acquisition of social and political status within the town.[56]

By the later fourteenth century, these changes in the ownership and management of property were accompanied by the development of written leaseholds, which placed more emphasis on the design and value of the house, rather than the land on which it stood.[57] The length of these leases,

---

Diane Owen Hughes, "Urban Growth and Family Structure in Medieval Genoa," *Past and Present* 66 (1975): 3–28; F. W. Kent, *Household and Lineage in Renaissance Florence* (Princeton, 1977), 21–55, 229–30.

[54] Rees Jones, "Household and English Urban Government," 80–82, 87. Similar examples from Winchester are given in Keene, *Survey of Medieval Winchester*, 1:219, 2:746–48, 752, 755–56, 788–89.

[55] Rees Jones, "Household and English Urban Government," 83–84.

[56] Rees Jones, "Household, Work and the Problem of Mobile Labour," 133–54.

[57] In particular landlords began to develop written leaseholds for their more prosperous tenants, who might otherwise have aspired to the ownership of a "freehold" property. Keene, *Survey of Medieval Winchester*, 1:187, 191–93; Rees Jones, "Property, Tenure and

which specified the exact term of years of the tenancy and the annual rent due, tended to increase in the fifteenth century, and the lump sum paid by the tenant on entering the lease also became more important than the annual rent owed. As a result, landlords increasingly invested in building and repairing houses before letting them (to justify the large lump sum the tenant paid to enter the lease) or offered a lower rent in return for the tenant rebuilding and maintaining the property to an agreed standard. Written leases nearly always contained a building clause specifying who was responsible for maintaining the buildings to an agreed standard. Thus the real value of the property came to reside more and more in the design and building quality of the house.

While the development of the written leasehold put more emphasis on the tenancy and quality of the house, it was a form of tenancy that was generally more available to men than women because it was regarded as a financial contract. A woman would not usually be regarded as a trustworthy leaseholder because her husband or father would have to underwrite all her debts. In the twenty-eight leases surviving for the York city corporation's estate between 1415 and 1422, all the leaseholders are male and no wives are mentioned.[58]

The decline of the social importance of the burgage plot and the development of new forms of leasehold tenure thus both conspired to put more emphasis on individual buildings or houses, at the same time that social patterns of landownership among town dwellers emphasized that houses should primarily be thought of as homes rather than investments. So the individual town house, rather than the burgage plot on which it was built, increasingly became the principal spatial unit for reproducing family identity. At the same time such self-sufficient houses became more complex. Prosperous householders, in particular, needed to accommodate a greater variety of spaces under a single roof as communal facilities shared with related neighbors became less common.

If we put these hypotheses together, we can see that for those townswomen fortunate enough to be property owners, there were important changes in the social use of law in the long fourteenth century and in the social use of housing, which materially affected their relationship to their homes. These changes worked to detach women, to some extent, from wider contexts of kinship, inheritance, and estate ownership and to focus their legal interests more on the temporary possession of a single house. This was often their conjugal home, although single women were also provided with independent homes by wealthy relatives. The secure ownership of a home was especially

---

Rents," 1, 289–91; Keene, "Landlords, the Property Market, and Urban Development," 109–10. Many tenants of rented property, especially poorer ones, continued to occupy their homes "at will" without any written contract.

[58] *York Memorandum Book B/Y*, 53–67. Widows and married couples, however, did assign outstanding portions of leasehold terms.

important for the female members of prosperous families because other forms of secure tenancy, such as the written lease, were less readily available to them than to men of the same class.[59] If the hypothesis can be sustained that there was a slow and gradual transition from stem- or extended-family groups occupying adjacent parts of burgage plots to more nuclear households occupying individual houses, then such a home was also increasingly likely to be detached and self-sufficient, in both function and form, from the homes of other relatives. The "housewife" in charge of such an autonomous household would thus need to take responsibility, either with her husband or by herself, for a wide variety of domestic and business activities, as indeed conduct literature of the time suggests.[60] Here is a powerful set of circumstances for the creation of an ideal of bourgeois female domesticity, shaped by the home itself, among the wealthier artisans and merchants of the town. It suggests that the physical environment of the independently owned house provided, and was perhaps increasingly seen to provide, a safe forum for the expression of feminine identity among both married and single women of property.

WOMEN AS TENANTS

We can extend this discussion of the status of women in relation to their homes by looking at the circumstances of those women who rented rather than owned their property. In this case we are primarily discussing "tenants at will," not leaseholders; that is, those who rented accommodation without any written contract and without any rights of inheritance of their tenancy by their heirs or assigns. Such tenants are listed in detail in many surviving urban rent accounts, although these have never been subjected to a sustained analysis according to gender. The following is a preliminary analysis of the later-medieval rent accounts of the Vicars Choral of York Minster. Their estate grew from under 100 to over 200 tenancies in the city during the course of the fourteenth century, and it included both larger houses of the hall-house type and many smaller rows of cottages or rents, of which the vicars constructed large numbers in the fourteenth century.[61]

An analysis of this estate's rented properties (table 1) certainly suggests a long-term change in the status of women tenants. Table 1 shows the numbers of male and female tenants, the percentage of total rents paid by them, and the percentage of the total cost of repairs made to properties tenanted by men and women. In the fifty years before the Black Death about 20 percent of the Vicars' tenants were women, and they paid a roughly propor-

---

[59] Tenants renting property by leasehold agreements before 1450 remained a privileged minority compared to the majority of tenants who rented "at will" (see below).

[60] "How the Good Wife Taught Her Daughter"; Riddy, "Looking Closely."

[61] Rees Jones, "Property, Tenure and Rents," 1, 207–11; Nigel Tringham, ed., *Charters of the Vicars Choral of York Minster: City of York and its Suburbs to 1546*, Yorkshire Archaeological Society Record Series 148, 1993, xxxii, xxxvi.

TABLE 1. The estate of the Vicars Choral in York, 1309–1472

Year	Total rent income[a]	Total cost of repairs	Men			Women		
			% tenants	% rent paid by men[a]	% repairs (by cost)	% tenants	% rent paid by women[a]	% repairs (by cost)
1309	£17 11s 0.5d	No data	64–87[b]	56–92[b]		13–36[b]	7–44[b]	
1328/9	£39 12s 1d	£1 4s 6d	80	75	67	20	18	21
1344/5	£38 13s 3d	19s 10d	76	74	98	21	18	2
1371[c]	£64 19s 9d	£4 0s 11d[d]	75	89	58–87[c]	25	11	13[e]–42[c]
1399	£72 6s 4d	£12 5s 3d	68	80	78	32	19	20
1426	£65 4s 6d	Approx. £2 13s[f]	76	89	90	24	11	10
1449	£32 4s 9d	No data	87	90		13	10	10
1471/2	£36 7s 1d	£4 2s 3d	90	95	39 min.	10	5	0 min.

Sources: YML, VC 4/1/1, 4, 8, 14; VC 6/2/10, 26, 38, 50, 54, 63; VC 6/6/7.

Note: The percentages given in each row do not always total 100 because not all tenancies and repairs were identified by the name of the tenant. £ = pounds; s = shillings; d = pence.

[a] Based on a calculation of rents recorded as collected, not rents recorded as owed. The Vicars accounted for their rental income twice a year, at Pentecost and Martinmas. All the figures given here are therefore for rental periods of six months.

[b] Proportions of male and female tenants are uncertain in 1309 because in 23% of the tenancies (accounting for 37% rents due), the name of the current tenant is not given. The proportions given here are therefore minimum–maximum range.

[c] From 1371 it is possible to distinguish assize rents from farms, and the latter are listed here. See text for discussion.

[d] Repair accounts are for 1369, the closest available surviving record. In 29% of repairs this year, the tenants of the house were not named.

[e] All on one householder—Emma Saddler.

[f] Full repair accounts are not available because by the mid-fifteenth century many of the repairs had become the responsibility of a different official, whose accounts did not always survive.

tional amount of rent, suggesting that on average women paid roughly the same level of rents as male tenants. But in the 75 years after the Black Death, the proportion of women tenants increased, rising to 32 percent of tenants by 1399.[62] Even more significantly, their economic status had obviously declined; they provided no more than 10–20 percent of the Vicars' rent income in the period 1370–1450, despite accounting for almost one third of the tenants. Another change occurred in the mid- and later fifteenth century when there appears to have been a significant decrease in women tenants to numbers well below those of the pre-plague period. By 1471/2 just 10 percent of the Vicars' tenants were female, and they contributed only 5 percent of the Vicars' rent income.

How might we explain these three phases in the changing number and status of female tenants on a single estate? The rental evidence might be used to support the hypothesis of Jeremy Goldberg, who has argued for an increase in the employed female population of York after the Black Death as women found more opportunities for work in a period of increased demand and reduced labor supply.[63] The growth in the numbers of female tenants after the Black Death might indeed indicate a few more women, both widowed and newly arrived in the city, eking out an independent living in low-paid work and able to afford independent tenancies in the cheaper properties on the estate. Similarly the decline in the number of such female tenants later in the fifteenth century would correspond well with Goldberg's argument that women were the first to be excluded from the workforce during an economic recession.[64]

There may also be other explanations. The overall increase in the number of female tenants after 1350 was not very great, and may not be statistically significant. It can be examined in more detail by comparing the accounts for the term Martinmas 1344 to Pentecost 1345 with those for the term Pentecost 1399 to Martinmas 1399.[65] In 1344/5 there were 29 female tenants on the estate, which at that time included a total of 145 tenancies, so that women accounted for 20 percent of all tenants. By 1399 there were 63 female tenants on the estate, which by then had increased to 238 tenancies. Female tenants were thus 26.47 percent of all tenants in 1399, only a slight increase from the figure of 20 percent in 1344/5. By 1399, however, the information that we have about free tenants is unreliable and often out of date; only in the lists of tenants of "farmed" tenancies do we have even reasonably accurate information.[66] If we only count farmed tenancies, then 53

---

[62] For further discussion of these figures, see below.

[63] Goldberg, *Women, Work and Life-Cycle*, 336–9.

[64] Ibid.

[65] YML, VC 4/1/8; VC 6/2/38. Values of rents do not seem to have varied between winter and summer terms. More money was generally spent on repairs in the summer months.

[66] Before 1371 the lists of tenants do not distinguish between those who "farmed" their tenancies "at the will" of the Vicars Choral and those who were free tenants owing "assize"

out of 185 (or 31.35 percent) farmed tenancies were let to women in 1399. This figure gives us a more accurate idea of the proportion of tenants who were women and who rented houses that the Vicars were responsible for maintaining, but is not directly comparable to pre-plague figures and, taken alone, exaggerates the increase in numbers of female tenants compared to 1344/5.

Much more significant than the increase in numbers of female tenants was the decline in the value of the rents owed and paid by them after the Black Death (see table 1). Before the Black Death the ratio of female tenants to rents they paid on the Vicars' estate was approximately 1:1, suggesting that, on average, female tenants paid the same levels of rent as male tenants. By contrast, in all but one of the years of sample data for 1370–1470 this ratio was more like 2:1, suggesting a dramatic decline in the capacity of female tenants to pay rents comparable to those paid by men. Once again a direct comparison of the accounts for 1344/5 and 1399 permits a more detailed picture to emerge. In the account for 1344/5 the inclusion of both "farms" and "free" rents exaggerates the number of tenants of both sexes who paid comparatively modest rents. In that term the value of rents paid by women ranged from nothing to 26 shillings. Seven women paid rents of 10 shillings or more, and 19 women paid rents of 5 shillings or less.[67] By contrast in 1399 only two woman paid rents of 10 shillings or more, and 55 women paid rents of 5 shillings or less.[68] This evidence suggests that female tenants were increasingly concentrated in the cheapest properties, and after the plague were much less likely to take responsibility for the more expensive houses that were largely rented to male tenants. This would certainly seem to support those who argue that even if there was an increase in female employment after the Black Death, it was in lowly paid

or "free" rents, which were generally small rents of fixed value. *Free or assize rents* were often the result of rent charges or quit-rents with which properties had been burdened by previous owners, often many years earlier. The Statute of *Quia Emptores* in 1290 had outlawed the creation of most new rents of this kind, but took some time to be fully effective. Free tenants usually retained full ownership of their property, together with control of its development and letting to subtenants. The free rents from such property thus did not reflect its true value. *Farms* were more comparable to the modern concept of rent. They represented rents from houses and properties of which the landlord had full possession and control, and thus reflected the market value of the property more closely. In general the Vicars Choral strove to maximize its control of property and to reduce the number of free tenants on its estate. By 1371 their accounts listed the two kinds of rent separately, and the free rents due to them were often not collected. Before 1371 it is sometimes possible to distinguish between the two kinds of rent in the account, but often it is difficult, just as the distinction was not always clear, at this date, to contemporaries. For further discussion, see Keene, *Medieval Winchester*, 185–89, 207–14.

[67] In addition, two women paid rents of between six and nine shillings, and two women's rents were unpaid ("*vacat*").

[68] For the sake of comparison this includes both farms and assize or free rents, but only five women were listed as free tenants in 1399. In addition six women paid rents of between six and nine shillings.

and relatively precarious employment.[69] Yet we have already seen that the overall increase in the numbers of women tenants was not great. What really requires explanation is the decline in their economic status.

The declining economic status of female tenants in post-plague York raises more questions than can be answered easily in a short essay, but two aspects of the local economy should, at least, be indicated. Although the period between the mid-1360s and mid-1380s was one of rental inflation on the Vicars' estate, from the 1390s the Vicars increasingly struggled to find tenants, and rents in general were progressively reduced.[70] The Vicars' efforts to find tenants after the plague may have prompted them to cast a wider net and draw from a wider social group than previously. Certainly by 1399 the Vicars were letting to women who were unable to pay the rent, as in that year three women were excused payment of their rent because they were poor.[71] Thus, poorer women may simply have been more visible in the rent accounts by 1400, rather than more numerous in the city. The higher profile of poorer women appearing in the rentals might also account for the numbers of these tenants who can be identified as involved in prostitution around c. 1400.[72]

None of this, however, explains why the numbers of women renting more expensive properties in the city also declined. It may be that local economic factors were important in determining their life opportunities. During much of the first half of the fourteenth century, York benefited economically from of its role as the royal center of operations for the wars against Scotland.[73] In the late fourteenth century a growth in cloth exports also boosted the local economy,[74] but the evidence of these rentals may indicate that opportunities for female employment in the cloth industry, later in the century, were less financially advantageous to them (and demanded simpler accommodation) than the extra work (such, perhaps, as brewing) available at least to some women while York was the temporary center of royal government earlier in the century. Different kinds of work were not

69 Mate, *Women in Medieval English Society*, 28–30 and works cited there.

70 Rees Jones, "Property, Tenure and Rents," 212–3, 215–7, 236–58. This chronology of decline corrects that found in J. N. Bartlett, "The Expansion and Decline of York in the Later Middle Ages," *Economic History Review* 2d ser., 12 (1959–60): 17–33. This initial increase and eventual fall in rental values also occurred on many rural estates when poor, "landless" men and women initially took up vacant rural holdings in the first decades after the Black Death; see J. L. Bolton, *The Medieval English Economy 1150–1500* (London, 1980), 209–11.

71 YML, VC 6/2/38.

72 The replacement of male by female tenants was particularly noticeable in the "rents" owned by the Vicars in Aldwark in the later fourteenth century. YML, VC 4/1/1–14, VC 6/2/10, 26, 38, 50, 54, 63. Cf. Goldberg, *Women, Work and Life-Cycle*, 151.

73 Bartlett, "The Expansion and Decline of York," 1–3; W. M. Ormrod, "Competing Capitals? York and London in the Fourteenth Century," in *Courts and Regions in Medieval Europe*, ed. S. Rees Jones, R. Marks, and A. J. Minnis (Woodbridge, 2000), 81–88.

74 Goldberg, *Women, Work and Life-Cycle*, 39–81; Jennifer I. Kermode, *Medieval Merchants: York, Beverley, and Hull in the Later Middle Ages* (Cambridge, 1998), 265–75.

equally available to all kinds of women. If the ability of women "house-holders" to earn a living was at least as good, and possibly even better, before the Black Death as after, then this has major implications for our understanding of the history of marriage. Goldberg's argument that expanded work opportunities encouraged women to postpone marriage in the period after the Black Death would also need to be considered in the period before the Black Death, at least in York where we also now have some evidence of numbers of moderately prosperous women apparently renting houses independently on terms comparable to male tenants.[75] This evidence suggests that, whether married or not, significant numbers of women took primary responsibility for the tenancy of their own homes, both before and after the Black Death.[76]

The continued and substantial decline of the status and then the number of female tenants over the later fourteenth and fifteenth centuries can also be placed in the context of the other social customs relating to the housing of women that we have identified. The general fall in the status of women tenants may reflect, for instance, the familial preference among wealthier property-owning families for turning women into homeowners whenever financially possible, in a legal climate that made it difficult for such women to rent houses on secure leasehold tenancies. But this new legal development may also, in turn, have actively contributed to the declining status and numbers of women tenants on the Vicars' urban estate.

We can also use estate accounts as evidence for the choices that landlords or female tenants made in maintaining properties rented by women. The overall impression is that the status of a tenant was more important than their gender in determining the amount of money that the vicars spent on repairing their property (see table 1). As the status of female tenants declined, however, the sums spent on their repairs may be perceived as more gendered. Other than this, there is little clear indication that the kinds of repairs to female-tenanted property were different from the kinds of repairs made to the property of male tenants. There are two tantalizing features,

[75] The proportion of female tenants prior to 1350 fits the model for a "northwestern" European marriage regime if one assumes that most of them were single, especially since the number of single women listed as tenants must have been significantly less than the number of women without husbands. Maryanne Kowaleski, "Singlewomen in Medieval and Early Modern Europe: The Demographic Perspective," in *Singlewomen in the European Past, 1250–1800*, ed. Judith M. Bennett and Amy M. Froide (Philadelphia, 1999), 45. But see note 76 below.

[76] The marital status of female tenants is rarely indicated in these accounts. A few are described as widows, but usually only when a wife has taken over a tenancy from a recently deceased husband. Others may also have been widowed, married, never married, or in some less formal partnership. For some of the poorer women listed in the accounts it may be unsafe to make assumptions about "marital" status based on an understanding of marriage customs in wealthier sections of society. If the woman is named as the tenant, however, it suggests that she was considered responsible for the rent, whatever her marital status.

though, which suggest an agenda for future research. In 1399 the Vicars spent a large sum on repairs, which was concentrated on upgrading their tenants' houses with three items in particular: new barrel wells, tile and plaster chimneys, and new locks for doors.[77] The wells and chimneys were constructed for tenants of both sexes, but the vast majority were built for male-headed households. New locks on doors, a cheaper repair, were also provided for both sexes but here the overwhelming majority were provided for women.[78] Does this suggest that if we looked in even more detail, female preferences in house building might emerge from the records?

The repair accounts also suggest that different levels of privacy were enjoyed in different kinds of homes. The Vicars' estate contained both larger homes, of the type likely to include a hall, and rows of cottages. Part of their responsibility as landlords was to erect and maintain privies and wells. The larger houses were equipped with their own privies and wells, but the rows of cottages were usually provided with communal facilities such as the communal latrines built for a row of small houses in Stonegate in 1328–9, or the communal well constructed for another court of houses in Goodramgate in 1364.[79] The tenants of such properties, who included a large proportion of females after 1350, thus enjoyed less privacy and a more "communal" way of life. Indeed, the desire to fit such houses with locks may suggest a defensive reaction against this lack of privacy.[80]

Conclusion

Steven Rigby has convincingly suggested that we ought to consider women as a fourth estate in medieval society, that "all women were inferior . . . to men of their own class." He further suggests that differences between women were derived entirely from their marital status and the status of the men on whom they depended. Women's place within a "household" further isolated individual women, preventing the formation of a common identity.[81] Rigby's conclusions are derived mainly from studies of female labor. If we consider the status of women from the perspective of the built environment, however, a slightly different conclusion may be drawn.

The rent accounts for the Vicars' estate in York suggest that relatively large numbers of women were regarded as independent tenants both before and after the Black Death, although there was a significant decline in their economic status after 1350 and in their numbers from the mid-fifteenth century. Until we have comparable data from other towns, it seems

[77] YML, VC 6/2/38.
[78] Of course this difference also reflects the simple fact that the landlord spent more on improvements to expensive properties than to cheap ones.
[79] YML, VC 6/2/10, VC 6/10.
[80] I am grateful to Maryanne Kowaleski for this observation.
[81] Rigby, *English Society*, 278–80.

likely that these variations over time reflected variations in the local economy, with different kinds of women prospering in different periods, perhaps depending on the kinds of employment available to them. We do not know their marital status, but we do find that urban families who owned property were willing to set up single women as well as widows as householders. This desire of independent women to run their own homes may be reflected in the high take-up of cheap tenancies by poorer women after 1350. The perceived lower status of female tenants in this later period, combined with the obstacles independent women faced in entering secure leaseholds, may have further increased the preference for home ownership among slightly wealthier artisan and mercantile women and further reduced the numbers of such women appearing in rent accounts, especially as overall demand for property diminished in the fifteenth century.

Women as homemakers were a significant feature of the later medieval townscape whether they "owned" or rented their home, and whether they were married or not. Despite a cultural preference for male heirs, families seem to have been anxious to provide homes for female relatives as well. Yet the type of house occupied would significantly affect a woman's potential earnings. Larger houses offered more opportunities for subletting and for sustaining a greater variety of productive activities than smaller ones did. This was equally true for both sexes. The occupants of small "rents" were particularly disadvantaged, and indeed the occupation of such houses may even have carried a social stigma that inhibited both business and marital opportunities for men as well as women.[82] In this respect, the division of interest between larger and smaller householders created a social divide that was the product of a well-established and politicized hierarchy of labor that inhibited the articulation of the common interests of women just as it did those of men.

Certainly women's exclusion from political activity, strong cultural incentives to marry, and their role as mothers all substantially limited women's economic potential, individually and collectively. The presence of these other limitations, however, may have rendered the control of a home even more important for women than for men. Homes provided security and status and, for some, the means to earn a living. The independent control of that home thus empowered some women. It provided them with a small alternative to economic dependence on a man. Yet just as their homes, rather than their marriages, gave some women status, the design of those homes also reinforced differences of power, wealth, and opportunity among women. Class was more important than gender in the design of the later medieval urban home.

[82] Rees Jones, "Household and English Urban Government," 85–86.

CHAPTER ELEVEN

Looking Closely: Authority and Intimacy in the Late Medieval Urban Home

Felicity Riddy

Public and Private Authority

A parliamentary decree of 1461, aiming to control the antisocial pastimes of dicing and playing at cards, ordered that "noon Hosteler, Taverner, Vitailler, Artificer or Housholder, or other, use any such Pley, or suffre to be used any such Pley in their houses, or elleswhere where they may lette [prevent] it."[1] Household heads, that is, were required by central government to act as sources of public authority and agents of good order. In the course of the fourteenth and fifteenth centuries, English towns increasingly placed obligations of this kind on householders. The ancient system known as Frankpledge, by which groups of men stood surety for one another's conduct, had been organized on a neighborhood basis; that is, people's behavior was felt to be the responsibility of the locality. This Frankpledge system remained in place in urban communities throughout the medieval period.[2] However, with the development of craft guilds during the fourteenth and fifteenth centuries, a new source of urban authority emerged. Increasingly, individual guild masters were held to be responsible for the orderliness of their households and were answerable to the civic authorities for the conduct of household members, which included wives, children, apprentices, and servants.[3] This authority extended even to the

---

[1] *Rotuli Parliamentorum; ut et Petitiones, et Placita in Parliamento*, 6 vols. (London, 1832), 5:448. I am grateful to Dr. Cordelia Beattie, University of Edinburgh, for this reference.

[2] See W. A. Morris, *The Frankpledge System* (London, 1901).

[3] Sarah Rees Jones, "The Household and English Urban Government," in *The Household in Late Medieval Cities, Italy and Northwestern Europe Compared*, ed. Myriam Carlier and Tim Soens (Louvain-Apeldoorn, 2001), 71–87.

212

inside of the home, as the parliamentary decree shows. Looking at this shift, we might say that by the late middle ages in England the government of towns had brought patriarchal household heads into being, or at least made them visible by giving them a public authority.

The fact that the English words "houshold" and "housholder" only came into use in the latter part of the fourteenth century seems to confirm this; the first recorded instances are from the 1380s.[4] "Houshold" partly displaces the older French-derived term "meinie," which was applied to collectivities of people who were not necessarily linked to a place; by contrast "houshold" was from the first associated with a house, and thus with the idea of co-location, if not co-residence. There is no single term used of the person in charge of a "meinie," which suggests that "housholder" was coined for a new function—perhaps the maintenance of order with which I began. It certainly seems to have been most frequently recorded in official contexts, as in "The Baillifs and the Comens have chosen . . . xxiii worthi Burgeys, receauntz [resident] housholders."[5] These worthy burgesses were men of substance, who no doubt lived in the multiroom timber-frame houses—with their own kitchens, parlors, business premises, and privies—that must have been so visible a feature of the late medieval urban scene.[6] These were employers as well as family men, who mostly worked from home alongside the other members of their households. Working from home was a mark of status that distinguished the householder from the day-laborer who, as Charles Phythian-Adams has pointed out, probably spent most of his waking hours working away from his one- or two-room cottage and his family.[7] Urban householders, then, were domestic men and, from the civic perspective, figures of authority.

The civic requirement for visible forms of authority (also buttressed at a national level, as the quotations above show), was lent intellectual support by the assumptions of Aristotle's *Politics* and *Ethics* and Augustine's *City of God*, which were the subject of extensive academic commentary from the thirteenth century on.[8] For both Aristotle and Augustine the distinction between the *oikos* or *domus* (household) and the *polis* or *civitas* (political community) was fundamental to their analyses of social living. For Aristotle, the household comes into being to supply the daily needs of the family for survival; the state then comes into being when families band together, first

---

[4] See *Middle English Dictionary, Part H.5*, ed. Sherman M. Kuhn and John Reidy (Ann Arbor, 1967), 1010–12: "hous-hold n." and "hous-holder(e n."

[5] *Rotuli Parliamentorum*, 5:121.

[6] See Jane Grenville, *Medieval Housing* (London, 1997), 157–93; John Schofield, *Medieval London Houses* (New Haven, 1995), 51–53; Sarah Rees Jones, "Women's Influence on the Design of Urban Homes," chap. 10 in this volume.

[7] Charles Phythian-Adams, *Desolation of a City: Coventry and the Urban Crisis of the Late Middle Ages* (Cambridge, 1979), 80–81, 88.

[8] See M. S. Kempshall, *The Common Good in Late Medieval Political Thought* (Oxford, 1999). I am indebted to Matthew Kempshall for advice on late medieval Augustinianism.

in villages and then in larger communities for the sake of the good life, which is a higher order of existence. Aristotle describes rule in the household, though, in terms of rule in the state: the household head, he explains, exercises a constitutional rule over his wife, a royal rule over his children, and a tyrannical rule over his slaves.[9] So although they have different functions and although the state has precedence over the household, it is assumed that authority within the home is analogous to authority in the public sphere. Similarly, for Augustine the household is a microcosm of the city: "domestic peace has reference to civic peace: that is, the ordered concord of domestic rule and obedience has reference to the ordered concord of civic rule and obedience."[10] And both writers assume that the head of the household will be male; as Aristotle puts it, "the male is by nature superior, and the female inferior; and the one rules, and the other is ruled; this principle, of necessity, extends to all mankind."[11]

A modern master narrative of the home that also draws on the public-private distinction is that of Georges Duby in *A History of Private Life II: Revelations of the Medieval World*, published in English in 1987.[12] Duby sees the public-private distinction as demarcated by "different kinds of power":

> Think of two realms in which peace and order were maintained in the name of different principles. . . . In one group the purpose was to govern the *res publica*, the *populus*, the group of men (women had no place here) who, assembled, constituted the state, administered communal property, and shared responsibility for the common good. . . . Its administration is the responsibility of the magistrate, . . . of the king and the law.[13]

The other realm was that of the *res familiaris*, "the cornerstone of family life, where family refers to a community distinct from the community of all the people, defined by its natural meeting place, or perhaps I should say its natural place of confinement, the house. This private community was governed not by law but by 'custom.' "[14]

In fact, *A History of Private Life II* forgets about the public sphere after the introduction and focuses, as its title suggests it will, only on the *res familiaris*. Moreover, representing the household as a private community enables the book to develop on sociological rather than political lines. The

---

[9] Aristotle, *The Politics and the Constitution of Athens*, ed. Stephen Everson (Cambridge, 1996), I. 12: 27.

[10] Augustine, *The City of God Against the Pagans*, ed. and trans. R. W. Dyson (Cambridge, 1996), 945.

[11] Aristotle, *Politics*, ed. Everson, I. 5: 17.

[12] Georges Duby, "Introduction: Private Power, Public Power," in *A History of Private Life*, vol. 2, *Revelations of the Medieval World*, ed. Philippe Ariès and Georges Duby, trans. Arthur Goldhammer (Cambridge, Mass., 1987), 6–7. Originally published as *Histoire de la vie privée*, vol. 2, *De l'Europe féodale à la Renaissance* (Paris, 1985).

[13] Ibid., 7.

[14] Ibid., 7.

overarching narrative is of the processes by which a convivial and sociable kind of domestic living became increasingly individualistic and solitary, both literally and metaphorically, in the course of the later middle ages. It is about how, from the fourteenth century on, various new kinds of privacy are discernible within the household, including an inner privacy of the self. The strain of reconciling political and sociological models of publicness and privateness is shown in a passage in which Duby talks about the limitations of the customary authority of the head of the household, conceived of typically as male. He suggests that various kinds of countervailing autonomy were available to the wife and children; for example, canon law required a daughter to give her consent to marriage and so she could, theoretically, thwart her father's will. Wives, Duby argues, had other kinds of autonomy: "Masculine power ended on the threshold of the room in which children were conceived and brought into the world and in which the sick were cared for and the dead washed. In this most private sanctum, women rule over the dark realm of sexual pleasure, reproduction and death."[15] This view seems to be the result of trying to bring together the two different kinds of privacy he has evoked: a spatial one to do with separateness and a discursive one to do with power. It produces a bizarre variant of the separate-spheres model familiar from the nineteenth century, with a boundary between male and female zones drawn at the chamber door. I find it hard to accept Duby's view that male power ceased in the bedroom—as if this were not the quintessential domain of the phallus; as if marital sex was never coerced by the husband, with the support of canon legal thinking on the marriage debt; as if women's authority in relation to medical care was not contested by male experts with their apprenticeships or their university degrees; as if women's unpaid and therefore unregulated work in the home was only a source of autonomy and not also of exploitation. Duby's line of argument seems to collude with ancient and medieval ideologues by drawing the public-private divide in such a way as to contain women within the home, at the same time representing their sway over the dark realm of the chamber in terms that suggests they are a kind of collective Morgan la Fée. This article attempts to demystify female autonomy by suggesting an alternative view: that the circumstances of everyday domestic living—especially urban living—mitigated any simple model of male power and female subordination.

Home and Intimacy

By stressing "the circumstances of domestic living," I want to draw attention to what it means for a group of people to live in close proximity with one another. This is an area from which medievalists can learn from a

---

[15] Ibid., 80.

strand of modern research into contemporary housing that has been influenced by the "embodied turn" in sociology.[16] Urban domestic living is not simply the close proximity of neighbors, which in the fourteenth and fifteenth centuries was to some extent, at least, governed by its own conventions and laws, but the intertwined living of people of different generations who ate, slept, and worked alongside one another in the multiroom houses to which I have already referred that were a marked feature of the late medieval urban scene. Such houses were not particularly spacious; they were multiroom only in comparison with the one- or two-room houses of the poor and are characterized by modern historians of housing as "medium-sized."[17] They ranged in size from around four to around eight rooms on two or three floors. The habits of living that developed in these houses, which might be characterized as bourgeois domesticity, can be understood in the fourteenth and fifteenth centuries as a process—always ongoing and always at risk of defeat—of ordering and giving meaning to the messy and embodied involvement of people with one another in the home. As Craig M. Gurney points out,

> home (in various unique ways) accommodates bodies. The word accommodating . . . denote[s] compromise and reconciliation as well as . . . dwelling or residing. This is to draw attention to the fact that we train, manage, regulate, discipline and present our bodies at home in ways we cannot elsewhere.[18]

The multiroom urban homes I have in mind were places in which people shared beds and bedrooms; in which trestle tables were ubiquitous, and rooms rapidly rearranged for work, eating, and leisure; in which there may have been separate privies but only partial privacy, at best, for attending to personal hygiene. Poor families, crammed into one room, must have lived much of their lives outdoors, buying ready-cooked food because they did not have kitchens, using public privies, and letting their children play in the street. The larger houses of the gentry allowed space between people within the home, so that close-up living—living on top of one another—was probably not how everyday family life was experi-

---

[16] See, e.g., Craig M. Gurney, "Accommodating Bodies: The Organization of Corporeal Dirt in the Embodied Home," in *Organizing Bodies: Institutions, Policy and Work*, ed. Linda McKie and N. Watson (Basingstoke, 2000), 55–78. I am grateful to Professor Janet Ford, Center for Housing Policy, University of York, for alerting me to this work.

[17] See Schofield, *Medieval London*, 51–53; W. A. Pantin, "Medieval English Town-House Plans," *Medieval Archaeology* 6–7 (1962–63): 202–39. Pantin's right-angle hall house seems to be reflected in Schofield's Type 3 house, as Jane Grenville points out; see *Medieval Housing*, 169. See also Rees Jones, "Women's Influence," chap. 10 in this volume.

[18] Gurney, "Accommodating Bodies," 55.

enced at the aristocratic level.[19] The inhabitants of middling-sized houses knew the embodiment of the people they lived with from very close up and developed value systems relating to intimacy in order to deal with this.

Intimacy is regarded by some historians, especially following Lawrence Stone, as a marker of modernity.[20] This chronology does not seem to be borne out by the medieval meanings of the word "homly," the native equivalent of domestic, which suggest that the home, whether or not it was also a workplace or a shop, was understood as an intimate sphere in which private identities were formed. The meanings of "homly" cluster round ideas of familiarity, closeness, affection, privacy, intimacy, and everydayness. Its opposite is "strange"; in a passage in the Middle English translation of Suso's *Orologium Sapientiae*, written around 1400, this is brought out explicitly: "Sumtyme . . . þou art so homelye, so godelye and . . . sumtyme in contrarye maner so strange & so ferre."[21] The contrast here is not between home and work or home and the street, but between home and estrangement. If, as Richard Sennett suggests, the city is the place where strangers meet, then home is where one is known.[22] We might think of the way Nicholas Love describes the Blessed Virgin at the marriage at Cana in the early fifteenth-century *Mirror of the Blessed Life of Jesus Christ*: "she . . . was þe eldest and most worþi of þe þre sisters. And þerfore she was not byden nor cleped [summoned] þidere as oþere strangeres weren, bot she was þere in hir sistere house homely as in hir owne house, ordeynyng, and mynistryng as maistresse þerof."[23] Not a stranger or even a guest, she belongs there by right of close kinship, "homely as in her owne hous": she does not have to be invited; she knows where everything is kept, and she can tell the kids to shut up and play elsewhere as if they were her own (because this is what "ordeynyng and mynistryng as maistresse therof" presumably includes).

The intimacies of home were often specifically loving; *The Book of Vices and Virtues* says, "Þe ȝifte of pite . . . is swetnesse of hert, þat makeþ a man swete and debonere [meek], homliche, ful of charite."[24] The mystic Julian of Norwich talks of having "a gostly sight of [God's] homely louyng. I saw

[19] See C. M. Woolgar, *The Great Household in Late Medieval England* (New Haven and London, 1999), 46–82; Mark Girouard, *Life in the English Country House: A Social and Architectural History* (Harmondsworth, 1980), 29–80.

[20] Lawrence Stone, *The Family, Sex and Marriage in England, 1500–1800* (London, 1977).

[21] C. Horstmann, "Orologium Sapientiae or the Seven Poyntes of Trewe Wisdom, aus MS Douce 114," *Anglia* 10 (1888): 323–89, at 332.

[22] Richard Sennett, *The Fall of Public Man* (New York, 1974), 48.

[23] *Nicholas Love's Mirror of the Blessed Life of Jesus Christ: A Critical Edition Based on Cambridge University Library Additional MSS 6578 and 6686*, ed. Michael G. Sargent (New York, 1992), 81.

[24] *The Book of Vices and Virtues*, ed. W. N. Francis, EETS o.s., 217 (London, 1942), 143.

that he is to vs all thing that is good and comfortable to our helpe."[25] In religious writings Jesus is the exemplar of an affectionate domestic familiarity in his relations with his followers: "hou louely he spekes to hem, and how homely he sheweþ him self to hem, drawyng hem to his loue withinforþe by grace and without forþe by dede, familiarely ledyng hem to his modere house, and also goyng with hem oft to hir duellynges."[26] Here "homely" is part of the complex of love, closeness, and domestic living.

Plainness and directness seem also to have been hallmarks of homeliness. It quite often seems to be positioned against elegance, sophistication, or fashion: Chaucer uses "homliche" to mean straightforwardly;[27] Hoccleve uses "hoomlynesse" to mean lack of manners;[28] it can collocate with "boistous" and "rude."[29] In the *Alliterative Morte Arthure* of around 1400, Arthur meets Sir Cradock on the road to Rome, in pilgrim's garb "with hatte and with heyghe schone homely and rownde" (3485).[30] These are not the pointy shoes fashionable in England at the end of the fourteenth century, but serviceable walking boots with room for the toes to spread. Not just shoes, but hairstyles as well, could be "homli": in his translation of Bartholomaeus Anglicus, Trevisa tells the reader that "Such a wif is worthi to be ipreised þat fondiþ more to plese here housbonde wiþ heer homlich iwounde þan wiþ heer gailiche ipinchid."[31] [Such a wife is more deserving of praise who tries to please her husband with hair plainly wound than with hair showily crimped.] Home was the everyday, where you were among your own ordinary things: the worn cushions, the broken mazer, the dog's chain, the birdcage for a thrush, the cloak trimmed with fitchew fur, the piece of plate with the greyhound feet, the bedcover with stars on it, the rat trap, the primer, the bronze jars, the child's cart, and the child's chair. All these things are named in York domestic inventories of the four-

[25] *A Book of Showings to the Anchoress Julian of Norwich*, ed. Edmund Colledge and James Walsh, Studies and Texts 35, 2 vols. (Toronto, 1978), 1:299.

[26] *Nicholas Love's Mirror*, ed. Sargent, 80.

[27] Geoffrey Chaucer, "Boece," III, pr.12, 199: "And thise thinges ne schewedest thou naught with noone resouns ytaken fro withouten, but by proeves in cercles and homliche knowen"; see *The Riverside Chaucer*, ed. Larry D. Benson et al. (Oxford, 1988). All Chaucer quotations are from this edition.

[28] "Letter of Cupid," ll. 132–33: "But on madding he be so deepe broght, / Þat he shende al with open hoomlynesse [a noticeable lack of manners]"; see *Hoccleve's Works*, vol. 2, *The Minor Poems*, ed. I. Gollancz, EETS extra ser., 73 (London, 1925).

[29] E.g., *Nicholas Love's Mirror*, ed. Sargent, 150–51: "men vsen in bodily fedyng and festes, first to be seruede with buystes [crude] and homely metes, and after with more delicate and deynteþes"; *A Dialogue Between Reason and Adversity*, ed. F. N. M. Diekstra (Nijmegen, 1968), 13: "Homly folk and rude brouȝt me in to þis worlde."

[30] *King Arthur's Death: The Stanzaic Morte Arthur and Alliterative Morte Arthure*, ed. Larry D. Benson (Exeter, 1986).

[31] *On the Properties of Things: John Trevisa's Translation of Bartholomaeus Anglicus, De Proprietatibus Rerum*, ed. M. C. Seymour et al., 2 vols. (Oxford, 1975), 1:309.

teenth and fifteenth centuries.[32] We can begin to see from all this how homeliness might offer a position for anticourtly critique; that is, the urban home might offer a critical perspective on the public sphere.

It is worth considering the kinds of feelings and attitudes associated more generally with the home in fourteenth- and fifteenth-century England. The word "home" in Middle English may be a town or a country, or more generally the place where you were born, the place you go back to at the end of your journey or at the end of the day. Home was both public and private; kings and armies go home to England, while husbands go home to their wives. Home in the private sense was a house, the house that seems to have been central to the idea of the household; "house and home" often collocate in Middle English, though they do not mean quite the same thing. "House" is the building; "home" is the focus of feelings associated with where you belong and what you are most attached to. So the thirteenth-century *Vices and Virtues* can speak of those who, in hope of Christ, forsake "fader and moder, wif and children, hus and ham, and alle worldes wele and blisse."[33] Family, home, and happiness are all wrapped up together here in a bundle of feelings about what it is that the apostolic life forgoes: settledness, intimacy, the most archaic forms of relationship, content. The grim thirteenth-century poem, "The latemest day," warns the man who is too attached to the things of this world that "al hit wole a-gon / Is lont and is lude, is hus and is hom."[34] [It will all pass: his land and his property, his house and his home.] The seemingly stable constituents of identity—what you own, where you live—are already on their way. These early examples both come from the writings of clerics, men exiled from family life, who, we assume, left the parental home young and did not replicate it themselves. So perhaps in clerical discourses "home" has a particular force as a signifier of what is most painful to give up.

But of course it was not only clerics who left home: The thirteenth and early fourteenth centuries were a period of massive urban growth sustained by immigration. After the Black Death and the later recurrences of plague, towns maintained their populations—insofar as they did—only through a continual influx of incomers. Bearing this in mind may help us to identify specifically urban senses of home. Whatever adventurousness or desperation or longing it was that drove people from their birthplaces must also have ensured that many never went back because what they went to towns to find could not be found where they were born. Often the more successful townspeople remembered in their wills the places they

---

[32] *Probate Inventories of the York Diocese, 1350–1500*, ed. and trans. P. M. Stell and Louise Hampson (unpublished typescript, York, 1999).

[33] *Vices and Virtues: Being a Soul's Confession of Its Sins*, ed. F. Holthausen, EETS o.s., 89 and 159 (London, 1888–1921), 1:35.

[34] *English Lyrics of the Thirteenth Century*, ed. Carleton Brown (Oxford, 1932), 46.

had come from and the people they had left behind. Their memories of home seem to be not merely a matter of retrospection but of nostalgia, structured on an awareness of loss, especially sharp on the deathbed when you know that you will never take the road home again. The London merchant Richard de la Pole, less notorious than his younger brother William, left his native Hull in Yorkshire for London in 1329, made his fortune there, and retired to a manor in Northamptonshire. When he died in 1345 he left money in his will for mending the roads north out of London and west out of Hull.[35] This seems a strikingly ambivalent good work: it enables the ambitious and dissatisfied to take the same route out that he had taken years before, but at the same time it enables the homesick to go home.

Authority and Intimacy

Turning to the home itself, we can find many examples that represent it from the male point of view as the place where one's wife and children are. It is the place where the woman is naturalized as the fulfiller of bodily needs: not a question of academic theory or even of morality but a matter-of-fact acceptance of the everyday state of affairs: "And so he went home and sett hym down to his meatt, and his wife sett bread befor hym"; "And þis done, onone hur husband come home fro huntyng and bad hur oppyn hym þe chamber dure, and he wold lay hym down and slepe a while"; "Hur husbond come home passand seke and bad hur make hym a cuche þat he myght lig on."[36] In these passages the roles of wife and husband are not transferable: she is not coming home, expecting him to have made a meal for her; she does not tell him to open the chamber door or make up the couch so that she can sleep. He is mobile, she is stationary; he gives orders; she sees to the needs of the body: food and rest. These quotations come from preachers' exempla—the stories used to enliven sermons—and have an unusual engagement with the familiar and everyday, which is of course why they are used. But we need to be most wary of the everyday; this is where the discourses of domination and power are so familiar that they can go unnoticed. So my point is not that women did not leave the home, that men never opened chamber doors for women or gave them food or looked after them when they were sick; it is simply that the language of everyday life was saturated with a sense that women, home, and bodily needs go together and that these are what make the pull of home so strong for men. The same familiar scene is depicted in the late-fifteenth-century poem *The Castle of Labour*, which is a dream-allegory about the dangers of idleness and its consequence, poverty. Toward the end of the

[35] *Testamenta Eboracensia or Wills Registered at York, Part I*, ed. James Raine, Surtees Society 4 (London, 1836), 8.
[36] *An Alphabet of Tales*, ed. Mary Macleod Banks, 2 vols., EETS o.s., 126, 127 (London, 1904, 1905; reprinted as 1 vol., Millwood, N.Y., 1987), 26, 393, 117.

poem, the narrator leaves the nightmare castle of labor and enters the house of rest, which also turns out to be his own home:

> I sawe rest whiche dyde me abyde
> Within his hous withouten blame,
> And my wyfe, on the other syde,
> Dressed my souper without dyffame.
> There rested I in goddes name,
> Famylyarly, nat as a straunger,
> Thankynge god of inmortall fame
> That I escaped was that daunger.
>
> Unto the table I wente that tyde,
> Entendynge to soupe without outrage.
> My wyfe sate on the other syde,
> After my custome and olde vsage.
> There had we brede, wyne and potage,
> And of flesshe a smale pytaunce;
> Without to any hurte or damage
> We souped togyder at our pleasaunce.
>
> My wyfe voyded the table clene
> And vnto me aprochde nere.
> Than on my shulder dyde she lene,
> After hyr custome and manere.
> There tolde I her of the daunger
> Whiche I was in the nyght before,
> How that she slepte with mery chere
> The whyle that I was troubled sore.[37]

Home means the known place, rest, a wife preparing a simple meal and clearing it away, familiar routines, small gestures of intimacy. The woodcut that illustrates this moment in Pynson's 1505 edition adds an eager dog watching his master eat while his mistress tends a pot on the fire.[38] This ideology has a powerful institutional underpinning: "Bracton," the great legal systematization of the thirteenth century, writing of the age of legal maturity for women of the propertied class says: "A woman may be of full age whenever she can and knows how to order her house and do the things that belong to the arrangement and management of a house, provided she understands what pertains to 'cove and keye,' which cannot be before her fourteenth or fifteenth year since such things require discretion and under-standing."[39] Understanding "what pertains to 'cove and keye'" means

---

[37] Alexander Barclay, *The Castle of Labour*, 2d ed. ([London]: Richard Pynson, 1505), sig. Iii–Iiii. My punctuation and minor corrections.

[38] Ibid., sig. Iiii.

[39] *Bracton on the Laws and Customs of England*, ed. George Woodbine, trans. S. E. Thorne, 4 vols. (Harvard, 1961), 2:250–51.

how to run a household, so adult womanhood is defined by the common law as housekeeping. Two hundred years later the fifteenth-century English political polemicist, Sir John Fortescue, had turned this into an ideology of separate spheres, as part of an argument about women's unfitness for public rule: "a man devotes his attention to affairs outside, the woman hers to the internal business of the family. Whence it is the duty of a woman . . . to keep quiet at home, and to look after the concerns of the household."[40] Looking after "the concerns of the household" means servicing the demands of the body: eating, sleeping, washing, getting dressed and undressed, preparing the food and clearing it away; raising the children; tending the sick and the dying. In the houses of the great these activities were mediated by servants; in the middling-sized urban homes they were the direct responsibility of the wife and mother.

Home, then, was the "locus of care," as the title of a recent book has it.[41] Home understood the body as needy, vulnerable, hungry, cold, growing up and growing old, and endlessly leaky. "The everyday body" is the term I have coined for the body understood in this way—the body in the home: not intellectualized or medicalized; not the lower half of a body-mind hierarchy; but something more like what Simone de Beauvoir calls "the body as situation."[42] It is the material predicament in which we find ourselves: "fundamentally *ambiguous*, . . . subject at once to natural laws and to the human production of meaning."[43]

This kind of embodiedness works against the hierarchical structures that were assumed by urban and national lawmakers. Viewed from the perspective of the everyday body, even the patriarchal home is democratic: after all, one tired and hungry man is much like another. He brings his needs to the woman, and she satisfies them. Aristotle's analysis of domestic authority seems to allow for this. In arguing, in a passage I have already quoted, that the rule of the husband over that of the wife is "constitu-

---

[40] Sir John Fortescue, "De Natura Legis Naturae," trans. Chichester Fortescue, in *The Works of Sir John Fortescue*, ed. Thomas Fortescue, 2 vols. (London: privately printed, 1869), 1:191–333, at 257. I am grateful to Dr. Cordelia Beattie for this reference. Fortescue later retracted the argument of which this is part. The aim of "De Natura Legis Naturae," apparently written in exile in the 1460s, was to deny the legitimacy of the Yorkist claim to the throne, on the grounds that it gave precedence to a daughter over a brother. Deeply tendentious though it is, it is evidence of a certain strand of conservative thinking about women and public life.

[41] *The Locus of Care: Families, Communities, Institutions, and the Provision of Welfare Since Antiquity*, ed. Peregrine Horden and Richard Smith (London, 1998).

[42] Simone de Beauvoir, *The Second Sex*, ed. and trans. H. M. Parshley (London, 1997), 68–69. Originally published as *Le Deuxième Sexe* (Paris, 1949).

[43] Toril Moi, *What Is a Woman? And Other Essays* (Oxford, 1999), 69. Author's italics. I discuss the everyday body in "Temporary Virginity and the Everyday Body: Bourgeois Self-Making in *Le Bone Florence of Rome*," in *Pulp Fictions of Medieval England: Essays in Popular Romance*, ed. Nicola McDonald (Manchester, forthcoming).

tional," he acknowledges a fundamental equality: "for the idea of a constitutional state implies that the natures of the citizens are equal, and do not differ at all."[44] In the constitutional state the citizens rule and are ruled in turn; in the domestic sphere, as Aristotle explains it, the wife just never happens to get her turn at authority. Nevertheless, we should not neglect her point of view, disenfranchised from power as she is, and yet daily and routinely reminded within the home that "the natures of the citizens are equal." It was the practice in late medieval towns for women to tend the sick and dying in their homes and to wind the bodies of the dead: this is clear from postmortem inventories that record payment for this work.[45] Although funeral rites, of course, aimed to construct social difference in death, the women who wound the bodies knew something else: how dying dethrones the patriarch. He cannot keep his food down; he befouls his sheets; he cries out in pain. Margery Kempe of Lynn is represented as knowing this about her husband when he became senile in his last years, and that knowledge is shown as a source of power in her constant confrontations with ecclesiastical, civic, and state authorities. Certainly her *Book* records its protagonist telling an extraordinary story to a hostile priest in which she likens him to a bear that eats flowers and then "whan he had etyn hem, turnyng his tayl ende . . . voydyd hem owt ageyn at the hymyr party [shameful part]."[46] This is not so much a Rabelaisian grasp of the body's grotesqueness, I suggest, as a reductively domestic one: eating and defecating are central activities to be managed by household routines; they are the business of the kitchen and the privy. Margery Baxter, tried for heresy in Norwich in 1429, was accused of having denied the doctrine of the Real Presence. A witness claimed that she had said that if the sacrament is God, "a thousand and more priests make a thousand such gods and afterwards eat these gods and, having eaten them, discharge them through their posteriors into foul smelling privies, where you can find plenty of such gods if you want to look."[47] For Julian of Norwich, the slightly older contemporary of these two Margeries, the humanity of Jesus includes defecating as well: "And that it is he that doyth this, it is schewed ther wher he seyth he comyth downe to vs in the lowest parte of oure nede. For he hath

---

[44] Aristotle, *Politics*, ed. Everson, I. 12: 27.

[45] *Probate Inventories*, ed. Stell and Hampson: John Cadeby, Beverley mason, 1439: "A woman for wrapping the body of the deceased 2d," 80; Thomas Gryssop, York chapman, 1446: "A woman for looking after the deceased during his illness 1s. 8d," 91; William Duffield, York canon residentiary, 1452: "Isabel Snaw for washing the clothes of the deceased, 6s 8d . . . Alice Kendall and another woman for wrapping the body of the deceased in sindone 1s. 8d," 118; Katherine North, York, 1461: "To a woman for binding her 2d," 232.

[46] *The Book of Margery Kempe*, ed. Lynn Staley (Kalamazoo, Mich., 1996), 127.

[47] *Women in England c 1275–1525*, ed. and trans. P. J. P. Goldberg (Manchester, 1995), 292, from *Heresy Trials in the Diocese of Norwich, 1428–31*, ed. Norman Tanner, Camden Society, 4th ser., 20 (London, 1977), 45. I owe this reference to Sarah Rees Jones.

no dispite of that he made, ne he hath no disdeyne to serue vs at the symplest office that to oure body longyth in kynde."[48] [And that it is he that does this, is shown where he says he comes down to us in the lowest part of our need. He does not despise what he made nor does he disdain to serve us at the humblest task that belongs to the body by way of nature.] Jesus excretes like us.

That death (like defecation) is a leveler is a medieval sermon cliché, but it means something different in the home from in the pulpit. Patriarchal authority is never absolute, and perhaps least so in the home where it is seen from terribly close up. What the child learns in the intimacy of the home without even knowing it is her parents' physical vulnerability. If we accept what I have already suggested, that women, more than men, were involved in the household tasks relating to the management of the body, then we might also agree that, as a concept, the everyday body is gendered. It is produced by the person who cannot afford to be squeamish, who just has to get on with cleaning up the vomit on the floor or, as Margery Kempe is represented as having to do, changing the linen of an incontinent husband. The regulations for nursing in the infirmary at Syon Abbey include these instructions for the sister in charge of the care of the sick:

> Ofte chaunge ther beddes and clothes, ʒeue them medycynes, ley to ther plastres, and mynyster to them mete and drynke, fyre and water, and al other necessaryes, nyghte and day, as nede requyrethe, after counsel of the phisicians, and precepte of the soueryne, not squaymes [squeamish] to wasche them, and wype them, or auoyde them [empty their bowels], not angry or hasty or unpacient thof one haue the vomet, another the fluxe, another the frensy.[49]

The physician counsels, the sovereign—the person in charge—issues precepts: the nurse unsqueamishly gets on with the business of care that in the home is carried out without need of formal instruction.

Peregrine Horden has written that the household was not a republic of care. By this he means that throughout the medieval period there were limits on the capacity of small domestic units to sustain their sick or enfeebled members independently. Horden postulates support networks extending from the home into neighborhoods and kin groups, particularly networks

---

[48] *Book of Showings*, ed. Colledge and Walsh, 2:307. That this passage refers to defecation is clear from what precedes it: "A man goyth vppe right, and the soule [nourishment] of his body is sparyde [closed] as a purse fulle feyer. And when it is tyme of his necessary, it is opynyde and sparyde ayen fulle honestly."

[49] Quoted by Claire Jones, "An Assortment of Doctors: The Readers of Medical Books in Late Medieval England," *Journal of the Early Book Society* 3 (2000): 136–51, at 140, from G. J. Aungier, *The History and Antiquities of Syon Monastery, the Parish of Isleworth, and the Chapelry of Hounslow* (London, 1840), 395.

of women.[50] As a unit for the management of the body, it seems that the household was porous rather than independent, and this is why Horden says that it is not a republic of care. But in another sense it is a republic: care is, I suggest, disruptive of hierarchies and unimpressed by status. In the course of the fifteenth-century romance *Le Bone Florence of Rome*, which survives in an urban domestic manuscript, the heroine is subject to brutal and gratuitous demonstrations of male power.[51] She has been hung up by her hair, cast out into the forest, and embraced till her ribs crack; most of the men she meets have tried to rape her, either singly or en masse. But all is reversed when they become ill or disabled and bring their damaged bodies to her to be healed: one has a festering wound (1943); another has a terrible skin disease (2021–2); another shakes with palsy (2024); while a fourth has to be carried in a wheelbarrow (2029). Florence does not shrink from all this: unsqueamishly, "Sche handylde þem wyth hur hande" (2110), and they are cured.

The everyday body is not only visible in respect of care, however; it is also the subject of the civilizing processes of the courtesy texts, those little poems of advice for adolescents that were read in bourgeois homes. Mercantile and artisan households employed servants as a matter of course— or, rather, exchanged them, since they were often young people from homes of similar status.[52] Practical texts like "Urbanitatis" or "The Young Children's Book" aimed to teach these young people how to manage the body that sneezes, burps, yawns, farts, spits, and itches: "Fro spettyng and snetyng [sniffing] kepe þe also; / Be priuy of voidance [breaking wind], and lette it go" (19–20); "When þou sopys, make no noyse / With thi mouth as do boys [urchins]" (127–8); "At thi tabull noþer crache [scratch] ne claw, / That men wylle say þou art a daw. / Wype not thi nose nor þi nos-thirlys [nostrils], / Then men wylle sey þou come of cherlys" (139–42); and so on.[53] These poems are all about establishing conventions of behavior in the conditions of intimacy that I am arguing characterized the urban home, marking oneself off from those lower-status people ("boys" and "cherlys") who intrude their bodies into other people's consciousnesses. Norbert Elias

[50] Peregrine Horden, "Household Care and Informal Networks: Comparisons and Continuities from Antiquity to the Present," in *The Locus of Care*, ed. Horden and Smith, 21–67.

[51] The manuscript is Cambridge University Library, MS Ff. 2. 38; see *Le Bone Florence of Rome*, ed. Carol Falvo Heffernan (Manchester, 1976). References are to this edition.

[52] See P. J. P. Goldberg, *Women, Work and Life-Cycle in a Medieval Economy: Women in York and Yorkshire c. 1300–1520* (Oxford, 1992), 168–86; idem, "What Was a Servant?" in *Concepts and Patterns of Service in the Later Middle Ages*, ed. Anne Curry and Elizabeth Matthew (Woodbridge, 2000), 1–20; Felicity Riddy, "Mother Knows Best: Reading Social Change in a Courtesy Text," *Speculum* 71 (1996): 66–86.

[53] The first quotation is from "Urbanitatis," and the second from "The Young Children's Book." Both are cited from *The Babees Book*, ed. Frederick J. Furnivall, EETS o.s., 32 (London, 1868), 13–15, 17–25.

argues in *The Civilizing Process: The History of Manners*, another master narrative of modernity, that texts such as these show that people of the middle ages "stood in a different relationship to one another than we do. . . . their emotional life also had a different structure and character."[54] Elias regards them as more shameless than moderns, these people who did not use forks; "what was lacking in this *courtois* world . . . was the invisible wall of affects which seems now to rise between one human body and another, repelling and separating."[55] He seems not to have known about Absolon in Chaucer's "Miller's Tale," the part-time barber-surgeon who "was sumdeel squaymous / Of fartyng" (3337–8). Absolon's fastidiousness is often interpreted as effeminate, but perhaps we should see him as "civilized" in Elias's sense. He curls his hair, wears shoes with fancy designs, and is squeamish about the body. Alison, the carpenter's teenaged wife, by contrast, has not yet learned the lessons of the courtesy texts: she sticks her backside out of the window for a laugh, intruding her body into other people's consciousnesses, including the reader's.

In contemporary America and Britain huge amounts of money are spent on devices designed to eliminate personal odors in the home; our supermarket shelves groan with room fresheners, carpet deodorizers, toilet perfumes, and all manner of commercial products relating to personal hygiene. This may suggest that we have become, as Elias argues, fastidiously civilized. It may also suggest that what we have done is to commodify the "leaky and oderiferous" everyday body—that we have moved it into the marketplace.[56] The repulsion and separation that Elias values may themselves be a product of consumerism rather than of civilization. After all, medieval urban homes, too, knew about room fresheners: in the "Miller's Tale," the room where Nicholas lodges in the house of John, the Oxford carpenter, is "Ful fetisly ydight with herbes swoote" (3205).[57] One of John Mirk's sermons alludes to the custom of spring-cleaning: at Easter the fireplace in the hall is cleaned out and "arayde with grene rusches, and swete flowers strawed all about . . . For . . . ȝe wyll not suffyr no þing in your howse þat stynkyþe or saureth euell, wherby þat ȝe may be dosesyd."[58] The medieval courtesy texts, with their unembarrassed awareness of bodily functions that need to be regulated, seem to suggest that people in the home knew each other to be animals, or—to put it another way—that the idea of common humanness generated by the domestic sphere was embodied.

[54] Norbert Elias, *The Civilizing Process: The History of Manners and State Formation and Civilization* (Oxford, 1994), 55. Originally published as *Über der Prozess der Zivilisation*, 2 vols. (Basel, 1939).

[55] Ibid., 55–56.

[56] "Our bodies are leaky and oderiferous containers": Gurney, "Accommodating Bodies," 55.

[57] I am grateful to Mary Erler for reminding me of this.

[58] *Mirk's Festial*, ed. T. Erbe, EETS extra ser., 96 (London, 1905), 129–30. I am grateful to Fiona Dunlop, University of York, for pointing out this passage to me.

One of the dominant models of humanness in the period was, of course, the humanity of Christ. There is no need to rehearse the evidence for a change in the representation of Christ's humanity in the late middle ages, so that the hieratic figure of earlier times becomes a realistically depicted, suffering contemporary. There is a complex medieval theology surrounding the idea of God made man, but as Jesus is represented among laypeople in the discourses of affective devotion—naked, suffering, vulnerable, frightened of dying, bleeding, and in need of care—his is the everyday body at home. And the way in which his body, alive and dead, is tended, and by whom—Mary Magdalene washing his feet, Veronica wiping his face, the Marys tending his corpse—fits into the medieval women's networks of care that I have already referred to. It is something of a cliché now to call Christ's crucified body feminized. Perhaps the perspective of home allows us to think of it somewhat differently: as the body the home knows about, not in itself gendered masculine or feminine. Knowledge of it, unsqueamishness in dealing with it, may be female, but the body is not. What is transgressive about the body of the crucified Christ, then, might not be that it dissolves the gender binary but that it dissolves the public/private one.

Homeliness itself, however, is located at the point where boundaries are breached or dissolved. One reason why the term occurs so frequently in religious writings is because God's intimacy with the devout soul is precisely such a dissolution of boundaries: "Loo, what myght thys noble lorde do more wurschyppe and ioy to me than to shew to me that am so lytylle thys marvelous homlynesse?"[59] It is God's condescension—his ignoring of the boundaries that separate the low from the high—that is so often remarked on by devotional writers and that is a perpetual source of wonderment to Julian of Norwich. Intimacy suspends differences of status. Lords were not supposed to be "homli"; the public sphere was marked by proper distance. So the *Secreta Secretorum* counsels the ruler not to "haunte the company of his sugetis, and specially of chorlis and ruralle folke, for bi ouyr moche homelynes he shalle be the lasse honourid."[60] But the breaching of boundaries goes both ways, of course. The obverse of condescension is boldness or presumption, speaking on equal terms, or behaving as if you are at home even when you are not. An early fifteenth-century poem, "Why I Can't Be a Nun," says this directly: "Than at the yates in we yede [went], / Boldly as thowgh we had be at home" (188–9),[61] while Margaret Paston describes an occasion in 1450 when "the seyd enmys ben so bolde that they kom vp to þe lond and pleyn hem on Caster sondys and in othere plases as

[59] Colledge and Walsh, eds., *Book of Showings*, 2:313–14.
[60] *Three Prose Versions of the Secreta Secretorum*, ed. Robert Steele, EETS extra ser., 74 (London, 1898), 12–13.
[61] *Six Ecclesiastical Satires*, ed. James M. Dean (Kalamazoo, Mich., 1991).

homely as they were Englysch-men."[62] And the *Promptorium Parvulorum*—
a Latin dictionary in a manuscript from around 1440—glosses "Boldenesse
or homelynesse" as "Presumpcio."[63] The irritation of John Paston II with
Margaret Maltby, his uncle's widow, who had possession of some family
deeds and would only hand them over for cash, seems to have been occa-
sioned by what he saw as bourgeois effrontery: "It is a peyne to deele wyth
hyre. . . . She is in many thyngys full lyke a wyffe off London and off Lon-
done kyndenesse, and she woll needys take advise off Londonerys,
wheche I telle here can nott advyse her howghe she scholde deele weell
wyth any body off worshyp."[64] Margaret Maltby had brought four of her
neighbors to the meeting, and answered him back. Lynn wives seem to
have behaved in the same way: *The Book of Margery Kempe* is full of encounters between its protagonist and men in authority to whom she is represented as speaking as she would at home: "Than seyde the suffragan to the
seyde creatur, 'Damsel, thu wer at my Lady Westmorlond.' 'Whan, sir?'
seyde sche. 'At Estern,' seyd the suffragan. Sche, not replying, seyd, 'Wel,
ser?' "[65] Or before this, the encounter with the Archbishop of York, who
says to her: " 'I am evyl enformyd of the; I her seyn thu art a ryth wikked
woman.' And sche seyd ageyn, 'Ser, so I her seyn that ye arn a wikkyd
man.' "[66] Nagging wives are proverbial; bossy wives get carved in miseri-
cords and drawn in margins; but the wife who holds her ground and gives
as good as she gets is perhaps something different: the product of the egalitarian discourses of intimacy within the bourgeois home.

[62] *Paston Letters and Papers of the Fifteenth Century*, ed. Norman Davis (Oxford, 1971–76),
1:237–8.

[63] *Promptorium Parvulorum*, ed. A. Way, 3 vols. (London, 1843–64), 1:43.

[64] *Paston Letters*, ed. Davis, 1:513–14.

[65] *The Book of Margery Kempe*, ed. Staley, 132.

[66] Ibid., 125.

REFERENCES

Aarts, Florent G. A. M., ed. *Þe Pater Noster of Richard Ermyte: A Late Middle English Exposition of the Lord's Prayer.* Nijmegen: Janssen, 1967.

Adaptation of Peraldus's "Summa de Vitiis et Virtutibus" and Friar Laurent's "Somme le Roi." Mediaevalia Groningana, no. 24. Groningen: Forsten, 1998.

Aelred of Rievaulx. *A Rule of Life for a Recluse.* Translated by Mary Paul MacPherson. In *Treatises; the Pastoral Prayer.* Cistercian Fathers Series, no. 2. Spencer, Mass.: Cistercian Publications, 1971.

Akbari, Suzanne. "Nature's Forge Recast in the *Roman de Silence.*" In *Literary Aspects of Courtly Culture,* edited by Donald Maddox and Sara Sturm-Maddox, 39–46. Rochester: D. S. Brewer, 1994.

Alan of Lille. *De planctu Naturae.* Edited by N. M. Häring. *Studi Medievali,* terza serie, 19.2 (1978): 749–879.

Albert, Jean-Pierre. "La legende de Sainte Marguerite un mythe maieutique?" *Razo* 8 (1988): 19–33.

Alexander, Jonathan, and Paul Binski, eds. *Age of Chivalry: Art in Plantagenet England 1200–1400.* London: Royal Academy of Arts with Weidenfeld and Nicolson, 1987.

Allen, Peter. "The Ambiguity of Silence: Gender, Writing, and *Le Roman de Silence.*" In *Sign, Sentence, Discourse: Language in Medieval Thought and Literature,* edited by Julian Wasserman and Lois Roney, 98–112. Syracuse: Syracuse University Press, 1989.

Allen, Prudence. *The Concept of Women: The Aristotelian Revolution, 750 BC–AD 1250.* Montreal and London: Eden Press, 1985.

———. "Hildegard of Bingen's Philosophy of Sex Identity." *Thought* 64 (1989): 231–41.

Ambrosini, Federica. "Ceremonie, feste, lusso." In *Storia di Venezia.* Vol. 5, *Il rinascimento: società ed economia,* edited by Alberto Tenenti and Ugo Tucci. Rome: Istituto della Enciclopedia Trecanni, 1996.

Anderson, M. D. *Drama and Imagery in English Medieval Churches.* Cambridge: Cambridge University Press, 1963.

Antoninus of Florence. *Confessionale Anthonini.* Paris: Jehan Petit, [1507?].

Aquinas, Thomas. *Scriptum super sententiis.* Paris: P. Lethielleux, 1947.

——. *Summa theologiae*. Edited and translated by the Fathers of the English Dominican Province. 61 vols. London: Blackfriars, 1964–81.

Archer, Rowena E. "Rich Old Ladies: The Problem of Late Medieval English Dowagers." In *Property and Politics: Essays in Later Medieval English History*, edited by A. J. Pollard, 15–35. Gloucester: Alan Sutton, 1984.

Aristotle. *The Politics and the Constitution of Athens*. Edited by Stephen Everson. Cambridge: Cambridge University Press, 1996.

Arnold, John. *Inquisition and Power: Catharism and the Confessing Subject in Medieval Languedoc*. Philadelphia: University of Pennsylvania Press, 2001.

Arntz, Mary Luke, ed. *Richard Rolle and Þe Holy Boke Gratia Dei: An Edition With Commentary*. Salzburg Studies in English Literature: Elizabethan and Renaissance Studies, no. 92:2. Salzburg: Institut für Anglistik und Amerikanistik, 1981.

Ashley, Kathleen, and Pamela Sheingorn, eds. *Interpreting Cultural Symbols: Saint Anne in Late Medieval Society*. Athens: University of Georgia Press, 1990.

Aspegren, Kerstin. *The Male Woman: A Feminine Ideal in the Early Church*. Edited by René Kieffer. Stockholm: Almquist & Wiksell, 1990.

Aston, Margaret. *Lollards and Reformers: Images and Literacy in Late Medieval Religion*. London: Hambledon, 1984.

——. "Segregation in Church." In *Women in the Church*, edited by W. J. Sheils and Diana Wood, 238–42. Studies in Church History, vol. 27. Oxford: Basil Blackwell, 1991.

Atkinson, Clarissa W. *The Oldest Vocation: Christian Motherhood in the Middle Ages*. Ithaca: Cornell University Press, 1991.

Augustine. *The City of God Against the Pagans*. Edited and translated by R. W. Dyson. Cambridge: Cambridge University Press, 1996.

Aungier, G. J. *The History and Antiquities of Syon Monastery, the Parish of Isleworth, and the Chapelry of Hounslow*. London: J. B. Nichols and Son, 1840.

Auvray, Lucien, ed. *Registres de Grégoire IX*. 4 vols. Paris: A. Fontemoing, 1896–1955.

Aymar, A. "Le sachet accoucher et ses mystères." *Annales du Midi* 38 (1926): 273–347.

Backhouse, Janet. *The Bedford Hours*. New York: New Amsterdam, 1990.

Baird, Joseph, and John Kane, eds. and trans. *La Querelle de la Rose: Letters and Documents*. Chapel Hill: University of North Carolina Press, 1978.

Baker, A. T., ed. "An Anglo-French Life of Saint Paul the Hermit." *Modern Language Review* (1908–9): 491–504.

——, ed. "An Anglo-French Life of St Osith." *Modern Language Review* 6 (1911): 476–502.

——, ed. "La vie de saint Edmond, archevêque de Cantorbéry." *Romania* 55 (1929): 332–81.

——, ed. "Vie anglo-normande de sainte Foy par Simon de Walsingham." *Romania* 66 (1940–41): 49–84.

——, ed. "Vie de saint Panuce." *Romania* 38 (1909): 418–24.

Baker, A. T., and Alexander Bell, eds. *Saint Modwenna*. ANTS, vol. 7. Oxford: Blackwell for ANTS, 1947.

Banker, James R. *Death in the Community: Memorialization and Confraternities in an Italian Commune in the Late Middle Ages*. Athens: University of Georgia, 1988.

Banks, Mary Macleod, ed., *An Alphabet of Tales*. 2 vols. EETS, o.s., vols. 126, 127. London: Kegan Paul, 1904, 1905. Reprinted as 1 vol. Millwood, N.Y.: Kraus Reprint, 1987.

Barbaro, Francesco. *De Re Uxoria*. In *The Earthly Republic: Italian Humanists on Government and Society*, edited by Benjamin G. Kohl and Ronald G. Witt. Philadelphia: University of Pennsylvania Press, 1978.

Barclay, Alexander. *The Castle of Labour*. 2d ed. [London]: Richard Pynson, 1505.

Barron, Caroline M. "The 'Golden Age' of Women in Medieval London." *Reading Medieval Studies* 15 (1989): 35–58.

——. "Introduction: The Widow's World." In *Medieval London Widows 1300–1500*, edited by Caroline M. Barron and Anne F. Sutton. London: Hambledon Press, 1994.

——. "London 1300–1540." In *The Cambridge Urban History of Britain*. Vol. 1, *600–1540*, edited by D. M. Palliser, 395–440. Cambridge: Cambridge University Press, 2000.

——. "The Parish Fraternities of Medieval London." In *The Church in Pre-Reformation Society: Essays in Honour of F. R. H. du Boulay*, edited by Caroline M. Barron and Christopher Harper-Bill, 13–37. Woodbridge: Boydell, 1985.

Barrow, Julia. "A Twelfth-Century Bishop and Literary Patron: William de Vere." *Viator* 18 (1987): 175–89.

Bartlett, Anne Clark. " 'A Reasonable Affection': Gender and Spiritual Friendship in Middle English Devotional Literature." In *Vox Mystica: Essays on Medieval Mysticism in Honor of Professor Valerie M. Lagorio*, edited by A. C. Bartlett et al., 131–45. Cambridge: D. S. Brewer, 1995.

Bartlett, J. N. "The Expansion and Decline of York in the Later Middle Ages." *Economic History Review*, 2d series, 12 (1959–60): 17–33.

Bateson, Mary. "The Register of Crabhouse Nunnery." *Norfolk Archaeology* 11 (1892): 1–71.

Baugh, A. C., ed. *The English Text of the 'Ancrene Riwle': Edited from British Museum MS. Royal 8.C.1.* EETS, o.s., vol. 232, 1956.

Beattie, Cordelia. "A Room of One's Own? The Legal Evidence for the Residential Arrangements of Women Without Husbands in Late Fourteenth- and Early Fifteenth-Century York." In *Medieval Women and the Law*, edited by N. J. Menuge, 41–56. Woodbridge: Boydell, 2000.

Beauvoir, Simone de. *The Second Sex*. Edited and translated by H. M. Parshley. London: Vintage, 1997.

Beckwith, Sarah. "Passionate Regulation: Enclosure, Ascesis, and the Feminist Imaginary." *South Atlantic Quarterly* 93 (1994): 803–24.

——. "Problems of Authority in Late Medieval English Mysticism: Language, Agency, and Authority in *The Book of Margery Kempe*," *Exemplaria* 4 (1992): 172–99.

Bede. *Ecclesiastical History of the English People*. Edited and translated by Bertram Colgrave and R. A. B. Mynors. Oxford: Oxford University Press, 1969.

Beissel, Stephan. *Geschichte der Verehrung Marias in Deutschland während des Mittelalter.* Freiburg-im-Breisgau: Herdersche Verlagshandlung, 1909.

Bell, David N. *The Image and Likeness: The Augustinian Spirituality of William of St Thierry.* Cistercian Studies Series, no. 78. Kalamazoo, Mich.: Cistercian Publications, 1984.

——. *What Nuns Read: Books and Libraries in Medieval English Nunneries.* Kalamazoo, Mich.: Cistercian Publications, 1995.

Bell, Susan Groag. "Medieval Women Book Owners: Arbiters of Lay Piety and Ambassadors of Culture." *Signs* 7 (1982): 742–68.

Benedetti, Marina, ed. *Milano 1300: I processi inquisitoriali contro le devote e i devoti di santa Guglielma.* Milan: Libri Scheiwitter, 1999.

Bennett, Adelaide. "A Book Designed for a Noblewoman: An Illustrated *Manuel des Péchés* of the Thirteenth Century." In *Medieval Book Production: Assessing the Evidence*, edited by Linda L. Brownrigg, 163–81. Los Altos Hills, Calif.: Anderson-Lovelace, 1990.

Bennett, Judith M. *Ale, Beer and Brewsters in England: Women's Work in a Changing World, 1300–1600.* Oxford: Oxford University Press, 1996.

——. "Confronting Continuity." *Journal of Women's History* 9 (1997): 73–94.

——. *Medieval Women in Modern Perspective.* Washington, D.C.: American Historical Association, 2000.

——. "Medieval Women, Modern Women: Across the Great Divide." In *Culture and History: 1350–1600: Essays on English Communities, Identities, and Writing*, edited by David Aers, 147–75. Detroit: Wayne State University Press, 1992.

——. "The Village Ale-Wife: Women and Brewing in Fourteenth-Century England." In

Women and Work in Preindustrial Europe, edited by Barbara Hanawalt, 20–36. Bloomington: Indiana University Press, 1986.

——. "When the Master Takes a Mistress." Paper delivered at Fordham University's Medieval Studies Conference, New York, March 31, 2001.

——. *Women in the Medieval English Countryside: Gender and Household in Brigstock Before the Plague*. Oxford: Oxford University Press, 1987.

Benson, Larry D., ed. *King Arthur's Death: The Stanzaic Morte Arthur and Alliterative Morte Arthure*. Exeter: Exeter University Press, 1986.

Beriou, Nicole. "La Confession dans les écrits théologiques et pastoraux du XIIIe siècle: Médication de l'ame ou démarche judiciare?" In *L'Aveu: Antiquité et Moyen Age*. Actes de la table ronde organisée par l'Ecole française de Rome avec le concours du CNRS et de l'Université de Trieste, Rome, 28–30 mars 1984. Rome: Ecole Française de Rome, Palais Farnèse, 1986.

Berman, Harold J. *Law and Revolution: The Formation of the Western Legal Tradition*. Cambridge: Harvard University Press, 1983.

Bethell, Denis. "The Lives of St Osyth of Essex and St Osyth of Aylesbury." *Analecta Bollandiana* 88 (1970): 75–127.

Bibliotheca hagiographica graeca. Edited by Francois Halkin. 3d ed. Brussels: Société des Bollandists, 1957.

Bibliotheca hagiographica latina. Edited by Francois Halkin. Vol. 2. Brussels: Société des Bollandists, 1900–1901.

Bihl, Michael, ed. "Statua generalia ordinis edita in capitulis generalibus celebratis Narbonae an. 1260, Assisii an. 1279 atque Parisiis an. 1292. Editio critica et synoptica." *Archivum Franciscanum Historicum* 34 (1941): 13–94, 284–358.

Binney, Erskine, ed. "Accounts of the Wardens of the Parish of Morebath, Devon: 1520–1573." *Devon Notes and Queries*, supplementary volume, 1903–4. Exeter, 1904.

Bistort, Guilio. *Il magistrato alle pompe nella republica di Venezia*. Bologna: Forni editore, 1912.

Blaauw, William Henry. *The Barons War: Including the Battles of Lewes and Evesham*. London: Bell and Daldy, 1871.

Blamires, Alcuin. "Women and Preaching in Medieval Orthodoxy, Heresy, and Saints' Lives." *Viator* 26 (1995): 135–52.

Blanton-Whetsall, Virginia. "St Æthelthryth's Cult: Literary, Historical, and Pictorial Constructions of Gendered Sanctity." Ph.D. diss., State University of New York, 1998.

Bloch, Marc. *Feudal Society*. Translated by L. A. Manyon. 2 vols. Chicago: University of Chicago Press, 1970.

Bloch, R. Howard. "Silence and Holes: The *Roman de Silence* and the Art of the Trouvère." *Yale French Studies* 70 (1986): 81–99.

Blumenfeld-Kosinski, Renate. "Constance de Rabastens: Politics and Visionary Experience in the Time of the Great Schism." *Mystics Quarterly* 25 (1999): 147–68.

——. *Not of Woman Born: Representations of Caesarean Birth in Medieval and Renaissance Culture*. Ithaca: Cornell University Press, 1990.

——. "Satirical Views of the Beguines in Northern French Literature." In *New Trends in Feminine Spirituality: The Holy Women of Liège and Their Impact*, edited by Juliette Dor, Lesley Johnson, and Jocelyn Wogan-Browne, 237–49. Turnhout: Brepols, 1999.

——, ed. *Selected Writings of Christine de Pizan*. Translated by Kevin Brownlee and Renate Blumenfeld-Kosinski. New York: W.W. Norton & Co., 1997.

Blumreich, Kathleen. "Lesbian Desire in the Old French *Roman de Silence*." *Arthuriana* 7 (1997): 47–62.

Boccaccio, Giovanni. *The Decameron*. Translated by Mark Musa and Peter Bondanella. New York: Mentor Books, 1982.

Boholm, Asa. "The Coronation of Female Death: The Dogaressas of Venice." *Man* 27 (1992): 91–104.

Bolton, Brenda. "Thirteenth-Century Religious Women: Further Reflections on the Low Countries 'Special Case.' " In *New Trends in Feminine Spirituality: The Holy Women of Liège and Their Impact*, edited by Juliette Dor, Lesley Johnson, and Jocelyn Wogan-Browne, 129–58. Turnhout: Brepols, 1999.

Bolton, J. L. *The Medieval English Economy 1150–1500*. London: Dent, 1980.

Bonaventure. *S. Bonaventurae . . . Opera Omnia*. Florence: Quaracchi, 1898.

Bonfield, Lloyd. *Marriage Settlements, 1601–1740: The Adoption of the Strict Settlement*. Cambridge: Cambridge University Press, 1983.

Bonnassie, Pierre. *From Slavery to Feudalism*. Translated by Jean Birrell. Cambridge: Cambridge University Press, 1991.

Bowman, Winifred M. *England in Ashton-Under-Lyne*. Cheshire: John Sherratt and Sons for Ashton-Under-Lyne Corp., 1960.

Bozon, Nicholas. *Seven More Poems by Nicholas Bozon*. Edited by Sr. Amelia Klenke. Franciscan Institute Publications Historical Series, vol. 2. New York: Franciscan Institute, and Louvain: Nauwelaerts, 1951.

Bracton, Henry. *On the Laws and Customs of England*. Edited by George Woodbine and translated by S. E. Thorne. 4 vols. Harvard: Harvard University Press, 1961.

Bradley, Ritamary. "In the Jaws of the Bear: Journeys of Transformation by Women Mystics." *Vox Benedictina* 8 (1991): 116–75.

Braeckmans, Louis. *Confession et communion au moyen age et au concile de Trente*. Gembloux: J. Duculet, 1971.

Brahney, Kathleen. "When *Silence* Was Golden: Female Personae in the *Roman de Silence*." In *The Spirit of the Court*, edited by Glyn Burgess and Robert Taylor, 52–61. Dover: D. S. Brewer, 1985.

Braun, Joseph. *Tracht und Attribute der Heiligen in der deutschen Kunst*. Stuttgart: J. B. Metzler, 1943.

Braunfels, Wolfgang. *Die Verkündigung*. Düsseldorf: L. Schwann, 1949.

Breisach, Ernst. *Caterina Sforza: A Renaissance Virago*. Chicago: University of Chicago Press, 1967.

Bridget of Sweden. *Revelaciones Extravagantes*. Edited by Lennart Hollman. Uppsala: Almqvist & Wiksell, 1956.

Brown, Andrew. *Popular Piety in Late Medieval England: The Diocese of Salisbury, 1250–1550*. Oxford: Oxford University Press, 1995.

Brown, Carleton, ed., *English Lyrics of the Thirteenth Century*. Oxford: Clarendon Press, 1932.

Brown, Patricia Fortini. "Measured Friendship, Calculated Pomp: The Ceremonial Welcomes of the Venetian Republic." In *"All the World's a Stage": Pageantry in the Renaissance and Baroque*, edited by Barbara Wisch and Susan Scott Munshower, 136–87. University Park, Pa., Pennsylvania State University Press, 1990.

Brown, Peter. *The World of Late Antiquity, AD 150–750*. London: Thames and Hudson, 1971.

Brownlee, Kevin. "Discourses of the Self: Christine de Pizan and the *Romance of the Rose*." In *Rethinking "The Romance of the Rose": Text, Image, Reception*, edited by Kevin Brownlee and Sylvia Huot, 234–61. Philadelphia: University of Pennsylvania Press, 1992.

Bryant, Lawrence M. "The Medieval Entry Ceremony at Paris." In *Coronations*, edited by J. M. Bak, 81–118. Berkeley: University of California Press, 1990.

Burgess, Clive. " 'A Fond Thing Vainly Invented': An Essay on Purgatory and Pious Motive in Late Medieval England." In *Parish, Church and People: Local Studies in Lay Religion, 1350–1750*, edited by Susan Wright, 56–84. London: Hutchinson, 1988.

Burke, Peter. *Popular Culture in Early Modern Europe*. New York: Harper Torchbooks, 1978.

Burns, E. Jane. *Bodytalk: When Women Speak in Old French Literature*. Philadelphia: University of Pennsylvania Press, 1993.

Butler, Judith. *Gender Trouble: Feminism and the Subversion of Identity*. New York: Routledge, 1990.

Büttner, Frank Olaf. "'Mens divina liber grandis est': Zu einigen Darstellungen des Lesens in spätmittelalterlichen Handschriften." *Philobiblion* 16 (1972): 92–126.

Bynum, Caroline Walker. *Holy Feast and Holy Fast: The Religious Significance of Food to Medieval Women*. Berkeley: University of California Press, 1987.

Caesarius of Heisterbach. *The Dialogue on Miracles*. Translated by H. Von E. Scott and C. C. Swinton Bland. London: G. Routledge & Sons, Ltd., 1929.

———. *Dialogus miraculorum*. Edited by Joseph Strange. Cologne: H. Lempertz & Co., 1851.

Calendar of Patent Rolls, 1367–70. London: Her Majesty's Stationery Office, 1913.

Canning, Kathleen. "Feminist History after the Linguistic Turn: Historicizing Discourse and Experience." *Signs* 19 (1994): 368–404.

Carlin, Martha. "Fast Food and Urban Living Standards in Medieval England." In *Food and Eating in Medieval Europe*, edited by Martha Carlin and Joel T. Rosenthal, 27–51. London: Hambledon Press, 1998.

Carolus-Barre, M. Louis. "Un nouveau parchemin amulette et la legende de Sainte Marguerite patronne des femmes en couches." *Academie des inscriptions et belles-lettres comptes rendus* (1979): 256–75.

Carpenter, Jennifer, and Sally-Beth MacLean, eds. *Power of the Weak: Studies on Medieval Women*. Urbana: University of Illinois Press, 1995.

Casegrande, Giovanna. "Women in Confraternities between the Middle Ages and the Modern Age: Research in Umbria." *Confraternities: The Newsletter of the Society for Confraternity Studies* 5 (1994): 3–13.

Casini, Matteo. *I gesti del principe: la festa politica a Firenze e Venezia in età rinascimentale*. Venice: Marsilio, 1996.

Cassian, John. *Conferences*. Translated by Colm Lubhéid. New York: Paulist Press, 1985.

Catalogus codicum hagiographicorum bibliothecae regiae bruxellensis. Part I. Brussels: Pollenuis, Ceuterick et Lefebure, 1886.

Cazelles, Brigitte. *The Lady as Saint: A Collection of French Hagiographic Romances of the Thirteenth Century*. Philadelphia: University of Pennsylvania Press, 1991.

Cazenave, Annie. "Aveu et contrition. Manuels de confesseurs et interrogatoires d'inquisition en Languedoc et en Catalogne (XIIIe–XIVe siècles)." In *La piété populaire au moyen âge*, 333–52. Actes du 99e Congrès National des Sociétés savantes, Bescançon, 1974. Paris, 1977.

Chambers, R. W. "On the Continuity of English Prose from Alfred to More and His School." In *The Life and Death of Sir Thomas More by Nicholas Harpsfield*, edited by Elsie Vaughan Hitchcock, EETS, o.s., vol. 186. London, Oxford University Press, 1932; repr. 1957 as EETS o.s., vol. 191A.

Chance, Jane. "Speaking *in Propria Persona*: Authorizing the Subject as a Political Act in Late Medieval Feminine Spirituality." In *New Trends in Feminine Spirituality: The Holy Women of Liège and Their Impact*, edited by Juliette Dor, Lesley Johnson, and Jocelyn Wogan-Browne, 269–94. Turnhout: Brepols, 1999.

Chaucer, Geoffrey. *The Riverside Chaucer*. 3d ed. Edited by Larry D. Benson et al. Boston: Houghton Mifflin, 1987.

Cheetham, Francis W. *English Medieval Alabasters*. Oxford: Phaidon and Christie's, 1984.

Cheney, Christopher. "Rules for the Observance of Feast Days in Medieval England." *Bulletin for the Institute of Historical Research* 34, no. 90 (1961): 117–47.

Chewning, Susannah Mary. "Mysticism and the Anchoritic Community." In *Medieval*

Women in Their Communities, edited by Diane Watt, 116–37. Cardiff: University of Wales Press, 1996.

Chojnacka, Monica. *Working Women in Early Modern Venice*. Baltimore: Johns Hopkins University Press, 2001.

Chojnacki, Stanley. "La posizione della donna a Venezia nel Cinquecento." In *Tiziano e Venezia: Convegno internazionale di studi, Venezia, 1976*, 65–70. Vicenza: N. Pozza, 1980.

——. *Women and Men in Renaissance Venice*. Baltimore: Johns Hopkins University Press, 2000.

Christine de Pizan. *The Book of the City of Ladies*. Translated by E. J. Richards. New York: Persea Books, 1982.

——. *Book of the City of Ladies*. Edited by E. J. Richards. In *La Città delle Dame*. Milan: Luni, 1997.

——. *Lavision-Christine*. Edited by Mary Louis Towner. Washington, D.C.: Catholic University of America, 1932.

——. *Le Livre de la mutacion de Fortune*. Edited by Suzanne Solente. 4 vols. Paris: A. & J. Picard, 1959–66.

——. *The Treasure of the City of Ladies or the Book of the Three Virtues*. Translated by Sarah Lawson. Harmondsworth: Penguin, 1985.

Clayton, Mary, and Hugh Magennis, eds. *The Old English Lives of St. Margaret*. Cambridge: Cambridge University Press, 1994.

Cloke, Gillian. *"This Female Man of God": Women and Spiritual Power in the Patristic Age, AD 350–450*. London and New York: Routledge, 1995.

Clover, Carol J. "Regardless of Sex: Men, Women and Power in Early Northern Europe," *Speculum* 68, no. 2 (1993): 364–88.

Coakley, John. "Friars as Confidants of Holy Women in Medieval Dominican Hagiography." In *Images of Sainthood in Medieval Europe*, edited by Renate Blumenfeld-Kosinski and Timea Szell, 222–46. Ithaca: Cornell University Press, 1991.

——. "Gender and the Authority of the Friars: The Significance of Holy Women for Thirteenth-Century Franciscans and Dominicans." *Church History* 60 (1991): 445–60.

Coleman, Joyce. *Public Reading and the Reading Public in Late Medieval England and France*. Cambridge: Cambridge University Press, 1996.

Coleman, William E. *Philippe de Mézières' Campaign for the Feast of Mary's Presentation*. Toronto: Pontifical Institute of Mediaeval Studies, 1981.

Collijn, Isak, ed. *Acta et processus canonizacionis Beate Birgitte*. Uppsala: Almqvist & Wiksells, 1924–31.

Connolly, Margaret, ed. *Contemplations of the Dread and Love of God*. EETS, o.s., vol. 303. 1993.

Constable, Giles. *The Reformation of the Twelfth Century*. Cambridge: Cambridge University Press, 1996.

Constable, Giles, and Bernard Smith, eds. *Libellus de diversis ordinibus et professionibus qui sunt in æcclesia*. Oxford Medieval Texts. Oxford: Clarendon Press, 1972.

Cooke, Alice, ed. *Ecclesiastical Court Book of Walley*. Chetham Society, vol. 44. 1901.

Cooper, Kate Mason. "Elle and L: Sexualized Textuality in *Le Roman de Silence*." *Romance Notes* 25 (1985): 341–60.

Corbet, Patrick. *Les saints ottoniens: Sainteté dynastique, sainteté royale et sainteté féminine autour de l'an Mil*. Sigmaringen: J. Thorbecke, 1986.

Cotton, Charles, ed. "Churchwardens' Accounts of the Parish of St. Andrew, Canterbury 1485 to 1625. Part I." *Archaeologia Cantiana* 32 (1917): 181–246; "Part II." *Archaeologia Cantiana* 33 (1920): 1–46.

Cowper, J. M., ed. "Accounts of the Churchwardens of St. Dunstan's Church, Canterbury. Part II, A.D. 1508–80." *Archaeologia Cantiana* 17 (1887): 77–139.

Cox, J. Charles. *Bench-ends in English Churches*. Oxford: Oxford University Press, 1916.

Cré, Marleen. "Women in the Charterhouse? Julian of Norwich's *Revelations of Divine Love* and Marguerite Porete's *Mirror of Simple Souls* in British Library, MS Additional 37790." In *Writing Religious Women: Female Spiritual and Textual Practices in Late Medieval England,* edited by Denis Renevey and Christiania Whitehead, 43–62. Cardiff: University of Wales Press, 2000.

Cullum, Patricia, and Jeremy Goldberg. "How Margaret Blackburn Taught Her Daughters: Reading Devotional Instruction in a Book of Hours." In *Medieval Women: Texts and Contexts in Late Medieval Britain: Essays for Felicity Riddy,* edited by Jocelyn Wogan-Browne et al., 217–26. Turnhout: Brepols, 2000.

Da Canal, Martino. *Les Estoires de Venise.* Edited by Alberto Limentani. Florence: Leo S. Olschki Editore, 1972.

Davis, Isabel. "John Gower's Fear of Flying: Transitional Masculinities in the *Confessio Amantis.*" Paper delivered at the conference on "Rites of Passage," York, 2001; forthcoming in *Rites of Passage,* edited by P. J. P. Goldberg et al. Woodbridge: Boydell.

Davis, Natalie Zemon. "The Reasons of Misrule." In *Society and Culture in Early Modern France,* 97–123. Stanford, Calif.: Stanford University Press, 1965.

———. "Women on Top." In *Society and Culture in Early Modern France,* 143–47. Stanford, Calif.: Stanford University Press, 1965.

Davis, Norman, ed., *Paston Letters and Papers of the Fifteenth Century.* 2 vols. Oxford: Clarendon Press, 1971–76.

Davis, Robert C. "The Geography of Gender." In *Gender and Society in Renaissance Italy,* edited by Judith C. Brown and Robert C. Davis, 19–38. London: Longman, 1998.

Dean, James M., ed. *Six Ecclesiastical Satires.* Kalamazoo, Mich.: Western Michigan University for TEAMS, 1991.

Dean, Ruth J., and Maureen B. M. Boulton. *Anglo-Norman Literature: A Guide to Texts and Manuscripts.* ANTS OP, vol. 3. London: ANTS, 1999.

Deschamps, Paul, and Marc Thibout. *La peinture murale en France au début de l'époque gothique.* Paris: Centre National de la Récherche Scientifique, 1963.

Desjardins, Gustave, ed. *Cartulaire de l'Abbaye de Conques en Rouergue.* Documents historiques publiés par la Société de l'École des Chartes. Paris: Picard, 1879.

D'Evelyn, Charlotte, and Anna J. Mills, eds. *The South English Legendary.* 3 vols. EETS, o.s. vols. 235, 236, 244. 1956–59.

Diekstra, F. N. M., ed. *A Dialogue Between Reason and Adversity.* Nijmegen: Van Gorcum, 1968.

———, ed. *Book for a Simple and Devout Woman.* Medieavalia Groningana 24. Groningen, 1998.

Dilkes, Thomas Bruce, ed. *Bridgwater Borough Archives.* Vol. 3. Somerset Record Society, vol. 58. 1945.

Dobson, E.J., ed. *The English Text of the "Ancrene Riwle": Edited from B.M. Cotton MS. Cleopatra C.vi.* EETS, o.s., vol. 267. 1972.

Doree, Stephen G., ed. *The Early Churchwardens' Accounts of Bishops Stortford 1431–1558.* Hertfordshire Record Society, vol. 10. 1994.

Doyle, A. I. "Book Production by the Monastic Orders in England (c. 1375–1530): Assessing the Evidence." In *Medieval Book Production: Assessing the Evidence,* edited by Linda Brownrigg, 1–19. Los Altos Hills, Calif.: Anderson Lovelace and Red Gull Press, 1990.

Drew, Charles. *Early Parochial Organisation in England: The Origins of the Office of Churchwarden.* St. Anthony Hall Publications, no. 7. York: Borthwick Institute, 1954.

Dronke, Peter. *Women Writers of the Middle Ages: A Critical Study of Texts from Perpetua (d. 203) to Marguerite Porete (d. 1310).* Cambridge: Cambridge University Press, 1984.

Duby, Georges. "Introduction: Private Power, Public Power." In *A History of Private Life.* Vol. 2, *Revelations of the Medieval World,* edited by Philippe Ariès and Georges Duby, translated by Arthur Goldhammer, 6–7. Cambridge, Mass.: Harvard University Press, 1987.

———. *The Knight, the Lady and the Priest: The Making of Modern Marriage in Medieval France.* Translated by Barbara Bray. New York: Pantheon, 1985.

———. *Medieval Marriage.* Translated by Elborg Forester. Baltimore: Johns Hopkins University Press, 1978.

———. *La Société aux XIe et XIIe siècles dans la région maconnaise.* Paris: A. Colin, 1953.

———. *Women of the Twelfth Century.* Translated by Jean Birrell. 3 vols. Chicago: University of Chicago Press, 1998.

Duffy, Eamon. "Holy Maydens, Holy Wyfes: The Cult of Women Saints in Fifteenth- and Sixteenth-Century England." *Studies in Church History* 27 (1990): 175–96.

———. *The Stripping of the Altars: Traditional Religion in England c.1400–c.1580.* New Haven: Yale University Press, 1992.

Dugdale, William. *Monasticon Anglicanum.* 10 vols. Edited by J. Caley, H. Ellis, and B. Bandinel. London: Longman, 1817–30.

Duggan, Anne, ed. *Queens and Queenship in Medieval Europe.* Woodbridge: Boydell, 1997.

Dunn, Charles W. Introduction to *The Romance of the Rose.* Translated by Harry Robbins. New York: Dutton, 1962.

Earenfight, Theresa. "Maria of Castile, Ruler or Figurehead? A Preliminary Study in Aragonese Queenship." *Mediterranean Studies* 4 (1994): 45–61.

Economou, George. *The Goddess Natura in Medieval Literature.* Cambridge: Harvard University Press, 1972.

Elisabeth of Hungary. "La vie de sainte Elisabeth d'Hongrie." Edited by Ludwig Karl. *ZRPh* 24 (1910): 295–314.

Elliott, Dyan. "Authorizing a Life: The Collaboration of Dorothea of Montau and John Marienwerder." In *Gendered Voices: Medieval Saints and Their Interpreters,* edited by Catherine Mooney, 168–91. Philadelphia: University of Pennsylvania Press, 1999.

———. "*Dominae* or *Dominatae*? Female Mystics and the Trauma of Textuality." In *Women, Marriage, and Family in Medieval Christendom: Essays in Memory of Michael M. Sheehan, C.S.B.,* edited by Constance Rousseau and Joel Rosenthal, 47–77. Kalamazoo, Mich.: Medieval Institute Publications, 1998.

———. *Fallen Bodies: Pollution, Sexuality, and Demonology in the Middle Ages.* Philadelphia: University of Pennsylvania Press, 1999.

———. "The Physiology of Rapture and Female Spirituality." In *Medieval Theology and the Natural Body,* edited by Peter Biller and Alastair Minnis, 141–73. Woodbridge: York Medieval Press, 1997.

———. *Spiritual Marriage: Sexual Abstinence in Medieval Wedlock.* Princeton: Princeton University Press, 1993.

Elvey, E. M., ed. *The Courts of the Archdeaconry of Buckingham: 1483–1523.* Buckingham Record Society, vol. 19. 1975.

Erbe, T., ed. *Mirk's Festial.* EETS, extra series, vol. 96. 1905.

Erler, Mary C. "Syon Abbey's Care for Books: Its Sacristan's Account Rolls 1506/7–1535/6." *Scriptorium* 39 (1985): 293–307.

———. *Women, Reading and Piety in Late Medieval England.* Cambridge: Cambridge University Press, 2002.

Erler, Mary C., and Maryanne Kowaleski, eds., *Women and Power in the Middle Ages.* Athens: University of Georgia Press, 1988.

Esser, Caietanus. *Opuscula sancti patris Francisci Assisiensis.* Rome: Grottaferrata, 1978.

Evans, Joan, ed. *The Flowering of the Middle Ages.* 1966. Reprint. London: Thames and Hudson, 1985.

Eve, Julian. *A History of Horsham St Faith, Norfolk: The Story of a Village.* Rev. ed. Norwich: Catton Printing, 1994.

Evergates, Theodore, ed. *Aristocratic Women in Medieval France.* Philadelphia: University of Pennsylvania Press, 1999.

——. *Feudal Society in the Bailliage of Troyes under the Counts of Champagne, 1152–1284.* Baltimore: Johns Hopkins University Press, 1976.

Ferrante, Joan M. " 'Licet longinquis regionibus corpore separati': Letters as a Link in and to the Middle Ages." *Speculum* 76 (2001): 877–95.

——. *To the Glory of Her Sex: Women's Roles in the Composition of Medieval Texts.* Bloomington: Indiana University Press, 1997.

Finlay, Robert. "The Venetian Republic as a Gerontocracy: Age and Politics in the Renaissance." *Journal of Medieval and Renaissance Studies* 8 (1978): 157–78.

Fisher, John H., ed. *The Tretyse of Love.* EETS, o.s., vol. 223. 1951.

Fleming, John. *Reason and the Lover.* Princeton: Princeton University Press, 1984.

——. *The "Roman de la Rose": A Study in Allegory and Iconography.* Princeton: Princeton University Press, 1969.

Fleming, Peter. *Family and Household in Medieval England.* Basingstoke: Palgrave, 2000.

Fletcher, Anthony. *Gender, Sex and Subordination in England, 1500–1800.* New Haven: Yale University Press, 1995.

Fortescue, Sir John. "De Natura Legis Naturae." Translated by Chichester Fortescue. In *The Works of Sir John Fortescue,* edited by Thomas Fortescue. 2 vols. London: privately printed, 1869.

Foster, C. W., ed. *Lincoln Wills: 1427–1532.* 3 vols. Lincoln Record Society, vols. 5, 10, 24. 1914, 1918, 1930.

Foster, J. E., ed. *Churchwardens' Accounts of St. Mary the Great, Cambridge, from 1504–1635.* Cambridge Antiquarian Society, vol. 35. 1905.

Foucault, Michel. *Essential Works of Foucault 1954–1984.* Vol. 3, *Power,* edited by James D. Faubion; translated by Robert Hurley et al. New York: The New Press, 2000.

——. *The History of Sexuality.* Vol. 1, *An Introduction,* translated by Robert Hurley. New York: Vintage Books, 1980.

——. *The History of Sexuality.* Vol. 3, *The Care of the Self,* translated by Robert Hurley. New York: Vintage Books, 1988.

——. *The Order of Things: An Archaeology of the Human Sciences.* New York: Vintage Books, 1994.

——. *Power/Knowledge: Selected Interviews and Other Writings 1972–1977.* Edited by Colin Gordon. Translated by Colin Gordon et al. New York: Pantheon Books, 1980.

Fradenburg, Olga, ed. *Women and Sovereignty.* Edinburgh: Edinburgh University Press, 1992.

Francis, W. N., ed. *The Book of Vices and Virtues.* EETS, o.s., vol. 217. 1942.

Franco, Giacomo. *Habiti l'huomeni et donne Venetiane.* Venice: G. Franco, 1610.

Frecero, Carla. "Marguerite de Navarre and the Politics of Maternal Sovereignty." In *Women and Sovereignty,* edited by Louise Olga Fradenburg, 132–149. Edinburgh: Edinburgh University Press, 1992.

French, Katherine L. " 'I Leave My Best Gown as a Vestment': Women's Spiritual Interests in the Late Medieval English Parish." *Magistra* 4 (1998): 57–77.

——. "Maidens' Lights and Wives' Stores: Women's Parish Guilds in Late Medieval England." *Sixteenth Century Journal* 29 (1998): 399–425.

——. *The People of the Parish: Community Life in a Late Medieval English Diocese.* Philadelphia: University of Pennsylvania Press, 2001.

——. " 'To Free them from Binding': Women in the Late Medieval English Parish." *Journal of Interdisciplinary History* 27 (1996): 387–412.

Frye, Susan, and Karen Roberton, eds. *Maids and Mistresses, Cousins and Queens: Women's Alliances in Early Modern England.* Oxford: Oxford University Press, 1999.

Furnivall, F. J., ed. "How the Good Wife Taught Her Daughter." In *The Babees Book*. EETS, o.s., vol. 32. 1868.

——, ed. *The Babees Book*. EETS, o.s., vol. 32. 1868.

Gabriel, Astrik L. "The Educational Ideas of Christine de Pisan." *Journal of the History of Ideas* 16 (1955): 3–22.

Garland, Lynda. "The Life and Ideology of Byzantine Women: A Further Note on Conventions of Behavior and Social Reality as Reflected in Eleventh- and Twelfth-Century Historical Sources." *Byzantion* 58 (1988): 361–89.

Garrison, Christine Wille. "The Lives of St Ætheldreda: Representation of Female Sanctity from 700–1300." Ph.D. diss., University of Rochester, 1990.

Gaunt, Simon. "The Significance of Silence." *Paragraph* 13 (1990): 203–4.

Geary, Patrick J. *Living with the Dead in the Middle Ages*. Ithaca: Cornell University Press, 1994.

Georgianna, Linda. "Coming to Terms with the Norman Conquest: Nationalism and English Literary History." In *Literature and the Nation*, edited by Brook Thomas, 33–53. Tübingen: Gunter Narr, 1998.

——. *The Solitary Self: Individuality in the "Ancrene Wisse."* Cambridge: Harvard University Press, 1982.

Gerson, Jean. *The Concept of "Discretio spirituum" in John Gerson's "De probatione spirituum" and "De distinctione verarum visionum a falsis."* Translated by Paschal Boland. Washington, D.C.: Catholic University of America Press, 1959.

——. *Jean Gerson: Selections from A deo exivit, Contra curiositatem studentium and De mystica theologia speculativa*. Translated by Steven Ozment. Leiden: E. J. Brill, 1969.

——. *Oeuvres complètes*. Edited by Palémon Glorieux. Paris: Desclée, 1960–1973.

Gibson, Gail McMurray. *The Theater of Devotion: East Anglian Drama and Society in the Late Middle Ages*. Chicago: University of Chicago Press, 1989.

Gilchrist, Roberta. *Gender and Material Culture: The Archaeology of Religious Women*. London: Routledge, 1994.

Giles, Kate. "Framing Labour: The Archaeology of York's Medieval Guildhalls." In *The Problem of Labour in Fourteenth-Century England*, edited by J. Bothwell, P. J. P. Goldberg, and W. M. Ormrod, 65–84. Woodbridge: Boydell, 2000.

Gilligan, Carol. *In a Different Voice: Psychological Theory and Women's Development*. Cambridge: Harvard University Press, 1982.

Girouard, Mark. *Life in the English Country House: A Social and Architectural History*. Harmondsworth: Penguin Books, 1980.

Given, James. *Inquisition and Medieval Society: Power, Discipline, and Resistance in Languedoc*. Ithaca: Cornell University Press, 1997.

Goldberg, P. J. P. "Household and the Organisation of Labour in Late Medieval Towns: Some English Evidence." In *The Household in Late Medieval Cities, Italy and Northwestern Europe Compared*, edited by Myriam Carlier and Tim Soens, 59–70. Louvain-Apeldoorn: Garant, 2001.

——. "The Public and the Private: Women in the Pre-Plague Economy." In *Thirteenth-Century England*, vol. 3, edited by J. Bothwell, P. J. P. Goldberg, and W. M. Ormrod, 75–89. Woodbridge: Boydell, 1991.

——. "What Was a Servant?" In *Concepts and Patterns of Service in the Later Middle Ages*, edited by Anne Curry and Elizabeth Matthew, 1–20. Woodbridge: Boydell, 2000.

——. *Women, Work and Life-Cycle in a Medieval Economy: Women in York and Yorkshire c. 1300–1520*. Oxford: Clarendon Press, 1992.

——, ed. and trans. *Women in England c 1275–1525*. Manchester: Manchester University Press, 1995.

Gowing, Laura. *Domestic Dangers: Women, Words, and Sex in Early Modern London*. Oxford: Oxford University Press, 1996.

Graziato, Gisela, ed. *Le promissioni del Doge di Venezia dalle origini alla fine del duecento.* Venice: Il Comitato, 1986.

Grenville, Jane. "Houses and Households in Late Medieval England: An Archaeological Perspective." In *Medieval Women: Texts and Contexts in Late Medieval Britain: Essays for Felicity Riddy,* edited by Jocelyn Wogan-Browne et al., 309–28. Turnhout: Brepols, 2000.

——. *Medieval Housing.* London: Leicester University Press, 1997.

Grubb, James. *Provincial Families of the Renaissance: Private and Public Life in the Veneto.* Baltimore: Johns Hopkins University Press, 1996.

Grubb, Judith Evans. *Law and Family in Late Antiquity: The Emperor Constantine's Marriage Legislation.* Oxford: Clarendon Press, 1995.

Grundmann, Herbert. *Religiösebewegungen im Mittelalter: Untersuchungen über die geschichtlichen Zusammenhänge zwischen der Ketzerei, den Bettelorden und der religiösen Frauenbewegung im 12. Und 13. Jahrhundert.* 2d ed. Hildesheim: Olms Verlagsbuchhandlung, 1961.

——. *Religious Movements in the Middle Ages: The Historical Links between Heresy, the Mendicant Orders, and the Women's Religious Movement in the Twelfth and Thirteenth Century with the Historical Foundations of German Mysticism.* Translated by Steven Rowan. Notre Dame: University of Notre Dame Press, 1995. Orig. pub. in German, 1935. rev. ed., 1961.

Gundersheimer, Werner. "Women, Learning and Power: Eleonora of Aragon and the Court of Ferrara." In *Beyond Their Sex: Learned Women of the European Past,* edited by Patricia Labalme, 43–65. New York: New York University Press, 1980.

Gunn, Alan. *The Mirror of Love: A Reinterpretation of "The Romance of the Rose."* Lubbock: Texas Tech Press, 1952.

Gurney, Craig M. "Accommodating Bodies: The Organization of Corporeal Dirt in the Embodied Home." In *Organizing Bodies: Institutions, Policy, and Work,* edited by Linda McKie and N. Watson, 57–78. Basingstoke: Macmillan, 2000.

Guzzetti, Linda. "Le donne a Venezia nel XIV secolo: Uno studio sulla loro presenza nella società e nella famiglia." *Studi Veneziani* n.s. 35 (1998): 15–88.

Gy, Pierre-Marie. "Le Précepte de la confession annuelle (Latran IV, c. 21) et la détection des hérétiques: S. Bonaventure et S. Thomas contre S. Raymond de Peñafort." *Revue des sciences philosophiques et théologiques* 58 (1974): 444–50.

Hagen, Susan K. *Allegorical Remembrance: A Study of the Pilgrimage of the Life of Man as a Medieval Treatise on Seeing and Remembering.* Athens: University of Georgia Press, 1990.

Hairston, Julia. "Skirting the Issue: Machiavelli's Caterina Sforza." *Renaissance Quarterly* 53 (2000): 687–712.

Hall, R. A. et al., eds. *Medieval Tenements in Aldwark, and Other Sites.* The Archaeology of York, 10/2. York: Council of British Archaeology, 1988.

Hamel, Christopher de. *Syon Abbey: The Library of the Bridgettine Nuns and their Peregrinations after the Reformation: An Essay by Christopher de Hamel, with the Manuscript at Arundel Castle.* London: Roxburghe Club, 1991.

Hanawalt, Barbara A. "At the Margins of Women's Space in Medieval Europe." In *"Of Good and Ill Repute": Gender and Social Control in Medieval England,* edited by Barbara A. Hanawalt, 70–87. Oxford: Oxford University Press, 1998.

——. *The Ties That Bound: Peasant Families in Medieval England.* Oxford: Oxford University Press, 1986.

Hand, John Oliver. *"Saint Anne with the Virgin and the Christ Child* by the Master of Frankfurt." *Studies in the History of Art* 12 (1982): 43–52.

Hanna, Ralph. "Reconsidering the Auchinleck Manuscript." In *New Directions in Later Medieval Manuscript Studies,* edited by Derek Pearsall, 91–102. York: York Medieval Press, 2000.

——. "Will's Work." In *Written Work: Langland, Labor, and Authorship,* edited by Steven

Justice and Kathryn Kerby-Fulton, 23–66. Philadelphia: University of Pennsylvania Press, 1997.

Hannay, Margaret P., ed. *Silent But for the Word: Tudor Women as Patrons, Translators, and Writers of Religious Works*. Kent, Ohio: Kent State University Press, 1985.

Hanswernfried, Muth. *Tilman Riemenschneider. Die Werke des Bildschnitzers und Bildhauers, seiner Werkstatt und seines Umkreises im Mainfränkischen Museum, Würzburg*. Würzburg: Stürtz, 1982.

Haraway, Donna. *Simians, Cyborgs, and Women: The Reinvention of Nature*. New York: Routledge, 1991.

Harrington, Susanmarie. *Women, Literacy, and Intellectual Culture in Anglo-Saxon England*. Ph.D. diss., University of Michigan, 1990.

Harvey, Barbara. "Work and *Festa Ferianda* in Medieval England." *Journal of Ecclesiastical History* 23, no. 4 (1972): 289–308.

Haskins, Charles Homer. "Robert le Bougre and the Beginnings of the Inquisition in Northern France." In *Studies in Mediaeval Culture*, 193–244. Oxford: Clarendon Press, 1929.

Hazlitt, W. Carew. *Faiths and Folklore of the British Isles*. Vol. 2. 1905. Reprint. New York: Benjamin Bloom, 1965.

Heffernan, Carol Falvo, ed. *Le Bone Florence of Rome*. Manchester: Manchester University Press, 1976.

Hennecke, Edgar. *New Testament Apocrypha*. Vol. 1, *Gospels and Related Writings*. Edited by William Schneemelcher. English translation by J. B. Higgins et al. and edited by R. McL. Wilson, 374–78. Philadelphia: Westminster Press, 1963.

Henry of Freimar. *De quatuor instinctibus*. In *Insignis atque preclarus de singulari tractatu de quatuor instinctibus*. Venice: Iacobus Pentius for Laz. De Soardis, 1498.

Herlihy, David. "Land, Family and Women in Continental Europe, 701–1200." In *Women in Medieval Society*, edited by Susan M. Stuard, 13–46. Philadelphia: University of Pennsylvania Press, 1976.

Hicks, Eric, ed. *Le Débat sur le Roman de la Rose*. Paris: H. Champion, 1977.

Hindle, Steve. "The Shaming of Margaret Knowsley: Gossip, Gender and the Experience of Authority in Early Modern England." *Continuity and Change* 9 (1994): 371–93.

Hobhouse, Edmund, ed. "Croscombe Church-Wardens' Accounts." In *Church-Wardens Accounts of Croscombe, Pilton, Yatton, Tintinhull, Morebath, and St. Michael's Bath*. Somerset Record Society, vol. 4. 1890.

Hoccleve, Thomas. *Hoccleve's Works*. Vol. 2, *The Minor Poems*. Edited by I. Gollancz. EETS, o.s., vol. 73. 1925.

Hollister, C. Warren. *Medieval Europe: A Short History*. 7th ed. New York: McGraw-Hill, 1995.

Holthausen, F., ed. *Vices and Virtues: Being a Soul's Confession of Its Sins*. EETS, o.s., vols. 89 and 159. 1888–1921.

Holum, Kenneth. *Theodosian Empresses: Women and Imperial Dominion in Late Antiquity*. Berkeley: University of California Press, 1982.

Horden, Peregrine. "Household Care and Informal Networks: Comparisons and Continuities from Antiquity to the Present." In *The Locus of Care: Families, Communities, Institutions and the Provision of Welfare Since Antiquity*, edited by Peregrine Horden and Richard Smith, 21–67. London: Routledge, 1998.

Horstmann, C. "Orologium Sapientiae or the Seven Poyntes of Trewe Wisdom, aus MS Douce 114." *Anglia* 10 (1888): 323–89.

Houlbrooke, R. A. "Women's Social Life and Common Action in England from the Fifteenth Century to the Eve of the Civil War." *Continuity and Change* 1 (1986): 171–89.

Howell, Margaret. *Eleanor of Provence: Queenship in Thirteenth-Century England*. Oxford: Blackwell, 1998.

Howell, Martha C. *The Marriage Exchange: Property, Social Place and Gender in Cities of the Low Countries, 1300–1550*. Chicago: University of Chicago Press, 1998.

Hughes, Diane Owen. "From Brideprice to Dowry in Mediterranean Europe." Reprinted in *The Marriage Bargain: Women and Dowries in European History*, edited by Marion A. Kaplan, 13–58. New York: Haworth Press, 1985.

———. "Sumptuary Law and Social Relations in Renaissance Italy." In *Disputes and Settlements: Law and Human Relations in the West*, edited by John Bossy, 66–99. Cambridge: Cambridge University Press, 1983.

———. "Urban Growth and Family Structure in Medieval Genoa." *Past and Present* 66 (1975): 3–28.

Hunt, Richard. "The Sum of Knowledge: Universities and Learning." In *The Flowering of the Middle Ages*, edited by Joan Evans, 179–202. London: Thames and Hudson, 1985.

Huot, Sylvia. "Seduction and Sublimation: Christine de Pizan, Jean de Meun, and Dante." *Romance Notes* 25 (1985): 372–73.

Hurlburt, Holly S. " 'La Serenissima Domina Ducissa': The Dogaresse of Venice, 1250–1500." Ph.D. diss., Syracuse University, 2000.

Hutton, Ronald. *The Rise and Fall of Merry England: The Ritual Year, 1400–1700*. Oxford: Oxford University Press, 1994.

Immel, Hans, ed., *Passio Kiliani*. Commentary by Cynthia J. Hahn. Graz, Austria: Akademische Druck- u. Verlagsanstalt, 1988.

Jackson, Richard. *Ordines Coronationis Franciae: Texts and Ordines for the Coronation of Frankish and French Kings and Queens in the Middle Ages*, vol. 1. Philadelphia: University of Pennsylvania Press, 1995.

———. *Vive le Roi!: A History of the French Coronation from Charles V to Charles X*. Chapel Hill, N.C.: University of North Carolina Press, 1984.

Jacques de Vitry. *The Exempla or Illustrative Stories from the Sermones Vulgares of Jacques de Vitry*. Edited by Thomas Frederick Crane. Folklore Publications, no. 26. London, 1890.

———. *The Life of Marie d'Oignies*. Translated by Margot King. Saskatoon: Peregrina Publishing, 1986.

———. *Two Lives of Marie D'Oignies*. Translated by Margot King. Peregrina Translations Series. Toronto: Peregrina, 1998.

———. "Vita B. Mariae Oigniacensis." In *AA SS* (June 5): 547–72. Paris: Victor Palmé, 1865.

Jantzen, Grace. *Power, Gender, and Christian Mysticism*. Cambridge Studies in Ideology and Religion, vol. 8. Cambridge: Cambridge University Press, 1995.

Jean de Meun. *Roman de la Rose*. Edited by Daniel Poirion. Paris: Garnier-Flammarion, 1974.

Jenkins, Jacqueline. "Lay Devotion and Women Readers of the Middle English Prose Life of St Katherine." In *The Cult of St Katherine in Medieval Europe*, edited by Jacqueline Jenkins and Katherine J. Lewis. Turnhout: Brepols, forthcoming.

Johnson, Lynn Staley. "The Trope of the Scribe and the Question of Literary Authority in the Works of Julian of Norwich and Margery Kempe." *Speculum* 66 (1991): 820–38.

Jones, Claire. "An Assortment of Doctors: The Readers of Medical Books in Late Medieval England." *Journal of the Early Book Society* 3 (2000): 136–51.

Jones, Karen, and Michael Zell. "Bad Conversation? Gender and Social Control in a Kentish Borough, c. 1450–c. 1570." *Continuity and Change* 13 (1998): 11–31.

Julian of Norwich. *A Book of Showings to the Anchoress Julian of Norwich*. 2 vols. Edited by Edmund Colledge and James Walsh. Studies and Texts, no. 35. Toronto: Pontifical Institute of Mediaeval Studies, 1978.

Kantorowicz, Ernst. *The King's Two Bodies: A Study in Mediaeval Political Theology*. Princeton: Princeton University Press, 1957.

Karl, Ludwig, ed. "Die Episode aus der Vie de Madeleine." *ZRPh* 34 (1910): 363–70.

Kazhdan, Alexander P., and Michael McCormick. "The Social World of the Byzantine Court." In *Byzantine Court Culture from 829 to 1204*, edited by Henry Maguire, 167–98. Washington, D.C.: Dumbarton Oaks, 1997.

Keats-Rohan, K. S. B. "Prosopography and Computing: A Marriage Made in Heaven?" *History and Computing* 12 (2000): 1–11.

Keene, Derek. "Landlords, the Property Market and Urban Development in England." In *Power, Profit and Urban Land: Landownership in Medieval and Early Modern Northern European Towns*, edited by Finn-Einar Eliassen and Geir Atle Ersland, 93–119. Aldershot: Scolar Press, 1996.

——. *Survey of Medieval Winchester, Winchester Studies*. 2 vols. Oxford: Oxford University Press, 1985.

——. "Tanners' Widows, 1300–1350." In *Medieval London Widows*, edited by Caroline M. Barron and Anne F. Sutton, 1–27. London: Hambledon Press, 1994.

Keene, Derek J., and Vanessa Harding, comp. *Historical Gazetteer of London before the Great Fire. Part 1. Cheapside*. 57 microfiches. Cambridge: Chadwick Healey, 1987.

Keller, Hans-Erich, ed. *La vie de sainte Marguérite/Wace; édition, avec introduction et glossaire par Hans-Erich Keller, commentaire des enluminures du ms. Troyes 1905 par Margaret Alison Stones*. Beihefte zur Zeitschrift für romanische Philologie, Band 229. Tübingen: M. Niemeyer, 1990.

Kempshall, M. S. *The Common Good in Late Medieval Political Thought*. Oxford: Clarendon Press, 1999.

Kent, F. W. *Household and Lineage in Renaissance Florence*. Princeton: Princeton University Press, 1977.

Kerby-Fulton, Kathryn. "Hildegard and the Male Reader: A Study of Insular Reception." In *Prophets Abroad: The Reception of Continental Holy Women in Medieval England*, edited by Rosalynn Voaden, 1–18. Cambridge: D. S. Brewer, 1996.

Kermode, Jennifer. *Medieval Merchants: York, Beverley and Hull in the Later Middle Ages*. Cambridge: Cambridge University Press, 1998.

King, Margaret L. "Book-Lined Cells: Women and Humanism in the Early Italian Renaissance." In *Beyond Their Sex: Learned Women of the European Past*, edited by Patricia H. Labalme, 91–116. New York: New York University Press, 1984.

——. "Personal, Domestic and Republican Virtues in the Moral Philosophy of Giovanni Caldiera." *Renaissance Quarterly* 28 (1975): 554–57.

Kitto, John V., ed. *St. Martin-in-the-Fields: The Accounts of the Churchwardens, 1525–1603*. London: Simpkin, Marshall, Kent, Hamilton and Co. Ltd., 1901.

Klapisch-Zuber, Christiane. "The Griselda Complex: Dowry and Marriage Gifts in the Quattrocento." In *Women, Family and Ritual in Renaissance Italy*, translated by Lydia G. Cochrane, 213–46. Chicago: University of Chicago Press, 1985.

——. "Zacharias, or the Ousted Father: Nuptial Rites in Tuscany between Giotto and the Council of Trent." In *Women, Family and Ritual in Renaissance Italy*, translated by Lydia G. Cochrane. 178–212. Chicago: University of Chicago Press, 1985.

Klausner, David N., ed. *Records of Early English Drama: Herefordshire and Worcestershire*. Toronto: University of Toronto Press, 1990.

Kleinschmidt, Beda. *Die heilige Anna: Ihre Verehrung in Geschichte, Kunst und Volkstum*. Düsseldorf: Schwann, 1930.

Kolve, V. A. *Chaucer and the Imagery of Narrative: The First Five Canterbury Tales*. Stanford: Stanford University Press, 1984.

Kowaleski, Maryanne. *Local Markets and Regional Trade in Medieval Exeter*. Cambridge: Cambridge University Press, 1995.

——. "Singlewomen in Medieval and Early Modern Europe: The Demographic Perspective." In *Singlewomen in the European Past, 1250–1800*, edited by Judith M. Bennett and Amy M. Froide, 38–81, 325–44. Philadelphia: University of Pennsylvania Press, 1999.

———. "Women's Work in a Market Town: Exeter in the Late Fourteenth Century." In *Women and Work in Preindustrial Europe*, edited by Barbara Hanawalt, 145–64. Bloomington: Indiana University Press, 1986.

Kowaleski, Maryanne, and Judith M. Bennett. "Crafts, Guilds, and Women in the Middle Ages: Fifty Years After Marian K. Dale." In *Sisters and Other Workers in the Middle Ages*, edited by J. M. Bennett et al., 11–38. Chicago: University of Chicago Press, 1989.

Krueger, Roberta. *Women Readers and the Ideology of Gender in Old French Verse Romance.* Cambridge: Cambridge University Press, 1993.

Kuhn, Sherman M., and John Reidy, eds. *Middle English Dictionary, Part H.5.* Ann Arbor: University of Michigan Press, 1967.

Kümin, Beat. *The Shaping of a Community: The Rise and Reformation of the English Parish c. 1400–1560.* Aldershot, Hants.: Scolar Press, 1996.

Labalme, Patricia, and Laura Sanguinetti White. "How to (and How Not to) Get Married in Sixteenth-Century Venice (Selections from the Diary of Marin Sanudo)." *Renaissance Quarterly* 52 (1999): 43–72.

Lacey, Kay E. "Women and Work in Fourteenth– and Fifteenth–Century London." In *Women and Work in Pre-Industrial England*, edited by Lindsey Charles and Lorna Duffin, 24–82. London: Croom Helm, 1985.

Langlois, Ch.-V. *Histoire de France illustrée depuis les origines jusqu'à la révolution.* 9 vols. Edited by E. Lavisse. Paris: Hachette, 1911.

Lea, Henry Charles. *A History of Auricular Confession and Indulgences in the Latin Church.* Philadelphia: Lea Bros., 1896.

Lecoy de la Marche, A., ed. *Anecdotes historiques, légendes et apologues tirés du recueil inédit d'Etienne de Bourbon.* Paris: Librairie Renouard, 1877.

Legge, M. Dominica. *Anglo-Norman Literature in the Cloisters.* Edinburgh: Edinburgh University Press, 1950.

Lehfeldt, Elizabeth A. "Ruling Sexuality: The Political Legitimacy of Isabel of Castile." *Renaissance Quarterly* 53 (2000): 31–56.

Lehrman, Sara. "The Education of Women in the Middle Ages." In *The Roles and Images of Women in the Middle Ages and Renaissance*, edited by Douglas Radcliff-Umstead, 133–44. Pittsburgh: University of Pittsburgh Press, 1975.

Leinhardt, Samuel. *Social Networks: A Developing Paradigm.* New York: Harcourt Brace Jovanovich, 1977.

Lemay, Helen. "Women and the Literature of Obstetrics and Gynecology." In *Medieval Women and the Sources of Medieval History*, edited by Joel T. Rosenthal, 189–209. Athens: University of Georgia Press, 1990.

Le Roux de Lincy, M., ed. *Le Livre des Proverbes Français.* 2d ed. Paris, 1859.

Levi-Strauss, Claude. *The Elementary Structures of Kinship.* Boston: Beacon Press, 1969.

———. *The Raw and the Cooked.* Translated by John and Doreen Weightman. New York: Harper & Row, 1969.

Leyser, Henrietta. *Hermits and the New Monasticism: A Study of Religious Communities in Western Europe, 1000–1150.* New York: St. Martin's Press, 1984.

Leyser, Karl. *Rule and Conflict in an Early Medieval Society: Ottonian Saxony.* Bloomington: University of Indiana Press, 1978.

L'Hermite-Leclercq, Paulette. "La Réclusion volontaire au moyen âge: une institution religieuse spécialement féminine." In *La condición de la mujer en la Edad Media*, 136–54. Madrid: Universidad Complutense, 1986.

Lochrie, Karma. *Covert Operations: The Medieval Uses of Secrecy.* Philadelphia: University of Pennsylvania Press, 1999.

Loftus, E. A., and H. F. Chettle. *A History of Barking Abbey.* Barking: Wilson and Whitworth, [1954].

Love, Nicholas. *Nicholas Love's Mirror of the Blessed Life of Jesus Christ: A Critical Edition*

Based on Cambridge University Library Additional MSS 6578 and 6686. Edited by Michael G. Sargent. New York: Garland, 1992.

Lubkin, Gregory. *A Renaissance Court: Milan under Galeazzo Maria Sforza*. Berkeley: University of California Press, 1994.

Lugano, Placido Tommaso, ed. *I processi inediti per Francesca Bussa dei Ponziani (1440–1453)*. Vatican City: Biblioteca apostolica vaticana, 1945.

Lydgate, John. "The Legend of Seynt Margarete." In *The Minor Poems of John Lydgate*, edited by Henry Noble McCracken, 173–92. EETS, o.s., vol. 107. 1910.

MacBain, William, ed., *The Life of Saint Catherine by Clemence of Barking*. ANTS 18. Oxford: Blackwell for ANTS, 1964.

MacCormack, Carol. "Nature, Culture, and Gender: A Critique." In *Nature, Culture, and Gender*, edited by C. MacCormack and M. Strathern, 1–24. Cambridge: Cambridge University Press, 1980.

MacCormack, Carol, and Marilyn Strathern, eds. *Nature, Culture, and Gender*. Cambridge: Cambridge University Press, 1980.

Mack, Frances M., ed. *Seinte Marherete*. EETS, o.s., vol. 193. 1934. Reprint. 1958.

Mackenney, Richard. *Tradesmen and Traders: The World of the Guilds in Venice and Europe, c. 1250–c.1650*. Totowa, N.J.: Barnes & Noble Press, 1987.

MacLean, Sally-Beth. "Hocktide: A Reassessment of a Popular Pre-Reformation Festival." In *Festive Drama*, edited by Meg Twycross, 233–41. Cambridge: D. S. Brewer, 1996.

Majeska, George. "The Emperor in His Church: Imperial Ritual in the Church of St. Sophia." In *Byzantine Court Culture from 829 to 1204*, edited by Henry Maguire. Washington, D.C.: Dumbarton Oaks, 1997.

Martin Luther und die Reformation in Deutschland. Exhibition Catalog. Frankfurt am Main: Insel, 1983.

Masters, Betty, and Elizabeth Ralph, eds. *The Church Book of St. Ewen's, Bristol: 1454–1485*. Bristol and Gloucestershire Archaeological Society, vol. 6. 1967.

Mate, Mavis E. *Women in Medieval English Society*. Cambridge: Cambridge University Press, 1999.

Matteotti, John. "Vita S. Francesca Romana." In *AA SS*. Paris: Victor Palme, 1865.

McCarthy, Adrian James, ed. *Book to a Mother: An Edition with Commentary*. Salzburg Studies in English Literature: Elizabethan and Renaissance Studies, no. 92:1. Salzburg: Institut für Anglistik und Amerikanistik, 1981.

McCracken, Peggy. " 'The Boy Who Was a Girl': Reading Gender in the *Roman de Silence*." *Romanic Review* 85 (1994): 517–36.

McDonnell, Ernest. *Beguines and Beghards in Medieval Culture, with Special Emphasis on the Belgian Scene*. New Brunswick, N.J.: Rutgers University Press, 1954.

McKitterick, Rosamond. *The Uses of Literacy in Early Medieval Europe*. Cambridge: Cambridge University Press, 1990.

McNamara, Jo Ann. "Canossa: The Ungendered Man and the Anthropomorphized Institution." In *Render Unto Caesar*, edited by Sabrina Petra Ramet and Donald Treadgold, 131–50. Washington D.C.: American University Press, 1995.

——. "Chastity as a Third Gender in the Work of Gregory of Tours." In *The World of Gregory of Tours*, edited by Kathleen Mitchell and Ian Wood, 199–210. Leyden: Brill, 2002.

——. "City Air Makes Men Free and Women Bound." In *Text and Territory: Geography and Literature in the European Middle Ages*, edited by Sylvia Tomasch and Sealy Gilles, 141–58. Philadelphia: University of Pennsylvania Press, 1998.

——. "Cornelia's Daughters: Paula and Eustochium." *Women's Studies* 11 (1984): 9–27.

——. "Gendering Virtue." In *Plutarch's Advice to the Bride and Groom and A Consolation to His Wife: English Translations, Commentary, Interpretive Essays, and Bibliography*, edited by Sarah B. Pomeroy, 151–61. Oxford: Oxford University Press, 1999.

———. "The Herrenfrage: The Restructuring of the Gender System, 1050–1150." In *Medieval Masculinities: Regarding Men in the Middle Ages*, edited by Clare A. Lees, 3–29. Minneapolis: University of Minnesota Press, 1994.

———. "*Imitatio Helenae*: Sainthood as an Attribute of Queenship in the Early Middle Ages." In *Saints*, edited by Sandro Sticca, 51–80. Binghamton: Center for Medieval and Renaissance Studies, State University of New York, 1996.

———. "The Need to Give: Suffering and Female Sanctity in the Middle Ages." In *Images of Sainthood*, edited by Renate Blumenfeld-Kosinski and Timea Szell, 199–221. Ithaca: Cornell University Press, 1991.

———. "Sexual Equality and the Cult of Virginity in Early Christian Thought." *Feminist Studies* 3, no. 3/4 (1976): 145–58.

———. *Sisters in Arms: Catholic Nuns Through Two Millennia*. Cambridge: Harvard University Press, 1996.

———. "An Unresolved Syllogism: The Search for a Christian Gender System." In *Conflicted Identities and Multiple Masculinities: Men in the Medieval West*, edited by Jacqueline Murray, 1–24. New York: Garland, 1999.

———. "Wives and Widows in Early Christian Thought." *International Journal of Women's Studies* 2, no. 6 (1979): 575–92.

McNamara, Jo Ann, and John E. Halborg (with Gordon Whatley). *Sainted Women of the Dark Ages*. Durham, N.C.: Duke University Press, 1992.

McNamara, Jo Ann, and Suzanne Wemple. "Marriage and Divorce in the Frankish Kingdom." In *Women in Medieval Society*, edited by Susan M. Stuard, 95–124. Philadelphia: University of Pennsylvania Press, 1976.

———. "The Power of Women Through the Family," *Feminist Studies* 1 (1973): 126–41. Reprinted in *Clio's Consciousness Raised*, edited by Mary Hartman and Lois Banner, 103–18. New York: Harper and Row, 1974; and in *Women and Power in the Middle Ages*, edited by Mary C. Erler and Maryanne Kowaleski, 83–101. Athens: University of Georgia Press, 1988.

Meale, Carol M., ed. *Women and Literature in Britain 1150–1500*. Cambridge: Cambridge University Press, 1993, rev. ed. 1996.

Mechthild of Magdeburg. *The Flowing Light of the Godhead*. Translated by Frank Tobin. New York: Paulist Press, 1998.

Mens, A. "L'Ombrie italienne et l'ombrie brabançonne: Deux courants religieux parallèles d'inspiration commune." *Etudes franciscaines* annual supplement 17 (1967): 14–47.

Merchant, Carolyn. *The Death of Nature: Women, Ecology, and the Scientific Revolution*. San Francisco: Harper & Row, 1980.

Meredith, Peter, ed. *The Mary Play from the N.town Manuscript*. London: Longman, 1987.

Messner, Michael A., and Donald F. Sabo, eds. *Sport, Men, and the Gender Order: Critical Feminist Perspectives*. Champaign, Ill.: Human Kinetic Books, 1990.

Metz enluminée: Autour de la Bible de Charles le Chauve; Trésors manuscrits des églises messines. Metz: Editions Serpenoise, 1989.

Millett, Bella. "*Ancrene Wisse* and the Book of Hours." In *Writing Religious Women: Female Spiritual and Textual Practices in Late Medieval England*, edited by Denis Renevey and Christiania Whitehead. Cardiff: University of Wales Press, 2000.

———. " 'Women in No Man's Land': English Recluses and the Development of Vernacular Literature in the Twelfth and Thirteenth Centuries." In *Women and Literature in Britain 1150–1500*, edited by Carol M. Meale, 86–103. Cambridge: Cambridge University Press, 1993.

Millett, Bella, with the assistance of George B. Jack and Yoko Wada, "*Ancrene Wisse*," the *Katherine Group and the Wooing Group*. Vol. 2 of *Annotated Bibliographies of Old and Middle English Literature*. Cambridge: D. S. Brewer, 1996.

Milsom, S. F. C. *Historical Foundations of the Common Law*. London: Butterworths, 1969.

Mirk, John. *Instructions for a Parish Priest*. Edited by Edward Peacock. EETS, o.s., 31a. 1902.

——. *Mirk's Festival*. Edited by Theodor Erbe. EETS, extra series 96. 1905. Reprint, 1987.

Moi, Toril. *What Is a Woman? And Other Essays*. Oxford: Oxford University Press, 1999.

Moltmann-Wendel, Elisabeth. *A Land Flowing with Milk and Honey: Perspectives on Feminist Theology*. Translated by John Bowden. New York: Crossroad, 1986.

Mooney, Catherine, ed. *Gendered Voices: Medieval Saints and Their Interpreters*. Philadelphia: University of Pennsylvania Press, 1999.

Moore, R. I. *The First European Revolution, 900–1200*. Oxford: Blackwell, 1998.

Morris, W. A. *The Frankpledge System*. London: Longmans, Green, 1901.

Morton, James, ed. and trans. *Ancrene Riwle. The Ancren Riwle: A Treatise on the Rules and Duties of Monastic Life, Edited and Translated from a Semi-Saxon MS. of the Thirteenth Century*. Camden Society, vol. 57. 1853.

——, ed. *The Legend of St Katherine of Alexandria. Edited from a Manuscript in the Cottonian Library*. London: Bentley, 1841.

Muir, Edward. *Civic Ritual in Renaissance Venice*. Princeton: Princeton University Press, 1981.

Mulder-Bakker, Anneke B. "The Prime of Their Lives: Women and Age, Wisdom and Religious Careers in Northern Europe." In *New Trends in Feminine Spirituality: The Holy Women of Liège and Their Impact*, edited by Juliette Dor, Lesley Johnson, and Jocelyn Wogan-Browne, 215–36. Turnhout: Brepols, 1999.

Murray, Alexander. "Confession As a Historical Source in the Thirteenth Century." In *The Writing of History in the Middle Ages*, edited by R. H. C. Davies and J. M. Wallace-Hadrill, 268–305. Oxford: Clarendon Press, 1981.

Mustanoja, Tauno F., ed. *The Good Wife Taught Her Daughter. The Good Wyfe Wold a Pylgremage. The Thewis of Gud Women*. Helsinki: Annales Academiae Scientiarum Fennicae, vol. 61. 1948.

Neel, Carol. "The Origins of the Beguines." In *Sisters and Workers in the Middle Ages*, edited by Judith M. Bennett, Elizabeth A. Clark, Jean F. O'Barr, B. Anne Vilen, and Sarah Westphal-Wihl, 240–60. Chicago: University of Chicago Press, 1989.

Nelson, Janet. "Early Rites of Queen-Making and the Shaping of Medieval Queenship." In *Queens and Queenship in Medieval Europe*, edited by Anne Duggan, 301–15. Woodbridge: Boydell, 1997.

Netzer, Nancy, ed. *Catalogue of Medieval Objects: Metalwork*. Boston: Museum of Fine Arts, 1991.

Newett, Margaret. "The Sumptuary Laws of Venice in the Fourteenth and Fifteenth Centuries." In *Historical Essays by Members of the Owens College, Manchester*, edited by T. F. Tout and J. Tout, 245–78. New York: Longmans Green & Co., 1902.

Newman, Barbara. *God and the Goddesses: Vision, Poetry, and Belief in the Middle Ages*. Philadelphia: University of Pennsylvania Press, 2002.

——. "Possessed by the Spirit: Devout Women, Demoniacs, and the Apostolic Life in the Thirteenth Century." *Speculum* 73 (1998): 463–68.

——. *From Virile Woman to WomanChrist: Studies in Medieval Religion and Literature*. Philadelphia: University of Pennsylvania Press, 1995.

Nichols, John A., ed. "The History and Cartulary of the Cistercian Nuns of Marham Abbey, 1249–1536." Ph.D. diss., Kent State University, 1974.

Nicol, Donald. *The Byzantine Lady: Ten Portraits, 1250–1500*. Cambridge: Cambridge University Press, 1994.

Nider, John. *Confessionale sue manuale confessorum fratris Johannis Nyder ad instructionem spiritualium pastorum valde necessarium*. Paris: Jehan Petit, n.d.

——. *Consolatorium timorate conscientie*. Paris: Jehan Petit, [1502].

——. *Formicarium*. Douai: B. Belleri, 1602.

Nidurst, René. "Lettre inédite de Robert d'Arbrissel à la comtesse Ermengarde." *Bibliothèque de l'Ecole de Chartes* 3, no. 5 (1854): 209–35.

Niezen, R. W. "Hot Literacy in Cold Societies: A Comparative Study of the Sacred Value of Writing." *Comparative Studies in Society and History* 33, no. 2 (April 1991): 225–54.

Norbert, Elias. *The Civilizing Process: The History of Manners and State Formation and Civilization*. Oxford: Blackwell, 1994.

Norton, Christopher, David Park, and Paul Binski. *Dominican Painting in East Anglia: The Thornton Parva Retable and the Musée de Cluny Frontal*. Woodbridge: Boydell, 1987.

Obrist, Barbara. "The Swedish Visionary: Saint Bridget of Sweden." In *Medieval Women Writers*, edited by Katharina Wilson, 227–51. Athens: University of Georgia Press, 1984.

O'Faolain, Julia, and Lauro Martinez, comps. *Not in God's Image*. New York: Harper and Row, 1973.

Ogilvie-Thomson, S. J., ed. *Walter Hilton's "Mixed Life," Edited from Lambeth Palace MS 472*. Elizabethan and Renaissance Studies, no. 92: 15. Salzburg: Institut für Anglistik und Amerikanistik, 1986.

O'Keeffe, Katherine O'Brien. *Visible Song: Transitional Literacy in Old English Verse*. Cambridge: Cambridge University Press, 1990.

Oliva, Marilyn. *The Convent and the Community in Late Medieval England: Female Monasteries in the Diocese of Norwich, 1350–1540*. Woodbridge: Boydell, 1998.

——, ed. *Charters and Household Accounts of the Female Monasteries in the County of Suffolk*. Woodbridge: Suffolk Record Society, forthcoming.

Ormrod, W. M. "Competing Capitals? York and London in the Fourteenth Century." In *Courts and Regions in Medieval Europe*, edited by S. Rees Jones, R. Marks, and A. J. Minnis, 81–88. Woodbridge: Boydell, 2000.

Ortner, Sherry B. "Is Female to Male As Nature Is to Culture?" In *Woman, Culture, and Society*, edited by Michelle Zimbalist Rosaldo and Louise Lamphere, 67–87. Stanford: Stanford University Press, 1974.

——. "The Virgin and the State." *Feminist Studies* 4 (1978): 17–28.

Ortner, Sherry B., and Harriet Whitehead, eds. *Sexual Meanings: The Cultural Construction of Gender and Sexuality*. Cambridge: Cambridge University Press, 1981.

Owen, A. ed. *Le Traité de Walter de Bibbesworth sur la langue française*. Paris: Presses Universitaires de France, 1929.

Palmer, D. J. *The Rise of English Studies: An Account of the Study of English Language and Literature from Its Origins to the Making of the Oxford English School*. London: Oxford University Press for the University of Hull, 1965.

Park, David. "Wall Painting." In *Age of Chivalry: Art in Plantagenet England 1200–1400*, edited by Jonathan Alexander and Paul Binski, 125–30. London: Royal Academy of Arts with Weidenfeld and Nicolson, 1987.

Parker, Rozsika. *The Subversive Stitch: Embroidery and the Making of the Feminine*. New York: Routledge, 1984.

Parsons, John Carmi. "Family, Sex and Power: The Rhythms of Medieval Queenship." In *Medieval Queenship*, edited by John Carmi Parsons, 1–11. New York: St. Martins Press, 1993.

——. "Of Queens, Courts, and Books: Reflections on the Literary Patronage of Thirteenth-Century Plantagenet Queens." In *The Cultural Patronage of Medieval Women*, edited by June Hall McCash, 175–201. Athens: University of Georgia Press, 1996.

Payling, S. J. "The Economics of Marriage in Late Medieval England: The Marriage of Heiresses." *Economic History Review* 2d series, 54 (2001): 413–29.

——. "The Politics of Family: Late Medieval Marriage Contracts." In *The McFarlane Legacy: Studies in Late Medieval Politics and Society*, edited by R. H. Britnell and A. J. Pollard, 21–47. New York, 1995.

———. "Social Mobility, Demographic Change and Landed Society in Late Medieval England." *Economic History Review* 2d series, 45 (1992): 51–73.

Pearsall, Derek. "Frederick James Furnivall (1825–1910)." In *Medieval Scholarship: Biographical Studies on the Formation of a Discipline*. Vol. 2, *Literature and Philology*, edited by Helen Damico, 125–38. New York, Garland, 1998.

———, ed. *Piers Plowman by William Langland: An Edition of the C-text*. York Medieval Texts. London: Arnold, 1978.

Penn, Simon A. C. "Female Wage-Earners in Late Fourteenth-Century England." *The Agricultural History Review* 35 (1987): 1–14.

Percy, Joyce W. *York Memorandum Book B/Y*. Surtees Society, vol. 186. 1973.

Peter d'Ailly. *De falsis prophetis*. In *Opera omnia*, vol. 1, by Jean Gerson. Edited by L. E. du Pin. Antwerp: Sumptibus Societatis, 1706.

Petroff, Elizabeth. *Body and Soul: Essays on Medieval Women and Mysticism*. New York: Oxford University Press, 1994.

———. *Women's Visionary Literature*. New York: Oxford University Press, 1986.

Phythian-Adams, Charles. *Desolation of a City: Coventry and the Urban Crisis of the Late Middle Ages*. Cambridge: Cambridge University Press, 1979.

Pliny. *Natural History*. Edited and translated by H. Rackham et al. 10 vols. Cambridge: Harvard University Press; London: William Heinemann, 1938–62.

Poly, Jean-Pierre, and Eric Bournazel. *The Feudal Transformation, 900–1200*. Translated by Caroline Higgitt. New York: Holmes and Meier, 1991.

Pomeroy, Sarah. *Goddesses, Whores, Wives, and Slaves*. New York: Schocken, 1975.

Poos, L. R. *A Rural Society after the Black Death: Essex 1350–1525*. Cambridge: Cambridge University Press, 1991.

Poovey, Mary. "Feminism and Deconstruction." *Feminist Studies* 14, no. 1 (1988): 52–65.

Power, Eileen. *Medieval English Nunneries*. Cambridge: Cambridge University Press, 1922.

Psaki, Regina, trans. *Le Roman de Silence*. New York: Garland, 1991.

Pseudo-Kodinos. *Traité des Offices*. Edited by Jean Verpeaux. Paris: Éditions du centre national de la recherche scientifique, 1976.

Purcell, Dominic. "The Priory of Horsham St Faith and Its Wall Paintings." *Norfolk Archaeology* 35 (1970–73): 469–73.

Raine, James, ed. *Testamenta Eboracensia or Wills Registered at York, Part I*. Surtees Society, vol. 4. 1836.

Raymond of Peñafort. *Summa de poenitentia et matrimonio*. Rome, 1603. Reprint, Farnham, Hants.: Gregg, 1967.

Reames, Sherry, with Martha Blalock and Wendy Larson, eds. *Middle English Legends of Women Saints*. Kalamazoo, Mich.: Medieval Institute Publications, 2002.

Rees Jones, Sarah. "Historical Introduction." In *Medieval Urbanism in Coppergate: Refining a Townscape*. The Archaeology of York, vol. 10/6, edited by R. A. Hall and K. Hunterman et al., 684–98. London: Council for British Archaeology, 2002.

———. "The Household and English Urban Government." In *The Household in Late Medieval Cities, Italy and Northwestern Europe Compared*, edited by Myriam Carlier and Tim Soens, 71–87. Louvain-Apeldoorn: Garant, 2001.

———. "Household, Work and the Problem of Mobile Labour: The Regulation of Labour in Medieval English Towns." In *The Problem of Labour in Fourteenth-Century England*, edited by J. Bothwell, P. J. P. Goldberg, and W. M. Ormrod, 133–53. Woodbrige: Boydell, 2000.

———. "Property, Tenure and Rents: Some Aspects of the Topography and Economy of Medieval York." D. Phil. diss., University of York, 1987.

Reinsch, R., ed. "La vie de Madeleine." *Archiv* 64 (1880): 85–94.

Rézeau, Pierre. *Les Prières aux saints à la fin du moyen âge*. 2 vols. Geneva: Droz, 1982.

Richards, E. J. "Virile Woman *and* WomanChrist: The Meaning of Gender Metamorphosis in Christine." In *"Riens ne m'est seur que la chose incertaine": Études sur l'art d'écrire au Moyen Âge offertes à Eric Hicks*, edited by Jean-Claude Mühlethaler and Denis Billotte, 239–52. Geneva: Slatkine, 2001.

Richer of Sens. *Richeri gesta Senoniensis ecclesiae.* Edited by G. Waitz. *MGH SS* vol. 25. Hannover: Hahniani, 1880.

Riddy, Felicity "Mother Knows Best: Reading Social Change in a Courtesy Text." *Speculum* 71 (1996): 66–86.

———. "Temporary Virginity and the Everyday Body: Bourgeois Self-Making in Le Bone Florence of Rome." In *Pulp Fictions of Medieval England: Essays in Popular Romance*, edited by Nicola McDonald. Manchester: Manchester University Press, forthcoming.

———. "'Women Talking about the Things of God': A Late Medieval Subculture." In *Women and Literature in Britain 1100–1500*, edited by Carol M. Meale, 104–27. Cambridge: Cambridge University Press, 1993.

Rigby, S. H. *English Society in the Late Middle Ages: Class, Society and Gender.* London: Macmillan, 1995.

———. "Gendering the Black Death: Women in Later Medieval England." *Gender and History*, 12, no. 3 (2000): 745–54.

Riley, Henry Thomas. *Memorials of London and London Life in the Thirteenth, Fourteenth and Fifteenth Centuries.* London: Longman, 1868.

Robb, David M. "The Iconography of the Annunciation in the Fourteenth and Fifteenth Century." *Art Bulletin* 18 (1936): 480–526.

Robertson, D. W., Jr. *A Preface to Chaucer: Studies in Medieval Perspectives.* Princeton: Princeton University Press, 1962.

Robertson, Elizabeth. *Early English Devotional Prose and the Female Audience.* Knoxville: University of Tennessee Press, 1990.

Roche-Mahdi, Sarah, ed. and trans. *Silence: A Thirteenth-Century French Romance.* East Lansing, Mich.: Colleagues Press, 1992.

Rocke, Michael. "Gender and Sexual Culture in Renaissance Italy." In *Gender and Society in Renaissance Italy*, edited by J. Brown and Robert C. Davis, 150–70. London: Longman, 1998.

Rogers, Nicholas. "The Original Owner of the Fitzwarin Psalter." *Antiquaries' Journal* 69 (1989): 257–60.

Romano, Dennis. "Gender and Urban Geography." *Journal of Social History* 23 (1989): 339–53.

Roper, Lyndal. *The Holy Household: Religion, Morals, and Order in Reformation Augsburg.* Oxford: Clarendon Press, 1989.

Rosaldo, Michelle Zimbalist. "The Use and Abuse of Anthropology: Reflections on Feminist and Cross-Cultural Understanding," *Signs* 5 (1980): 389–427.

———. "Woman, Culture, and Society: A Theoretical Overview." In *Woman, Culture, and Society*, edited by Michelle Zimbalist Rosaldo and Louise Lamphere, 17–42. Stanford: Stanford University Press, 1974.

Rosand, David. "Venezia Figurata." In *Interpretazioni Veneziane: Studi di Storia dell'Arte in onore di Michelangelo Muraro*, edited by David Rosand, 177–96. Venice: Arsenale editrice, 1984.

Rosenwein, Barbara, and Lester Little. *Debating the Middle Ages.* New York: Blackwell, 1998. 105–210.

Rosser, Gervase. "Going to the Fraternity Feast: Commensality and Social Relations in Late Medieval England." *Journal of British Studies* 33 (1994): 430–46.

Rotuli Parliamentorum; ut et Petitiones, et Placita in Parliamento. 6 vols. London: Record Commission, 1832.

Royal Commission of Historical Monuments England. *An Inventory of Historical Monu-*

ments in the City of York, vols. 3 and 5. Oxford: Her Majesty's Stationery Office, 1972, 1981.

Rubin, Gayle. "The Traffic in Women: Notes on the 'Political Economy' of Sex." In *Toward an Anthropology of Women*, edited by Rayna R. Reiter, 157–210. New York: Monthly Review Press, 1975.

Rubin, Miri. *Corpus Christi: The Eucharist in Late Medieval Culture*. Cambridge: Cambridge University Press, 1991.

Russell, D. W., ed. *La Vie seint Richard evesque de Cycestre*. ANTS, vol. 51. London: ANTS, 1995.

Sanday, Peggy Reeves. *Female Power and Male Dominance: On the Origins of Sexual Inequality*. Cambridge: Cambridge University Press, 1981.

Sandler, Lucy Freeman. *Gothic Manuscripts 1285–1385. I: Texts and Illustrations*. Vol. 5, *A Survey of the Manuscripts Illuminated in the British Isles*. London: Harvey Miller and Oxford University Press, 1986.

Sansovino, Francesco. *Venetia: Città nobilissima et singolare*. Farnborough, England: Gregg International, 1968.

Sanudo, Marino. *Vitae Ducum Venetorum*. Vol. 22, *Rerum Italicarum Scriptores*, edited by Ludovico Muratori. Milan: Societas Palatinae, 1733.

Savage, Anne. "The Solitary Heroine: Aspects of Meditation and Mysticism in *Ancrene Wisse*, the Katherine Group and the Wooing Group." In *Mysticism and Spirituality in Medieval England*, edited by W. Pollard and R. Boenig, 63–84. Woodbridge: Boydell, 1997.

Savage, Anne, and Nicholas Watson, trans. *Anchoritic Spirituality: "Ancrene Wisse" and Associated Works*. Classics of Western Spirituality. New York: Paulist Press, 1991.

Sawicki, Jana. "Foucault and Feminism: A Critical Reappraisal." In *Critique and Power: Recasting the Foucault/Habermas Debate*, ed. Michael Kelly, 347–64. Cambridge: MIT Press, 1994.

Scase, Wendy. "St Anne and the Education of the Virgin: Literary and Artistic Traditions and Their Implications." In *England in the Fourteenth Century*, edited by Nicholas Rogers, 81–96. Harlaxton Medieval Studies, vol. 3. Stamford: Paul Watkin, 1994.

Schiller, Gertrud. *Iconography of Christian Art*. Vol. 1. Translated by Janet Seligman. Greenwich, Conn.: New York Graphic Society, 1971.

——. *Ikonographie der christlichen Kunst*. Vol. 4.2, Gütersloh: Gerd Mohn, 1980.

Schofield, John. *Medieval London Houses*. New Haven: Yale University Press, 1995.

——. "Urban Housing in England, 1400–1600." In *The Age of Transition. The Archaeology of English Culture 1400–1600*, edited by David Gaimster and Paul Stamper, 127–44. Oxford: Oxbow Books, 1997.

Schofield, John, and Alan Vince. *Medieval Towns*. London: Leicester University Press, 1994.

Schofield, Roger. "English Marriage Patterns Revisited," *Journal of Family History* 10 (1985): 2–20.

Schreiner, Klaus. "Marienverehrung, Lesekultur, Schriftlichkeit: Bildungs- und frömmigkeitsgeschichtliche Studien zur Auslegung und Darstellung von 'Maria Verkündigung.'" *Frühmittelalterliche Studien* 24 (1990): 314–68.

——. "'... wie Maria geleicht einem puch': Beiträge zur Buchmetaphorik des hohen und späten Mittelalters." *Archiv für Geschichte des Buchwesens* 11 (1971): cols. 1437–64.

Schulenberg, Jane Tibbetts. *Forgetful of Their Sex: Female Sanctity and Society, ca. 500–1100*. Chicago: University of Chicago Press, 1998.

Scott, Joan. "Gender: A Useful Category of Historical Analysis." *American Historical Review* 91 (1986): 1053–75.

——. *Gender and the Politics of History*. New York, 1988.

Searle, Eleanor B. *Predatory Kinship and the Creation of Norman Power, 840–1066*. Berkeley: University of California Press, 1988.

Sekules, Veronica. "Women and Art in England in the Thirteenth and Fourteenth Centuries." In *Age of Chivalry: Art in Plantagenet England 1200–1400*, edited by Jonathan Alexander and Paul Binski, 41–48. London: Royal Academy of Arts with Weidenfeld and Nicolson, 1987.

Sellers, Maud, ed. *York Memorandum Book, A/Y, part 1*. Surtees Society, vol. 120. 1912 for 1911.

Sennett, Richard. *The Fall of Public Man*. New York: Norton, 1974.

Seymour, M. C., et al., eds. *On the Properties of Things: John Trevisa's Translation of Bartholomaeus Anglicus, De Proprietatibus Rerum*. 2 vols. Oxford: Clarendon Press, 1975.

Sharpe, Reginald R., ed. *Calendar of Letter-Books . . . of the City of London, Letter-Book I (c. 1400–1422)*. London: Corporation of London, 1909.

———. *Calendar of Letter-Books . . . of the City of London, Letter Book K*. London: Corporation of London, 1911.

Sheingorn, Pamela. "Appropriating the Holy Kinship: Gender and Family History." In *Interpreting Cultural Symbols: Saint Anne in Late Medieval Society*, edited by Kathleen Ashley and Pamela Sheingorn, 169–98. Athens: University of Georgia Press, 1990.

———. "The Holy Kinship: The Ascendancy of Matriliny in Sacred Genealogy of the Fifteenth Century." *Thought: A Review of Culture and Idea* 64 (1989): 268–86.

Shemek, Deanna. "Circular Definitions: Configuring Gender in Italian Renaissance Festival." *Renaissance Quarterly* 48 (1995): 1–40.

Sherman, Claire Richter. "The Queen in Charles V's 'Coronation Book': Jeanne de Bourbon and the 'Ordo ad Reginam Benedicendam.' " *Viator* 8 (1977): 255–98.

———. "Taking a Second Look: Observations on the Iconography of a French Queen." In *Feminism and Art History: Questioning the Litany*, edited by Norma Broude and Mary D. Garrard. New York: Harper and Row, 1982.

Shilton, Dorothy O., and Richard Holworthy, eds. *Medieval Wills from Wells*. Somerset Record Society, vol. 40. 1925.

Shirley, Janet. *Guarnier's Becket*. Chichester: Phillimore, 1975.

Simons, W., and J. E. Ziegler. "Pheonomenal Religion in the Thirteenth Century and Its Image: Elisabeth of Spalbeek and the Passion Cult." In *Women in the Church*, edited by W. J. Sheils and Diana Wood, 117–26. Studies in Church History, vol. 27. Oxford: Basil Blackwell, 1991.

Smith, Richard M. "Coping with Uncertainty: Women's Tenure of Customary Land in England c. 1370–1430." In *Enterprise and Individuals in Fifteenth-Century England*, edited by Jennifer Kermode, 43–67. Stroud: Alan Sutton, 1991.

———. "Hypothèses sur la nuptialité en Angleterre aux XIIIe-XIVe siècles." *Annales E. S. C.* 38 (1983): 120–24.

———. "Women's Property Rights Under Customary Law: Some Developments in the Thirteenth and Fourteenth Centuries." *Transactions of the Royal Historical Society* 5th series, vol. 36 (1986): 165–94.

Södergaard, Östen, ed. *La Vie d'Edouard le confesseur, poème anglo-normand du XIIe siecle*. Uppsala: Almqvist & Wiksell, 1948.

———, ed. *La vie sainte Audrée: Poème anglo-normand du XIIIe siècle*. Uppsala: Almqvist & Wiksell, 1955.

Soliman, Donato. *Il ministero della confessione nella legislazione dei frati minori*. Studi e testi Francescani, no. 28. Rome: Edizione francescane, 1964.

Spector, Stephen, ed. *The N-Town Play: Cotton MS Vespasian D.8*. Vol. 1, *Introduction and Text*. EETS, supplementary series, vol. 11. 1991.

Sperling, Jutta Gisela. *Convents and the Body Politic in Late Renaissance Venice*. Chicago: University of Chicago Press, 1999.

Stafford, Pauline. "Women and the Norman Conquest." *Transactions of the Royal Historical Society* 6th series, 4 (1996): 221–50.

Staley, Lynn, ed. *The Book of Margery Kempe.* Kalamazoo: Western Michigan University for TEAMS, 1996.

Stallard, A. D., ed. *The Transcript of the Churchwardens' Accounts of the Parish of Tilney, All Saints, Norfolk: 1443–1589.* London: Mitchell, Hughes and Clarke, 1922.

Staniland, Kay. *Embroiderers.* Toronto: University of Toronto Press, 1991.

Steele, Robert, ed., *Three Prose Versions of the Secreta Secretorum.* EETS, extra series, vol. 74. 1898.

Stell, P. M., and Louise Hampson, eds. and trans. *Probate Inventories of the York Diocese, 1350–1500.* York: University of York: Unpublished typescript, 1999.

Stevens, Martin. *Four Middle English Mystery Cycles: Textual, Contextual, and Critical Interpretations.* Princeton: Princeton University Press, 1987.

Stevenson, Lorna, and Jocelyn Wogan-Browne, eds. *A Computer Concordance to the Katherine Group and the Wooing Group.* Cambridge: D. S. Brewer, 2000.

Stiller, Nikki. *Eve's Orphans: Mothers and Daughters in Medieval English Literature.* Westport, Conn.: Greenwood, 1980.

Stock, Lorraine. "The Importance of Being Gender 'Stable': Masculinity and Feminine Empowerment in *Le Roman de Silence.*" *Arthuriana* 7 (1997): 28–29.

Stone, Lawrence. *The Family, Sex, and Marriage in England, 1500–1800.* London: Weidenfeld and Nicolson, 1977.

Stuard, Susan Mosher. "The Dominion of Gender: Women's Fortunes in the High Middle Ages." In *Becoming Visible: Women in European History,* edited by Renate Bridenthal, Claudia Koonz, and Susan Stuard, 153–72. 2d ed. Boston: Houghton Mifflin, 1987.

Sulpitius Severus. *The Life of Saint Martin.* Translated by Alexander Roberts. *Select Library of Nicene and Post-Nicene Fathers of the Church.* Vol. 11: 3–17. Ann Arbor: Eerdmans, 1964 (reprint).

——. *Vie de Saint Martin.* Edited by Jacques Fontaine. In *Sources Chrétiennes.* No. 133. Paris: Editions du Cerf, 1967.

Swayne, Henry James Fowle, ed. *Churchwardens' Accounts of St. Edmunds and St. Thomas, Sarum: 1443–1702.* Wiltshire Record Society, vol. 1. 1896.

Tanner, Norman, ed. and trans. *Decrees of the Ecumenical Councils.* London: Sheed & Ward, 1990.

——, ed. *Heresy Trials in the Diocese of Norwich, 1428–31.* Camden Society, series 4, vol. 20. London: Royal Historical Society, 1977.

Taylor, Andrew. "Authors, Scribes, Patrons and Books." In *The Idea of the Vernacular: An Anthology of Middle English Literary Theory, 1280–1520,* edited by Jocelyn Wogan-Browne, Nicholas Watson, Andrew Taylor, and Ruth Evans, 353–65. University Park, Pa.: Pennsylvania State University Press, 1999.

Taylor, Charles. *Sources of the Self: The Making of Modern Identity.* Cambridge: Harvard University Press, 1989.

Tentler, Thomas. *Sin and Confession on the Eve of the Reformation.* Princeton: Princeton University Press, 1977.

Terpstra, Nicholas. *Lay Confraternities and Civic Religion in Renaissance Bologna.* Cambridge: Cambridge University Press, 1995.

Thomas, A. H., ed. *Calendar of Plea and Memoranda Rolls of the City of London 1381–1412.* Cambridge: Cambridge University Press, 1932.

Thomas, Marcel. *The Golden Age: Manuscript Painting at the Time of Jean, Duke of Berry.* New York: George Braziller, 1979.

Thomas of Cantimpré. *Bonum universale de apibus.* Douai, 1627.

——. *The Life of Christina of Saint-Trond.* Translated by Margot King. Saskatoon: Peregrina, 1986.

——. *The Life of Lutgard of Aywières.* Translated by Margot King. Saskatoon: Peregrina, 1987.

———. *The Life of Margaret of Ypres.* 3d ed. Translated by Margot King. Toronto: Peregrina, 1999.

Thompson, Sally. *Women Religious: The Founding of English Nunneries after the Norman Conquest.* Oxford: Clarendon Press, 1990.

Thomson, R. M., ed. *The Chronicle of the Election of Hugh, Abbot of Bury St Edmunds and Later Bishop of Ely.* Oxford: Clarendon Press, 1974.

Thorpe, Lewis, ed. *Le Roman de Silence.* Cambridge: Heffer, 1972.

Thrupp, Sylvia. *The Merchant Class of Medieval London.* Ann Arbor: University of Michigan Press, 1948.

Tobler, Adolf, and Erhard Lommatzsch, eds. *Altfranzösisches Wörterbuch.* Stuttgart: Wiesbaden, 1965.

Tolhurst, J. B., ed. *The Ordinale and Customary of the Benedictine Nuns of Barking Abbey.* 2 vols, HBS, vols. 65, 66. London: Harrison and Sons, 1927, 1928.

Tolkien, J. R. R., and N. R. Ker, eds. *The English Text of the Ancrene Riwle: "Ancrene Wisse": Edited from MS. Corpus Christi College Cambridge 402.* EETS, o.s., vol. 249. 1962.

Tondro, Maximilian. "Memory and Tradition: The Ephemeral Architecture for the Triumphal Entries of the Dogaresse of Venice in 1557 and 1597" Ph.D. diss., Cambridge University, 2002.

Trethewey, W. H., ed. *The French Text of the "Ancrene Riwle": Edited from Trinity College Cambridge MS. R. 14. 7.* EETS, o.s., vol. 240. 1958 for 1954.

Tringham, Nigel, ed. *Charters of the Vicars Choral of York Minster: City of York and its Suburbs to 1546.* Yorkshire Archaeological Society Record Series, vol. 148. 1993.

Tristram, E. W. *English Wall Painting of the Fourteenth Century.* London: Routledge and Paul, 1955.

Tristram, E. W., and M. R. James. "Wall-Paintings in Croughton Church, Northamptonshire." *Archaeologia* 76 (1927): 179–204.

Turner, Ralph V. "*Miles Literatus* in Twelfth- and Thirteenth-Century England: How Rare a Phenomenon?" *American Historical Review* 83 (1978): 928–45.

Tuve, Rosemond. *Allegorical Imagery: Some Mediaeval Books and Their Posterity.* Princeton: Princeton University Press, 1966.

Tyson, Diana B. "The Adam and Eve Roll in Corpus Christi College Cambridge MS 98." *Scriptorium* 52 (1998): 301–16.

———. "Patronage of French Vernacular History Writers in the Twelfth and Thirteenth Centuries." *Romania* 100 (1979): 180–222.

Usener, Hermann, ed. "Passio a Theotimo." In *Acta S. Marinae et Christophori. Festschrift zur Fünften Säcularfeier der Carl-Ruprechts Universität zu Heidelberg,* 15–47. Bonn: Universitäts Buchdruckerei von Carl Georgi, 1886.

van Houts, Elisabeth M. C. *Memory and Gender in Early Medieval Europe 900–1200.* Basingstoke: Macmillan, 1999.

Verdeyen, Paul. "Le Procès d'inquisition contre Marguerite Porete et Guiard de Cressonessart (1309–1310)." *Revue d'histoire ecclésiastique* 81 (1986): 47–94.

Vicinus, Martha. *Independent Women: Work and Community for Single Women 1850–1920.* Chicago: University of Chicago Press, 1985.

Victoria County History of Essex. Vol. 2. Edited by William Page and J. Horace Round. London: Constable, 1907.

Victoria County History of Suffolk. Vol. 2. Edited by William Page. London: Constable, 1907.

Victoria County History of Wiltshire. Vol. 3. Edited by R. B. Pugh and Elizabeth Crittall. London: Oxford University Press for the Institute of Historical Studies, 1956.

Voragine, Jacobi de. *Legenda Aurea Vulgo Historia Lombardica Dicta.* Edited by Theodor Graesse, 400–403. Lipsiae: Librariae Arnold, 1850.

Walberg, E., ed. *La Vie de Saint Thomas le Martyr par Guernes de Pont-Sainte-Maxence.* Oxford: Oxford University Press, 1922.

Wallace, David, ed. *The Cambridge History of Medieval English Literature*. Cambridge: Cambridge University Press, 1999.

Walters, Lori. "Fortune's Double Face: Gender and the Transformations of Christine de Pizan, Augustine, and Perpetua." *Fifteenth-Century Studies* 25 (1999): 97–114.

Ward, Benedicta, trans. *Apophthegmata Patrum: The Desert Christian: Sayings of the Desert Fathers : The Alphabetical Collection*. New York: Macmillan, 1980.

Ward, Jennifer, ed. and trans. *Women of the English Gentry and Nobility*. Manchester: Manchester University Press, 1995.

Warner, Marina. *Monuments and Maidens: The Allegory of the Female Form*. New York: Atheneum, 1985.

Warren, Nancy Bradley. "Kings, Saints, and Nuns: Gender, Religion, and Authority in the Reign of Henry V." *Viator* 30 (1999): 307–22.

———. *Spiritual Economies: Female Monasticism in Later Medieval England*. Philadelphia: University of Pennsylvania Press, 2001.

Watson, Nicholas. "*Ancrene Wisse*, Religious Reform, and the Late Middle Ages." In *A Companion Guide to "Ancrene Wisse*," edited by Yoko Wada. Cambridge: D. S. Brewer, 2003.

———. "Fashioning the Puritan Gentry-Woman: Devotion and Dissent in *Book to a Mother*." In *Medieval Women: Texts and Contexts in Late Medieval Britain: Essays for Felicity Riddy*, edited by Jocelyn Wogan-Browne et al., 169–84. Turnhout: Brepols, 2000.

———. *Richard Rolle and the Invention of Authority*. Cambridge Studies in Medieval Literature, no. 13. Cambridge: Cambridge University Press, 1991.

Way, A., ed. *Promptorium Parvulorum*. Camden Society, 1st series, vols. 25, 54, 89. 1843–64.

Weatherly, Edward, ed. *Speculum Sacerdotale*. EETS, o.s., vol. 200. 1936.

Weaver, F. W., ed. *Somerset Medieval Wills: 1383–1500*. Vols. 1–3. Somerset Record Society, vols. 16, 19, 21. 1901, 1903, 1905.

Weedon, Chris. *Feminist Practice and Poststructuralist Theory*. Oxford: Oxford University Press, 1987.

Weir, David R. "Rather Never Than Late: Celibacy and Age at Marriage in English Cohort Fertility, 1541–1871." *Journal of Family History* 9 (1994): 340–54.

Wemple, Suzanne Fonay. *Women in Frankish Society: Marriage and the Cloister 500 to 900*. Philadelphia: University of Pennsylvania Press, 1981.

Westlake, H. F. *The Parish Gilds of Mediaeval England*. London: Society for Promoting Christian Knowledge, 1919.

Whitehead, Christiania. "Making a Cloister of the Soul in Medieval Religious Treatises." *Medium Aevum* 67 (1998): 1–29.

Wilkinson, John J., ed. "Accounts for the Building of Bodmin Church: 1469–1472." In *Camden Miscellany VII*. Camden Society, o.s., vol. 14. London, 1874.

Willard, Charity Cannon. *Christine de Pizan: Her Life and Works*. New York: Persea Books, 1984.

William of Auvergne. *Opera omnia*. 2 vols. Edited by L. E. du Pin. Paris: A. Pralard, 1674.

William of Nangis. *Gesta Philippi tertii Francorum regis ann. 1276*. Vol. 20, *Recueil des historiens des Gaules et de la France*, edited by Danon and Naudet. Paris: Aux dépens des libraires associés, 1840.

Wilson, Bronwen. " 'Il bel sesso, e l'austero Senato': The Coronation of Dogaressa Morosina Morosini Grimani." *Renaissance Quarterly* 52 (1999): 73–139.

Winstead, Karen A. *Virgin Martyrs: Legends of Sainthood in Late Medieval England*. Ithaca: Cornell University Press, 1997.

Wogan-Browne, Jocelyn. "The Apple's Message: Some Post-Conquest Hagiographic Accounts of Textual Transmission." In *Late-Medieval Religious Texts and Their Transmission*, edited by A. J. Minnis, 39–53. London: D. S. Brewer, 1994.

———. " 'Reading is Good Prayer': Recent Research on Female Reading Communities," *New Medieval Literatures* 5 (2002): 229–97.

——. "Re-routing the Dower: The Anglo-Norman Life of St. Etheldreda by Marie [of Chatteris?]." In *Power of the Weak: Studies on Medieval Women*, edited by Jennifer Carpenter and Sally-Beth MacLean, 27–56. Urbana: University of Illinois Press, 1995.

——. *Saints' Lives and Women's Literary Culture c.1150–1300: Virginity and Its Authorizations*. Oxford: Oxford University Press, 2001.

——. "Whose Bible Is It Anyway? Women and Holy Writings in Anglo-Norman England." In *Proceedings of the Patristic, Medieval, and Renaissance Conference*. Villanova, Pa.: Augustinian Historical Institute, forthcoming.

—— et al., eds. *Medieval Women: Texts and Contexts in Late Medieval Britain: Essays for Felicity Riddy*. Turnhout: Brepols, 2000.

Wogan-Browne, Jocelyn, and Glyn S. Burgess, eds. *Virgin Lives and Holy Deaths: Two Exemplary Biographies for Anglo-Norman Women*. London: Dent, 1996.

Wood-Legh, K. L., ed. *Kentish Visitations of Archbishop William Warham and His Deputies, 1511–1512*. Kent Archaeological Society, Kent Records, vol. 24. 1984.

Woolgar, C. M. *The Great Household in Late Medieval England*. New Haven and London: Yale University Press, 1999.

Wordsworth, Christopher, and Henry Littlehales. *The Old Service-books of the English Church*. London: Methuen, 1904.

Wyclif, John. *The English Works of Wyclif*. Edited by F. D. Matthew. EETS, o.s., 74, 1880. Rev. ed., 1902. Reprint, 1973.

Zatta, Jane. "The *Vie Seinte Osith*: Hagiography and Politics in Anglo-Norman England." *Studies in Philology* 96 (1999): 367–93.

Zettersten, Arne, ed. *The English Text of the "Ancrene Riwle": Edited from Magdalene College, Cambridge MS. Pepys 2498*. EETS, o.s., vol. 274. 1976.

Zettersten, Arne, and Bernhard Diensberg, eds. *The English Text of the Ancrene Riwle: The 'Vernon' Text*. EETS, o.s., vol. 310. 2000.

CONTRIBUTORS

DYAN ELLIOTT is Professor of History and Adjunct Professor of Religious Studies at Indiana University. She is author of *Spiritual Marriage: Sexual Abstinence in Medieval Wedlock* (Princeton University Press, 1993), *Fallen Bodies: Pollution, Sexuality, and Demonology in the Middle Ages* (University of Pennsylvania Press, 1999), and *Proving Woman: Female Spirituality and Inquisitional Culture in the Later Middle Ages* (forthcoming).

MARY C. ERLER is Professor of English at Fordham University. She is the author of *Women, Reading and Piety in Late Medieval England* (Cambridge University Press, 2002) and has written on devotional reading for the *Cambridge History of the Book in Britain*, vol. 3, *1400–1557*. She is interested in vowed women, in female reading and book ownership, and in early printing (she edited the work of the Tudor printer-poet Robert Copland [University of Toronto Press, 1993]). Her essays have appeared in *The Library*, *Modern Philology*, *Renaissance Quarterly*, *Viator*, and other journals.

KATHERINE L. FRENCH is an Associate Professor of History at State University of New York-New Paltz. With Beat Kümin and Gary Gibbs, she is editor of *The Parish in English Life* (Manchester University Press, 1997). She is author of *The People of the Parish: Community Life in a Late Medieval English Diocese* (University of Pennsylvania Press, 2001) and is currently working on a book on women in English parish life.

HOLLY S. HURLBURT received her Ph.D. in History at Syracuse University in 2000 and is currently an Assistant Professor at Southern Illinois University, Carbondale. Her research focuses on women, family, gender, and ritual in medieval and Renaissance Venice. Her book on the dogaresse of Venice, tentatively titled *First Wives of Venice*, will be published by Palgrave/St. Martin's Press.

MARYANNE KOWALESKI is Professor of History and Director of Medieval Studies at Fordham University. She is author of *Local Markets and Regional Trade in Medieval Exeter* (Cambridge University Press, 1995) and articles on medieval trade and maritime history, and editor of two volumes of medieval account rolls. Her publications on medieval women include the co-edited volume (with Mary Erler) *Women and Power in the Middle Ages* (University of Georgia Press, 1988) and articles on women and work, the demographic history of singlewomen, and urban families.

WENDY R. LARSON received her Ph.D. from the University of Wisconsin at Madison and is currently an Assistant Professor in the English department at Roanoke College in Salem, Virginia. She is working on a history of the cult of St. Margaret of Antioch.

JO ANN MCNAMARA was Professor of History at Hunter College for many years with added instruction in the Ph.D. program in history at the Graduate Center of the City University of New York. She taught courses in medieval history, including the medieval family and medieval women, and ancient and medieval Christianity. Her books include *A New Song: Celibate Women in the First Three Christian Centuries* (Haworth, 1983) and *Sisters in Arms: Catholic Nuns through Two Millennia* (Harvard University Press, 1996). In her retirement, she is working on a gendered history of the first millennium.

BARBARA NEWMAN is Professor of English and Religion at Northwestern University. She is the author of *God and the Goddesses: Vision, Poetry, and Belief in the Middle Ages* (University of Pennsylvania Press, 2002) and *From Virile Woman to WomanChrist: Studies in Medieval Religion and Literature* (University of Pennsylvania Press, 1995), as well as three books about Hildegard of Bingen. She has held fellowships from the American Council of Learned Societies, the Guggenheim Foundation, and the Kaplan Center for the Humanities at Northwestern, and is a fellow of the Medieval Academy of America.

SARAH REES JONES is Senior Lecturer in Medieval History at the Centre for Medieval Studies, University of York. She has completed several studies in conjunction with the York Archaeological Trust that reconstruct sites excavated in the city. Her publications include articles on the urban household, the history of urban citizenship, and Margery Kempe, as well as co-edited volumes on such topics as the government of medieval York and "pragmatic utopias." She is currently working on a monograph on medieval York.

FELICITY RIDDY is the author of *Sir Thomas Malory* and has edited *Selected Poems of Henryson and Dunbar* (with Priscilla Bawcutt). She has published many articles on medieval literature and is now working on a book on late medieval urban domesticity. For three years she was Director of the Centre for Medieval Studies at the University of York, where she is now Deputy Vice-Chancellor and Professor of English.

PAMELA SHEINGORN is Professor of History at Baruch College, City University of New York, and Professor of History and Theatre at the Graduate Center, City University of New York, where she is Executive Officer of the Ph.D. Program in Theatre. She is co-author of *Writing Faith: Text, Sign, and History in the Miracles of Sainte Foy* (University of Chicago Press, 1999) and of *Myth, Montage, and Visuality in Late Medieval Manuscript Culture: Christine de Pizan's Epistre d'Othea* (University of Michigan Press, 2003), as well as co-editor of *Same-Sex Love and Desire among Women in the Middle Ages* (Palgrave, 2001), and the annual *Studies in Iconography*.

NICHOLAS WATSON has an M.Phil. from Oxford University, a Ph.D. from the University of Toronto, and is Professor of English and American Literature and Language at Harvard University. He has researched extensively on religious writing in England, with a particular focus on mystical works and on works written by and for women. His books include *Richard Rolle and the Invention of Authority* (1991) and *Anchoritic Spirituality: "Ancrene Wisse" and Associated Works* (with Anne Savage, 1991). He is presently finishing an edition of the works of Julian of Norwich (with Jacqueline Jenkins) and working on a companion volume to this edition. His long-term goal is to write a history of vernacular religious writing in England between the Fourth Lateran Council (1215) and the Reformation.

JOCELYN WOGAN-BROWNE is Professor of English at Fordham University and has taught in the United Kingdom, Europe, Australia, and the United States. Her most recent publication is *Saints' Lives and Women's Literary Culture c. 1150–1300: Virginity and Its Authorizations* (Oxford University Press, 2001). She is co-editor of *The Idea of the Vernacular: An Anthology of Middle English Literary Theory, 1280–1520* (Pennsylvania State University Press, 1999), *Medieval Women: Texts and Context in Late Medieval Britain: Essays for Felicity Riddy* (Brepols, 2000), and other collaborative works and has edited, translated, and published articles on literature for and by women in medieval England. She is currently working on various projects in the French literature of England, including a translation series.

INDEX

Note: Italic page numbers indicate illustrations.

Abou-el-Haj, Barbara, 132
Adelheid (Holy Roman empress), 24, 25
Aelred of Rievaulx, 54–55, 61, 61 n. 21, 62, 68 n. 31
Agency: forces determining possibility of, 3; and power, 1. *See also* Women's agency
Agnes (German empress), 35
Alan of Lille, 135–36, 137, 140, 143, 150, 153, 155
Albert the Great, 47, 107
Allen, Prudence, 23
Amice de Haddon, 124
Anchoresses: and apocalyptic thinking, 62; athletic coach-like approach toward, 59–61; and cult of St. Margaret, 95; and hagiography, 79–80; hermits compared to, 54, 55, 69; instructions for, 54, 72; and interiority, 53, 55, 58, 65–66; and lay spirituality, 62–69; as readers, 80; and religious orders, 54, 56–57, 58
Ancrene Wisse: athletic coach-like attitude of author, 59–61; and communities of women, 80, 81; and confession, 55–56; geography of, 80–81, 84; and hagiography, 79–80; and inner self, 55, 63, 69–70, 80; and lay spirituality, 56, 58, 62–69, 72; and misogyny, 54, 56, 58, 59, 60, 69; modern editions of, 73; and nationalism, 9, 73; and religious orders, 56–57; and satire, 68–69, 68 n. 31;

scholarly study of, 91; and self-containment, 69–70; and women's power, 5–6, 54, 59; and women's religious lives, 72
Anglo-Norman Text Society, 74
Anglo-Norman texts, 9, 74, 91–92, 93
Anne of Burgundy (duchess of Bedford), 121, 123
Anne, Saint, teaching the Virgin Mary: images of, 108, 110, *110*, *111*, 112, *113*, 116, *119*, 121, *123*, *124*, *125*, *126*, *127*, 128, *129*, *130*, 131, 132, *133*, 134; and Incarnation history, 110, 112, 113, 116, 106, 108, 124, 126, 128, 132–33; and literacy, 13, 106, 108, 124, 126, 128, 132–33; St. Anne Trinity, 112–13, *114*, *115*, 116, *117*, *118*, *120*, 121, *122*, *123*
Annunciation, 107, 112
Antichrist, 48
Antoninus of Florence, 44, 51
Aristocratic women: education of, 131; and Faith of Agen and Conques, 82, 82 n. 30; and family/kinship networks, 7, 19–22, 24–29; and patronage, 86–87, 88; and political interests, 26, 175; and property rights, 20, 198; and public power, 7, 18–19, 21, 25–26, 27; roles/responsibilities of, 188; as surrogates for husbands, 26–27. *See also* Class; Elite women
Aristotle: concept of gender, 23, 26, 154; and dichotomy of form and matter, 144; and domestic authority, 213–14, 222–23

Ascetic practices: and *Ancrene Wisse*, 55, 59, 61–62; and lay spirituality, 66; and mysticism, 6

Ashley, Kathleen, 113

Aude, 50

Audrée of Ely, 77, 78, 79, *85*, 90

Augustine, Saint (Canterbury), 32

Augustine, Saint (Hippo), 52, 213, 214

Augustus (Roman emperor), 28

Babington, Katherine, 92

Backhouse, Janet, 121

Barbaro, Francesco, 178, 178 n. 13

Barking Abbey, 71, 75, 86

Bartholmaeus Anglicus, 218

Baxter, Margery, 223

Beauvoir, Simone de, 222

Becket, Marie, 75

Becket, Saint Thomas, 75, 77, 78, 79, 82, 90

Bedford Hours, *121, 123*

Beguines: and *Ancrene Wisse*, 58; as community of women, 72; and confession, 3, 32, 34, 36, 37, 40–41, 42, 139; imitations of, 38–39; and Jean de Meun, 139–40; and patriarchal status quo, 14; and penitential system, 35, 40–41; and purgatory, 35, 35 n. 12; and scrupulosity, 46

Beissel, Stephan, 113

Bennett, Judith, 8–9, 22, 128

Black Death: and family/kinship networks, 202; and tenants, 11, 202, 204, 206, 207, 208; and urban senses of home, 219; and working women, 8, 9, 11, 204, 206, 207–9, 210

Blanton-Whetsall, Virginia, 84

Boethius, 150

Bona of Savoy, 184, 184 n. 31

Bonaventure, Saint, 34, 40 n. 27, 42

Bone Florence of Rome, Le, 225

Book of Vices and Virtues, The, 217

Book to a Mother, 63, 64, 65, 68

Book to a Simple and Devout Woman, 68, 69

Books of Hours: Hours of the Virgin, 128; Latin primer, 126; Little Hours of the Virgin, 58; Primer of Claude of France, 128, 129, *130*; Sarum Book of Hours, 124, 126

Boudicca (British queen), 27, 28

Bozon, Nicholas, 75

Braun, Joseph, 110, 112, 113, 116

Bridget of Sweden, 35

Brown, Peter, 18

Brunhild (Merovingian queen), 25, 26

Burgage tenements, 201, 202, 203

Burke, Peter, 172

Bury St. Edmunds monastery, 84, 86, 90

Butler, Judith, 2

Bynum, Caroline Walker, 34

Byzantine empresses, 184–85, 186, 187, 187 n. 38, 188

Campsey manuscript: and communities of women, 10, 87, 88, 89, 90, 92, 93; and elite women, 14, 76, 78, 82, 88, 89, 90; and female authorship, 75–76, 75–76 n. 15, 77; geography of, 81–82, *83*, 84, *85*, 86, 88, 89, 92–93; and hagiography, 74–79, 81–82, 84, 86, 89, 92; and lineages, 86, 87, 88, 92–93; and master narratives, 91, 92; and networks, 88, 88 n. 44, 92–93; and texts, 9–10, 77, 81, 87–88

Canon law, 157, 215

Carolingian period, 8, 19–20, 24, 25

Carrasco, Magdalena, 132

Cassian, John, 53

Castle of Labour, The, 220–21

Catherine de Westhusen, 49

Catherine of Alexandria, 77, 78, 79, 80, 82, 89, 100

Cecily de Chanville, 89

Chambers, R. W., 73

Chance, Jane, 7

Chanson de Roland, 74

Charlemagne, 24

Charles V (king of France), 184, 186, 187

Chaucer, Geoffrey, 138, 139, 140, 195, 218, 226

Childbirth: and Christine de Pizan, 155; and communities of women, 174; and coronation rituals, 185; and parish guilds, 169; and St. Anne, 113; and St. Margaret, 12, 94–96, 97, 98, 99, 100–102, 104

Children: and aristocratic women, 26; and class, 216; and home, 220; and inheritance, 200–201, 200 n. 46; and intimacy, 217, 224

Chocke, Margaret, 162

Christianity: and interiority, 52, 53; and marriage practices, 27, 28; and parish activities, 172. *See also* Roman Catholic Church

Christina Mirabilis, 39

Christina of Markyate, 71

Christine de Pizan: *Book of the Mutation of Fortune, The*, 148–52, 154, 155; *City of Ladies, The*, 148, 149, 151, 152, 154, 155; *Epistle of the God of Love*, 148; and female authorship, 75 n. 15; and female identity, 151; and Jean de Meun, 137, 139, 148, 149, 153–54, 155; *Lavision-Christine*, 140, 148, 152–55; and literacy, 105, 134; and Nature, 14, 136, 140, 148–50, 151, 152, 153–55; *Querelle de la Rose*, 148

Church and state, separation of, 29

Churchwardens, 157, 161, 168, 169

Clanchy, M. T., 124, 126

Class: and family/kinship networks, 19; and female patronage, 13, 104; and intimacy, 227; and literacy, 126, 128, 131; and marital status, 23, 210; and Nature, 143–44; as organizing principle of society, 8, 23, 24; and

Etheldreda of Ely, Saint, 75, 77, 78, 79, 84, 87
Evergates, Ted, 21
Eyck, Jan van, 101–2

Faith of Agen and Conques, 77, 78, 79, 82, 82 n. 30, 86
Family identity, and housing practice, 11, 202, 203
Family/kinship networks: and aristocratic women's power, 7, 19–22, 24–29; and Black Death, 202; changes in structure, 20, 21; and clergy, 23; and home, 217; and households, 201–2, 204; and property ownership, 198–201, 209; and public/private dichotomy, 214; and single-gender system, 24; and tenants, 202; women's detachment from, 203; women's influence through, 2
Female spiritual writing, 6–7
Female subcultures: clergy's fear of, 165, 172; effect on women, 13–14; and parish activities, 164–65; and parish guilds, 169, 169 n. 73
Feminist history: and female subcultures, 13–14; Foucault's effect on, 2; and free subject versus victimization, 3; and historical recovery, 3, 10; and transformations, 9
Fertility, 11, 12 n. 26
Feudalism, 18, 19 n. 6, 22
Fitzwarin Psalter, 122
Fortescue, Sir John, 222
Foucault, Michel, 1, 2, 3, 27
Fournier, Bishop, 50
Fourth Lateran Council, 3, 9, 34, 40, 41, 54
Frances of Rome, 35
Francis, Saint, 42
Franciscan order, 33, 34, 41–42
Frankpledge, 212
Fredegund (Frankish queen), 26
French, Katherine, 4, 10
Freud, Sigmund, 52
Fulk (bishop of Toulouse), 32

Gatenby, John, 199
Geary, Patrick, 87, 92
Gender: and *Ancrene Wisse*, 55, 56, 58, 59, 60; Aristotelian concept of, 23, 26, 154; and becoming male, 136, 147, 151, 152, 155; and Christine de Pizan, 149–55; and dangerous activity, 193; and domestic sphere, 5, 190–97; and everyday body, 224; and Nature, 135–36, 140, 142, 143–44, 149, 154, 155; as organizing principle of society, 23, 24; and parish support, 160–61; performative nature of, 2; and property, 191; and rituals, 188–89; and *Roman de Silence*, 142, 142 n. 19, 143–44, 146–48; and scrupulosity, 47; and single-gender system, 24, 25–26, 28, 29–30

Gender relations: and housing practice, 11; and lay spirituality, 5–6; and women's power, 5, 15–16
Gender roles: and communities of women, 175; and Hocktide celebrations, 169–72; and home, 220; and parish activities, 4, 156–59, 156 n. 1, 172; and parish guilds, 168
Gender system shift: and master narrative, 7–8, 22, 29–30; and women's position in marriage, 25, 28
Germanic kings and queens, 26
Gerontocracy, 180
Gerson, Jean, 36–37, 40, 44, 45–47, 48, 50
Gibson, Gail McMurray, 128, 131
Gilchrist, Roberta, 190
Giotto, 106
Goddesses, 135, 149, 155. *See also* Nature
Goldberg, Jeremy, 190, 196, 206, 209
Goody, Jack, 133
Great woman model, 2, 16
Gregorian reforms, 9, 22
Gregory the Great, 32, 45, 47, 48, 49
Grundmann, Herbert, 54
Guainerius, Anthonius, 94–95
Guglielmites, 50
Guiard de Cressonessart, 41
Guide for Anchoresses. See Ancrene Wisse
Guilds: and cottages, 194; craft guilds, 10, 202, 212; regulations of working hours, 192; and Venetian dogaresse's entrance procession, 177, 177 n. 10. *See also* Parish guilds
Guillaume de Lorris, 136
Guillaume le Clerc, 84
Gurney, Craig M., 216
Gy, Pierre-Marie, 40

Hagiography: and becoming a man, 151; and Campsey manuscript, 74–79, 81–82, 84, 86, 89, 92; and communities of women, 71; contexts of, 87, 92; cultural functions of, 113; and Katherine Group, 73, 74, 79–80; pictorial hagiography, 132; as romance, 81. *See also* Saints
Hahn, Cynthia, 132
Hall houses, 191 n. 6, 192, 204, 210
Hanawalt, Barbara, 128, 190, 196
Heldris of Cornwall, 136, 140–47, 149, 151, 166; *Roman de Silence*, 14, 136, 140–48, 142 n. 19, 151
Helena (Roman empress), 27
Henry of Freimar, 44
Heraclitus, 17
Heretical revelations: and confession, 3, 33, 40, 40 n. 27; and inquisition, 49–50, 50 n. 70, 51
Herlihy, David, 18

Literary culture, 10, 74, 76, 79–80, 81, 87–88
Little Hours of the Virgin, 58
Livia (Roman empress), 28
Livingstone, Amy, 21
Livre de la mutacion de Fortune, Le, 136
Lollardy, 63, 65
Lothar, 24
Louis the Pious, 24
Love, Nicholas, 63, 107, 217
Lutgard of Aywières, 42, 46
Lydgate, John, 97

Male-female relationships: and attraction between holy women and clergy, 42–44, 42 n. 35; and confession, 3–4, 33, 35–36, 41–42, 48, 51, 164; and fraudulent raptures, 39–40; and Hocktide celebrations, 172; and scrupulosity, 47
Maltby, Margaret, 228
Margaret of Antioch, Saint: artifacts of, 100–102, *101*, *103*, 104; as childbirth advocate, 12, 94–102, 104; emergence from belly of dragon, 95, 96, 98–100; prayers to, 97–98, 102, *103*
Marguerite Porete, 40–41
Marital status: and class, 23, 210; cultural incentives to marry, 211; and demography, 11–12, 12 n. 26; and guilds, 194; and house as status object, 204; and joint title to property, 200, 200 n. 46; and parish guilds, 165, 167, 168–69; and political activity, 5, 24, 27–28, 182, 188; and tenants, 194, 195, 209 nn. 75, 76; and urban home design, 195; and Venetian dogaresse's entrance procession, 5, 179, 180; and women's property ownership, 197–98; and working women, 209. *See also* Single women
Marriage practices, 21, 22, 23, 25–26, 27
Martyrs, 28, 51, 98, 167
Mary Magdalene, Saint, 48, 77, 78, 79, 82, 84, 89, 227
Mary of Brabant, 37
Mary of Oignies, 32, 34, 35, 46, 54
Mary Play from the N.town Manuscript, The, 106, 108 n. 12, 133
Master narrative: and Campsey manuscript, 91, 92; and gender system shift, 7–8, 22, 29–30; gendering of, 15; and historical periods, 27; and home, 214; multiple meanings of, 7; and power structure shift, 22; and reliance on political and institutional themes, 9, 18, 29; and St. Margaret, 100, 104
Maud (queen of England), 78
McNamara, Jo Ann, 7–8, 9, 13
Meditationes vitae Christi, 107
Men: and *Ancrene Wisse*, 55, 62, 64–65, 66, 67; and egalitarianism of ecclesiastical society,

23; as gendered beings, 22; and home, 220; and marital status and housing, 194, 195; married, as second-class citizens, 23; and parish guilds, 165–66, 167, 168; and parish offices, 4, 156, 157; and parish seating arrangements, 163; and parish support, 160; and public authority, 213, 214, 215; and safety of work, 195, 196; as tenants, 205, 206, 207, 209, 210; and women's parish activities, 159
Menstruation, 47
Merovingian period, 25, 26
Metaphrastes, Simeon, 98
Middle ages: as historical period, 18, 27, 29; as visual culture, 132; women's social role in, 36
Millett, Bella, 57–58
Mirk, John, 158–59, 164, 226
Misogyny: and *Ancrene Wisse*, 54, 56, 58, 59, 60, 69; and clergy, 172; and Jean de Meun, 139, 148; and *Roman de Silence*, 141 n. 17, 142, 146
Modwenna of Britain, Saint: and Campsey manuscript, 77, 78, 79; and communities of women, 87; sites associated with, 82, 84, 84 n. 34, *85*
Monasteries: and *Ancrene Wisse*, 72; and Campsey manuscript, 78; and copyists, 88, 88–89 n. 46; and female subcultures, 14; hermit's rejection of, 53; and manly women, 28; opposition to, 65; women's access to positions of power in, 8
Moore, R. I., 22
Morality: and Christine de Pizan, 152; and moral safety in home, 193; and Nature, 143, 149
More, Sir Thomas, 6, 68, 69
Morgan, Nigel, 121
Muth, Hanswernfried, 116
Mysticism: and confession, 36–37; and fraudulent female raptures, 38–39, 38 n. 27; and goddesses, 135; Jantzen redefinition of, 6; and Mary of Oignies's life, 32

Na Prous Boneta, 50
Nationalism, 6, 9, 13, 73, 74, 91
Nature: and Christine de Pizan, 14, 136, 140, 148–55; and gender, 135–36, 140, 142, 143–44, 149–50, 154, 155; and Heldris of Cornwall, 136, 140–47; and Jean de Meun, 136–40, 150, 153, 155
Networks. *See* Family/kinship networks; Social networks
Newman, Barbara, 14, 55
Nicholas of Dunstable, 86
Nider, John, 44, 47–48
Niezen, R. W., 133

Norman conquest of England, 8, 73
Nunnery culture, 76

Old English Martyrology, 98
Oostsanen, Cornelisz van, 121, 122
Osith of Chich: and Campsey manuscript, 77, 78, 79, 90; and communities of women, 87; sites associated with, 82, 84, 84 n. 33, 85
Otto the Great, 24
Ottonian empresses, 26, 27

Panuce, 77, 79
Paris, Matthew, 76, 78
Parish activities: and gender roles, 4, 156–59, 156 n. 1, 172; and leadership roles, 158, 168, 172
Parish fund-raising, 4, 159–60, 162–63, 165–67, 172
Parish guilds, 4, 165, 166–68, 169, 172; and stores, 165–69
Parish seating arrangements, 4, 162, 163–64, 163 n. 32, 172–73
Parish support: and fund-raising, 4, 159–60, 162–63, 165–67, 172; and gifts and testamentary bequests, 160–61, 172; women's specific instructions for, 161–62, 172
Park, David, 112
Parker, Rozsika, 132
Parsons, John Carmi, 76
Paston, John, II, 228
Paston, Margaret, 227–28
Pater Noster of Richard Hermit, The, 63, 64
Patriarchal authority: and Ascension Day festival, 183; and female gossip, 10; and home, 224; and household heads, 213; and marriage rituals, 188–89, 189 n. 44; and Venetian dogaresse's entrance procession, 178, 183, 186–87; and women's chastity, 178, 178–79 n. 14; and women's use of confession, 37
Patriarchal equilibrium, 9
Patriarchal ideology, 134, 175, 178
Patronage: and Campsey manuscript, 86–87, 88; and cult of St. Margaret, 95, 100, 102, 104; definition of, 12–13, 95–96; and property ownership, 20, 198; and queens, 78; and St. Anne teaching the Virgin Mary, 121, 122, 124; and St. Anne Trinity, 116; women's use of, 2, 16
Paul, Saint, 27
Paul the hermit, 77, 79
Pepys Rule, The, 65, 66, 66 n. 29, 67
Perpetua (martyr), 151
Peter of Brocia, 37
Peter, Saint, 48
Philip III (king of France), 37
Phythian-Adams, Charles, 213

Plato, 52, 153
Pliny, 42
Plow Monday celebrations, 165
Plutarch, 27
Pole, Richard de la, 220
Political interests: and aristocratic women, 26, 175; and burgage tenements, 202; and consorts, 25, 26, 175, 176, 177, 179, 180, 181, 184, 185; and coronation rituals, 184, 185, 187; and households, 213; and marital status, 5, 24, 27–28, 182, 188; and public/private dichotomy, 215; and Venetian dogaresse's entrance procession, 177, 179, 180, 181, 182–83, 182 n. 27, 185; and womens' economic interests, 211
Power, and agency, 1
Primer of Claude of France, 128, 129, 130
Primogeniture, 20, 21
Privacy, 191, 210, 215, 216. *See also* Public/private dichotomy
Promptorium Parvulorum, 228
Property: aristocratic women's control of, 20, 198; and Campsey manuscripts, 78; and domestic status of tenants, 195; and gender, 191; and house as status object, 201–4; and jointures, 200, 200 n. 46; ownership/management changes in, 202; and parishes, 158; and single women, 201, 201 n. 51, 203, 211; and women owners of, 197–201, 211; and women as tenants, 204–10
Prosopography, 12, 16
Protevangelium of James, 106
Pseudo-Kodinos, 187
Pseudo-Matthew, 106, 107
Public authority, 6, 20, 22, 212–14, 220–28
Public/private dichotomy, 2, 5, 214, 219, 222–23, 227
Purgatory, 35, 35 n. 12
Pusey, E. B., 73
Pynson, Richard, 221

Queens: and coronation rituals, 184–88, 185 n. 33, 186 n. 35; and husband/wife partnership, 27, 28; and patronage, 78; and political interests, 25, 26; as regents, 185. *See also* Consorts

Radegund (Merovingian queen), 25
Raymond of Peñafort, 34, 44, 49
Rees Jones, Sarah, 6, 11, 12
Reform movements, 8, 63
Reformation, 4, 56, 172
Reynes, Robert, 128
Riario, Girolamo, 184
Richard of Chichester, 76, 77, 78, 79, 82, 86
Richard of St. Victor, 89
Richer of Sens, 33, 38

Riddy, Felicity, 5, 6, 10, 11, 196
Riemenschneider, Tilman, 116, *120*
Rigby, Steven, 210
Rituals: and communities of women, 174–75, 177–78, 178 n. 12, 179, 183 n. 28, 187, 187 n. 39; and consorts, 183–84, 189; coronation, 184–88, 185 n. 33, 186 n. 35, 187 n. 38; and gender, 188–89; marriage, 180–83, 181 n. 21, 188. *See also* Venetian dogaresse's entrance procession
Robert le Bougre, 33, 38, 51
Robert of Arbrissel, 35–36
Robert of Bedford, 89
Rogers, Nicholas, 124
Rolle, Richard, 53 n. 3, 55, 61, 62, 62 n. 22
Roman Catholic Church: and coronation rituals, 185, 186, 187 n. 38; hierarchy in, 22; and imperial power, 29; and indissoluble monogamy, 26; and penitential system, 35, 37. *See also* Clergy; Monasteries
Roman Empire, 7, 18, 27–28, 29
Rosser, Gervase, 170
Rossetti, Dante Gabriel, 132
Rous, Reginald, 92
Rubin, Gayle, 19

Saint Alexis, 74
Saints: and fund-raising, 166–67; images of, 4, 172–73; and parish guilds, 165, 166, 172; and women's parish support, 162, 173. *See also* Hagiography; *specific saints*
Sansovino, Francesco, 181–82
Santa Maria delle Vergini convent, 183
Sarum Book of Hours, 126
Schiller, Gertrud, 112
Schofield, John, 191, 192 n. 8, 196 n. 32
Scriveners, 88, 88–89 n. 46
Scrupulosity, 4, 45–50
Searle, Eleanor, 19
Seinte Katerine, 73, 80
Sekules, Veronica, 122
Selby, William, 199, 201
Sennett, Richard, 217
Sforza, Caterina, 184, 184 n. 31
Sheingorn, Pamela, 13
Sherman, Claire Richter, 184, 185 n. 34, 186 n. 35, 187 n. 38
Silvestris, Bernard, 135–36, 140
Simon of Walsingham, 82, 86
Simple Tretis, A, 65, 66–68
Single women: and demography, 12, 12 n. 26; and house as status object, 204; and parish activities, 158; and parish fund-raising, 165, 167; and parish guilds, 165, 168, 169; and property inheritance, 201, 201 n. 51, 203, 211; as tenants, 209, 209 n. 75
Skipwith, Adam, 199, 200
Social networks: and Campsey manuscript,

88, 88 n. 44, 92–93; and everyday body, 224–25; and parish guilds, 165; and Venetian dogaresse's entrance procession, 179, 186; women's influence through, 2; and women's leadership, 168
Soly, Walter, 164
South English Legendary, 99
Speculum Sacerdotale, 159
Spiritual discernment, 44, 45
St. Anne Trinity, 112–13, *114, 115*, 116, *117, 118, 120*, 121, *122, 123*
St. Denis, abbot of, 37, 38
Stephen of Bourbon, 49
Stevens, Martin, 133–34
Stiller, Nikki, 133
Stoic writers, 27, 52
Stone, Lawrence, 217
Stoss, Veit, 116
Strensall, William, 199, 200
Stuard, Susan Mosher, 8
Sumptuary laws, 179, 182
Sybil (fraudulent mystic), 38–39
Sybil de Cheney, 82
Syon Abbey, 71, 224

Tacitus, 27, 28
Tateshal, Joan, 124
Tenants: and Black Death, 11, 202, 204, 206, 207, 208; and cottages, 192, 194, 202, 204; and farmed tenancies, 206–7, 206–7 n. 66; and free rents, 207, 207 n. 66; and marital status, 194, 195, 209 nn. 75, 76; and master householder, 195, 202; tenants at will, 204; working women as, 11, 194, 204–10, 211; and written leaseholds, 202–3, 202–3 n. 57, 204, 204 n. 59
Teutberga, 24
Theodosian empresses, 27
Theophano (German empress), 25
Thomas Aquinas, 23–24, 45, 48, 154
Thomas de Pizan, 149
Thomas, Marcel, 121
Thomas of Cantimpré, 34, 42–44, 42 n. 35
Toky, Richard, 195
Tolkien, J. R. R., 73
Town houses, 191, 192 n. 10, 194, 203
Trevisa, John, 218
Tristam, E. W., 112
Tristan, 74
Tron, Dea Morosini (dogaressa of Venice), 176
Tunnock, Richard, 199, 200
Tyrel, Alice, 76
Tyson, Diana, 87

Urban home design: and class, 211, 216; and flexible use of space, 191, 216; and kitchens, 193–94, 194–95 n. 22, 216; and leasehold tenure changes, 203; and privacy,

191, 210; and safety, 192–93, 195, 196; and social hierarchies, 195; trends in, 191, 191 n. 6; and space segregation, 191–92, 192 n. 8, 193, 194, 194–95 n. 22, 196; women's influence on, 190

Venetian dogaresse's entrance procession: and communities of women, 4, 10, 175, 177–79, 182, 187 n. 39; coronation rituals compared to, 184–88, 185 n. 33; and doge's election, 176–77; familial issues of, 182–83, 185–86; and fertility references, 176, 185–86; marriage ritual compared to, 180–82, 181 n. 21, 183; and political interests, 177, 179, 180, 181, 182–83, 182 n. 27, 185; processional elements of, 177, 177 n. 11; and real/symbolic tension, 4–5, 182–83, 189
Vescy, William, 200
Vicars Choral, 204–10, 206–7 n. 66
Victorian era, ideologies of femininity, 13, 132
Virgin Mary: education of, 106–8, 109, 128, 134; and Hocktide celebrations, 166–67; images of St. Anne teaching the Virgin Mary, 13, 108, 110, 110, 111, 112, 113, 116, 119, 121, 123, 124, 125, 126, 127, 128, 129, 130, 131, 132, 133, 134; and St. Anne Trinity, 112–13, 114, 115, 116, 117, 118, 120, 121, 122, 123
Voaden, Rosalynn, 80
Voragine, Jacopo da, 98, 99, 100–101, 102

Wace, 97
Walter of Bibbesworth, 126, 128
Watson, Nicholas, 5–6, 10, 14
Wemple, Suzanne, 7, 17, 21, 27
Widows, 11, 57, 78, 210
William of Auvergne, 49
Wingfield, Anne, 92
Wiseman, Barbara, 71
Wives: brides of Christ, 28, 55, 78, 80; guilds, 166; house-, 11, 220–22; and power, 28
Wogan-Browne, Jocelyn, 9–10, 13, 14, 104
Women's agency: definition of, 1–2; and demography, 11–12, 16; and female subcultures, 13–14; and multiple narratives, 15–16; and patronage, 2, 12–13, 16
Women's collective impact: and St. Anne teaching the Virgin Mary, 13; and St. Margaret cult, 12, 95, 96, 104; and working women, 11
Women's public preaching/teaching, 6, 57, 66, 66 n. 29, 80
Wooing Group, 72, 73
Working women: and Black Death, 8, 9, 11, 204, 206, 207–9, 210; domestic status of, 195; and economic conditions, 208, 209, 210–11; and gendered nature of work, 193, 194; and safety, 195, 196; status of, 8, 9, 210; as tenants, 11, 194, 204–10, 211
Wyclif, John, 48